Smithsonian Series in Ethnographic Inquiry
WILLIAM L. MERRILL AND IVAN KARP, SERIES EDITORS

Ethnography as fieldwork, analysis, and literary form is the distinguishing feature of modern anthropology. Guided by the assumption that anthropological theory and ethnography are inextricably linked, this series is devoted to exploring the ethnographic enterprise.

ADVISORY BOARD
Richard Bauman (Indiana University), Gerald Berreman (University of California, Berkeley), James Boon (Princeton University), Stephen Gudeman (University of Minnesota), Shirley Lindenbaum (New School for Social Research), George Marcus (Rice University), David Parkin (University of London), Roy Rappaport (University of Michigan), Renato Rosaldo (Stanford University), Annette Weiner (New York University), Norman Whitten (University of Illinois), and Eric Wolf (City University of New York).

The Guaymí

Indians

and Mining

Multinationals

in Panama

conditions not of their choosing

Chris N. Gjording

Smithsonian Institution Press

Washington and London

Editors: George Vranas and Peter Johnson
Production Editor: Duke Johns
Designer: Linda McKnight

Library of Congress Cataloging-in-Publication Data

Gjording, Chris N.
  Conditions not of their choosing : the Guaymí
Indians and mining multinationals in Panama /
Chris N. Gjording.
      p. cm.
  Originally presented as the author's thesis.
  Includes bibliographical references and index.
  ISBN 0-87474-472-5 (alk. paper)
  1. Guaymí Indians—Mines and mining.
  2. Guaymí Indians—Government relations.
  3. Guaymí Indians—Social conditions.
  4. Corporación de Desarrollo Minero Cerro
Colorado. 5. Copper industry and trade—
Panama. 6. Panama—Politics and government—
1946– I. Title.
  F1565.G8G65 1991
  972.87'004978—dc20   90-45490

British Library Cataloguing-in-Publication Data is
available

Manufactured in the United States of America
98 97 96 95 94 93 92 91 5 4 3 2 1

To Michael B. Herzog

CONTENTS

PREFACE

Sólo el rey Urracá siempre tuvo su tesón de aborrecimiento contra
los españoles, llorando toda su vida no podellos acabar: al cual en
su tierra sin illo más a buscar, cognosciendo que nunca vez le
hicieron guerra que muchos dellos no saliesen della muertos y bien
descalabrados; y así en su tierra y casa murió.*

> —Bartolomé de las Casas, *Historia de las Indias*

In the heart of the Guaymí Indian lands
of western Panama looms the mountain Cerro Colorado, long known as a mountain that gives birth to
rivers, and in the 1970s discovered to be the repository of one of the
world's largest copper deposits. On these lands, the descendants of
Urracá, survivors of the Spanish conquest and of numerous subsequent
incursions by settlers, cattle ranchers, and government representatives,
engaged in their latest uneven struggle for survival.

In the 1970s and early 1980s, threats to Panamanians in general
and to the Guaymíes in particular came not from Spanish conquistadors

---

*Only the Indian king Urracá persisted in his detestation of the Spaniards,
anguished the rest of his life that he could never wipe them out. Finally
the Spaniards left him alone, because whenever they warred against him,
they suffered many dead and gravely wounded. Thus Urracá died on his
own lands, in his own home.

but from being small, poor, indebted, uninfluential nodes in a complex web of western political and economic relationships whose dynamics were beyond their control. The visible representatives of overwhelming power no longer answered to names like Balboa and Pedrarias Dávila, but to names like the United States government, the International Monetary Fund, the World Bank, transnational banking companies, and in the story told here, multinational mining firms like Texasgulf, Inc. and Rio Tinto-Zinc, Ltd., agents of the western world's voracious appetite for natural resources.

Long a national symbol in Panama's fight against United States domination, Urracá was frequently mentioned also among the Guaymí Indians as they tried to organize themselves. The Guaymíes and most Panamanians sought to ensure that they, like their ancestors, would be able to live and die in their own houses and on their own lands.

This case study focuses on social, economic, political, and cultural dimensions of the Cerro Colorado copper mining project from 1970 to 1981. Part 1 provides background material on the Cerro Colorado project, on Panama, and on the Guaymí Indians. Part 2 discusses the mining project in detail, including sketches of the multinational corporations involved: Canadian Javelin, Ltd., Texasgulf, Inc., and Rio Tinto-Zinc, Ltd. The discussion shows the tremendous risk and expense of the multibillion-dollar project in comparison with the resources of Panama as an underdeveloped country.

Part 3 shows that the large, complex, controversial project provoked a variety of responses and reactions in Panama and internationally, depending on different understandings of its impact due to the use of conflicting criteria. These criteria arose from perceptions of the needs and interests of the groups and sectors affected by the mining project. Most of the responses discussed in this book are those of the Guaymí Indians and those others who worked with them. The Guaymíes discovered that the mining project, contrary to government promises, held little benefit for them; they worked to organize themselves into an effective force, demanding to be taken seriously in negotiations concerning the project. Others, especially personnel of the Catholic Church, worked closely with the Guaymíes in these efforts. Viewed narrowly, this book argues that the people affected by Cerro Colorado could not control the dynamics of the project, nor did they have the power to influence decisions whose consequences would inevitably bring about major changes in their lives. The massive, complex project involved decisions and activities on decidedly unequal levels of dynamics.

Viewed more broadly, the present case study may further "delineate the general processes at work in . . . capitalist development while at the same time following their effects on the micro-populations" affected. In doing so, it seems to document another moment of a "people without history" who "emerge as participants in the same historical trajectory [as those] who claim history as their own" (Wolf 1982:23).

GENESIS OF THIS STUDY

By birth I am a citizen of the United States, from the Pacific Northwest. By vocation I am a Catholic priest, a member of the Society of Jesus (Jesuits). By education I am an anthropologist, alumnus of the Graduate Faculty of Political and Social Science of the New School for Social Research in New York City. Between 1977 and 1985, as a U.S. Jesuit anthropologist, I studied the Cerro Colorado copper mining project in Panama, with emphasis on its potential impact on the Guaymí Indians.

I did little of this work alone. I became involved in this investigation at the invitation of fellow Jesuits in Panama, who knew of my professional interests related to this sort of issue. With them I formed part of a varied group that set itself the objective of making available reliable information and analyses of the mining project in all its implications. Our aim was to provide a series of mini-studies that would be accessible primarily to those people of Panama who had no voice in the project's planning, but who would most feel the project's impact. We wanted to cooperate with them in their struggle to be heard.

"Varied" hardly captures the backgrounds of the members of this small interdisciplinary group. We brought to our efforts specialized education in sociology, political economics, communications, anthropology, and experience working with rural peoples of Central America. We were men and women; citizens of Panama, Spain, Canada, Great Britain, and the United States; Jesuit priests, committed lay Christians, agnostics, and a self- described "Marxist-Leninist atheist." Two of us worked full-time on this project, usually with one or another contracted third person; the rest joined in as possible or when needed.

The Cerro Colorado project was transnational, as were we. The Centro de Estudios y Acción Social—Panama (CEASPA) in Panama City, founded in 1977 by Jesuit economist Xabier Gorostiaga, provided overall coordination. The Jesuit-staffed Catholic parish of San Félix-Remedios in eastern Chiriquí Province brought in those working directly with the Guaymí Indians; I served as liaison between the Chiriquí Jesuits and CEASPA, which provided the funding for my work in Panama. Robert Carty and the Latin America Working Group (LAWG) in Toronto, Ontario, Canada—besides supplying the Panamanian contingent with articles, clippings, analyses, rumors, and questions unavailable in Panama—kept tabs on the major Canadian connections. Contacts in England, Europe, the United States, New Zealand, and Australia gave us helpful comparisons to illuminate what we were seeing in Panama.

Although the Cerro Colorado project rivaled the Panama Canal in its implications for the nation, the debate about the project involved only the narrow interests of the most powerful people in the country. In the highly charged political climate that the mining project provoked, the arguments raged on the basis of narrow, partisan analyses: the government and cosponsoring mining transnationals marshalled their evidence to assure the world that they had solved all problems; extreme right-wing opponents screamed that the sponsors ignored the most disastrous problems; and major Panamanian business associations with their open political links angled for their slice of the multi-billion dollar pie. It deeply troubled us that no one was looking at broad-based popular interests, especially those of the Guaymí Indians. In the words of Bishop Daniel Núñez, whose diocese includes Cerro Colorado: *"Almost no one has spoken for them,* their cause has been irrelevant" (Núñez y Consejo 1979:2; original emphasis).

Our group mapped out a strategy and set to work collecting and analyzing all the relevant information we could get our hands on. The political climate in Panama influenced that strategy. The government sponsored no hearings, closed or open, at which we could try to present our analyses. We had no access to the key decision-makers, no direct way to argue our perceptions with them, in hopes of influencing their decisions. Because of the polarized political climate and threatened reprisals, we could not openly advocate positions, nor even conduct our inquiry openly. My research was backed by the required official approval of the Patrimonio Histórico, the government agency responsible for supervising anthropological investigations. Nonetheless, in the presence of representatives of other government agencies, especially personnel of the Cerro Colorado project working in eastern Chiriquí, I generally followed the advice I received from people of the Patrimonio Histórico and other government agencies, and kept to myself the fact that I was an anthropologist.

Nonetheless, we moved around over much of the country and, by mail, the world; we showed up to listen in on so many meetings that some mining company personnel attributed to us Superman-like powers. We nervously chased down countless rumors, whether about impending announcements of the beginning of construction or about possible government reprisals against various ones of us. We argued among ourselves about the significance of projections of world economic recovery, the strategies of transnational mining and financial institutions, and the goals of national governments. At times we agreed to put together a critical study on some aspect of the situation, but then could not agree on the propitious moment for its release. In the week-to-week pressure and excitement, we forgot our goals and strategies; in later sessions, we went back to the basics, regrouped, and moved forward again.

As a small group of people who would not be particularly affected by the project, we had no standing on our own to insist on our right to a hearing. We sought to support the people most directly—and adversely—affected by the project, to work with them to make the case that they were entitled to present their interests and defend their lifeways that were bound up in the project. We established a working relationship with Panama's Catholic bishops, provided them with arguments and analyses, and waited impatiently to see what they would make of it all. They published strong pastoral letters, one on Cerro Colorado and the Guaymíes, and another on Cerro Colorado and the nation, and we could see that they appreciated our work. The main lines of our analysis of the project reached popular sectors of Panama through activities that took place in conjunction with these pastoral letters. At the same time, the bishops' stand gave us some backing and some breathing space; those mulling over possible reprisals now knew they could provoke a church–state confrontation that no one wanted.

For us, the principal protagonists in this struggle were the Guaymí Indians. We assented to the request of some Guaymíes for our help in the preparation of a study they could use in their own discussion of the mining project. By fighting to keep this little study out of Guaymí hands, the government mining corporation did more to give it credibility in Guaymí eyes than any amount of argumentation could have. But the government's representatives could not be persuaded that the Guaymíes raised their own serious questions about the mining project; instead, they mounted a campaign of petty harassment against church people as those responsible for stirring up the waters.

Our group members, collectively and separately, published our vision of the Cerro Colorado project in bits and pieces, but made no attempt to write an account of the entire process. However, I had a dissertation to write, so I took on the task of presenting my vision of the mining project and the process. My dissertation, with revisions, is this book. What follows now is a discussion of my approach to this study, an approach which in the main was that of our group.

METHODOLOGY OF THIS STUDY

In its diverse ramifications and manifestations, the Cerro Colorado project itself forms the unit of inquiry that sets the overall boundaries of this book. This mining project integrates a wide range of topics: the world copper market; the assurance of relatively unlimited supplies of metals; transnational corporations, market shares, and transnational financial institutions; the global economy and its recovery; the government of Panama and the nation's economic development; environmental and social impacts and their assessments; Guaymí communities; and so on. While any of these topics could itself form a unit of inquiry, the key here is the attempt to treat them all as aspects of the Cerro Colorado project.

But we conducted our investigation for specific purposes, and these defined the vantage point of our inquiry: the Cerro Colorado project viewed *from the poor—desde los pobres—*of Panama. We viewed "the poor" from two aspects: Panama as a less developed country, and the Guaymí Indians as a distinct "poor" within Panama. I adopt the same vantage point.

All investigators work to some purpose and from some vantage point. The importance of our vantage point emerges when it is contrasted with that of the mining transnationals and the Panamanian government, the sponsors of the mining project. Whereas the sponsors presumably adopted the same unit of inquiry, they conducted their studies in line with their interest in bringing the copper mine into production. Their analyses of costs took account of projections of inflation, interest rates, and the relative value of investment capital at different times and in different uses; but these analyses only accidentally took account of costs to Panama's poor, especially the Guaymíes. Their analyses of benefits used computer models to project different levels of gross national product and government income; but the models themselves took no account of how Panama came to be a poor, indebted country in the first place, and assumed that a bigger gross national product would mean a better life for all.

In contrast, our vantage point *desde los pobres,* rather than limiting or partializing the inquiry, made it more comprehensive. With respect to Panama as a less developed country, our group understood Panama's geographic vocation, the "path between the seas" (McCullough 1977), as the major factor shaping the nation's history. National dynamics were always subordinated to the primary influence of the transit area, itself constructed and controlled by major foreign powers—Spain, and later the United States. Dependency theory helped shape our understanding: in the expansion of the capitalist world system, Panama became, in the terminology of Andre Gunder Frank (1969), a dependent satellite exploited by a metropolitan center—in the language of Immanuel Wallerstein (1974), one of the periphery countries subservient to those at the core. Dependency theory, by pointing "to wider linkages [to] be investigated if the processes at work in the periphery [were] to be understood" (Wolf 1982:23), ensured that we would not consider Panama in isolation.

We discussed the "transnational vs. national dynamics" of the mining project in order to employ the analytical strength of dependency theory while also examining the pertinent national interests. It took little imagination for me to add Guaymí "local dynamics" to the above, in order to sketch a framework that encompassed the levels of dynamics of the project itself and provided tools to look at the unequal power relationships involved. This approach, it seems to me, gave relative weight to the actions and decisions of the different agents of the project within their spheres of influence; at the same time, it allowed discussion of ways their spheres of influence were limited. Thus, for example, Catholic bishops could criticize the Panamanian government for glossing over the enormous risks of the mining project, and yet note the dire straits of Panama's economic crisis of the 1970s and Panama's severely limited power to make decisions either about its economy or about the project itself.

Our vantage point proved itself comprehensive rather than partializing in another fashion, through what Eric Wolf calls a virtue of anthropology's particularism. Wolf speaks of the "drive for generalization," the all too often unidirectional efforts that "proceed from general suppositions and models to statistical statements that discount the individual case, or 'average' it into oblivion." Anthropologists "constitute a countervailing force" when they "set their data, obtained from flesh and blood informants in a local setting, against the more general measurements, garnered and aimed at a higher level, and thus provide a further test of their validity" (1974:91–92). The sponsors of Cerro Colorado, in their approaches to the study of the mining project, insisted that their generalizations disclosed the full truth about the processes and their consequences. The validity test from the vantage point of the poor—Panama and the Guaymíes—revealed the partiality of those generalizations.

Put differently, our approach was holistic, a term that points to "the characteristic quest of the anthropologist, which is to study the life of a group in its multiple relationships" (Wolf 1974:92). Our vantage point, I think, allowed us not only to keep in view the full network of these multiple relationships, but also to perceive their full force. With Eric Wolf (1982:386),

> I think of relationships as possessing force: relationships subject human populations to their imperatives, drive people into social alignments, and impart a directionality to the alignments produced. . . .
> As Marx said, men make their own history but not under conditions of their own choosing. They do so under the constraint of relationships and forces that direct their will and their desires.

In their full force, the principal relationships constituting the processes of the Cerro Colorado project were "quite asymmetrical, which is to say often downright unpleasant, relationships of political and economic power" (Adams 1977:271). As the project sponsors showed, the "measurement" of these asymmetrical forces and their "unpleasantness"— their oppressive effects—varied in sign and degree depending on the vantage point from which the measurements were carried out. From their viewpoint, the mining project could bring only "progress" to the "backward" Guaymíes, who might suffer some "minor inconveniences." But viewed from Guaymí communities in the area of Cerro Colorado, these same minor inconveniences took shape as the destruction of crops and water supplies, as grave threats to life and livelihood; sponsors' perceptions of the Guaymíes as "backward" seemed yet another demonstration of only slightly disguised prejudice.

We could discover the full force of these asymmetrical relationships of political and economic power by viewing them from the vantage point where that force most rawly asserted itself. Within Panama as a poor country, that force weighed most heavily on the Guaymí Indians, the people with fewest resources to exert adequate counterforce in their own interests. The brute power of these forces starkly contrasted with the defenselessness of the Guaymíes. It seemed that in the contemporary complex world, the full force of these relationships was often hidden, disguised, or difficult to discover until one happened on the vantage point in which this force appeared in relatively naked form.

This vision in turn provided us the means to more concrete appreciation of the somewhat more abstract implications of the same forces. "Economic risks" for indebted Panama took on fuller meaning when amplified from a narrower range of concerns for potential investors to include the deterioration of basic education, health care, housing, and transportation among Panama's majority poor.

A description of my participation in all these efforts reads like almost any account of an anthropologist's research: library work, searches for sources, travel abroad, field research, more library work and interviews, and, after several warmups, writing up the results. In anticipation of going to Panama, I studied what materials I could find in the New York area. For the mining project, besides newspaper and journal accounts, I chanced upon a good contact with Texasgulf Inc., the corporation then responsible for the development of the project; executives provided me with some written materials and a few good interviews. For the Guaymí Indians, in addition to finding published materials, I discovered that the anthropologists Philip Young and John Bort were extremely helpful and encouraging, both in the United States and in Panama. On my return to the United States after fieldwork, I interviewed a few people at the World Bank about aspects of the project, renewed certain contacts at the United Nations Centre for Transnational Corporations, and talked with several others associated with the Texasgulf side of the project. I chose mid-1981, the death of Panamanian leader Omar Torrijos, as the cutoff date for trying to bring the information in this book up to date. I finished the first writing (my dissertation) in the Spring of 1985, in Spokane, Washington, the first revisions requested by the publisher in the Spring of 1987, in El Progreso, Yoro, Honduras, and the final editing in July of 1990, back again in Spokane.

From June 1978 through November 1980 (except the summer of 1979), my investigative activities in Panama included about eleven months of fieldwork in the Guaymí area and the rest of the time in related research in eastern Chiriquí Province and in Panama City. (Figures 1 and 2 in Chapter 1 will provide some orientation.) My first period with the Guaymíes of eastern Chiriquí Province served to let them translate into images and experiences the published materials of Young and Bort, whose ethnographic work proved to be a sure foundation for me. To this end, I spent about three months working out of Hato Pilón, San Félix District. For another three months I moved my base of operations to Hato Chamí, Remedios District, to get to know the mining project area and the Guaymíes there. To become acquainted with some other aspects of the impact of the mining project, I spent two months working out of the community of Tebujo, Tolé District. I made other brief visits to Hato Pilón and environs and returned a number of times to Hato Chamí and the mining project area. I also spent about a month in Bocas del Toro Province, mainly working out of the Guaymí community of Canquintú.

My problem-oriented fieldwork required that I move around quite a bit; I could do my work only by talking with a lot of people in a lot of places. While some people proved better sources than others, I developed no group of informants. Initial contacts always led to others—family members, friends, even enemies. I gathered bits and pieces of information here and there, moved around, returned to earlier sources to check inconsistencies and contradictions, and continued to meet new people, until gradually a consistent account of the processes that interested me began to emerge.

I conversed with Guaymíes in Spanish, their (and my) second language. Guaymí men's Spanish usually more than sufficed for wide-ranging discussions, although I regretted that my ignorance meant they could not express themselves to me with the nuances of Ngawbere, their first language. But most Guaymí women were effectively monolingual, so that I had few conversations with women. Despite the Guaymí custom that women not talk with men other than their husbands or close kin, I was sufficiently accepted in some households that women probably would have spoken with me. We sometimes conversed through translators, but these conversations were no substitute for the give and take of direct communications. Since I could not learn Ngawbere, I had no way around this problem; I have no doubt that this limitation contributes to male bias in this book, a bias whose dimensions I cannot specify.

Throughout my stay in Panama, my fellow Jesuits of the parish residence in the town of Remedios provided me an overall base of operations. There, and in the town of San Félix, I became acquainted with the local campesinos, cattle ranchers, shop keepers, local politicians, and other folks. I also visited the banana plantations of Chiriquí and of Bocas del Toro, and the coffee and vegetable region of the western Chiriquí highlands. I spent some time in the coastal area of Tolé, talking with campesinos who lived near the mining project's proposed port and tailings disposal site. And of course, I became well acquainted with church workers.

Although I offer this book as an analysis of the processes involved in the Cerro Colorado mining project, for much of the presentation my writing style is descriptive. All descriptions, mine included, are selective. I tried to apprentice myself to the master ethnologist Paul Radin, selecting elements "in such a way that we feel we are dealing with real and specific men and women, with real and specific situations, and with a real and specific tradition" in order to provide "a description of a specific period and as much of the past . . . as is necessary for the elucidation of the particular period" (Radin 1933:177, 184–85).

Finally, the objectives and activities of my work need not be viewed as beyond the boundaries of what anthropologists might consider proper endeavors, even if few anthropologists explicitly conceptualize their work in the same terms as I have mine. Developing subfields with names like "applied anthropology" and "action anthropology," numerous anthropologists spend their careers in collaborative activities among people whose ways they study. And many anthropologists have carried out fieldwork focused on the lives and lifeways of the world's poor and oppressed, under names such as "primitives," "Native Americans," "peasants," "rural-to-urban migrants," "laborers," and other subjugated or besieged "minorities." Consciously or not, these anthropologists became " 'students and spokespersons' of the poor who cannot speak for themselves" (Wolf 1974:92, quoting Lewis 1964:xxiv).

I am a Jesuit priest and an anthropologist; these two parts of me became integrated in the lives of these poor. Like the Jesuits who invited me to Panama, I was influenced by recent Catholic social theology, especially the Latin American tendencies popularly known as liberation theology. Liberation theology springs from church people's growing awareness of the misery, oppression, and injustice in which Latin America's vast majorities live. As the Latin American bishops wrote, this awareness leads to acceptance of a "preferential option for the poor . . . aimed at their integral liberation" (CELAM 1979:n. 1134).

This option for the poor urges us to get beyond names and categories like "Indians" and "peasants" and even "poor," to the discovery that these are Francisco and Eneida and Chepita, fellow human beings. To the outsider, their ordinary human activities may be more interesting or even fascinating because they are "Indians" and "peasants," or because they appear simple and direct—not stupid or backward. They may even spark outside interest simply because they are "poor." But in reality, they live their lives as best they can; and their poverty is important not for its romantic potential, but because its result is that too often they die too soon.

All of this invites solidarity with these fellow human beings, in the quest for their "integral liberation"—their attempt to find ways to live more and better, to die later rather than sooner. The larger fact is that many children die from gastrointestinal and respiratory complications brought about by inadequate basic nutrition and hygiene—causes that a medical person might say could be readily eliminated if only they ate as they would instead of as they could. The specific experience of this fact was brought home to me in Hato Pilón one day, as I stood in tears by an inconsolably anguished Guaymí mother burying her two-year old son who died after several days of diarrhea.

In the course of my work on this project, I came to appreciate first hand what many of my religious colleagues already knew in Central America: despite the image that some people have, the Catholic Church in Latin America has little real power to bring about socio-political and economic change when these changes are opposed by the government and military leaders in office. Church-sponsored agencies may own radio stations and publishing houses, and through them try to mobilize public opinion; but states, often dominated by the military, control the laws and their implementation. Constitutional guarantees of freedom of expression and of due process mean nothing when the government decides to revoke a license (as in Panama during the period discussed in this book) or simply to condone, or even sponsor, the destruction of the facilities through a well-placed bomb (as in El Salvador in the 1970s and 1980s). Some church personnel may possess certain talents for investigation and analysis, even for convincing others of the validity of their points of view; but they have no effective defenses when the state sets out to discredit them (as in Panama during the period discussed in this book) or even to eliminate them (as in El Salvador and Guatemala in the 1970s and 1980s).

We were influenced, willy-nilly, by the experiences of our companions in nearby countries. Three of my Jesuit companions arrived in Panama in 1977, after they had been kidnapped by the armed forces of El Salvador and expelled from that country, only two months after another Jesuit, Rutilio Grande, had been machine-gunned there. (More than a decade later, such violence in El Salvador persists: despite worldwide revulsion and protest, the military's brutal slaughter of six prominent Jesuit priests in El Salvador in November, 1989, along with their housekeeper and her daughter, has scarcely been investigated, and most likely will go unpunished.)

These experiences helped us to maintain our expectations at a modest level, and to avoid any temptation to think ourselves possessed of immense influence over the course of the events described in this book. They also reinforced our conviction that our task was to try to keep the focus of everyone's attention on the Guaymíes and other poor of Panama, and away from ourselves.

I also came to another appreciation in my work in Panama. Despite the very inconsistent history of the Catholic Church (in Latin America and elsewhere), at least at times church representatives manage to take stands and adopt positions that quite accurately embody the stances mapped out in official church documents that too often sound too good to be true. In what I describe in this book, I make no claims that the Catholic Church's representatives always act this way; I only claim that, in this case, our official statements and our activities showed remarkable coherence.

In solidarity with the poor, then, and with my own inconsistencies and contradictions, I accepted the invitation to participate with others in the Cerro Colorado study. As student and unofficial spokesperson, I offer this study, with its deficiencies, as a voice of some poor who would like nothing better than to speak for themselves, but cannot yet make themselves heard. I hope that among all the other anthropologies, it may be a modest contribution from an anthropology of solidarity or of liberation. Its message might well be: "Tell them we too are people."

WORDS AND NAMES

Throughout this book I refer to the principal indigenous group discussed as the Guaymí Indians (plural: Guaymíes). They are known by other names as well, most commonly Ngawbe.

In the text, I use, without italics, a few Spanish words that have found their way into English dictionaries or into common United States usage. These are: cacique, campesino, conquistador, cordillera, latino, and macho. A few other Spanish words occur with sufficient frequency that their continued italicization would be distracting; consequently, they are italicized only on their first occurrence. They are:

carta orgánica
 The document setting out the legal framework for Guaymí limited self-rule.
caserío (plural *caseríos*)
 The small agglutinations of Guaymí houses into hamlets or villages or settlements.

comarca
> The defined geographical area of western Panama reserved for the Guaymíes and within which they would exercise authority according to the prescriptions of the *carta orgánica*.

corregidor (plural *corregidores*)
> An appointed local-level official, like a registrar, charged with certain responsibilities within a *corregimiento*.

corregimiento (plural *corregimientos*)
> A political subdivision of a political/geographic district, which in turn is a subdivision (like a county) of a province. *Corregimientos* bear some similarities to sub-county political entities in the United States, such as voting districts, precincts, wards, or beats.

jefe inmediato (plural *jefes inmediatos*)
> The local representative of the Guaymí cacique.

For convenience, the abbreviations and acronyms commonly used throughout the book have been defined in a brief glossary. Unless otherwise noted, all English translations of originally Spanish materials are mine.

Several individuals appear in this book protected by pseudonyms. They received the following names: Miguel Cruz, Ricardo Smith, León Palacios, Marcelo Bruno, Martín Manteca, Federico Santos, the Rodríguez family, and the Aparicio family. Persons who appear under their own names are public figures: Guaymí caciques, and personages of the Panamanian government and mining corporation, the multinational mining firms or the Catholic Church. Some others, although readily identifiable in Panama, receive partial anonymity through the use of their titles or roles only.

ACKNOWLEDGMENTS

In Panama, many Guaymí Indians willingly shared their lives with me, talked about their situation, and provided me with places to stay and food to eat. CEASPA invited my full participation in a very engrossing collaborative venture. Jorge Sarsanedas, José María Andrés, Xabier Gorostiaga, Tarsicio Parrado, Néstor Jaén, and Salvador Carranza, in good Jesuit fashion, received me as a brother and companion. Alaka Wali and I often compared notes on our work in Panama; later, in New York, we collaborated in pulling together the historical materials in Chapter 2. Charlotte Elton, and Jesuits César Jerez, Ricardo Falla, and Jorge Sarsanedas gave me good advice—not always followed—on some sensitive areas of the manuscript.

In the United States, Philip Young and John Bort responded to my interest in the Guaymí Indians with enthusiastic assistance in anything I could think of to ask them. Rayna Rapp, William Roseberry, and Shirley Lindenbaum of my doctoral committee at the New School for Social Research encouraged me warmly and constantly; Roseberry helped me over several rough spots and suggested some good revisions. William Merrill of the Smithsonian Institution offered very constructive criticisms. Jane Rinehart and Michael B. Herzog, both of Gonzaga University in Spokane, Washington, helped me resolve some difficult editing problems. Duke Johns of the Smithsonian Institution Press worked patiently with me, so that my relationship with the publisher was a smooth one. David S. Anderson, cartographer of the Geography and Anthropology Department of Eastern Washington University, greatly improved my original maps when he remade them for publication. My Jesuit companions, John (Jake) Paret and Ivan Nikolic, made St. Ignatius in Brooklyn home for me; later, the Herzogs, Mahoneys. Rineharts, Preecs/Coxes, Elizabeth Cole, and Jack Kennedy made Spokane, Washington, feel like a real family time. My sister, Karin Gjording, has affected my work more than she knows.

Michael B. Herzog met with me daily for a year and a half, in response to my request for his help to finish my doctoral dissertation, the original version of this book. Without his help, I would never have finished; I put myself in his hands, and he taught me the process of writing. To this friend and brother, unfailing source of good counsel, with deepest heartfelt gratitude, I dedicate this book.

PART 1

Introduction and Background

CHAPTER 1

Overview of the Cerro Colorado Project

On April 19, 1980, the rustic meeting place of the Extraordinary Guaymí General Congress became the scene of an unprecedented confrontation. Four thousand Guaymí delegates gathered in Soloy, in the foothills of eastern Chiriquí, to consider the pros and cons of the Cerro Colorado copper mining project and the related Teribe-Changuinola hydro-electric project, multibillion-dollar investments that the Panamanian government and multinational corporate partners planned to develop in the Guaymí area of western Panama—Cerro Colorado in the eastern part of the Pacific province of Chiriquí, Teribe-Changuinola in the western part of the Caribbean province of Bocas del Toro (Figure 1).

On the third and final day of the congress, Ricardo Rodríguez, Minister of Government and Justice of the Panamanian government, harangued the delegates in response to their resolutions rejecting both projects. He accused the congress of "blackmail" and of marching under an ill-advised "political banner" (i.e., playing politics) in linking their insistence on the definition of their legal land rights to their discussion of the mega-projects. He attributed their actions to manipulation by know-nothings "with old mental structures." He lamented that the congress had been led astray by outside agitators, non- Guaymíes who sought their own interests at the expense of what was clearly (to him) to the advantage of the Guaymíes in their supposedly close relationship with the national government he represented. The Guaymíes should support Cerro Colorado because it would solve all their problems (quo-

3

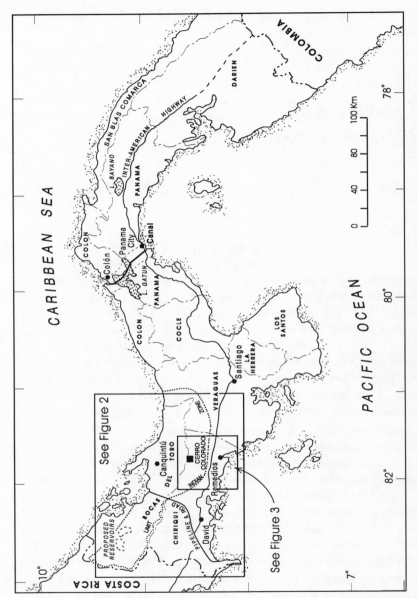

Figure 1. Republic of Panama

4

tations and summary from the minutes of the congress in Congresos Guaymíes 1980:47–48).

Rodríguez, instead of contenting himself with his opening platitudes assuring the Guaymíes that the government would always take care of them, had departed from the ordinary rhetoric of these occasions. Then he sat in shock and obvious discomfort as the Guaymíes followed his lead with their own departure from the ordinary rhetoric of the occasion. Instead of thanking the Minister for coming and assuring him of their unswerving confidence in General Torrijos' promises to grant them their legal land rights, several delegates accepted the invitation of congress officials to give their reactions to the statements of Rodríguez. As succinctly summarized in the minutes of the congress:

> People of the Congress intervened, refuting all the expressions emitted by the Minister, with solid arguments which left clear that the Guaymí people are not being manipulated; that the Guaymí position with respect to Cerro Colorado and the Hydroelectric Projects is based on problems and concrete facts and not a simple political banner, much less blackmail; that the Guaymí people want progress and development but not in the form that the State and Government [sic] wants to impose, via huge projects that guarantee no real benefit and which only proceed in detriment of the Guaymí people, toying with them via promises. (Congresos Guaymíes 1980:48)

This tense confrontation[1] left no doubt that ten years of government pronouncements and unfulfilled promises, rumors, and Cerro Colorado exploratory activities had drained most of the reservoir of Guaymí good will. The government had sought to convince them, and everyone else, that the Cerro Colorado project guaranteed a better future for all of Panama and for all Panamanians. It argued that if all Panama would profit from the exploitation of Panama's copper, eastern Chiriquí in particular would feel the positive impact. This region, "one of the poorest in the country, with high indices of mortality, morbidity, illiteracy, malnutrition and underemployment," would see "urban development, modernization, progress." The mine would transform the region, which provided none of the infrastructure needed for the project, into an area with "an important nucleus of industrial production and of services, the attraction of public investment in education, health, infrastructure, etc.": industry, a thriving city, a major port, excellent roads. Eastern Chiriquí would become a major pole of attraction and development within Panama, bringing to an end the nation's problems with rural-to-urban migration (CODEMIN 1979d:35).

In eastern Chiriquí, all the people—townsfolk, ranchers, campesinos, and the Guaymí Indians—would be the beneficiaries. Townsfolk would become city people, with all the economic and social advantages of city life: business opportunities, educational facilities, health care, recreation. Ranchers would have nearby markets, putting an end to the rising costs of transporting their cattle to Panama City or to the transit area's embarkation points for export. Campesinos could get good prices for all their agricultural produce, and be assured of local jobs to supplement their farming income.

And the always-neglected Guaymí Indians, inhabitants of the project area, could leave behind their poverty-stricken backward ways and take their rightful place in twentieth-century Panama (see especially CODEMIN 1979c). For the Guaymíes, project sponsors promised special benefits. Of course, any losses would be fully compensated. The project would greatly improve their economic situation: they would benefit from projects to improve production and nutrition, would have good markets for their agricultural products, and would even receive help with marketing traditional handicrafts and would learn marketable new ones. With the project in their backyard, they would be at an advantage in the competition for steady jobs, and the project would insure that they met the minimal standards for technical training.

The mining project would guarantee improved housing, sanitation and health care for the Guaymíes. Better educational facilities would enable their children to become fully integrated into Panamanian national life. Their leaders would participate in project decisions that affected Guaymí lands and life. And the sponsors, aware that the Guaymíes had no understanding of this major project (its scope, methods, impact, and meaning), launched an educational campaign, making themselves available to explain the project, answer concerns, put rumors to rest, and in general consult with the people affected. The sponsors claimed that, with regard to the Guaymíes, they were carrying out extensive investigations into all aspects of the anticipated impact of the project, and were developing measures to minimize anything negative (see CODEMIN 1979a:34–35).

Nonetheless, as the Guaymíes made clear in Soloy, for most of the planning and debate they seemed not to exist at all. *"Almost no one has spoken for them,* their cause has been irrelevant" (Núñez y Consejo 1979:2; emphasis in original). They most of all had unanswered questions; they most of all knew the unpromised impact. They lived with constant rumors. And more than hopes, they lived in increasing fear of the project.[2]

BACKGROUND MATTERS

Geographic Setting

The location and mammoth scope of the Cerro Colorado project more than justified Guaymí fears. The mountain Cerro Colorado, with an elevation of 1500 meters, lies on the Continental Divide of western Panama, in the northeastern corner of the province of Chiriquí, in the heart of the lands occupied by the Guaymí Indians. It is 260 km almost due west of Panama City, about 425 km by road (Figure 1). The Guaymíes refer to Cerro Colorado as a mountain that gives birth to rivers. At the foot of Cerro Colorado lies a principal source of the headwaters of the San Félix River, which drains an area of about 234 km[2]; within 5 km of Cerro Colorado lie the headwaters of the Cuvíbora River, which drains about 143 km[2]. And just to the north, on the Atlantic side of the Continental Divide, in the province of Bocas del Toro, lie the headwaters of the Cricamola River, which drains about 383 km[2] (Alvarado 1979:2–3). The San Félix River is the principal river of the two districts of Remedios and San Félix; the Cuvíbora and the Tabasará, into which the Cuvíbora flows, are the principal rivers of the district of Tolé. The Cricamola is the major river of the eastern region of the district of Chiriquí Grande (Figure 2).

The Continental Divide area of western Panama is a tropical mountain region with heavy rainfall. Average rainfall in the Cerro Colorado area of Chiriquí is between 3500 and 4000 mm annually; the rainy season begins around May and reaches its wettest around October or November.[3] On the Atlantic side, average rainfall is 4500 to 5000 mm, spread throughout the year (CSMRI 1977:XI–14, 16).

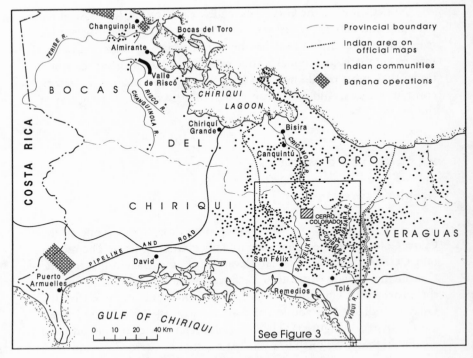

Figure 2. Western Panama indigenous area

Early Exploration and Development Plans

In 1932 Robert Terry, a Sinclair Oil geologist, located veins mineralized with copper on Cerro Colorado.[4] From time to time after that, geologists looked it over, wondering about the prospects for a copper mine. In 1955–57 Bob Stewart, a geologist of the Panama Canal Company, undertook some preliminary exploration of the site; he concluded that Cerro Colorado had at least 100 million tons of 0.5 percent copper. Stewart tried to interest North American copper companies in the deposit, but his efforts were unsuccessful (E/MJ 1977:194; CODEMIN 1979d:11).

In the 1960s, in the general climate of United Nations development decades, the Alliance for Progress, and theories of "stages of growth" for third world development, Panama showed interest in finding and developing its mineral resources. But attention shifted away from Cerro Colorado to other possible mineral sites in Panama. Between 1965 and 1969, the United Nations Development Programme (UNDP) teamed up with the government of Panama to sponsor exploration; as part of the exploration program, the UNDP helped Panama establish a laboratory to assay ore samples. By 1966 the UNDP had confirmed the presence of copper and molybdenum at Petaquilla and Botija, in an area of the province of Colón, to the east of Cerro Colorado. This discovery, more carefully mapped out by the UNDP by 1969, "sparked the search for copper in that country on a wide scale" (Carman 1979:56). However, under the joint UNDP–government program, the Cerro Colorado deposits were reserved for later study.

Mining companies looked closely at the Petaquilla and Botija copper–molybdenum deposits, estimated to be 300 million tons of average 0.65 percent copper ore (MS 1975). The government of Panama, near the beginning of the tenure of the National Guard General Omar Torrijos Herrera, offered this area for bids on August 31, 1969. Although the terms were judged "relatively harsh," since they included "provisions for joint government– private industry operations," major multinational corporations from the United States, Great Britain, France, Italy, Japan and Canada showed interest (E/MJ 1969b:112; 1970:102).[5]

While the mining industry considered its options on the Petaquilla deposits, the Torrijos government worked on another deal. In mid-1969, Torrijos opened negotiations for exploration concessions for what must have been Cerro Colorado—described as an area along the Continental Divide, an area unworked by the UNDP (E/MJ 1969:142). This area was most likely opened at the request of a small mining company from Montreal, Canadian Javelin, Ltd. (see E/MJ 1971:27). Only two companies (both Canadian) bid on this concession: Canadian Javelin, through its Panamanian subsidiary Pavonia, S.A., and Placer Development, Ltd. Canadian Javelin, offering a premium of $51,000 to only $10,000 from Placer, won the concession and began exploration late in 1970 (E/MJ 1971:27). With the entry of Canadian Javelin, Panama began its attempt to become a copper producer.

Scale of the Proposed Project

Between 1970 and 1981, three mining firms—Canadian Javelin, Texasgulf, and Rio Tinto-Zinc—spent millions of dollars working in these mountains, exploring the Cerro Colorado deposits.[6] Extensive drilling and sampling revealed that Bob Stewart had seriously underestimated the magnitude of the deposits. Cerro Colorado turned out to be one of the world's largest proven reserves, with 1,380 million metric tons (m.t.) of low-grade porphyry copper ore (mixed with great quantities of sulfur), along with recoverable traces of molybdenum, gold, and silver (Table 1). The Cerro Colorado deposits presented Panama with the possibility of becoming one of the world's major producers of copper.

Panamanian leaders envisioned a future in which copper mining would provide major economic benefits: almost $500 million injected into the Panamanian economy during the construction of the mine, and more than $2.5 billion in income to the government during twenty years of mining (CODEMIN 1979a:27, 32). With the mining project, they hoped to alter Panama's lopsided economic dependence on canal-related activities and gain much greater control over Panama's destiny.

The sponsors of the project proposed an open-pit copper mine, a concentrator, and a smelter (Figure 3). They thought it would take four or five years to remove the 80 million metric tons of "overburden" as they dug the 4-km by 5-km pit, which would range from 800 meters to 1500 meters above sea level (CODEMIN 1977:10; see Table 2 for the land requirements for the mining project). While they prepared the pit, they would build the other major parts of the project: the concentration plant at the foot of Cerro Colorado; the dam and reservoir south of Cerro Colorado to obtain the water needed for the concentrator; a 65-km slurry pipeline, to transport the concentrated copper to the smelter in the port area: a 65-km highway from the mine area to the Pacific port; the port itself, needed both to bring in supplies for the mine and to load copper for export; and the smelter and its accompanying sulfuric acid plant.

The mining project had a series of ancillary requirements: places to dispose of the overburden, the waste rock encountered during mining operations, and the tailings from the concentrator; quarries to provide lime and silica for the concentration and smelting of the copper; two construction camps for up to 3,500 workers each; a city (15,000 to 30,000 people) for the 2,000–3,500 permanent employees, their families, and the services they would need; and the electrical energy needed to operate all the aspects of the mining project. In addition, the spon-

TABLE 1
Cerro Colorado Statistics

Mine Area	
Potential Reserves	1,380 million m.t. of 0.78% copper 0.010% molybdenum 5.1 grams/m.t. silver 0.08 grams/m.t. gold
Mineral Production	27 million m.t./year
Sterile Rock	86 million m.t./year

Concentrator
  Capacity
  Concentrates
  Tailings
	
	27 million m.t./year
	759,000 m.t./year
	26.2 million m.t./year

Reservoir	10 million m³ of water 113.55 million liters/day

Port Area	
Port	2 piers for ships of 20,000 dead weight tons
Smelter Capacity	187,000 m.t./year of blister copper
Sulfuric Acid Plant Capacity	825,000 m.t./year

SOURCE: CODEMIN 1979a.

sors foresaw the need for storage facilities for equipment and spare parts, repair stations, offices, training areas, and a variety of lesser items, such as furniture, office supplies, clothing, and so on.

All the construction would require 7,000 or more workers, whose jobs would include building the two temporary towns they would live in during the construction period. Each year of mining operations, using 16-cubic-meter electric shovels and 166 m.t. electric dump trucks,

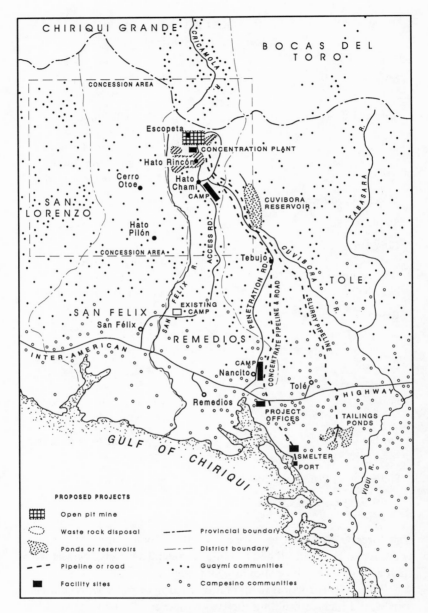

Figure 3. Cerro Colorado installation and surroundings

TABLE 2

Cerro Colorado Land Requirements

Installation	Land Needed (approx. km²)	Souce of Calculation
Mine Area Total, Cerro Colorado	314.2	
Open pit mine, 4 km × 5 km		2
Waste rock deposit, 4 km × 5 km		2
Unoccupied, 4 km on all sides		3
Construction Camp, Hato Chamí	3.0	4
Ridge, Hato Chamí to Boca del Monte, about 3 km × 1 km		
Reservoir, Cerro Laguna	4.5	4
4.5 km × 1 km		
Road (80% in Guaymí area)	6.3	1
63 km × 100 m		
Other Installations	3.2	4
(Slurry pipelines, electrical lines, etc.), calculated as 50% of road area		
Construction Camp, El Nancito	3.0	4
Port and Smelter	1.5	1
Tailings Dam	15.0	1
Total Land Needs	*350.7*	
Total, in Guaymí Area	*329.3*	
Plus Changuinola I	280.0	5
Hydroelectric energy for mine		
New Total Land Needs	*630.7*	
New Total, in Guaymí Area	*609.3*	

SOURCES: 1 = Cámara de Comercio 1979:67–68.
          2 = Texasgulf mining plans and maps.
          3 = F.T. Davis interview with DeRoo et al.
          4 = Author's calculations, based on maps and knowledge of terrain.
          5 = IRHE 1979a.

the sponsors intended to remove and process 113 million m.t. of the mountain. According to their studies, processing would begin with the separation and disposal of 86 million m.t. of "waste rock" which lacked significant copper content or whose mineral content was too low for profitable processing with present technology and expected copper prices.[7] The other quarter of what they dug up would be concentrated, smelted, loaded on ships, and sold abroad. Each year, the concentrator would produce 759,000 m.t. of 25 percent copper, 35 percent sulfur concentrate and 26.3 million m.t. of tailings; from the concentrate, the smelter would produce 187,000 m.t. of 99 percent pure blister copper, a by-product (with the addition of water) of 845,000 m.t. of 93 percent sulfuric acid, and 475,000 m.t. of slag (CODEMIN 1979a:10). The traces of molybdenum, gold, and silver would be sold within the smelted copper, then removed in the refinery.

Cerro Colorado would be one of the world's biggest copper mines; it would also be the most expensive. By late 1979, the sponsors calculated that it would cost more than $2 billion to build the mine and purchase all the equipment needed to operate it. They hoped to finance the project through loans made to the operating company they had established as the owner of the project. They also counted on the ability of the government of Panama to obtain lower interest development loans for some parts of the project excluded from the construction budget: the city, the roads, and the Changuinola I hydroelectric project.

However the project was financed, it had to pay for itself. The sponsors projected that in the worst case, Cerro Colorado could sell copper for $1.27 a pound and still pay all its debts; they thought copper would sell for around $1.50 a pound when Cerro Colorado began producing, leaving both plenty of margin and the likelihood of profits from the outset (CODEMIN 1979a:17, 20).[8]

The information on the different aspects of the deposits, the proposals for how to do the mining, the estimates of costs, and the details of what was required to convert Cerro Colorado into a major copper mine, all came from the extensive exploratory studies carried out in turn by the three multinational firms that worked on Cerro Colorado. Canadian Javelin spent $23 million for its explorations, Texasgulf and CODEMIN spent $18 million, and Rio Tinto-Zinc about $10 million more. The money went for a variety of things: crews and housing; drilling test holes, extracting ore samples, laboratory work on the ore samples; small-scale testing of proposed concentration and smelting methods; computer studies of the ore deposit, mining plans, costs, projected income; engineering consultants to design project facilities; econometric studies of future copper demand and prices; studies of sources of financing and of markets for copper, and so on. Texasgulf put together forty-eight volumes of studies on the various aspects of the project.

Some of these millions covered expenses in laboratories and offices in Panama, the United States, and Canada. Money for computer, econometric, and beneficiation studies (testing of processing of the ore) was spent in the United States and Canada. Consultants hired were principally major firms from the United States; in turn, some of these subcontracted Panamanians for parts of their work.

And some of the money paid for the on-site work in Chiriquí. All three corporations undertook extensive drilling all over the Cerro Colorado area to map the Cerro Colorado deposits. Texasgulf dug a 400-meter adit into the center of the mountain to take out thousands of tons of samples for various tests. Canadian Javelin and Texasgulf built permanent-looking settlements, which they called camps, to house their workers: one on the face of the mountain, for about 50 people; another in Escopeta, at the foot of the mountain, with a medical center, and offices and laboratories for geologists, an ecologist, hydrologists, mining engineers, and other technical personnel, about 100 people in all; a camp for about 100 workers in nearby Cuernavaca; a camp for another 100 people, with equipment repair shop and medical center, in Hato Chamí; and a supply camp at the foot of the road to the mine area, near the town of San Félix.[9] Canadian Javelin built a road from the Escopeta camp up the face of Cerro Colorado to the drilling sites, and began a road to the town of San Félix; Texasgulf added other roads. Both Canadian Javelin and Texasgulf brought in vehicles (jeeps, pickups, road scrapers, bulldozers, dump trucks) to build and maintain the roads, to provide transportation for personnel, and to carry out other aspects of their exploration.

At peak times of exploration, the work force reached 200-250 men; just the maintenance of roads and equipment required around 100 men. The companies brought their own crews to do most of the technical work; Panamanians (and a few Guaymíes) mainly had jobs as laborers, drivers, mechanics, cooks, janitors, electricians, and crew foremen.

Cerro Colorado was, then, a huge, expensive project, with powerful actors and a great deal at stake. The sponsors seemed comfortable combining the power and resources of multinational mining firms and a national government, arguing that their combined efforts guaranteed a better future for all of Panama and for all Panamanians. For twelve years, Torrijos and his associates worked with multinational mining firms and financial institutions to transform Cerro Colorado's potential into a major copper mine. But, as this book argues, the road to making Panama a major copper producer turned out to be as rocky, winding, full of detours, and ultimately impassable, as the rain-drenched Guaymí trails in the mountains where the deposits lay buried.

Cerro Colorado became a major focus of attention and controversy in Panama, and in mining, financial, and solidarity circles elsewhere. The attention and controversy, centered on the real costs and benefits of the project for Panama itself and especially for the Guaymí Indians within Panama, took their course as moments in the history of Panama and of the Guaymíes. The following two chapters present the background materials necessary for a fuller appreciation of these moments.

CHAPTER 2

The Torrijos Years, 1968–1981: Contradictions of the Torrijos Revolution

I n the Panamanian presidential elections of 1968, Dr. Arnulfo Arias Madrid emerged victorious when the oligarchy failed to overcome its factional splits to back a candidate. A few days after his inauguration, the National Guard, protecting itself from Arias' attempts to neutralize it, overthrew him.[1] Colonel Omar Torrijos Herrera, the little-known military commander of Chiriquí Province, emerged as a member of the junta governing Panama and as commander-in-chief of the National Guard. In less than a year, Torrijos, now a brigadier general, alone governed Panama (LaFeber 1979:154–62); he remained the key figure in Panamanian politics until his death in a plane crash in mid-1981.

Torrijos announced his goal of building nothing less than a new Panama, a revolutionary Panama. His master plan envisioned construction of an edifice resting on three sets of pilings: sovereignty, economic independence, and popular programs to favor the poor. He sought sovereignty through the negotiation of new canal treaties to replace those that gave the United States the right to dominate affairs on the isthmus. He sought economic independence through a variety of plans and projects to achieve self-sufficiency in food, to diversify the economy, and to increase production, exports, foreign exchange, and foreign investment. And in poor areas of the country, he launched an unprecedented expansion of public services, in education, health care, sanitation facilities, housing, roads, and in a modest land reform program.

But no matter how revolutionary were Torrijos' rhetoric or plans,

17

he had to work with the architecture of the Panama he took over, domestically under the control of a well-established oligarchy, internationally a transnational service platform under the control of outside interests and powers. The 1903 canal treaties, and the activities of the United States since its major entry into Panama in the mid-nineteenth century, developed the patterns begun by the Spaniards early in the sixteenth century, patterns that came to convince Panamanians and the world that Panama was little or nothing aside from its "geographic vocation" as a transit area subservient to the dictates of major outside powers—powers that made their decisions based only on their perceptions of their own interests. Throughout the twentieth century, the Republic of Panama was a sovereign and independent nation mainly on paper; few details of the life of the nation and its citizens did not feel the impact of the severely compromised sovereignty symbolized altogether too well by the United States–operated Panama Canal, itself cutting through a lush U.S.-controlled strip of Panama (the Canal Zone) guarded by fourteen U.S. military bases. Panama's dependence upon and subservience to the socio-political and economic interests of other nations narrowed severely the range of choices open to any revolutionary.

HISTORY

Panama's "Geographic Vocation"

When Spanish explorers failed to uncover extensive deposits of precious metals, they shifted their attention to Panama's "principal geographic resource," the key to Panama's historical development: the unique combination of a narrow land mass and easy access to both the Caribbean (Atlantic) and the Pacific Oceans. The mountain chain that extends eastward from the Costa Rican border reaches its lowest point just where the isthmus is at its narrowest, still to the west of the foothills of the Serranía de San Blas, the northern extension of the Andes (West and Augelli 1976:461ff.). Along this trans-isthmian corridor, the Spanish carved out a river and overland trail crossing early in the sixteenth century; United States businessmen built and profited from the Panama Railroad in the mid-nineteenth century;

and the U.S. government dug and operated the Panama Canal early in the twentieth century.

These "paths between the seas" (McCullough 1977) determined Panama's development as a platform serving the travel and trade needs of major outside powers. Spain moved soldiers and goods across the isthmus en route to western South America, and hauled Peruvian gold and silver to the galleons waiting to hurry to Seville to replenish the always-bare coffers of the kings. The Panama Railroad initially contributed to the transport of people and goods between the eastern United States and the California gold fields; the railroad shortened the isthmian crossing from a dangerous journey of three to five days, to an easy train ride of no more than six hours (Schott 1967). The canal cut days off voyages between oceans, contributing to the rapid expansion of the United States as a major shipping and naval power.

Spanish colonization of the isthmus responded to the needs of the transit area. Administrators, merchants, ecclesiastical authorities, and those who provided labor for the transport of goods formed the population of the transit area; rural towns provided food, and small outposts dotted the Pacific coast as way stations along the Spanish road (*camino real*) to Central America.

The map of Panama's colonization also became the map of political and economic power, as well as the guide to the fluctuations that from the outset influenced the daily lives of the people. Merchants, with ready access to Spanish and other trade goods, controlled the internal economy; they also established suburban haciendas to provide food for the city, and to give themselves some hedges against the ups and downs of the import-export trade.[2] In 1522, crown beneficiaries (*encomenderos*) founded the town of Natá, the early center for the "interior" of the isthmus, to ensure provisions for the transit area, but during off years of the boom-and-bust economy of the transit area, Panama City's powerful merchants kept Natá's officially recognized residents (*vecinos*) from competing in the slackened transit area markets.[3] Slaves, later replaced by mules raised in the more temperate climes of Costa Rica, Nicaragua, and Honduras, provided the "animal power" for the difficult crossing. The Spanish moved west along the Pacific coast, founding towns such as Montijo, Remedios and Alanje as outposts or way stations on the road from Central America to Panama, the route used for the mule drives.[4] By the end of the sixteenth century, Panama's political power and basic economic activity were concentrated on the transisthmian cargo route between Peru and Spain (MacLeod 1973:51). The isthmus had begun to live out its "geographic vocation."

Responses to fluctuating cycles in transisthmian traffic shaped the continued development of Panama's political and economic landscape. Spain could not control its vast empire in the face of problems at home and competition from other growing European powers. With the Treaty of Utrecht in 1713, Spain yielded its trade monopoly. After 1748, Spanish galleons no longer came to Portobelo; the transit trade plunged into a decline from which it would not recover for nearly a century, when U.S. businesses built the railroad.[5] During the economic recession of the transit area, many merchants bought up or claimed large tracts of land in the western part of the country—a process of ruralization of the commercial bourgeoisie. Families that established these latifundias, in Coclé, Veraguas, and Chiriquí, maintained ties to Panama City through relatives who continued commercial operations.[6]

The building of the Panama Railroad (opened in 1855) stimulated a new boom period for those whose economic activities depended on service to the transit trade; Panama was flooded with people from the eastern seaboard of the United States scurrying to the California gold fields. Panamanian merchants expanded their enterprises to provide services to the railroad construction crews (7,000 men at their peak); the main enterprise of the commercial elite was real estate and housing for laborers, railroad officers, steamship personnel, and the transient population.

But the railroad boom brought with it new problems of widespread unemployment[7] and an increase in the share of economic activity in Panama held by foreigners. The railroad's stockholders in New York received the bulk of the tremendous profits;[8] foreign, mainly U.S., entrepreneurs rushed to Panama to compete with local interests for the service of those awaiting passage on United States ships to California. To maintain both their economic base and their social and political prestige, the members of the local merchant class redoubled their concentration on the commercial sphere or on the provision of services connected with the transit route. The boom spread to their relatives in the countryside, who expanded their cattle raising and shipping to the transit area. Panamanian merchants also forged close ties with the foreign merchants and entrepreneurs who controlled the economy, linking themselves not only through business associations, but also through marriage (Figueroa N. 1978: chap. 1).[9]

Even more importantly, the construction of the railroad rendered visible the shift in the source of external influence from Spain and Europe to the United States.[10] After sporadic explorations for canal routes, in 1846 the U.S. signed the Bidlack–Mallorino Treaty with the Republic of New Granada (Colombia and Panama), securing and protecting a right-of-way across the isthmus, while providing the legal framework for U.S. military intervention on the isthmus (see Farnsworth and McKenney 1983:14–15). Dating from the signing of this treaty, "the United States has continuously exercised some attribute of sovereignty over the isthmus, and conversely the sovereignty of Panama and its predecessors has been less than absolute" (Bray 1977:21).[11] The railroad could be built because of the Bidlack–Mallorino Treaty.[12]

From Independence to Torrijos, 1903–1968

Throughout this century, the Panama Canal has dominated the economic and political life of Panama, an independent republic since 1903. As the century began, wealthy Panamanians, in the throes of another "bust" cycle following the completion of transcontinental railroads in the United States and the collapse of the French efforts to build a canal, made a pact with the United States in return for assistance in attaining Panama's independence from Colombia.[13] The U.S. sought a way around payment of Colombian demands in exchange for concessions to take over the French canal. But the 1903 Hay–Bunau Varilla Treaty—the treaty no Panamanian ever signed—gave the U.S., "in perpetuity," control over the entire canal area, stretching from Colón to Panama City, including all buildings, grounds, facilities, and markets, in exchange for a one-time payment of $10 million, and a $250,000 annuity (LaFeber 1979:260). Despite the possibilities created by the multibillion-dollar investment and the employment of an average of 42,000 workers, local merchants reaped relatively little profit from the most productive sector of the economy; principally, they provided housing in Colón and Panama City, and some limited services. Nonetheless, it was in their interest to maintain friendly ties with the United States, because only in this way had they any involvement in major commercial activities. By 1915, when the canal went into full operation, both the local commercial sector and the U.S. were firmly entrenched in their control of Panamanian economics and politics.

The cycle of economic boom and recession, a fact of life since the colonial period, became even more important in the twentieth century as the canal increased Panama's dependence on external markets. The boom periods were 1904–30, 1940–46, and 1966–73; the periods of recession were 1930–40, 1947–55, and 1973–79.[14] During periods of economic growth, the handful of merchant families who controlled local politics consolidated their power,[15] whereas workers and the middle class made the periods of depression times of unrest and rebellion.

Instability and factionalism characterized the political scene, which was also subject to external influence; between 1914 and 1930, Panama was effectively a colony of the U.S., which controlled the economy, migration, city services, radio and telegraph communications, foreign policy, and participated in Panama's elections. The U.S. government insisted that Panama accept U.S. economic advisers to assist in pulling out of the recession following World War I; U.S. troops intervened in the Republic many times in the twentieth century. United States-based companies dominated the economy: the United Fruit Co. in agriculture, Chase National and National City in banking, Panama Power and Light Company in electric services (see LaFeber 1979:chap. 3).[16]

During times of depression, conflicts emerged and discontent was expressed by both a growing working class and a small middle class that consisted of teachers, government employees, professionals, small business people, and students. This middle class formed part of a "populist" movement that focused on nationalism. By 1924, the organized middle class was insisting on a more favorable canal treaty (see LaFeber 1979, Soler 1976).[17] The labor force had to overcome major problems in order to effectively coalesce as a united movement.[18] From the outset, the trade union movement was heavily influenced by the AFL–CIO, and union members were vulnerable to manipulation by both the middle class organization and the oligarchy (Gandásegui et al. 1980). Gradually, the oligarchy absorbed the middle class movement with its own espousal of the nationalist rhetoric; both the oligarchy and the middle class used United States domination and the canal treaty as a scapegoat, urging renegotiation as the solution to the country's domestic problems (LaFeber 1979). Most of the rural population of small farmers remained unorganized.

In the 1960s, under the influence of growing nationalism through-out Latin America and worried about the influence of the Cuban revo-lution, U.S. policy makers shifted their approach. These were the years of early United Nations development decades and the Kennedy and Johnson administrations' Alliance for Progress, which emphasized rural and infrastructural development through vast injections of foreign as-sistance, and through the encouragement of land reform, small indus-try, housing, education, and health projects.[19] However, "the founda-tions of the economy remained weak. And although [Panama] boasted the highest per capita rate of economic growth during the 1960s of any Latin American nation, inequality and poverty also continued to grow" (LaFeber 1979:150); the new assistance did little or nothing to overcome the structural weaknesses.[20]

Political factionalism and structural weaknesses of the economy formed the immediate conditions for the successful military coup d'état in 1968. But the deeper problems came from Panama's history as a transnational service platform with the accompanying economic depen-dence and severely compromised sovereignty.

> It remained clear, as has been demonstrated ad nauseam, that his-torically the much-acclaimed "Geographic Vocation" of our country could only be translated into terms of transisthmian movement when a hegemonic center was inclined to assume the power of deci-sion concerning the use of what traditionally has been considered our "Principal Geographic Resource" (Castillero C. 1973:20–21).

This history provided the rhetoric, if not the real agenda, of the years of the Torrijos revolution.

NATIONAL DYNAMICS: WINNING SUPPORT FOR TORRIJOS

From the time of the presidency of Remón (1962–68), who had been commander of the National Guard, it was axiomatic that whoever controlled the National Guard controlled Pan-ama. Not long after the overthrow of Arnulfo Arias (October 1968), Omar Torrijos had consolidated his control over the Guard. However he brought this about, he clearly succeeded in surrounding himself with officers either personally loyal to him, or at least unable to develop their own following among the rank-and-file members. Torrijos expanded and professionalized the Guard, giving new opportunities to mestizo and black recruits. He raised the pay, and organized the chain of command in such fashion that he alone knew everything that was going on.[21]

But Torrijos realized that no leader could stay in power in Panama simply with the support of the military (see LaFeber 1979:167). He announced a "revolution," one that would favor the majority of Panamanians and instill national pride through the achievement of sovereignty and economic independence. Torrijos presented himself as the leader of the broad majority of Panamanians: campesinos, workers, and even Indians. On the level of image, he shrewdly used his own background as the mestizo offspring of lower middle class school teachers from Veraguas, in striking contrast to the usual succession of major political leaders in Panama: lily-white members of wealthy oligarchy families. He also appealed openly to the macho urges of popular Panamanians, appearing live or on billboards throughout the country dressed in National Guard fatigues with a pistol at his belt, looking like the Marlboro man (LaFeber 1979:160). His speeches emphasized his image as the common Panamanian that so many wished to become. He travelled the country on his "domestic patrols," going to remote areas where no government officials ever visited, making personal contact with the people, assuring them that he knew their problems and was working to solve them.

The early reforms of the Torrijos revolution went well with his populist image. Torrijos promised to concentrate on rural development to favor campesinos, reversing Panama's centuries-long favoritism of the transit zone. He announced a major land reform to insure that all rural families had small parcels of land for their subsistence. He brought about the formation of hundreds of small collective farms (*asentamientos de campesinos*) providing members with a piece of land, government financial assistance for equipment and inputs (including seed, fertilizer, and insecticides), and technical assistance to organize themselves, their farming, and the marketing of their rice or other products. Through these reforms, he sought to make Panama self-sufficient in basic foods, taking advantage of what the development planners saw as Panama's ample resources of land and people (see Merrill et al. 1975).

He stressed basic education, building rural schools, training and assigning new teachers, and reforming the curriculum to include supervised experience in practical matters like farming and carpentry. He provided a strong impetus to improved health care in rural areas by building or upgrading health centers, assigning doctors and nurses, expanding the government health insurance program, and by providing low-cost medication and care for all, with or without pay, by inaugurating a program to train rural health assistants in basic sanitation, nutrition, and family planning, and by urging communities to form local committees to find ways to improve for themselves their general health standards.

In urban areas—mainly Panama City and some provincial capitals—the Torrijos revolution concentrated on solving the massive housing problems brought on by the extensive rural-to-urban migration. With the help of loans from the U.S. State Department's Agency for International Development (AID), Torrijos built hundreds of units of low-cost housing that people bought with government-subsidized mortgages. He also greatly increased the number of apartments available to working- and middle-class renters. These efforts, an important contribution to the construction boom of the early 1970s, were accompanied (albeit at times very slowly) by extensions of government water, sewage, electricity, and road services.

Among the working people of the transit area, the principal symbol of the Torrijos revolution was the 1972 revision of the labor code, making the organization of workers into unions much easier, giving workers government-enforced rights to collective bargaining, prohibiting employers from arbitrary dismissals of workers, establishing minimum wages, providing some protections for domestic workers, and so on. Union organizers suddenly found themselves deluged with requests to help form new unions; the government insured rapid recognition of the unions as the collective bargaining agents. Some organizers from more militant organizations worked to strengthen national affiliations that kept at least some distance from the government; but the majority of the new unions became members of affiliations that openly supported the government.[22]

Much of Torrijos' rhetoric was anti-oligarchy. Taking dead aim at the oligarchy's decades-long strangle hold on Panama's political life, he disbanded the 53-member national legislature and outlawed political parties, on the grounds that the legislature and the main parties were simply vehicles to guarantee the oligarchy's control of the levers of political power in Panama. He also pressured the television, newspapers, and radio, to make sure that the people of Panama heard his version of what was going on.[23] His Constitution of 1972 instituted the National Assembly of Representatives, whose 505 members were directly elected in the 505 *corregimientos* (voting districts) of Panama. These representatives, paid year-round, met each year during the month of October, to hear reports on the activities of the ministries of the government, and sometimes to debate legislation proposed by the government. During the remainder of the year, they were to represent the needs of their communities to the appropriate federal agencies.[24]

In addition to these reforms and social programs, Torrijos also sought to increase Panama's revenues; he directed a period of unprecedented government intervention in the economy. He sought to increase revenues through government expansion of export-oriented sugar production; he built processing factories *(ingenios)* and cultivated thousands of hectares of sugar cane. He subsidized the construction of better port and processing facilities for the small shrimp export industry so that it could better harvest this rich natural resource so abundant along Panama's coast. He invited all Panamanians to look with pride on the huge, modern airport he built in hopes of attracting more airlines and tourists. He negotiated the government's equity, first in petroleum transshipment facilities, then in a pipeline, designed to keep Panama on the route of Alaskan oil destined for the east coast of the United States.[25] He announced the government's commitment to undertake other massive projects, with foreign assistance but under Panamanian control: construction of container-ship port facilities; construction of major dry dock facilities; and discussion of a lock-free sea-level canal able to handle the massive ships too large for the present canal's locks. And he made the government the holder of 80 percent of the stock in the corporation formed to exploit Panama's extensive copper deposits at Cerro Colorado. He hoped that these moves would give Panama a much-needed injection of the feeling of real sovereignty, the ability to represent and meet its own needs, and to make its own decisions about its national life.

Torrijos also improved the country's infrastructure, inaugurating programs that simultaneously served the "masses," benefited the private sector, and provided symbols of sovereignty. The Ministry of Public Works built roads into communities previously accessible only by jeeps or horses, opening new outlets for local produce and making access easier for merchants. The same Ministry also upgraded existing roads. Torrijos nationalized the foreign-owned companies that held monopolies over basic utilities (water and sewers, electricity, telephones), establishing government-owned semi-autonomous corporations to provide these services. The government water and sewer company replaced the Canal Zone in providing water and sewage disposal for Panama City and Colón; it located new water sources, built aqueducts, expanded sewer lines, and constructed sewage-treatment facilities. The government electrical company (which replaced the General Electric-controlled Panama Power and Light Co.) and the Bayano Corporation, taking advantage of World Bank commitments to hydroelectric power, built the Bayano hydroelectric facility, the first of an ambitious series of hydroelectric projects that would be linked together into the national energy grid. Slowly but surely, petroleum-burning generating stations would be phased out; fairly quickly, many parts of the country had access to electricity for home use. The government telephone company, taking over from foreign interests, used microwave technology to expand the national telephone service, and extolled the need for telephones in every home. International telephone service was upgraded at the same time, beginning with direct international dialing for the banks of Panama City. Torrijos made clear that these were ways the revolutionary government was asserting Panamanian sovereignty over basic services needed by common Panamanians; he also urged business people to take advantage of the government-sponsored improvements in infrastructure by expanding existing industries or establishing new ones.

In his quest for support from the private sector, Torrijos took advantage of the continued divisions among its major branches. Even as his reforms went against the interests of some of the oligarchy, they favored others. Construction-related businesses profited tremendously from the economic boom of the early 1970s, which made Torrijos the darling of those who gained most from such activities: construction companies, cement companies, providers of iron, and, of course, property owners and realtors. The infrastructure projects kept many companies busy; the sounds and sights of major construction projects all over Panama City (and, to a lesser extent, in other provincial capitals) gave evidence to all that the economy was booming. The quickly covered skeletons of office towers, bank buildings, and luxury hotels and high-rise apartments dotted the skyline; no less part of the construction boom, homes and apartments for working class people dotted the area closer to the ground.

Some business people worried about "socialist" tendencies and potential government inefficiency; others supported Torrijos' moves to nationalize the foreign-owned monopolies that controlled Panama's utilities. They enjoyed indirect government subsidies through improved and cheaper electricity, better roads to move their products, and so on. And Torrijos' less-publicized courting of the transnational private sector offered increased opportunities for those Panamanian business people whose activities relied on this most important area of the Panamanian economy.

TRANSNATIONAL DYNAMICS: FINANCING THE REVOLUTION

As noted at the outset of this discussion of the Torrijos years, General Torrijos could carry out his "revolutionary" endeavors only within the limited choices and possibilities inherited from Panama's prior development. As shown above, this development resulted in a Panama where the transnational dynamics, most evident in the living out of the geographic vocation that had made Panama an international service platform, acted in accord with their own rhythms—rhythms that frequently jarred with those of the major national dynamics.

Just as Torrijos realized that he could not govern Panama only with the domestic support of the National Guard, he also realized that he could not achieve anything without significant international support. Between 1968 and 1972, the gross domestic product grew at an annual rate of 7.6 percent; but not even this economic boom and new corporate taxes could provide the revenues for the unprecedented government intervention in the economy. Torrijos needed loans, in quantities only possible through international commercial and development banks. These loans were not available to a sovereign and independent

Panama, but to the Panama that served the needs of international business. So, while he publicly represented himself as the populist leader embodying the basic desires of the majority of Panamanians, privately he made clear to the transnational private sector that Panama would continue to be Panama. In quiet contradiction to his revolutionary rhetoric urging a national dynamic of sovereignty and economic self-reliance, Torrijos accepted and even deepened Panama's historic vocation as a transnational service platform, and with it the ascendancy of transnational dynamics through dependence on outside forces.

Taking advantage of the fact that Panama's currency was, by treaty, the U.S. dollar, Torrijos invited bankers to make his country into an international financial center like London, New York, or Hong Kong. With legislation guaranteeing the privacy of all transactions, with no restrictions on the movement of money or on interest rates, and with virtually no conditions that promised benefits to Panama, he watched as banks hurried to open major offshore facilities; from twenty banks with total assets of $665 million in 1970, the banking sector surged to 94 banks with assets of $23 billion in 1979.[26] Taking advantage of the isthmus' location as the crossroads between North and South America, the volume of shipping attracted to the canal, and Panama's ports, Torrijos transformed the sleepy Colón Free Trade Zone into the second largest (after Hong Kong's) of the world's 200 free zones, making it the major meeting place and shopping center for South American importers and western and Asian manufacturers and exporters.[27] For little apparent reason other than minor registration revenues and perhaps good will, Torrijos also enacted tax and accounting legislation that made Panama into a haven for 55,000 "paper companies," holding companies or branches of multinational corporations whose only reason for having an office in Panama was to have an advantageous place to report transactions or profits, beyond the legal control of less "liberal" governments (Manduley 1980).

In making these moves, and in continuing to make Panama an attractive place for more substantial foreign investment, Torrijos assured himself of ready transnational support when he needed loans to pay for the many new programs undertaken by his government; the international private sector recognized that Torrijos, like his predecessors, was more than willing to do business with them on their terms. Loans flowed in, part of the "generous" spirit of the booming world economy of the early 1970s and, later, of the excess cash available from the windfall profits of the petroleum industry following the success of OPEC in driving up prices. The financing may have been easy to come by, but the spending spree increased Panama's debt at an alarming rate. "[B]y 1972 debt service alone swallowed up a quarter of all governmental revenues." In late 1973, amid rumors that Torrijos would be ousted, a consortium of banks "loaned the regime $115 million to refinance the embarrassing national debt and maintain public investment rates" (LaFeber 1979:175, 177). But as Panama's public debt increased and the government began borrowing in order to pay interest on earlier loans, bankers still came to the rescue, confident of what they considered implicit guarantees from the U.S. government, whose strategic interests could never allow this important client state to default.[28]

And the boom ended; the danger of default was real. In 1973, OPEC raised oil prices; the western world economy went into recession, and Panama plunged into a deep economic crisis. Real gross domestic product growth fell to 6.5 percent in 1973, then averaged only 1.6 percent from 1974 through 1977; real per capita growth declined from 1973 to 1977. Exports and imports fell off, but petroleum bills rose astronomically, even as Panama reduced oil consumption.[29] The public debt, $207.6 million in 1968, had risen to $1,053.1 million in 1975. By the time Panama's recession began to reverse itself in 1978, the public debt exceeded the gross domestic product ($2,383.5 million vs. $2,306.1 million), prompting the International Monetary Fund to worry that "Panama has arrived at a relationship between indebtedness and national income without precedent in the Western Hemisphere" (IMF 1979:4).[30] As government borrowing continued, an increasing portion of the debt was based on commercial bank credit, bringing rapidly rising international interest rates into play.

The bottom dropped out of the construction industry; unoccupied or partially finished buildings presented eloquent commentaries on the lasting benefits of the construction-based boom.[31] Unemployment reached an estimated 100,000, out of a work force of 600,000. In the mid-1970s, the government inaugurated a job-creation program that provided work for 17,000 people; but early in 1980, International Monetary Fund pressure forced the scrapping of the program.[32] The expensive sugar mills came on-stream just as international sugar prices fell to about a fourth of what they were when the construction began; Panama had to sell sugar for less than the production costs.[33] Direct foreign investment dropped drastically as the international business community coped with the recession and worried about Panama's investment climate while the treaty negotiations dragged on.[34] Later, interest rates and inflation soared; the imported goods on which Panama relied rose in price while prices for Panama's few exports dropped. Even after the recovery began in 1978–79, Panamanian business people, angered at the unprecedented intervention in the economy by a government that did not serve their interests, paid little attention to government urging that they increase their investments in Panamanian productive capacity.

RESPONSES TO THE ECONOMIC CRISIS

Torrijos worked simultaneously to confront the economic crisis and yet maintain his popular support, pinning his hopes on two major endeavors: the canal treaties and the Cerro Colorado copper project. Panamanian control of the canal would heal its wounded sovereignty and national pride, would provide the Canal Zone as new territory for the expansion of Panama City and Colón, and would greatly increase government revenues as Panama, for the first time, received just compensation for the international use of the canal. Development of the copper mine would allow Panama to take pride in its ownership of one of the world's major mining projects, while injecting hundreds of millions of dollars into the economy during the construction period. Longer range, both the canal and the copper mine would provide the revenue base that Panama had never had, under Panamanian control; and the copper mine would diversify the economy away from the extreme dependence on the country's geographic vocation.

During the economic crisis, Torrijos (as other Panamanian leaders of the twentieth century) focused the nation's attention away from domestic problems and onto the Panama Canal and Panama's relationship with the United States. He had already promised new, more just, canal treaties; beginning in 1973, he worked to keep that promise. In the name of the national unity and sacrifice needed to win concessions from the colossus to the north, Torrijos frequently exhorted the people to bear up under the effects of the worsening economy. Faced with mount-

ing opposition from the business sector, Torrijos shrewdly made concessions, relying on the loyalties of workers and campesinos to keep
under control their increasing unrest as they felt the effects of the
economic crisis. Panamanian workers held back on demands for wage
increases to keep pace with inflation, then watched helplessly as Torrijos
gradually watered down the benefits guaranteed in the 1972 labor reforms; people grumbled, but did not take to the streets to protest as the
government allowed price increases for basic foods and transportation.
The U.S. must see a united Panama; and the new treaties would bring
prosperity to the nation.[35]

During the negotiations, Torrijos never lost sight of the transnational sector. He roused nationalist spirits in passionate speeches, but
he stopped short of direct attacks on the United States as a colonial
power.[36] He kept the crowds under control; public demonstrations
never became riots. When foreign investors, themselves struggling to
confront the recession, stayed away in droves as they worried about the
stability of Panama's "investment climate," he reassured them that Panama wanted their investments; he offered incentives favoring capital-
intensive investment through duty-free import of machinery, generous
depreciation allowances, and tax exemptions for reinvestment. Contrary
to his promise to develop Cerro Colorado under Panamanian control,
he signed contracts that handed over effective control of the project to
foreign transnational corporations, in exchange for the glamor of keeping 80 percent of the equity.[37]

With the Torrijos-Carter canal treaties, signed in 1977 and ratified
in 1978, Torrijos did, in however compromised form, deliver to the
people of Panama on his promise to remove the lesion of diminished
sovereignty, an open wound since the signing of the notorious "in
perpetuity" Hay–Bunau Varilla Treaty of 1903, a few days after Panama
achieved its independence from Colombia.[38] But the new treaties did
not provide the revenues anticipated; the promised payments and loans
diminished substantially under the right-wing attacks of treaty opponents in the U.S. House of Representatives, who reworked the treaties
in putting together the enabling legislation for the economic packages.
Torrijos had to settle for much less than he wanted.[39]

And the Cerro Colorado project looked less and less like a solution
to the economic crisis. World copper price recovery from the effects of
the recession was agonizingly slow, while inflation and rising interest
rates doubled and redoubled the anticipated costs of developing the

copper mine. Under pressure from the International Monetary Fund and the World Bank, Panama changed partners, reduced its equity from 80 percent to 51 percent, and even then kept postponing the project's start-up date. When Torrijos died in July 1981, Cerro Colorado had yet to produce a pound of commercial copper.

The new canal treaties not only failed to give Panama a way out of its economic crisis; transnational dynamics limited Torrijos from keeping Panama distracted from other domestic issues. The Senate, playing to the Reagan forces that opposed both the treaties and Torrijos himself (as a "tin-horn communist dictator"), and hearing from the exiled Arnulfo Arias and allies in Miami, insisted on a "return to democracy" in Panama; U.S. politicians pressured Torrijos to open up the channels of dissent and opposition. Once the treaties were ratified, Torrijos announced a process that would culminate in direct election of a president and the inauguration of a new era of democracy for Panama. He resigned as head of government, stating that he wanted to dedicate all his energies to his work as commander of the National Guard; he gave more power to the civilian president, Aristides Royo, the former Minister of Education whom he nominated to replace Demetrio Lakas, and he legalized political parties.

Torrijos tried to institutionalize his revolution and his personal popularity by pulling together his forces into the Democratic Revolutionary Party *(PRD, Partido Revolucionario Democrático)*, less an organization uniting people of common convictions and more an agglomeration of the groups that depended on Torrijos and the government: the National Guard, many campesinos and Indians, a number of labor unions, a good portion of the middle class, most government workers, and some key elements of the private sector. Like so much else of the Torrijos years, the Democratic Revolutionary Party depended on the ability of the General himself to hold together its disparate and frequently contradictory factions; from the beginning, people openly speculated that Torrijos intended to be his party's nominee for president in the 1984 elections.[40]

Although the Panamanian private sector had strongly objected to Torrijos' disbanding of political parties, its members mounted no serious opposition as the oligarchy continued its internal struggles.[41] But the oligarchy retained its hold on the areas of the Panamanian economy not directly under the control of foreign interests. And even without political parties, their basic structures of organization remained intact;

Torrijos had made no moves against the various business groups (the Chamber of Commerce, Industry, and Agriculture; the Association of Cattle Ranchers; the Association of Rice Growers; the Association of Coffee Growers; and so on). When Torrijos legalized political parties, the traditional parties sprouted virtually full-blown from these underground hiding places.

After their success in forcing concessions from the government during the treaty negotiations, the business people and their parties sought to unite opposition to the government around other issues: the controversial Cerro Colorado mining project and, later, the educators' strike and the educational reforms. In 1978–79, opposition to the mining project presented itself as non-partisan; the business associations, refusing to lend their names to the most virulent attacks on the mining project, worked on technical questions surrounding the project: the debt, the environmental impact, the contracts, and so on. The Chamber of Commerce, using a dialogue that took place in paid newspaper advertisements, pressured CODEMIN, the government mining company, to take part in a long, nationally televised forum on the mining project; their questions did not mask their underlying opposition to the government itself (see Cámara de Comercio 1979).[42]

But the government took advantage of the fact that some radio commentators voiced shrill opposition to the mining project, broadcasting throughout the Republic their wildly exaggerated claims of the terrible effects the project would have—huge areas would be devastated, people's hair would fall out, men would be sterilized. Since this virulent opposition came from commentators of nationally known anti-government ideologies and affiliations, the government defused much of the questioning by making the mining project into a loyalty test. Pro-Torrijos, pro-revolution, pro-progress must mean pro-Cerro Colorado; anything short of unquestioning support for the project meant alliance with the oligarchy that was willing to keep the majority of Panamanians poor in order to promote its own interests. Given the failure of the traditional parties to develop grass-roots organizations and support, the government's approach was quite effective.[43]

Later in 1979, letting the flood of inconclusive "debate" on the mining project trickle down to a small stream, the business associations threw their financial and logistical support behind the public educators. The teachers, striking for the second year in a row, submitted a long list of demands for negotiation (including issues of working conditions, in-service training, facilities for students, the supply of needed textbooks and other materials, and even the government's entire educational re-form project). However, for the majority of the teachers, only the wage and benefit issues really mattered. In exchange for essential help from the opposition, the teachers elevated their relatively inconsequential complaints about educational reforms to a position equal in importance to their salary demands, and the fight changed its nature, now becoming a test of the government's ability to defend its programs against charges they were "communist."[44]

In Panama City and in provincial capitals, people turned out in the tens of thousands for two major demonstrations supposedly in support of the teachers. In fact, few knew much about why the teachers were striking, even less who was backing them; the demonstrations became popular manifestations against the continued effects of the economic crisis and the inability of the government to relieve people's suffering. Under such massive popular pressure, the government had to cave in; President Royo abrogated the educational reforms and came up with more money for the teachers.[45]

In all these struggles with the opposition, government officials cloaked themselves in the mantle of the popularity and the revolution of Panama's self-styled "maximum leader" *(jefe máximo)*. But Torrijos, rarely appearing in public after he resigned as head of state, had been unable to transfer his popularity to the civilian government or to the party he founded; his name and his image no longer provided clothing whose style captured the popular imagination. In 1980, when the government held elections for the newly created legislature, the opposition parties won a surprisingly solid minority of the contested seats, despite the fact that the Democratic Revolutionary Party controlled the levers of government, the voting lists, and the ballot boxes. Without Torrijos directly and visibly in charge, his revolution seemed to be stripped to the flesh, revealing a body politic and economy little changed from that of 1968.[46]

CONCLUDING ASSESSMENT OF TORRIJOS YEARS

When Torrijos died in a plane crash in mid-1981, he left to Panama at best a mixed legacy. Although he could claim success in negotiating the new canal treaties with the U.S., he had to accept continued U.S. military presence after the year 2000, when Panama is scheduled to take over complete control of the canal; Panamanian sovereignty remained subject to dictates from foreign powers. His economic policies not only failed to win a measure of economic independence for Panama; they deepened the country's role as a transnational service platform even as they plunged the nation into unprecedented indebtedness that will require years to overcome. Through the popular reforms he inaugurated, he established the basis of his contention that his was the first government in Panama's history to concern itself with the needs of the poor, and particularly the rural poor; but the pressures of the economic crisis forced him to substitute rhetoric and promises for action, back away from some of his programs and, in the end, leave the poor not much better off than before he came to power.

Like so many predecessors, Torrijos made concession after concession to the international private sector, while arguing their necessity precisely in order to strengthen the weaker national dynamics over against the historically established ascendancy of the transnational dynamics. Like so many predecessors, he found that the benefits to Panama were at best severely limited. The rapid expansion of the international financial center and the Colón Free Trade Zone added to the construction boom and created permanent new jobs; but a few thousand clerical jobs had little impact on Panama's unemployment problems, which in any case were concentrated in unskilled laborers. The banks did not invest their Panamanian holdings in Panama. The Free Zone not only provided very little revenue to the government, but the attraction of contraband trade may well have reduced government income from duties and tariffs. The "paper companies" provided a bit of revenue from filing fees, but no employment; frequently their Panamanian operations consisted of a small room with a single desk and a number of telephones, each for one of the several companies that paid the salary of the person who answered the phone. Transnational corporations evaluated potential real investments in Panama based on projections of profits, not on the basis of any special concern for Panama.

Domestically, Torrijos did nothing to foster the development of an organized populace that could analyze its own reality and look for ways to solve its own problems. Despite his rhetoric of support for popular movements, he saw any attempt to form truly representative popular organizations as a threat to his own power. The 505 local representatives, instituted with such fanfare in the new Constitution of 1972, generally won their elections after campaigns that, far from uniting local communities through a common quest for solutions to major problems, played on old divisions and brought forth new acrimony and bitterness. Except for the representatives of densely populated urban corregimientos like San Miguelito in Panama City, those elected could carry out projects of local improvements to the degree that they established themselves in personal relationships with key figures in the federal government; local backing carried little weight.[47]

In the main, Torrijos presented his reforms as his personal gifts to the nation, the beneficent father taking care of the needs of his children. Billboards proclaiming the gains of the revolution also prominently displayed pictures of the General. Campesinos, Indians, and many poor of urban areas felt great affection for and loyalty to him; they spoke in almost hushed voices about "the General" or "our leader." People were patient when promises were not kept, believing Torrijos when he laid the blame at the feet of the oligarchy or problems within the bureaucracy or the need to sacrifice in order to achieve independence of the U.S.[48]

But Torrijos' paternalism had its limits too. When he retired from the spotlight, his children refused to accept his hand-picked replacements as fit objects for their loyalties; his revolution depended too much on Torrijos himself, too little on the mature efforts of popular sectors of Panama. The massive demonstrations during the 1979 teachers' strike showed both the popular discontent with the continued effects of the economic crisis, and the lack of development of popular-based analysis of the root causes of the misery of the poor. A people trained to believe that only the government could solve their problems took to the streets not to challenge the belief, but to protest the failures.

In the end, the contradictions of the Torrijos revolution overwhelmed the benefits. Panama's history and the Torrijos model together ensured the outcome. Torrijos never attacked the roots of Panama's problems; necessarily or not, he accepted the limits imposed by Panama's history and the solutions proposed by the United States. He tried to institutionalize his approach, but it depended too much on his own charisma. When he died, his revolution had no roots in the population of Panama; the revolution died with him.

CHAPTER 3

Dynamics of the Guaymí Region

I n 1502, the Guaymíes caught their first glimpse of Europeans when Christopher Columbus directed his fourth voyage along the coast of present-day Bocas del Toro Province (Young 1971:38). A few years later, the indigenous survivors of the early excursions of Pedro Arias de Avila (Pedrarias Dávila) and other conquistadors of his ilk fled north from the Pacific coastal plain to the rugged, less hospitable mountain chain and beyond to the Caribbean. The predecessors of the Guaymíes still had to contend with some foreign traffic: occasional explorers searched for resources that would provide quick riches, or sought alternative routes across the isthmus; a few missionaries set up short-lived stations in their area. But the principal energies of the conquerors and their successors went into the development of the transit area, the "geographic vocation"; for the most part, the Indians lived their own lives in their remote regions while engaging in some trade with the residents of the small towns that dotted the Spanish road. In these surroundings, relatively free of further incursions from outsiders, the people passed more than three centuries during which their local dynamics were generally in the ascendancy over the regional or national dynamics. They rebuilt their devastated population, adapting traditional ways to new circumstances; these basic life patterns still characterized their lives in the latter part of the twentieth century (see Young 1970, 1980a).

GUAYMI LOCAL DYNAMICS

Landscape, Settlements, and Subsistence

In the 1970s, the shortest distance from Panama City to the Guaymí area was some 300 kilometers along the Inter-American Highway to western Veraguas and eastern Chiriquí provinces; no road connected Bocas del Toro Province with the remainder of the country. Stretches of the 60 kilometers of highway in eastern Chiriquí Province (districts of Tolé, San Félix, Remedios and San Lorenzo) wind through low, gently rolling hills, cut by small ravines. The ravines, carved by numerous creeks, slope down to the banks of the major rivers of this well-watered landscape (the Viguí, the Tabasará, the Tolé, the Santiago, the San Félix, and the San Juan), rivers that flow south into the nearby, occasionally visible Pacific Ocean. Here and there the road passes small plots of campesino maize or little patches of banana trees. In a few places along the highway, plots of several hectares of rice are visible, neatly cultivated by tractors—evidence of ownership by campesino cooperatives or cattle ranchers experimenting with diversification. More commonly the road flows through kilometer after kilometer of assiduously maintained barbed-wire fences marking the limits of well-tended cattle pastures, their lush, soft greens surrounding the scattered browns, yellows, and darker greens of the trees that dot the landscape. The mottled green and brown foothills and mountains to the north rise naturally as the extension of the low hills of the wide coastal plain; the white and gray cloud cover along their farthest rim merges earth and sky to cap the horizon.

A few times the highway doubles as the main street of a small town. More commonly, a paved street begins its course where it intersects with the highway, becoming at the same time the access road and the main street of the principal latino towns of the area, set back a few minutes from the highway. These streets typically pass in front of several beer gardens with their small enclosed bars and ample, covered, unwalled cement floors for patrons' tables and occasional dancing; two or three general stores owned and operated by first- or second-generation Chinese immigrant families; a public school; a small government-run hospital and dental clinic; a Catholic church; a small building housing the municipal government, the post office, and telegraph; and the zinc-roofed cement block or wood homes of medium-scale cattle ranchers,[1] members of campesino cooperatives, landless campesinos who find work tending cattle, and the other residents who make up the local community: the owner of a local rice mill, school teachers and administrators, doctors and nurses, a lawyer or two, local government officials, mechanics, masons, carpenters, wives and children of absentee husbands and fathers, elderly parents awaiting visits and financial help from grown children in the cities, and, always, a handful of people who barely manage, through scavenging and begging, to carve out a meager subsistence. One town's main street features a branch office of a national bank, another's the regional base for government agencies like the Instituto de Recursos Hidráulicos y Electrificación (IRHE, the electric company) or the Ministerio de Obras Públicas (MOP, for roads). Almost always, not far from the highway, the street passes in front of a small barracks housing the local contingent of Panama's National Guard, now renamed "Fuerzas de Defensa"; three or four soldiers seem to pass the hours sitting on the front porch, checking out the comings and goings of those who use the street, whether local residents or visitors.

Small groups of Guaymí Indians are easily recognized as they walk in modest single-file along the dirt shoulders of the main street of, for example, San Félix, or sit in quiet shaded clusters in front of its hospital or general store. From their necks to the tops of their bare feet, the Guaymí women and girls wear old-fashioned looking dresses in an array of yellows, blues, or reds, the dominant solid colors beautifully set off by three or four variegated strips of geometric patterns.[2] They load their purchases or their babies into net bags woven from agave fiber, and return—women on foot, men sometimes on horses—to their homes in the mountains to the north. Those who live nearby will be home within an hour or two.

On the edge of San Félix, the paved main street tails off into the narrow dirt access road built for the Cerro Colorado copper project, the only road in the Guaymí area that reaches all the way to the Continental Divide, about fifteen hours' walk from San Félix. Before this road reaches the bridge crossing the San Félix River, a trail branches off to the Guaymí communities of San Félix District. As the trail heads uphill, the change in topography serves as the unsurveyed boundary dividing latino lands below from the hilly country occupied predominantly by the Guaymíes. The trail continues more or less in a straight line, in places ascending the middle of a hill, in others cut into the side of a hill, or along a ridge, following the contours of the terrain. Frequently the trail descends precipitously to cross a creek; just as precipitously it ascends on the other side, regaining the lost altitude.[3] On both sides of the predominantly north-south ridges, the landscape falls away sharply into large valleys bounded by ridges that rise from the opposite sides. But the valleys, far from fulfilling the image evoked by the word, display broken hills, mountains, and ravines, and, barely visible through the varied greens, scattered groups of Guaymí houses.

Here and there, less-traveled trails angle off through the light forest and undergrowth. Close to rivers or year-round creeks, kin groups build clusters of six to eight houses in *caseríos* (villages or settlements) that dot many of the relatively flat areas of the rugged mountainous terrain of the Guaymí area; other kin groups live in dispersed caseríos, their houses as much as half a kilometer apart, nearer their farmlands but farther from neighbors and kin. On a few somewhat larger plains, as many as fifteen or twenty houses of several main families may form a single caserío. Their residents might have better government services— larger schools and better health subcenters; but they also tend to engage in endless fights over rights to available farm and pasture land among the resident kin groups.

The typical caserío consists of a handful of dirt-floored Guaymí houses, some constructed in traditional round or rectangular shapes with thatched roofs and pole walls, others left unwalled or one-walled, except for corner posts to support the beams and corrugated zinc roofs.[4] A scattered collection of animals constitutes the families' free-roaming domestic zoo. Chickens pass the day hunting and pecking the ground for bits of food, in competition with a few ducks and the occasional turkey. Skinny dogs beg mealtime scraps, with moderate success; pigs, sometimes tied, lounge in the shade of the trees.

On all sides, there is evidence of farming: small plots of corn, rice or root crops are planted nearby; broad-leaved banana trees rise along the steep banks of the creek beds; and small stands of coffee trees grow in hillside groves. There are small clumps of sugar cane, pastures containing a few cows and a horse or two, patches of secondary underbrush, and large scattered stretches of savannah grassland. Every year, beginning in December and continuing through the dry season, Guaymí men cut down the brush and trees in these plots. Around May, guessing at the onset of the rain, they burn the brush. Together with the women, the men plant grains of corn or rice in holes made with digging sticks. They plant root crops like *otoe* and manioc, either separately or mixed in with stalks of corn. Men, and sometimes women, laboriously weed the corn and rice; the rice requires a second round of weeding. The women, relying on considerable help from the men, harvest the grains during August and September, using sunny spells to dry the corn on the cob and the rice in its husks. They then store the grains for the months ahead. Mature root crops are harvested as needed for consumption; the people know from long experience that the ground itself provides the best preservation for them. The same experience teaches them to stagger the planting of banana and plantain trees throughout the year, to assure year-round supplies.

Around September, with the cutting and partial clearing away of undergrowth, the people begin the other agricultural cycle, broadcasting a second crop of corn and the only crop of beans in separate plots, and felling trees in crisscross patterns to provide support for the bean vines. They harvest these unweeded plots in January and February; at the end of the dry season they burn off these fields, along with the others, for reuse in the major planting cycle.[5] Ideally, after two plantings, the people let the fields lie fallow to recover their fertility.

Social Organization

According to Young (1971:105 ff), Guaymí family ties held together households and settlements, strongly influenced agricultural practices, and in general provided the primary means of social, economic, and political organization. Nuclear families lived in houses grouped in small caseríos with close relatives—preferably of the husband, often of the wife.[6] Family members visited back and forth and sent children with dishes of food at meal times. They lent and borrowed among households: rifles and shotguns for hunting, picks and shovels, cooking pots, and a variety of other implements. In one house or another, the residents were likely to find everything necessary to make the caserío self-sufficient, even when households were not (Young 1971:169). Outside the caserío, Guaymíes traveled in the area commonly known as the "indigenous zone" *(zona indígena),* the undemarcated area occupied principally by the Guaymíes, to visit more distant relatives, who provided them with food and lodging (see Figure 2). Older Guaymí celebrations like the *balsería* (a traditional stick game) and the *chichería* (a traditional ritual eating and drinking party), still occasionally practiced, built on relationships of real and fictive kin (Young and Bort 1976a, Bort 1977).

The men engaged in agricultural chores, like clearing land or weeding, in cooperative work parties *(juntas de trabajo)* with their own or their wife's parents, brothers, and cousins, in their own caseríos or in those of other family members, keeping track of obligations contracted and redeemed; the women prepared the necessary *chicha* (lightly fermented corn beer) and food.[7] Work parties also maintained the trails in the area of the caserío, cutting back the continuous growths of grasses and bushes and repairing the damage caused by heavy rains.

Guaymíes lived on and farmed lands collectively held by their kin groups; both men and women inherited from their parents rights to the use of these lands. Although Guaymí inheritance theoretically gave all adults rights to use lands of their grandparents' kin groups, normally a Guaymí farmer had three possibilities: land on which his father was raised, land on which his mother was raised, and land on which his wife was raised. In practice, he usually planted crops in two caseríos, exercising his own rights to farm land on which he himself was raised, and his wife's rights to land on which she was raised (Young 1971:151). While the oldest man of the caserío generally had the final say over the allotment of the kin group's agricultural plots, those with an interest in the decision generally arrived at an informal consensus that would take account not only of the different degrees of rights involved, but also previous practices (who had cultivated where) and the relative needs of the claimants.[8]

Good marriages[9] meant access to lands in different ecological micro-niches, a partial safeguard against the considerable variations in agricultural production brought on by unpredictable factors such as rainfall, terrain, altitude, or insects (Bort 1976:37). But other factors such as the illness or absence of a key member of a household, or luck in determining the onset of the rainy season, also could greatly influence household production. So, households relied on being able to survive difficult times by borrowing food from others, whether of their own caserío or another to which they were linked by extended family ties;

these informal loans would be repaid when the others ran into their own hardships (Young 1971:168 ff; Bort 1976:40). Kin networks formed the chief line of defense against any combination of factors that could jeopardize the precarious subsistence production.

When Guaymíes, kin or not, gathered to decide some question, they looked for consensus (see Bort 1976, Young and Bort 1976b). Depending on the issues involved, a group might arrive at a quick consensus, or might take years. If the issue was some conflict (for example, over damages to crops), the disputants might agree to mediation from someone whose neutrality and good judgment both sides recognized.[10]

In Guaymí society, only consensus decision-making would be effective; there were no mechanisms or structures to force a dissenting minority to go along with the will of a majority. The Guaymíes developed no permanent political organization uniting them beyond community or kin groups; they have remained politically acephalous (see Young and Bort 1979). When necessary (e.g., when under attack from neighboring groups), the predecessors of the Guaymíes apparently united under a warrior whose skills and accomplishments made him acceptable as a leader; but once the danger had been met, communities returned to their independence of one another (see Young 1970; Young and Bort 1979; Helms 1979). Given that the Guaymíes no longer engaged in warfare, lived in an area of abundant land, and spent their energy seeking little more than comfortable subsistence for themselves, communities had no need to develop permanent non-kin structures of organization, hierarchy, conflict resolution, and so on.[11]

Signs of Identity

With their swidden agriculture and dispersed settlements, strong localized kinship relationships and no organization that transcended them, the Guaymíes showed little sense of themselves as a "people" with consciously expressed common values, concerns, and interests. But endogamy, language, and territory, as well as their common history and shared values, provided most of them with ties to others beyond their kin networks. With rare exception, Guaymíes married Guaymíes. The majority of Guaymíes of Chiriquí and Bocas del Toro provinces spoke two mutually intelligible dialects of the language Ngawbere; those of eastern Tolé District (Chiriquí) and Veraguas Province spoke dialects of Muríre, which the Guaymíes usually referred to as Sabanero (see Young 1971:20–22). Even without official demarcation, the overwhelming majority of the Guaymíes occupied contiguous lands in Chiriquí and Bocas del Toro, such that people could travel for days without leaving lands populated only by other Guaymíes.

Until the prohibitions of the Mama Chi movement swept the zone, Guaymíes celebrated the *balsería* and the *chichería*, signs of ethnic identity that created fictive extensions of the kin networks. In these celebrations, people of an extended kin group, several caseríos, invited counterparts from other kin groups for four days of ritualized eating and drinking with, in the case of the *balsería*, a game that included throwing large balsa sticks at another's legs (see Young 1976b).[12]

Apparently from early times, the Guaymíes recognized no organized religion, in the sense of a belief system that united dispersed communities for large-scale public ceremonies. Certainly they celebrated some traditional rites (naming of children, puberty, funeral vigils), but apparently on the level of families/caseríos and somewhat privately.[13] They also had *sukias* or shamans, some of whom had fairly widespread fame, but nothing that might be considered a class of priests who engaged in public cults.

Nor did Catholic Christianity provide for the Guaymíes a deeply rooted set of symbols that would form part of their identity. The few chronicles of missionary activities give an impression of sporadic, unsustained forays into the mountains from the sixteenth to eighteenth centuries, but nothing after the beginning of the nineteenth century. Protestant groups in the twentieth century made their attempts to gain Guaymí adherents, but with generally little success (Young 1971: 52–53).[14]

Even so, most Guaymíes professed to be Catholics, although unbaptized and manifesting no more knowledge of the Catholic Church and its teachings than of any number of other institutions or movements of which they spoke. In this century, their contacts with the church suggest that they were happy with, or at least readily tolerant of, the church's renewed efforts to establish a permanent presence in Guaymí territory. In Bocas del Toro, priests who have worked in the Cricamola area since 1883 established a house in Canquintú around 1930, and have lived there fairly permanently since the 1950s. With a group of nuns, they established a school, a small medical clinic, and several cooperative agricultural projects—a rice husker to enhance rice marketing possibilities, a chicken and egg production program, and vegetable gardens—meant to serve in part as demonstrations of alternatives for the Guaymíes. In the small chapel in Canquintú, a number of Guaymí men, women, and children assisted at the daily celebration of Mass in Spanish; the priests struggled to learn Guaymí, but the task proved decidedly difficult. From the earliest days of the United Fruit Company in Bocas del Toro, early in the twentieth century, priests have also lived among Guaymíes working on the plantations (Cabarrús 1979:37–40).[15]

Around 1970, a group of priests and nuns arrived in Tolé, Chiriquí, setting high priority on work with the Guaymíes. The nuns set up a medical clinic in the Guaymí area in remote Llano Ñopo, near the Continental Divide; the priests taught in the government school in the caserío of Chichica, and supervised a boarding facility in the town of Tolé for students able to continue their studies beyond the grade levels available in their home areas. They also sponsored some small-scale agricultural projects (vegetable gardens, coffee seedlings, experiments with organic fertilizers), and financed a full-time agronomist in agricultural extension service, to help the Guaymíes find ways to improve production and nutrition. The priests based their more directly religious work on regularly scheduled visits to Guaymí communities, where they met with locally selected lay people, who were gradually learning to lead their neighbors in prayers, bible readings, and the singing of hymns.

Toward the end of 1977, other priests arrived in the neighboring parish, the districts of San Félix and Remedios (including the Cerro Colorado project), to dedicate their energy to work with the Guaymíes. They spent the first few years getting to know the Guaymí area, learning the specifics of Guaymí life and problems before making plans for other work with the Guaymíes. Later they established a series of small cooperative projects in the Guaymí area, including community fish ponds, technical and small-scale financial help for little dry-goods stores, and some vegetable gardens, as well as a boarding facility for Guaymí students continuing their studies in the town of San Félix. At the same time, and along the same lines as in the neighboring parish of Tolé, these priests slowly began the process of forming groups of volunteer local lay leaders who could help the community meet from time to time to analyze and seek solutions to various local problems, who might lead local religious celebrations, and who would, eventually, take charge of preparing those who wished to be baptized.[16]

In Chiriquí, the Guaymíes at first met the priests with tolerance tempered with undisguised suspicion. Frequently, but seemingly without hostility, they asked the priests what they had come for—to buy cattle or other goods? to sell things? to find sexual release with Guaymí women? Or had the priests brought gifts of food and clothing for them? Often they requested that the priests do baptisms.[17] As they grew less suspicious, many expressed their satisfaction that the priests came to visit, to spend time getting to know them, and to sit around their houses with them; they seemed to find these visitors, with their knowledge of very different worlds, an interesting diversion. At times some Guaymíes would lament that they had, in their view, no religion, something they considered important to provide "orientation" for their lives; they would refer to themselves as "lost" (perdidos) and would ask the priests to help them learn about God, learn to pray, and, in general, provide them with this missing "orientation."[18] And, as discussed in Part 3 of this book, interested Guaymíes found the church's representatives ready allies in the ongoing struggles over the Cerro Colorado mining project and Guaymí agitation for the legal definition of their comarca (an area of western Panama to be reserved for the Guaymíes and governed semi-autonomously according to legislation to be embodied in its corresponding carta orgánica).[19]

Land Shortages and Economic Strategies

Since the middle of the twentieth century the Guaymíes of Chiriquí Province have been faced with new transkin/trans-community "enemies" that challenged their traditional way of life. These included: the deterioration of resources through erosion and overworking of the land, pressures on the land from increasing population and a diminished land base, the problems created by increasing numbers of people leaving the area for seasonal or semi-permanent work outside (coffee, vegetable, and sugar cane harvests, and "cleaning" pastures), and the problems that arose as the Torrijos government worked to fully incorporate the Guaymíes into the mainstream of the life of the nation. Of this list of enemies, the most immediate for the Guaymíes was the land shortage.

By late in the twentieth century, the Guaymí population, probably on the increase since around 1800 (Young 1971:48), had recovered to a point where wider and wider areas experienced the pressures of insufficient lands; the Guaymí area, especially in Chiriquí, was critically over-populated (Young 1971:81, 1980b; J. Bort, personal communication).[20] By 1980 the Guaymí population had grown to more than 50,000 (Table 3); the overall population density for the Guaymí area was about 7.6 persons per km[2] (Table 4). Generously calculating that the arable land constituted 50 percent of that occupied by the Guaymíes (Young 1971:80–81), the effective population density was 15.2 persons per km[2], a very high density for swidden agriculturalists (Young 1980b). In Chiriquí Province, home of more than 60 percent of the Guaymíes, the situation was worse—28.2 persons per km[2], considering 50 percent of the land as arable.

As their own population increase put increasing pressure on their

TABLE 3

Indigenous Population of Western Panama by Province, 1930–80

| Province | YEAR | | | | | |
	1930	1940	1950	1960	1970	1980
Bocas del Toro	5,103	6,574	9,147	12,629	13,831	15,237
Chiriquí	9,851	12,000[a]	14,288	19,946	25,194	31,519
Veraguas	1,207	1,476	1,998	3,292	3,832	4,925
TOTAL	16,161	20,050	25,433	35,867	42,857	51,681

[a] Panamanian census data included a 1940 Chiriquí indigenous population of 19,135, a figure which Young (1971:48) rejects as inaccurate "in view of the trends evident from the figures for the two adjacent provinces"; the table presented here follows his "more reasonable estimate" of 12,000 for 1940, with the resultant change in the 1940 total: from 27,185 in the census material to the present 20,050. See also Young (1971:80).

SOURCES: Young (1971:48 Table 3 [from Panamanian census data]) for the years 1930–60; Estadística y Censo, for 1970–80.

TABLE 4
Guaymí Population Density, 1980

	Area[a] (km²)	1980[b] Population	Density (Persons/km²)	Density, 50% of land (Persons/km²)
TOTAL	6,793.9	51,681	7.6	15.2
Bocas del Toro	3,718.4	15,237	4.1	8.2
Chiriquí	2,231.3	31,519	14.1	28.2
Veraguas	844.2	4,925	5.8	11.7

[a]The calculations for *area* are adapted from information provided in the 1970 Census.

[b]Estimates based on 1980 census figures. The 1980 census breakdown of indigenous and non-indigenous population was not available at the time of writing.

SOURCE: Estadística y Censo.

land base, the Guaymíes found they had virtually nowhere to turn to acquire more land. Historically, when communities grew too large for the local land base, some members of the community moved away to form a new community on vacant lands (see Young 1971:76). But in Chiriquí, Pacific Veraguas, and eastern Bocas del Toro, no such vacant lands remained available to the Guaymíes; regional and national dynamics combined with the local dynamics of population growth to put the squeeze on the Guaymíes.

The coastal plains of Chiriquí and of Pacific Veraguas have been latino lands since the arrival of the Spaniards; later, European immigrants to Panama brought vegetable and coffee production into the fertile lands and cool climes of the volcanic highlands of western Chiriquí, gradually forcing the native inhabitants either to be absorbed as campesinos or to retreat to less desirable areas.[21] Cattle ranchers and campesinos in Veraguas continued to chip away at Guaymí lands, moving farther and farther into the mountains of the cordillera. Early in the twentieth century, the United Fruit Company took over extensive Guaymí lands along the Cricamola River on the coastal plain of eastern

Bocas del Toro, bringing in Caribbean blacks as laborers after the canal was completed; some of these blacks formed small fishing communities that dotted the coasts of the province.[22] During the 1930s, the construction of a decent connection by land between Chiriquí and the transit area gave rise to the expansion of cattle ranches and larger rice farms along the coastal plain.

Beginning in the 1930s, and with greater force in statutes passed in 1952 and 1958, the Panamanian government established a legal framework that supposedly protected the Guaymíes from further losses of land by recognizing as "indigenous reserves" the "regions presently occupied" by indigenous peoples.[23] Nonetheless, latinos of eastern Chiriquí, taking advantage of the government's failure to establish clear demarcations of the lands reserved for the Guaymíes, continued to chip away here and there—sometimes through simple theft, or often through purchases from Guaymíes who knew little of how to reckon the "value" of their land.[24] A carefully documented investigation (Sarsanedas 1978) showed how cattle ranchers of Tolé, especially since the 1950s, acquired pasture lands clearly within the Guaymí area, manipulating the legal system to obtain titles. From 1965 to 1973, the son of a locally prominent cattle rancher used his position as director of the regional office of the government agrarian reform institute to register, for family and friends, several hundred hectares of pasture lands that by law could not be alienated from the Guaymíes. All of these ranchers lived in the town of Tolé, not on their holdings in the Guaymí area; these pastures formed a relatively small part of their overall properties. In a 1975 case, the agrarian reform office recognized only that the Guaymíes were entitled to "preference" when reserve lands came up for sale, but approved the alienation of property to latinos when the protesting Guaymíes could not come up with the $3,000 purchase price (Sarsanedas 1978:41).[25]

In the early 1960s, Guaymí hardships and resentments formed part of the backdrop of the Mama Chi religious crusade, a revitalization movement based on commands received in visions of the Blessed Virgin Mary and her husband *[sic]* Jesus. The new gospel, which rapidly gained adherents, preached a return to old ways and advocated a complete break with the corruptions of the latino world, in preparation for a future filled with wonders and prodigies for the Guaymíes. After the

late 1964 death of the group's young visionary foundress,[26] the movement took on a more political turn that focused on the active, unarmed
struggle for the legal definition of the Guaymí reserve of land.[27]

The frequent Mama Chi gatherings, closed to outsiders, prompted
considerable fear among cattle ranchers,[28] but Guaymí protests were
unable to reverse any of these acquisitions. In 1969–70, government
authorities twice arrested Lorenzo Rodríguez, the cacique of Chiriquí
Province, on charges of "subversion" and "communism" as he worked
to organize Guaymíes to pressure the government for definitive demarcation of Guaymí lands; on the second occasion, some 200 supporters
arrived in Tolé to demand explanations of the arrest, returning with
Cacique Lorenzo to their homes after some tense moments of discussion.[29] Some latinos became very nervous; a rancher of Tolé claimed to
have organized a group of latinos armed with an arsenal of 150 rifles and
60,000 bullets, to repel Guaymí attackers who never arrived (Sarsanedas 1978:24, 46–49).

Fears of an uprising originated in the demagoguery of some latino
ranchers who tried to stir up the local campesinos, and fed on snatches
of rumors of Guaymí gatherings, all in near-complete ignorance of
the reality of the Guaymí situation. This reality was one of growing
scarcity of materials of everyday life. People traveled farther in their
search for firewood for cooking. House styles were changing from the
more durable, cooler, more private rounded homes with thatched roofs
to less durable, hotter, less private rectangular homes with corrugated
metal roofing; from many caseríos, materials for long-lasting thatched
roofs grew as far as several days' walk away.[30] But even these problems
seemed relatively minor alongside the other manifestations of the acute
Guaymí land shortage, especially in Chiriquí: diminished fallow time,
unresolvable land fights, and temporary or permanent out-migration.

When Philip Young did fieldwork with Chiriquí Guaymíes in the
mid-1960s, his observations and interviews persuaded him that the ideal
fallow time was around twelve years; he noted that a number of families
found themselves unable to leave the land alone for that length of time,
because they had insufficient backup lands (Young 1971:74–81). After
further research and reflection, Young decided that anything less than
twenty-five years of fallow resulted in environmental degradation; the
mid-1960s ideal of twelve years itself already indicated a longer standing
land shortage (Young 1980b:12–13).[31]

However, by the late 1970s, fallow time of four to seven years in Chiriquí and southern Veraguas was not uncommon; at times, only the paucity of secondary growth forced farmers to leave their land fallow for as long as seven or eight years. While some families still had access to enough land to allow longer periods of fallow (although much shorter than the ideal), more and more people were being forced into dangerously shortened fallow cycles. People complained that weeds were ever more abundant, insect "plagues" more frequent, and crop yields constantly diminishing. With insufficient ground cover and root systems, the heavy rains increased the erosion of the thin topsoil in the sharply sloping regions. The deterioration of the soil and diminished productivity translated into Guaymí life as longer and harder work for lower yields. Without capital for emergency measures such as chemical fertilizers and weed- and insect-killers, and with no usable knowledge of organic gardening techniques, Guaymíes could only seek more land to meet their families' food requirements; but even the cultivation of some areas of savannah, left alone when cattle infections reduced pasture requirements, could do little to alleviate the problem.

Young and, later, Bort mentioned land fights among the Guaymíes, noting the tremendous difficulty in solving the conflicts because of the flexibility of Guaymí kinship and inheritance (Young 1971:74, 148–53: Bort 1976:55–56). By the late 1970s, these fights had increased, even reaching the point of brother fighting sister, demanding that family lands be split into tiny parcels which, as parents complained, would be too small to provide food for anyone. Guaymí "rules" governing land use gave to all children seemingly equal rights to lands of their parents, themselves exercising rights inherited from their own parents, and so on. However, those who actually cultivated lands gained rights even if others could argue a closer relationship to the previous generation. Some used lands whose rights belonged to a second, now deceased, spouse of their mother or father; and some relied on lands loaned them by a deceased neighbor who was a distant relative. The potential for dispute was tremendous; the complexities of the conflicting claims made resolution of the disputes near impossible (see Young 1971:148-53).

In growing pockets or micro-niches of the Guaymí area, hardships of subsistence production pushed people in ever greater numbers to look for ways to supplement their incomes. Guaymíes traditionally met their cash needs through a variety of strategies, modified according to individual needs, seasonality, and available resources—the sale of cattle, the sale of excess corn and rice, seasonal wage labor on coffee, banana, or sugar cane plantations, or on cattle ranches, and the occasional sale of home manufactures such as net bags, straw hats, baskets, hammocks or stone pipes (Young 1971:93–104; Bort 1976:56–63).[32] Where climate and soil permitted, Guaymíes cultivated coffee for sale as well as for household consumption.

Of these strategies, seasonal wage labor seemed most widespread. Each dry season, individuals or entire families headed for the volcanic mountains of western Chiriquí to take part in the coffee and vegetable harvests. Some men obtained temporary jobs clearing and weeding the cattle pastures along the coastal plain in eastern Chiriquí. Occasionally Guaymíes joined other laborers cutting sugar cane in government or private fields of Veraguas. In the early 1930s, when the Chiriquí Land Company (a Panamanian subsidiary of United Brands, formerly the United Fruit Company) began its Puerto Armuelles operations in western Chiriquí, many Guaymíes took their families to the banana plantations, some for several years at a stretch. But in 1961, the Chiriquí Land Company became less of an option for employment because of increased mechanization of the plantations, and because a partially successful Guaymí-led fight for union recognition backfired after permanence became a condition of union membership, and union membership became a condition for employment (Young 1971:100).[33] Some families nonetheless continued to find work on the banana plantations, living and working outside the Guaymí area for periods of several years at a stretch. But, with the increasing pressures on local resources in the Guaymí area, many found themselves embroiled in conflicts on their return; in their absence, others took over their land. When they tried to reassert their rights, they added to the growing land fights in the area.[34]

In most cases, seasonal wage labor was not a strategy for Guaymíes to get extra money; what little they earned usually went immediately for food and shelter, sometimes for "luxuries" like radios and watches, and too often for alcohol (Young 1971:102–03). Unfortunately, families that regularly left the area for wage work often became burdens for their relatives on their return, since they had not been on hand to do some necessary farm work and frequently ran short of food. Also, they missed opportunities to redeem reciprocal labor obligations. This survival strategy, then, endangered through abuses the reciprocal aspects of kin relationships, and added to tensions and resentments in the Guaymí area (Bort 1976:57 ff).

In at least two instances, Guaymíes formed new settlements elsewhere, adapting to the contemporary situation a traditional Guaymí strategy of seeking new lands when present lands were insufficient to meet the families' needs. Beginning nearly twenty-five years ago, more than 2000 Guaymíes formed permanent settlements in the fertile area of the Valle de Riscó of northwestern Bocas del Toro, near the Changuinola River; they moved there from the corregimientos of Mununi and Piedra Roja in eastern Bocas del Toro, along the Continental Divide, just north of Cerro Colorado (see Map 2, above). Since 1960, the land shortage in this rugged area has apparently caused the emigration of nearly half the residents (see Table 5).[35]

In the second emigration, a handful of families from a caserío at the foot of Cerro Colorado in the Chiriquí corregimiento of Hato Chamí cleared dense forests to open new lands in the Upper Changuinola area of southwestern Bocas del Toro, far from other Guaymí settlements. The men of these pioneer families had extensive experience as wage laborers on coffee farms of the Santa Clara area, in the volcanic highlands of western Chiriquí; in 1975, they began opening up land and

TABLE 5

Population Change, Corregimientos of Mununi and Piedra Roja
(District of Chiriquí Grande, Bocas del Toro)

	1960 Population	1970 Population	% Change, 1960–70	1980 Population	% Change, 1970–80	% Change, 1960–80
TOTAL	*3,451*	*2,102*	*−39.1*	*1,822*	*−13.3*	*−47.2*
Mununi	1,781	1,199	−32.8	986	−17.8	−44.6
Piedra Roja	1,760	903	−45.9	836	− 7.4	−49.9

SOURCE: Estadística y Censo.

planting crops in the new area, entering from Chiriquí and crossing the
Continental Divide, about two days' walk from the nearest road. These
Guaymíes left the Cerro Colorado area because of the lack of arable land
and, they reported, because the work on Cerro Colorado was damaging
their land, causing flooding (probably runoff from construction and
maintenance work).[36]

Finally, many Guaymí families of eastern Chiriquí seemed to have
some family members living permanently outside the Guaymí area (Bort
1976:48), where they found (mostly unskilled) jobs as best they could:
as laborers for government ministries, as dishwashers in the cities, and
so on (Young 1971:100). Residents of the little towns of eastern Chiriquí
thought that there were more Guaymíes "hanging around" than there
used to be. Catholic clergy in the coffee and vegetable areas of the
highlands of western Chiriquí noted that a number of Guaymíes stayed
year-round, scrounging for work, instead of returning to eastern Chiriquí at the end of the seasonal harvests. Although there were no formal
organizations of Guaymíes in Panama City (as there were of Cunas),
some thought that the small Guaymí population of the capital had
increased in recent years. These moves were tantamount to abandoning
(at least for one's children) people's identities as Guaymíes.[37]

GUAYMÍ REGIONAL AND NATIONAL DYNAMICS

Even as the Guaymíes struggled to find
ways to meet the crises of their own land shortage, they faced other
complications brought on by direct government activities in their area:
the arrival of the Torrijos revolution. Torrijos and others frequently
reminded the Guaymíes that this government, unique in Panama's history, worked to show special respect for the Guaymíes while it provided
them with the same services granted to other sectors of Panama. In the
Guaymí area, the revolution brought education, improved health care,
and promises of speedy recognition of Guaymí land rights (the comarca) and of projects to improve subsistence.

Education

The government opened numerous schools
in an area which, prior to 1968, had no government schools at all; by the

late 1970s, many schools dotted the Guaymí area of Chiriquí, including middle or junior high schools *(ciclos básicos),* offering grades seven through nine, in Soloy (San Lorenzo District) and Chichica (Tolé District).[38] Little by little, the government worked with local communities to improve the facilities, allocating building materials that the residents had to transport up the mountains. Government-assigned teachers, despite being the only latinos living among the Guaymíes, generally showed admirable dedication under difficult circumstances.[39]

Nevertheless, government education received mixed reviews from the Guaymíes. On the one side, the educational system brought into the Guaymí area was the same as practiced throughout rural Panama. The teachers for the Guaymí area received the same training as those who went to teach in latino communities; no one thought to prepare them with special training for work in a cross-cultural environment, or even to help them recognize some of their more blatant latino prejudices toward Indians. When Guaymí children arrived to begin first grade, they usually knew no Spanish; teachers usually knew no Ngawbere. But not even the handful of Guaymí teachers, themselves quite latinoized by the educational system, gave much thought to providing bilingual instruction for at least the early years of school.

The curriculum emphasized subjects beyond the experience or possibilities of most Guaymíes. It taught about electricity to people who had never seen a light bulb; it provided study skills that required a desk, a chair, a lamp, and privacy to children who lived in one-room, barely walled homes; it stressed personal hygiene by means of hot baths, good soap, and the frequent washing of hands and faces to people whose bathroom and bathtub were the local creek. Teachers defended this curriculum as necessary to the noble burden of "civilizing" these "uncivilized" people, a goal only too consonant with the revolution's desire to have all Panamanians take their rightful place in the one nation. The texts for the Guaymíes, the same ones used everywhere in Panama, presented Panamanian history without Indian history and depicted "typical" homes and families more like those shown in U.S. television commercials than like anything typical of Panama.[40] Many teachers expressed considerable frustration about the slowness of Guaymí students and their lack of enthusiasm; but even the rare teachers who saw some of the problems of the educational system itself had no tools with which to create educational materials better suited to the Guaymíes.

On the other side, few Guaymí parents appreciated the importance of education, so obvious to the government. For many parents, it was no small act of faith to get themselves and the children up before dawn, and to provide whatever they could for breakfast so that the children would not set out on their long walk to school on an empty stomach. Even when parents desired to provide more active support to their student children, they lacked resources to provide good study environments or skills to help with homework. Most parents sent their younger children to school; but as the children grew older and could provide more help to the family, few parents insisted they continue their education when the children showed signs of wavering. If parents took their children with them for seasonal labor in western Chiriquí, the children missed the last couple months of the school year; teachers compensated where possible, allowing the children to move on to the next grade.[41]

The schools provided local communities with an opportunity to organize beyond recognized kin groups. Some communities took a very active role in the parents' club, which oversaw aspects of local education. In Cerro Otoe, the president of the parents' club convoked the members to address issues that had to do with the education of their children. Parents built the school using local materials and workers instead of relying on the government-provided cement and cinder blocks stored on the outskirts of San Félix, many hours away. Community members generally responded warmly to the teachers, who reciprocated with a low absentee rate. In other communities, parents were less active. In Hato Pilón, the latino head of the school ran the parents' club. In response to frequent harangues, the residents eventually managed to haul the building materials up from San Félix (a block or a desk at a time). With some money obtained by the elected representative, the community hired a novice Guaymí mason who, on his second attempt, built walls that did not fall over. Teachers complained about the difficulties in getting parental collaboration in Hato Pilón; but their own approach was quite paternalistic.

Both communities, however, seemed to be responding more according to form than according to new opportunities presented by the schools. In Cerro Otoe, the people most active in the affairs of the school were also the people who had put together the cooperatively owned store in their caserío and the Guaymí house in San Félix (see Bort 1976). A number of the people had spent quite a while outside the Guaymí area, whether growing up in latino families or working on the

Chiriquí Land Company banana plantations; they had more knowledge of the latino world and its ways, and more experience of how to organize themselves. Perhaps most important, the core of Cerro Otoe was one extended family. The larger Hato Pilón, on the other hand, formed around three principal families whose dynamics included old and current land conflicts as well as some notable personality clashes. Even so, the people of Hato Pilón pointed with considerable pride to their accomplishments in building their school.

Health

As novel as the introduction of government schools into the Guaymí area, was the improvement in health care for the Guaymíes, whose overall health situation looked fairly bleak. Guaymí infant mortality stayed at a frightening level; most infant deaths resulted from diseases associated with the lack of adequate nutrition or clean drinking water. Tuberculosis and other respiratory ailments took their toll among the adults. The Guaymí area suffered epidemics of diseases readily controllable through vaccinations.[42]

The revolutionary government improved the equipment and personnel of regional health centers in latino towns and adopted policies making payment for medical care and medicines vary according to income levels. Guaymíes assisted their sick family members on the hours-long trek down the mountain trails to the centers, then often slept on the ground near the center in order to continue to attend to their sick. The Guaymíes tended to look to the health centers as a vital resource in their struggle to fight off diseases, even if their confusion and disorientation regarding diagnoses, procedures, courses of treatment, and charges meant that this resource was often a last resort.[43]

The government credited itself with a systematic vaccination program in the Guaymí area, taking advantage of help from international health agencies. But this program in fact was hit-and-miss. Sometimes everything went smoothly, and large numbers of Guaymíes received vaccinations and boosters as planned.[44] At other times, however, Guaymíes travelled from miles around to communities to which they were summoned by radio announcements of scheduled vaccinations, often to find themselves waiting in vain for the arrival by horseback or helicopter of the vaccination teams, who sometimes were held up by bad weather, or by communications breakdowns that left them standing around waiting for horses, or who may not even have left their base in the provincial capital of David.[45]

Occasionally the Guaymíes received some explanation for the failure of the vaccination team; more often they heard nothing. After a few of these experiences, the Guaymíes were reluctant to keep these appointments until they knew that the health workers had actually arrived; but distances and communications meant that relatively few could arrive before the vaccination teams moved on. The vaccination people, without attending to their part in fostering this state of affairs, often interpreted these Guaymí actions as further signs that the Guaymíes were stupid, lazy, and incapable even of appreciating the worth of a valuable program offered to them free of charge.[46]

Comarca

Besides its frequent reminders to the Guaymíes of the special attention given them in education and health care, the Torrijos government noted that it showed them special respect through its recognition of their caciques and through its efforts to give legal definition and delineation to their territorial base (the comarca). General Torrijos himself, in his meetings with the caciques, assured them that he saw them as the principal Guaymí leaders; especially favored was Lorenzo Rodríguez, the cacique of Chiriquí Province. All encounters with government officials brought renewed promises that the comarca was imminent.

In promising the comarca, the government pledged itself to carry out long-ignored legislation to the same effect. For, despite laws and constitutional articles dating back at least to 1934, the only demarcation of Guaymí territory that had taken place was not through land surveys and legislation, but by means of the simple expedient of drawing an arbitrary line on government maps. And this demarcation excluded about half the territory that was occupied by the Guaymíes: much of Bocas del Toro and, in eastern Chiriquí, a number of corregimientos occupied exclusively by Guaymíes (e.g., Cerro Iglesias, in Remedios District; Hato Julí, Hato Pilón, Quebrada de Loro, Salto de Dupí, Hato Jobo, in San Félix District; and virtually the entire Guaymí area of San Lorenzo District; see Map 2, above).[47]

Article 95 of the 1946 Constitution committed the government to take the steps necessary to grant to Panama's indigenous people, without charge, the "necessary lands" with "corresponding title" for their livelihood, at the same time prohibiting the transfer of indigenous lands (*"prohibir su adjudicación a cualquier título"*) and recognizing the existence of already established reserves. Further legislation in 1952 recognized "lands actually occupied" as belonging to the indigenous peoples. But Article 116 of the revolutionary Constitution of 1972 backed away from this language, instead guaranteeing to indigenous communities the much vaguer "necessary lands and collective property," while reserving to the government the right to set out both the procedures for specifying these guarantees, and the limits within which indigenous lands could not be reduced to private property. Despite these promises, repeated on many occasions, the government did nothing to enact the further legislation needed to provide legal rights for the Guaymíes.[48]

Throughout the 1970s, the Guaymíes formed their commissions and took seriously each meeting with government representatives concerning the comarca. Despite the fact that they had no resources and no special training, several times they put together information or proposals as requested by the government. Over the years, different Guaymí commissioners walked the hundreds of miles of territory requested for the comarca, noting natural boundary markers, noting who lived where, and so on; then they laboriously wrote up the results of their investigations and submitted their proposals.

During these same years, various officials expressed their deep concern about the Guaymí situation and assured the Indians that establishment of the comarca was just a matter of time. In 1974, officials of the Ministerio de Hacienda y Tesoro, of the Commission on Legislation, and of the aborning CODEMIN promised the Guaymíes a "final resolution" to the problem; a memo of August 1974 stated that field studies and maps had already been done, and by November the problem would be solved. It wasn't. Around 1976 or 1977, General Torrijos met at his headquarters at Farallón with Cacique Lorenzo of Chiriquí, and negotiated a change of tactics with respect to the comarca; Torrijos would deliver the comarca in exchange for Guaymí support in three areas: the plebiscite on the Torrijos-Carter canal treaties; Guaymí inscription in the Torrijos political party; and Guaymí support for the Cerro Colorado mining project.[49] In the 1977 plebiscite, the Guaymíes voted in favor of the proposed treaties by a margin several times greater than the national margin of two to one. In 1979, when the National

Guard helicopters buzzed around the Guaymí area in the registration campaign for Torrijos' party, most Guaymí adults signed on, even though they had little idea what they were doing. And well into 1980, a handful of Guaymí leaders (including Cacique Lorenzo) managed to keep the lid on the sharpest public criticisms of the mining project (see Lobo 1980b). Still, no comarca.

In 1978 the government finally filled the slot, created in 1952, of national director of indigenous policies. The director led a group of Guaymí representatives and technical people from the government on a field study of the entire boundary line proposed by the Guaymíes, and promised a careful study of the situation of the lands held under private title within the Guaymí area. No Guaymí ever saw this study. The director resigned at the end of 1979, supposedly to continue his legal studies in Mexico. But rumors consistent with what was known of his character indicated that he resigned in frustration over the fact that the government would not stand behind its own promises to the Guaymíes, and he could not continue to lie to the Guaymí representatives.

Each change of government ministers meant, for the Guaymíes, beginning the process all over; officials always found a way around Guaymí questions about why they couldn't look up in their files the work already done, whether by the Guaymíes or by the government. Finally, as the government lurched toward the right, under the continuing pressure of the economic crisis and the failure of the private sector to invest in Panama's recovery, Torrijos sacked the liberal Adolfo Ahumada as Minister of Government and Justice, replacing him with a conservative, the arrogant, high-handed Ricardo Rodríguez. Rodríguez refused to meet with the Guaymí commissioners even to discuss naming a replacement for the former director of indigenous policies.[50] And more shocking, it was during his tenure that the government, despite its many promises and assurances to the contrary, admitted that no studies in preparation for the comarca had ever been started—clear evidence that the government had never intended to take seriously the Guaymí request for a comarca.

Representatives to the National Assembly

The Torrijos government also gave itself credit for the incorporation of the Guaymí area into the new National

Assembly, for the first time allowing the Guaymíes their own elected representatives on the national level. According to the government, the Guaymíes no longer had to depend on getting the ear of their latino legislators and political parties; they had their own people to guarantee attention to Guaymí interests. In accord with the new Constitution, but with virtually no preparation, in 1972 the Guaymí corregimientos joined the rest of the republic in the electoral process. Again in 1978, now with some years of experience, Guaymíes returned to the election booths.

But six years of experience did little to instruct Guaymíes—or others, for that matter—about the power and responsibilities of these representatives. Their formal obligations revolved around the annual month-long meeting (October 11 to November 11) of the National Assembly, held in Panama City. During the meeting of the Assembly (as noted in Chapter 2), the representatives received reports on the activities of various government ministries and, within limits, debated government-proposed legislation. The salary of $300 a month, received year-round, was a handsome sum by Guaymí standards; and representatives received added compensation for travel, room, and board during the meetings of the Assembly.

For the remainder of the year, the representatives were supposed to mediate between their corregimientos and government agencies in order to insure that the agencies met the real needs of the communities. The government allocated a small budget to each representative for local projects; but that budget depended on the representative's ability to convince the right people to disburse the funds before the overall budget was exhausted. Successful representatives understood the political process and gained access to key people in the government; few Guaymíes had either the awareness or the ability to follow suit. So, while the government touted the system of elected representatives as a great advance in the democratization of Panama, in reality, the results were little different from those of earlier systems: those who had the clout got things done; those who didn't got ignored.[51]

Summary and Transition

Guaymí land shortages and their resultant problems have come about in the clash of local and regional/national dynamics. Local dynamics gave rise to the complex kinship and inheritance patterns as well as to the population increase. Regional and national dynamics gave rise to the continued shrinking of the territorial base of the Guaymíes, to the ambivalent strategies for supplementing Guaymí subsistence, and to the closing off of one of the more effective strategies, temporary migration to the Chiriquí Land Company banana plantations. The Guaymíes, in order to find a way to confront these new enemies, needed some form of trans-kin organization.

However, because the Guaymíes focused their primary energies on their day-to-day survival, virtually no one recognized these land-related problems as ones that required agreement and concerted effort that went beyond the capabilities of local kin groups or communities.[52] Approaches to dealing with the problems tended to be locally centered, with some exchange of information; but few Guaymíes worked actively to establish mechanisms that would encourage trans-community collaboration. Consequently, one family's efforts to eradicate cattle infection were always jeopardized by the possibility that neighbors would not take similar steps, allowing the infection to remain in the area. No one tried to think of ways to reforest some of the more seriously eroded areas; people complained about the erosion and about the distances they traveled to seek fire wood, but there was no planning beyond what a family might do.

Within families as well as within communities, the consequences of increased migrant labor were felt, as laboring families missed out on communal labor obligations, borrowed or begged food, and were unable to meet their own generalized reciprocal obligations. While neighbors might comment critically about someone's decision to rent pasture land to latinos, fearing that the latinos would find some way to claim title to the land, such matters were decided only by those with rights to the land.

INTERPLAY OF LOCAL AND NATIONAL DYNAMICS

The Guaymíes have struggled to find ways to organize in response to the problems they face. The first signs of Guaymí organization brought unprecedented unity to much of the area, providing a principle of organization that transcended kin groups. As mentioned earlier, in the early 1960s the "Mama Chi" revivalist movement swept the area, rapidly gaining adherents to its gospel of separation between Guaymíes and latinos: a return to old ways cut off from the corruptions of the latino world, and its agitation for the legal definition of the integrity of Guaymí lands (besides Young 1971, 1976a, 1978, see also Sarsanedas 1978:25–26). The Mama Chi movement owed some of its success to people's acceptance of its apocalyptic predictions of the end of the world. But the world didn't end, and the Mama Chi movement diminished as quickly as it arose, dissolving back into the prevailing patterns of kin autonomy.

This movement did, however, provide a Guaymí response to their deteriorating life situation, a situation made all the more critical when people recognized they could no longer supplement their subsistence with temporary labor on the Chiriquí Land Company banana plantations. In providing a response, the Mama Chi movement also alerted some Guaymíes to the gravity of their problems and to the possibility of other, more efficacious responses. Even though the Mama Chi movement ended up as a historical incident of an ethnic group's inadequate response to major survival issues, it set the stage for new efforts to organize and meet problems.[53]

In recent years, power struggles have become part of the political landscape of the Guaymí area, as different groups of Guaymíes tried to form trans-kin and trans-community organizations to meet common problems. The power struggles revolved around the cacique(s), *jefes inmediatos* (local delegates of the cacique), and accompanying organization(s); around some elected representatives and government-sponsored approaches to Guaymí leadership; and around various groups that were formed to work with or against these others. All were vying for the support of ordinary Guaymíes who, by tradition, only slowly and cautiously committed themselves to follow the leadership of people who had no power to help families with their subsistence problems.

As the Mama Chi movement began to wane, some astute Guaymíes tried to inject a more directly political component into the movement; among these was Lorenzo Rodríguez, who became cacique of the Guaymíes of Chiriquí Province (and, according to his followers, *primus inter pares* of the three caciques) and worked hard to organize the people in order to press for the comarca.[54] Cacique Lorenzo engaged for years in a fairly lonely battle both to interest the Guaymíes in the importance of the comarca and to pressure the government to carry out its promises. His followers recalled that the National Guard had imprisoned him two or three times, but had been forced to release him when they could find no supporting evidence for the charge that he was a "communist subversive." He travelled from community to community, held small meetings, and sought backing, always trying to develop a grass-roots organization to agitate for the comarca.[55] Even his opponents conceded that Lorenzo at least had been, at one time, a *luchador,* a fighter for the Guaymíes.

In his relationship with the government, Lorenzo was pretty much on his own; his ability to get what he wanted depended more on his individual skills than on his popular backing. A proud man, unwilling to consider himself out of his league in dealings with Torrijos or other government officials, he was an apt target for government offers of personal benefits in subtle exchange for making concessions. As already noted, he made a deal for a compromised comarca in a private meeting with Torrijos. CODEMIN provided him helicopter transportation from time to time, and took care of his medical problems. Later, Lorenzo took a CODEMIN-sponsored trip to Canada, to view Texasgulf and other mining projects; on his return, he signed the pro-Cerro Colorado statement of his fellow travellers. He had little defense against the blandishments of being given a fancy international trip, having a new suitcase full of new clothing, staying in fancy hotels, eating in fancy restaurants, and generally getting royal treatment from the mining companies. Tired after years of uphill struggle to achieve the comarca, frustrated by the seeming apathy of many Guaymíes, and honored by the personal attention he received from General Torrijos, he "derived personal benefits from his dealings" with the government, in the process adding to his problems within the Guaymí area (Young and Bort 1979:96).

The cacique tried to mediate his presence and influence in local communities through jefes inmediatos (literally, "immediate chiefs," the Guaymí version of a local community chief [Young and Bort 1979: 92-93]). He held meetings with them, and went over drafts of the carta orgánica, which spelled out limited Guaymí "home rule"; presumably he discussed with them how they should work in their communities. But in many cases the jefes seemed to be left on their own to translate these discussions into action. Some of his jefes came away from these meetings insisting that Lorenzo had ordered the people to acknowledge that the cacique and his representatives had extensive powers: to determine who could come into the Guaymí area; to exercise authority over elected representatives; to replace the *corregidores* (local registrars) with jefes;[56] to define what was legal in some disputes; to resolve land conflicts; and to impose fines and other light punishments.

Many people found such orders completely unacceptable and simply ignored the decisions of the jefes, who in turn had no way to enforce them. A common way of phrasing this opposition was the statement: "The cacique isn't in charge here; he never comes around here." At times the jefes sought to resolve conflicts in which they were personally involved; people considered their moves self-serving, and denied them support. A number of jefes were not adept at discussion of some of the issues of concern to local people; they could not read or write, spoke Spanish poorly, knew little about how the government operated, and were rather easily written off as anti-progress secret adherents of the Mama Chi cult. Since they claimed to be quoting the cacique, their actions hardened local opposition to the cacique.[57]

In 1978, Cacique Lorenzo attempted to consolidate his strength by working for the election of his candidates as representatives to the National Assembly; but conflict and confusion in a number of corregimientos undercut his organizational work instead of moving it forward. For example, the election campaign and vote among three candidates in the corregimiento of Hato Pilón showed only too clearly the nature of the problems. There, as elsewhere, people evaluated the cacique's efforts as mediated through the controversial activities of the local jefe inmediato and of a National Guard–assisted government employee, an ethnologist who was at the time part of the staff of the Department of Social Development of CODEMIN.[58]

The ethnologist became involved in Guaymí politics during the plebiscite of 1977, when—unsurprisingly, in the context—she apparently viewed her commission to assist the National Guard in voter registration in the Guaymí area as a mandate to campaign for Guaymí support for the Torrijos-Carter treaties; the Guaymíes voted overwhelmingly in favor, assisting Torrijos in his national two-to-one margin of victory. In the 1978 elections for representatives to the National Assembly, her voter registration work included taking charge of many organizational elements of the elections.

Many opponents complained that she manipulated the organizational work on behalf of Lorenzo's candidates. People charged that in her trips to register Guaymíes to vote, she insisted that the identity cards could only be used to vote for the cacique's candidates. In Hato Pilón, Lorenzo's candidate received the materials to file his candidacy two weeks before the deadline, while his opponents received their materials just five days before the deadline; the cacique's candidate had the opportunity to obtain more signatures and claim stronger support.[59] Lorenzo's candidate in Hato Pilón lived in the caserío of Cuerima, a new settlement founded by the cacique. A number of people from Hato Pilón maintained that Cuerima lay within the boundaries of the neighboring corregimiento of Hato Julí, not Hato Pilón; the ethnologist obtained documents declaring the candidate a legal resident of the corregimiento of Hato Pilón.[60]

The day-to-day activities of the jefe inmediato of Hato Pilón complemented the occasional activities of ethnologist. The local jefe, an autocratic figure accused of seeking only his own power over others, simply stated over and over that all Guaymíes were obliged to follow the orders of the cacique and General Torrijos; he made known these orders.[61] People had to vote for Lorenzo's candidate because the cacique, backed by the General, said so.[62] Cuerima lay within the boundaries both of Hato Pilón and of Hato Julí because Cacique Lorenzo, who founded the community with people drawn from both corregimientos, said so. When the National Guard helicopter brought beef to feed the voters on election day, the jefe took it all, maintaining that it was the General's gift only to those who voted for Lorenzo's candidate.[63] When the visiting corregidor would not commit himself to campaign and vote for the cacique's candidate, the jefe sent a note denouncing the corregidor's failure to remain neutral and threatening legal action.[64]

The campaign itself was hard to find. Many homes displayed colored banners indicating support for one of the candidates; but often the banners represented only a bit of decoration or a favorable response to a request to display it.[65] There were no rallies, no speeches, no debates, just quiet conversations here and there. Cacique Lorenzo's candidate, who came in second in the polling, stayed away from the main caseríos of the corregimiento; one could only surmise about his qualifications and his platform from conversations with his supporters. The principal opponent and eventual winner, son of the corregidor, had only recently returned after years of living outside the Guaymí area in order to continue his education. He had completed considerably more years of school than either of his opponents, but he no longer spoke Ngawbere. During the campaign he visited much of the corregimiento, chatting about his plans for development projects: a road, a health subcenter, an improved school, agricultural projects, and collaboration with other elected representatives of the area. He spent more time playing baseball than he did campaigning.[66]

Generally, people responded with little enthusiasm to the whole electoral process, perhaps supporting a candidate but manifesting little expectation that the outcome would make any difference to them. Those who depended upon the local jefe for access to lands seemed to support his endeavors, even though some of them privately hinted they might vote for another candidate. The winner apparently drew support from his extensive family ties and from his father's good name in much of the corregimiento; but even those who knew and liked his plans had little expectation he could carry them out.[67]

But the winner also profited from negative reactions to the jefe and to the activities of the ethnologist. In April, a group of Guaymí-elected representatives from Chiriquí had sent a formal petition to Gen. Torrijos, asking him (in vain) to intervene in the work of the ethnologist, despite the fact that she did get some good things done for the Guaymíes.[68] After five pages of specific denunciations, they requested

> the immediate transfer of [the ethnologist] to some activity which has nothing to do, to develop, to orient, to coordinate, to dialogue or to consult with the indigenous sector of Chiriquí, for the reasons given in the previous pages.

For good measure, they also requested that the money allocated for her helicopter trips be transferred to something useful for the indigenous area.

After the elections, even more openly than before, a number of people commented on the "bad attitude" of the jefe: his overall aggressiveness, his insistence that his way was the only way, his giving arbitrary orders that few were inclined to follow. "This isn't the way to do things," they would say; "what is reasonable is on one side, what [the jefe] does is on the other. This isn't correct." They saw his actions as part of his continuing attempt to usurp power over the people of the area, to impose his will—and to change previous judgments in land conflicts in which he was involved.[69]

These perceptions in turn fed into negative perceptions of the cacique, in whose name the jefe and the ethnologist worked. Cacique Lorenzo had many opponents in San Félix District and in parts of Remedios District.[70] Aside from jealousies and personal issues, his strongest opposition raised serious questions about what he stood for and how he worked. A number of opponents maintained that he was still pushing the anti-progress line of the Mama Chi movement, a line which they thought condemned the Guaymíes to continuing deterioration of their economic base, ever-worsening poverty, and no hope for future generations.[71] They described their nervousness about the lack of job descriptions for the cacique or his assistants, and about limits to their claims of authority. They mentioned difficulties with the local jefes inmediatos. They maintained that Lorenzo opposed the government's schools in the Guaymí area; as evidence they cited statements and actions of the jefes inmediatos of their own area. They claimed that over the years Lorenzo had collected a substantial amount of money from local Guaymíes, and no one knew what the money had gone for. Many were even unwilling to commit themselves to the idea of a comarca, afraid that it would bring an autocratic internal government without solving any problems.[72]

Although Cacique Lorenzo seemed to have little passionate support, he did have more support than any other Guaymí individual or group in Chiriquí (Young and Bort 1979:36). His principal support, in Tolé District (where he lived) and in some areas of Remedios District (where he was from), came from those Guaymíes who agreed that they needed the comarca and who thought that Lorenzo was a viable leader in that battle. He had no important resources at his disposal; he could not deliver funding for development projects in local communities, he could not force the government to grant the comarca. But he could point to his years of struggle on behalf of the Guaymíes, and bask in the sunlight of his personal relationship with Torrijos, who was very popular with the Guaymíes; through this relationship, he could lay claim to prominence as a national figure, one whose friendship and advice the General himself came to seek.[73]

Even though a majority of Cacique Lorenzo's candidates became representatives, he had little control over them. Several renounced their affiliation with him within months of the elections; others rejected his choice of liaison between himself and the representatives. Like some of his jefes (although with more finesse), Lorenzo seemed to believe that the representatives ought blindly to follow his orders. But the power of the representatives did not come from the cacique or even from the people who elected them; it came from the government, which paid their salaries and provided them with small budgets for local projects. The cacique had little leverage.[74]

José Mónico Cruz, the charismatic cacique of Bocas del Toro Province, seemed to enjoy more support among the Guaymíes of his province than did Cacique Lorenzo in Chiriquí.[75] He won popular backing by going around the entire province, meeting and talking with people, and working with them on approaches to local problems. He was influential in getting "voluntary" schools established in many communities, then in getting the government to recognize a number of these schools; Guaymí education in Bocas del Toro seemed somewhat more under Guaymí control than was the case in Chiriquí.

Cacique Mónico, more than his Chiriquí counterpart, also seemed wary of the manipulations of the government; as a consequence, he seemed more independent in his approach to questions and problems. He rarely met alone with government or National Guard officials, preferring to have some of his trusted advisors with him; he rarely committed himself on matters on which he had not consulted with the people affected, no matter how much pressure was exerted to make him decide on the spot. He turned down helicopter rides when the National Guard came looking for him to mediate disputes in Valle de Riscó; instead, he made them reschedule meetings for when he could arrive in the ordinary Guaymí way: on foot and/or by dugout canoe. He was reluctant to jeopardize his backing even for the enhanced life style available to him and his family.[76]

In Bocas del Toro, Mónico's organization counted on the efforts of Guaymíes long active in union affairs on the Chiriquí Land Company plantations of Changuinola, where the Guaymíes constituted the majority of the labor force.[77] Union activists, closely tied to their families and sharpened by their union work, participated articulately in Guaymí congresses and meetings. They provided solid, Guaymí-centered analyses of the problems under discussion (the comarca, Cerro Colorado and Teribe-Changuinola) while working well behind the scenes; they also mobilized Guaymí economic support to sponsor local meetings.

Some Panama City Guaymíes, led by Ricardo Smith, with strong support from Miguel Cruz, formed the *Unión Indígena Guaymí* (UIG, pronounced "weeg"), an organization that professed loyalty to Cacique Mónico.[78] UIG leaders were Mónico's delegates on the Guaymí commission that negotiated the comarca with the government; in effect, they gave him a permanent presence in Panama City, and provided him some access to information about government personnel and approaches.

But UIG's leaders were not well known by the grass-roots Guaymíes, who at times saw them as people who flew in for meetings, engaged in non-Guaymí debates and arguments, threw around the weight of their advanced educations, and disappeared again back to the "soft life" of the capital.[79] And UIG, with its small active membership and few resources, could do little to make itself a focal point of local-level Guaymí organization. In 1980, Smith waged a strenuous campaign as a candidate for the newly created post of legislator, representing Bocas del Toro. Even though he claimed the backing of Cacique Mónico (whose backing seemed at best lukewarm), he fared very badly in the elections. Even he recognized that the outcome was far worse than could be attributed to irregularities in the elections themselves; after making noises about taking legal action, he quietly accepted the results.[80]

Cacique Mónico and UIG were the principal organizers of the First Guaymí General Congress in Canquintú (September 1979), called to discuss issues relating to the comarca and carta orgánica as well as to the mega-projects (Cerro Colorado and Teribe-Changuinola).[81] Cacique Lorenzo of Chiriquí did not take part in this congress; a Guaymí from Chiriquí read a note, supposedly signed by Lorenzo, offering his regrets and claiming bad health. But the fact that none of his principal supporters took part indicated that more than his health kept him home. His supporters complained that he had been *"ninguneado"* (reduced to a nobody) by the congress organizers who did not consult with him as they should have. The organizers said they had tried to meet and work with Lorenzo, but he would not cooperate.

An opportunistic group of Chiriquí Guaymíes took control of the organization of the follow-up Extraordinary Guaymí Congress of Soloy (April 1980); again, Cacique Lorenzo and his supporters did not participate. The organizing group of self-styled "leaders," claiming to unite the Guaymí leaders of Chiriquí, quite openly opposed Lorenzo, looking for ways to unseat him in favor of one of their own. But they seemed unable to agree on a replacement, and in any case sensed that Lorenzo had more support than they. So, while they criticized him for his failure to take part in major Guaymí congresses and tried to persuade others to suggest it was time to replace him, they also denied that they were after anything but collaboration with the cacique.[82]

Both Lorenzo's supporters and his opponents suggested that he was fearful that these congresses were vehicles to replace him. During the Soloy congress, Lorenzo held his own meeting, in Tolé, of his jefes inmediatos, those elected representatives who supported him, and others of his followers—even as he sent a note apologizing that his poor health (cataracts) kept him from travelling to the congress. According to his supporters, the cacique distanced himself from the congresses, arguing that their resolutions held no weight because they did not take into account the Chiriquí Guaymíes whom he claimed to represent. In public, he used the standard Guaymí response that, since he wasn't there, he didn't know what they had done and thus had no opinion on it.

Neither Cacique Mónico of Bocas del Toro nor UIG openly opposed Cacique Lorenzo; when asked for their views of his absence from major meetings, they shrugged and responded that any problems with his leadership were matters for the Guaymíes of Chiriquí to resolve. But they were clearly unhappy that Lorenzo would not participate in the congresses and that Chiriquí was underrepresented; they recognized that Lorenzo's absence weakened any agreements hammered out among the Guaymíes present. Even without openly opposing him, they challenged the Guaymíes of Chiriquí to get themselves organized around leaders who would lead. But they did not see the group of opportunists as an alternative for Chiriquí; the UIG people went to some lengths to wrest control of the Soloy congress and its agenda from this group, which planned to make the congress into a public relations opportunity for the government.[83]

In opposition to UIG, other Guaymí university students in Panama City founded the *Frente de Liberación Guaymí,* headed by a very bright law student from Veraguas. At congresses, the Frente used the Intendente as its rallying point; but the Intendente seemed little involved with the Frente.[84] The Frente, much more than UIG, made itself known in Guaymí communities principally through concerted efforts to gain adherents among students, e.g., the older (fifteen or more years) students of the junior high school of Chichica in Tolé. The Frente focused its differences with UIG around the question of Guaymí collaboration with the government; the Frente opposed negotiations, claiming that the Guaymíes had never gotten anywhere this way, and never would. Its members advocated a more confrontational approach.[85]

These overlapping, conflicting attempts to develop Guaymí organization, besides running into the lack of experience of the prime movers, in more subtle ways ran head-on into the realities of Guaymí history. As noted earlier, Guaymí history provided them with precedents for organizing temporarily to meet a common enemy, and with slow but sure consensus decision-making. But the ordinary Guaymíes could not readily recognize the contemporary problems as enemies, any more than they could see in congresses, UIG, the Frente, or elections, a Guaymí way of arriving at decisions. Since subsistence posed the main object of attention for most people, the kin organization, which directly influenced subsistence, commanded primary loyalty. Most of those trying to develop Guaymí political organization did not work directly with kin groups and consensus; they did not build on Guaymí history and reality.

In contrast, Cacique Mónico of Bocas del Toro Province exercised his leadership in ways the Guaymíes could recognize culturally. Many saw him as a man of practical wisdom, courage, charisma, and dedication. He surrounded himself with able counselors and heeded their counsel. One may assume he enjoyed the support of kin groups. He successfully defined many modern enemies for the people of his province, and could mobilize large numbers to do battle with these enemies. He worked well with most of the Guaymí elected representatives in the province. He helped communities mobilize local resources on their own behalf. But, as cacique of the most remote province, he did not receive nearly the attention from the government that his colleague from Chiriquí received. It seemed that the government considered him much less a threat.

Whether through conscious policies or by accident, the government contributed to and profited from Guaymí divisions while professing to promote Guaymí unity and interests. The government repeatedly insisted on its support for the caciques and its commitment to negotiations for the comarca, but its actions were more cosmetic than substantive. The government took credit for establishing and giving limited power to the elected representatives, backing them even when they were divided among themselves and from the caciques. When working with individual elected representatives, the government acted as though it saw the Guaymíes as a hierarchically organized society under the caciques, even when the caciques were divided. The government also supported its other governmental agencies that at times rendered judgments that contradicted those of Guaymí instances of authority. And the government backed the ranchers, who continued to usurp Guaymí territory, although the same government stated its opposition to the usurpations.

The activities both of the government and of the Guaymíes took on greater significance with the government's plans to exploit the massive copper deposits of Cerro Colorado. With the new interest in natural resources located within the area inhabited by the Guaymíes, the government's policies toward the Guaymíes and toward ownership and exploitation of resources became a matter of critical concern. For no longer were the Guaymíes faced with occasional small groups of explorers arriving on foot, on horseback, or in small ships, but with explorers arriving

> in helicopters and airplanes, with maps made by satellites, with studies undertaken by the United Nations, with logos of transnational corporations: owners of the spirit and the means of exploration, technology, and possessed by a hunger which impels them to devour the crumbs [left over] from previous epochs. (Lobo 1979a:17)

No longer did the Guaymíes only face the continuation of the gradual deterioration of their subsistence base and the gradual erosion of their supplementary strategies; now they also faced the full-scale assault of the latest and biggest mining technology of the twentieth century, bringing with it a whole world ignorant of and inimical to the Guaymí way of life.[86]

PART 2

The Mining Project: Who's in Control?

art 1 presented an overview of the Cerro Colorado mining project and discussed the general setting of Panama and the Guaymí Indians; it should serve as background for detailed consideration of the Cerro Colorado mining project and its impact. Part 2 provides a detailed summary and analysis of the different aspects of the mining project: the companies involved, the plans and problems, and the outcome.

Part 1 used the analytical framework of contrasting the local, regional, national, and transnational levels of dynamics, with the aim of specifying those levels of dynamics that exercised greater or lesser influence on the matters under discussion. Part 2 continues within the same framework, contrasting Panama's struggle to control the mining project (the national dynamic) with the realities of the world in which Panama engaged in this endeavor (the transnational dynamic). In this struggle, Panama's government battled to avoid subjecting its own goals and desires to the realities imposed upon it from outside: by the transnational corporations that became Panama's partners, by the financial institutions, and by the vagaries of the international copper market.

Cerro Colorado's varied career reflects the complexities of large-scale mineral developments in the present era. Canadian Javelin, Ltd., arrived in 1970 and departed in 1975. In 1975 the Panamanian government announced that it would develop the copper project itself. In February 1976, the government signed contracts with Texasgulf, Inc., which granted the company minority ownership (20 percent of the equity) but overall management of the project. In May 1980, following a series of developments and disagreements, Texasgulf signed out in favor of Rio Tinto-Zinc, Ltd., of London; RTZ, taking over as project manager, entered the Cerro Colorado project with 49 percent of the equity as Panama reduced its own share from 80 percent to 51 percent.

During eleven years of exploration and study, one change dominated all others—the ever-rising estimates of the cost of construction of the Cerro Colorado project. These diffeering estimates reflected different methods of calculation, design changes, infrastructure requirements, inflation, interest rates, differing "kinds" of U.S. dollars (discounted, inflation-weighted, and so on), as well as recalculations of Canadian Javelin's earliest optimistic forecasts. Canadian Javelin's proposals (in U.S. dollars) ranged from initial guesses of $100–200 million in late 1972 (NM n.d.) through $450 million in mid-1973 (MM 1974:91) to $700 million in late 1974 (TGM 1974)—the estimated cost at the time of Canadian Javelin's 1975 departure (MS 1975). Texasgulf's initial estimate of $800 million (TGM 1975c) rose through $1.4 billion in 1977 (TGM 1978), then climbed to over $2.0 billion by the time Texasgulf left the project. Rio Tinto-Zinc published an estimate of a whopping $3.2 billion (1981:16). In round numbers, from 1972 to late 1980, estimates for the total cost of Cerro Colorado increased by 3200 percent.

CHAPTER 4

The National Dynamics of Cerro Colorado: Panama's Struggle for Control

Preliminary exploration in the 1960s confirmed that Panama had exploitable copper reserves. General Torrijos, wanting to make Panama a major copper producer, knew his country could not by itself provide the expertise or financing needed for a mining project, so he sought help from multinational mining corporations. But the General wanted Panamanian control over any mineral development in the country. To that end, he insisted that any agreement include "provisions for joint government-private industry operations," terms that the mining industry judged "relatively harsh" (E/MJ 1969b:112, 1970:102). Nonetheless, several companies showed interest in Panamanian copper, and the government thought it could achieve its goal of Panamanian control. In the early years of work on the Cerro Colorado project, events tended to reinforce the government's perceptions.

CANADIAN JAVELIN IN PANAMA

Canadian Javelin, Ltd., of Montreal opened the work on the Cerro Colorado deposits in November 1970, following the successful negotiation of an agreement conceding it exploration rights for up to eight years over an area of 75,000 hectares in the mountains of eastern Chiriquí. Canadian Javelin also received the first rights to negotiate an exploitation agreement with the government of

Panama, in the event of proving the presence of a commercially exploitable copper deposit (CODEMIN 1975:10; E/MJ 1971:27; NM n.d.:2).[1]

Canadian Javelin entered an area completely lacking the infrastructure needed for its exploratory work. The first crews arrived on foot or on horseback, some twelve to fifteen hours after setting out from the Pan-American Highway, 22 miles distant; a brush-cutting crew of fifteen men worked for six weeks to "walk in" a small bulldozer (E/MJ 1972:61). The company cleared a rough landing strip in Escopeta, at the foot of Cerro Colorado; when possible, helicopters or a small plane brought in supplies, including some fairly heavy equipment. Occasionally the company arranged to move still heavier items with a transport helicopter of the Panamanian National Guard; ordinarily Guaymí Indians carried the disassembled diamond-drill rigs from one drilling site to another.[2] Canadian Javelin built a narrow, winding jeep road up the face of Cerro Colorado, then supervised Guaymí crews in the daily work of maintaining the road. In 1972 the company contracted Owl Investments, Ltd., of Grand Cayman for preliminary work on an access road from the town of San Félix to the camp at Escopeta; in 1973 Canadian Javelin paid $6.5 million to International Oceanic Construction Corporation and Almora, S.A., to build the 40-km dirt road.

The work crews built and lived in the Escopeta base camp; later they added another camp on the side of the mountain. Initially, the payroll reached 200 men (NM n.d.:2), but leveled out nearer 100 during the main drilling seasons. The work force included a handful of expatriate geologists, engineers, and drillers, and a far larger number of Guaymíes, hired to hand-clear paths, small roads, and drilling sites, and to carry things from one part of the property to another.

In July 1973, John Doyle of Canadian Javelin announced that the Cerro Colorado deposit contained 2.2 billion tons of 0.8 percent copper; he said that construction of a major mining operation would begin in August. He said Canadian Javelin would need about two years and US$560 million to build the project, which would include: a mine and mill to process about 176,000 metric tons per day of ore; a smelter with a capacity of 200,000 metric tons per year; and an electrolytic refinery with a capacity of 100,000 metric tons per year. He proposed to export about half of Cerro Colorado's production as concentrate, one-fourth as blister copper, and the remaining fourth as refined copper and wirebar. Doyle said he had already signed preliminary financing agreements with purchasers of the Cerro Colorado production. These reports appeared in the U.S. press accompanied by the news that the government of Panama was forming a committee to negotiate a mining agreement with Canadian Javelin (WSJ 1973a; MH 1973b).

In the course of further investigation of the deposits, Canadian Javelin discovered that the Cerro Colorado project was too big and too complicated for it to manage alone. Canadian Javelin formed a powerful consortium to finance and develop the Cerro Colorado deposit: Noranda Mines, of Toronto; C. Itoh and Company (representing the Japanese Nippon Mining Company, Dowa Mining Company, Sumitomo Metal Mining Company, Mitsubishi Mining Company, Mitsui Mining and Smelting Company, and Furukawa Mining Company); and British Kynoch Metals (for its shareholders, British Insulated Callender's Cables, Delta Metal Industries, and Imperial Metal Industries). Noranda would manage the construction of the project and, later, the mining, concentrating, and smelting operations on behalf of the consortium. British Kynoch signed a letter of intent covering marketing arrangements for the entire Cerro Colorado production for the first fifteen years; "British Kynoch and its shareholders are the largest copper consumers in the world" (TGM 1974). Canadian Javelin would provide the concession. But more precise equity and financing arrangements were never revealed, because negotiations between the consortium and the government of Panama broke down (see TGM 1974; MS 1974; WSJ 1975a, 1975b). Canadian Javelin had no mining concession, and in the actual event never obtained one.

It is contrary to ordinary practice for a multinational corporation to enter into expensive, high-risk exploration of a mineral deposit without assuring itself of the right to exploit the deposit; but Doyle and Canadian Javelin had carried out their work with only the assurance of the first right to negotiate an exploitation agreement. Why? In the absence of solid information, one can only speculate. Quite likely, even before going to work on Cerro Colorado, Doyle was already friendly with General Torrijos; he may well have underestimated the wily Panamanian leader.[3] Canadian Javelin may have hoped to be favored as a small, Canadian-based corporation, avoiding the problems of Latin American bitterness over "Yankee imperialism" in general and over U.S.-based giants like Anaconda or Kennecott in particular. Canadian Javelin clearly assumed it could obtain a mining concession without much problem; when the U.S. press first revealed that Doyle had no agreement to develop Cerro Colorado, Canadian Javelin said the question was "academic" because negotiations were virtually concluded (WSJ 1973c).

In fact, the negotiations were concluded in March 1975, when Panama bought out Canadian Javelin's exploratory work and sent the company home. Panama refused to budge on its major negotiating points: length of the exploitation concession and later ownership of the project. Panama offered five years for investment and construction, and twenty years of exploitation; the Canadian Javelin consortium insisted on at least thirty-five years, with the right of renewal. In the Panamanian offer, the concession and all installations would revert to Panama after twenty years of exploitation; Panama maintained that the original investment could be recovered within ten years (fifteen at the outside) and that these terms offered the consortium adequate return on its investment. But the consortium thought twenty years of exploitation inadequate for recovery of and appropriate return on its investment, and in any case was unwilling to sign over the project to Panama at the conclusion of the agreed time. On this point, Panama's experience with the "in perpetuity" canal treaty of 1903 played an important role; the government was determined not to enter into any other agreement that could leave control indefinitely in the hands of foreign interests. Since Torrijos touted the Cerro Colorado mine (and copper in general) as the resource that would "save" Panama, a great deal rode on the government's ability to demonstrate at least the external trappings, if not more, of sovereignty and control (see MS 1975; WSJ 1975a).

According to Alan Riding, the Panamanian position was the result of a compromise between " 'nationalists' who pressed for government control over the project and 'pragmatists' willing to see 100 per cent foreign control" (MS 1975). In this climate, it is unlikely that Panamanian negotiators could demonstrate much flexibility; any major change in their position would have required another series of difficult arguments within the government, with the risk that no new compromise could be achieved.[4]

Looking back, mining engineer Jaime Roquebert, CODEMIN's technical director and a member of the Panamanian team negotiating with the Canadian Javelin consortium, noted other obstacles that had prevented an agreement: the financial difficulties of Canadian Javelin;

Panamanian questions about Canadian Javelin's technical ability to operate such a large project; and Panamanian insistence on at least 51
percent of the ownership, which was also Canadian Javelin's minimum
(E/MJ 1977:193).

Panama had good reason to be concerned about Canadian Javelin's
financial problems and technical abilities; from Doyle's first major announcement about the Cerro Colorado project (September 1973), the
company and its Chairman found themselves embroiled in major controversies with the United States Securities and Exchange Commission.
In November, the SEC charged Doyle and Canadian Javelin with stock
fraud (NYT 1973b).[5] The controversies revolved around two fundamental points: the verification of the information distributed by Doyle
concerning the size of the deposit and the arrangements for development; and the crucial question of whether Canadian Javelin in fact had
an exploitation agreement with the government of Panama.

> In words unusually animated for a legal document, the [Securities
> and Exchange Commission] hit the controversial mining company
> with a suit accusing it of misleading the public with press releases
> "all in superlative language more fit for suitable use by midway car-
> nival hawkers than responsible officials of publicly held companies."
> (WSJ 1973b)

The complaint noted the lack of a feasibility study and other documentation necessary for stock investors to judge the situation of Canadian
Javelin.[6]

> During the period from June 22 to September 19 that the "chain of
> hyperbolic press releases," as the SEC called them, were being is-
> sued, Javelin stock rose considerably in price from its earlier low of
> $5.875 to $18 a share in September. (WSJ 1973b)

Even more serious was the question of Canadian Javelin's legal rights to
exploit Cerro Colorado. On October 24, 1973, the *Wall Street Journal*
reported that Canadian Javelin, despite its pronouncements, had no
mining concession from Panama; the SEC suspended trading in Canadian Javelin stock (WSJ 1973b). Doyle, while insisting the concession
was a non-problem, struggled to obtain rights from Panama; as noted,
he failed.

But whatever the weakness of Canadian Javelin, the consortium itself was "a most powerful financing and copper-consuming group" (FP 1975) and Noranda was a major mining company with considerable technical ability. So, the key sticking point in the breakdown of negotiations with Panama was most likely the question of Panamanian sovereignty and control, expressed in the duration of the contracts and the equity participation in the project.

When negotiations terminated, Canadian Javelin turned over all properties and works at Cerro Colorado to the government of Panama, which began to work out the compensation owed to Canadian Javelin.[7] Panamanian officials, concerned to reassure potential partners about Panama's favorable investment climate, pledged fair treatment of Canadian Javelin; General Torrijos announced the decision to "indemnify and compensate [Canadian Javelin,] returning their investment, plus a generous indemnization" (WSJ 1975c). The two sides began these negotiations as far apart as when they ended the mining concession negotiations; Jaime Roquebert said that the government rejected a Canadian Javelin demand for $125 million in compensation (LAER 1975:71). By the end of August 1975, Panama and Canadian Javelin announced agreement on a compensation package of $23.6 million: $5 million in cash, paid immediately, and $18.6 million in 8 percent 20-year tax-free direct obligation bonds of Panama. This amount was considerably less than Canadian Javelin's demand of $125 million; some analysts argued that the compensation was too low because Canadian Javelin's expenditures had been made in dollars that were worth more than those used to repay the company (NM 1975). However, in the absence of any serious published complaints from the not-at-all bashful head of Canadian Javelin, one might conclude that Canadian Javelin was unable to substantiate its $125-million claim and found the smaller package, despite inflation, to be a fair one.[8]

PANAMA'S STRATEGY: CONTROL THE PROJECT

When negotiations between the government of Panama and the Canadian Javelin consortium broke down in early March 1975, Panama announced its intention to undertake on its own the development of the Cerro Colorado deposits. Torrijos said his government was not against anyone, but

> merely pro-Panamanian. We don't wish both of our principal economic resources, the Panama Canal and the copper deposits of Cerro Colorado, to be in foreign hands unless they serve our national interests. Our people profoundly believe they must control their own destiny. The mining potential is far more significant than the Canal. (WSJ 1975c)

Torrijos planned to contract both a major financial institution for the organization and management of the financial aspects of the project, and a major mining company to extract and process the ore "for the account and benefit of Panama"; the operator would have to contribute 15 percent of the equity as insurance of efficient operation of the project (WSJ 1975c). The list of firms competing to develop Cerro Colorado with Panama had been shortened to four: Texasgulf, Inc., Noranda, Ltd., British South African Selection Trust, Ltd., and Union Minière of Belgium (LAWG 1980:5). Analysts thought Noranda, part of the Canadian Javelin consortium, had the inside track (TC 1975).

Panama based its initial strategy on a plan to increase its bargaining power with potential multinational corporate partners. The principal proponents of this plan were Xabier Gorostiaga, economic consultant to the Ministry of External Relations, and Ronald Müller of American University in Washington, D.C., contracted to give advice on the Cerro Colorado strategy.[9] They argued that Panama would not guarantee for itself effective control over the profits from the mining venture by retaining majority ownership of the project; majority ownership would only guarantee difficult problems in financing the construction of the project.[10] Rather, Panama could control the profits by exercising control over the revenues and the costs of the project. This control in turn would depend on Panamanian control of: gross sales, volume of copper produced, copper prices, and costs of equipment and other imported services.

To these ends, Gorostiaga and Müller urged Panama to "unbundle" the project, to contract separately for the technological-managerial, marketing, and financial aspects of the project, dividing the tasks and powers of its multinational corporate partners while retaining for itself the determination of sales contracts, a key to the controls mentioned above. They counseled the use of a service contract for technology and management, "leasing" MNC technology and experience.[11] Panama could look for financing from Europe and Japan, from the emerging capital-rich OPEC countries, or even from some oil-producing LDCs; in the process Panama would diversify its dependence on the United States and gain political support in the negotiation of new canal treaties.[12]

Torrijos had announced that Panama would retain 85 percent of the equity in the mining project. In view of Panama's foreign debt, Gorostiaga and Müller suggested Panama consider reducing its equity participation to around 60 percent, with the remaining 40 percent divided among different foreign sources, for example, 15 percent for Arab investors, 15 percent to Japanese and/or European customers, and 10 percent to the managing multinational mining firm. In fact, to reduce its risk and indebtedness, Panama could reduce its equity to below 50 percent and yet retain power over project costs and revenues, by keeping the remaining blocks smaller than its own—for example, 35 percent for itself vs. 30 percent, 25 percent, and 10 percent, for the investors, customers, and hired managers, respectively.[13]

Gorostiaga and Müller thought they had succeeded in persuading the government to try this strategy. They felt they had reached and convinced at least the "outer" inner circle of Torrijos' advisers. Although they themselves had not made it to the small "inner" inner circle, they heard that their proposal received a favorable hearing and was likely to be accepted.

Meanwhile, the government had turned the work on the Cerro Colorado project over to its recently formed Panamanian Copper Commission. The Commission contracted the Ministry of Public Works to improve the unfinished access road and to build a bridge across the San Félix River; it hired workers to maintain the equipment and buildings left by Canadian Javelin. It sent some of its members into the field to assess and compensate damages caused to Guaymí lands by construction of the Canadian Javelin road. And it negotiated the indemnification of Canadian Javelin.

Midway through 1975, the government elevated the status of the Commission, making it a semi-autonomous corporation of the state called Corporación de Desarrollo Minero Cerro Colorado (Corporation for Mineral Development Cerro Colorado). The new corporation gave itself the acronym CODEMIN.[14] Rodrigo (Rory) González, businessman head of the Commission and close friend of Torrijos,[15] became president of CODEMIN; Jaime Roquebert, mining engineer, became technical manager; and two anthropologists and an ethnologist formed the core of the Department of Social Development. Rubén Darío Herrera, economist and reputed member of the Party of the People *(Partido del Pueblo)*, became general manager.

In July 1975, to the surprise of all, the government of Panama announced the pre-selection of Texasgulf, Inc., as sole partner for the development of the Cerro Colorado project; with this announcement, the government sent packing the consultants and multinational corporate competitors. Noranda expressed immediate shock over the announcement; it had not yet made its final proposals. Industry analysts expressed surprise, noting that Noranda had much more experience in copper mining, and had been involved with the Cerro Colorado project as part of the Canadian Javelin consortium; Texasgulf was much smaller in copper and had considerably less experience in bringing new projects into operation. Also, Texasgulf had entered late, and could not have prepared its case thoroughly. Some also said that they were surprised Texasgulf would get involved in such a project by itself (TC 1975).

In the aftermath of the startling announcement of Panama's new partner, rumors insinuated that intrigue had entered into the selection of Texasgulf. The announcement followed almost immediately upon the unexpected return to Panama of Rodrigo González, who supposedly had set out for Western Europe to explore some elements of the Müller-Gorostiaga strategy. Instead of changing planes in New York City for his transatlantic flight, he went to Washington, D.C.; from there, he returned directly to Panama.[16] Why did he change his plans? With whom did he meet in Washington?

Perhaps the United States government, using the stalled canal treaty negotiations as bait, put very strong pressure on the Panamanian government to select a U.S. corporation for the Cerro Colorado project; at that stage, Texasgulf was the only U.S. multinational corporation in the running.[17] Perhaps someone offered González and, presumably, Torrijos some "special consideration" (i.e., a bribe or a kickback) in exchange for the Cerro Colorado contracts; Panamanian popular perceptions of both Torrijos and González suggested that they would have been amenable to this approach.[18] Alternatively, González may have discovered, perhaps in conversations at the World Bank, that Panama would be unable to unbundle the project.[19]

With or without intrigue, Panama had a very fundamental reason for its selection of Texasgulf: this corporation, alone among the multinational bidders, would concede the ownership terms demanded by Panama.[20] As Torrijos had insisted in March, Panama sought to keep this "principal economic resource" under Panamanian control; Panama would not allow Cerro Colorado to become a divisive factor in national life, as was the canal (MH 1975).

Through its selection of Texasgulf, Panama claimed this control. Panama received recognition of its sovereignty over the copper deposits, retained majority ownership of the mining project, negotiated the transfer of mining technology, and contracted to take complete control of the ownership and operation of the project no more than twenty years after commencement of actual mining.

Panama reached these objectives through the negotiation of two contracts with Texasgulf. The first, the Association Agreement, mapped out CODEMIN's partnership with Texasgulf in the jointly owned operating company, Empresa de Cobre Cerro Colorado, S.A. (Cerro Colorado Copper Corporation), formed to exploit the deposits; this equity contract made Panama the holder of 80 percent of the shares in the operating company and Texasgulf the owner of the other 20 percent. An appendix to this contract provided the Articles of Incorporation, the bylaws for the new corporation. In the second contract, the Administration Agreement, the operating company hired Texasgulf as sole administrator of the mining project; in exchange for management fees, Texasgulf was to study, design, construct, operate, and take care of sales for the Cerro Colorado Copper Corporation. During its term as administrator, Texasgulf would train Panamanian personnel for all phases of the Cerro Colorado operation, insuring that Panamanians ran the entire operation before the termination of the administration agreement. The administration agreement would expire after fifteen years of actual mining operations (Consejo de Legislación, Adm. II). After twenty years of mining, CODEMIN could purchase Texasgulf's 20 percent equity according to formulas included in the contracts (Consejo de Legislación, Assn. XIII).[21]

In Texasgulf, Panama found "an uncommon company"—a U.S.

corporation whose principal stockholder (more than 30 percent) was the Canada Development Corporation, a holding company of the Canadian government (LAWG 1980:5-6). Internationally, the government of Panama could point to Texasgulf as a U.S. corporation, using the Cerro Colorado contracts to signal Panamanian acceptance of continued U.S. economic hegemony as the canal treaty negotiations moved forward. Domestically, to an increasingly anti-Yankee Panamanian public, the government could emphasize Texasgulf's "Canadian character," taking advantage of the less provocative (and less known) image of Canadian business in Latin America.

Texasgulf's characteristics also enhanced Panama's prospects for financing the mine. Thanks to the Canada Development Corporation, four Canadians sat on the Texasgulf board of directors. In turn, Canada Development Corporation's own board of directors interlocked, through the representatives of two government ministries, with the board of the Export Development Corporation, the Canadian government's export credit agency. In July 1978, General Torrijos announced that the Export Development Corporation had sent a letter of intent with its offer to take the lead in arranging financing of $1.1 billion for the construction of Cerro Colorado; one might have anticipated an offer of Export Development Corporation financing for a Canada Development Corporation project in Panama.

Panama and Texasgulf agreed on two key provisions with regard to financing the mining project. The first stipulated that neither the government of Panama nor Texasgulf would be obliged to guarantee loans made to the jointly owned operating company (Consejo de Legislación, Assn. IX.2); their financial obligations would be limited to their respective equity contributions.[22] The second stated that substantial parts of the mining project could, for financing purposes, be better viewed as national development projects; roads, port facilities, and some other items of infrastructure would benefit Panama's overall development, even though the mining project made them necessary. If possible, Panama should finance these items with subsidized development loans from multinational lenders like the World Bank and the Inter-American Development Bank (Consejo de Legislación, Adm. IV.3.i). The loans themselves would be considered part of Panama's equity contribution (Consejo de Legislación, Assn. XI.7). Texasgulf would supervise the planning and construction (Consejo de Legislación, Adm. ibid.). In order to avoid enclaves like the Canal Zone or the United Fruit Company plantations, Panama insisted on determination of the site and characteristics of the new city for mineworkers; its construction, including financing, would be completely in Panama's hands (Consejo de Legislación, Adm. ibid.).

CODEMIN pointed to other advantages it gained by signing on with Texasgulf. The relationship with the Canadian government would have provided Texasgulf with valuable experience for working with the Panamanian government; presumably the company would know how to juggle corporate and government interests, and how to work with politicians and bureaucrats. Panama would determine the personnel remuneration and training policies for the project (Consejo de Legislación, Adm. VI.2.h), giving it tools to avoid the creation of a labor elite (see Zorn 1980:213–14). Panama liked Texasgulf's record of good management-employee relations and of good solutions to worker problems without the need of unions.[23] Jaime Roquebert of CODEMIN pointed to another aspect of Texasgulf's ability to manage its workers: the low ratio of employees to sales. Also, Texasgulf would bring its expertise in the production of phosphate fertilizers, making possible the conversion of smelter waste into a marketable by-product (E/MJ 1977:194).[24]

CODEMIN maintained that its contracts with Texasgulf allowed Panama to undertake the Cerro Colorado project under conditions that respected national sovereignty and allowed legitimate control over Panama's resources. It defended the contracts with Texasgulf as embodying a new, equal relationship between a third world host country and a transnational mining corporation: Panama owned 80 percent of the Cerro Colorado operating company, hired experienced management, obtained pre-negotiated termination dates for the contracts, provided for the transfer of technology to Panama, and obliged Texasgulf to train Panamanian personnel to take over all aspects of the mining project (CODEMIN 1976:8–9). In Texasgulf, Panama had also found a company that agreed to low-risk financing, could handle labor problems without unions, knew how to work in partnership with a government, and would transform smelter waste into phosphate fertilizer. No other bidder presented the same combination of qualities; in any case, apparently no other bidder would concede the equity terms and time limitations demanded by Panama. According to CODEMIN, the partnership with Texasgulf guaranteed that Panama would control the dynamics of copper production.

The on-schedule completion of Texasgulf's studies in May 1978 added to Panama's officially encouraged optimism of the moment. The country was preparing for the June 16 arrival of United States president Jimmy Carter to exchange the final ratification instruments of the Torrijos-Carter canal treaties. Arnulfo Arias' return from self-imposed exile in Miami heralded the new political opportunities after a decade of National Guard rule. Now the popular General Torrijos reminded Panamanians that the Texasgulf–CODEMIN contracts anticipated a decision to begin construction of the mining project ninety days after delivery of the feasibility studies (Consejo de Legislación, Assn. VIII). By 1983, Panama would be a major copper producer.

Through the remainder of 1978, all of 1979, and much of 1980, government leaders and CODEMIN sang the praises of the copper project. Dates, firm or rumored, for beginning Cerro Colorado construction quietly passed, without comment and without any new work at Cerro Colorado; replacement rumors and firm dates reassured everyone that the start of construction was imminent. Some groups took advantage of the more open political climate to raise questions or even to denounce the mining project; CODEMIN mounted an impressive publicity campaign that emphasized the fantastic potential of Cerro Colorado while dismissing even the serious questioning as politically motivated opposition to the Torrijos revolution.

The reasons for going forward with Cerro Colorado remained clear for the Panamanian sponsors, whether they expressed them in their unprecedented series of cleverly written full-page newspaper advertisements, or in slightly more measured arguments in official publications.

SOME COUNTRIES HAVE OIL . . . WE HAVE COPPER!

WHY CAN'T PANAMA BE LIKE JAPAN, GERMANY, FRANCE, OR THE UNITED STATES?

COPPER: BETTER BUSINESS THAN THE CANAL

THE WORLD NEEDS COPPER. WE NEED THE WORLD . . . AND WE HAVE COPPER!

COPPER PAYS THE EXTERNAL DEBT . . . AND MORE.

[With the hundreds of millions of dollars in salaries, taxes, and payments,] the economic perspective places our copper and its entire powerful industrial complex as the biggest, most important and most promising economic activity that we can undertake. Copper is progress, a powerful motor of development. (CODEMIN 1979c)

The economic benefits would be manifold, whether long-range, short-range, public, or private—and all risk-free. CODEMIN published tables of projected economic growth with and without Cerro Colorado, year-by-year projections for 25 years of government income from the project. Supposing a constant price of $1.40 per pound for copper from 1984 on,[25] the government would receive $2,600 million (in constant 1983 dollars) over the course of the first twenty years of production, an average of $130 million annually. Over half of this amount would be taxes paid into the national treasury "to strengthen health, nutrition, education, cultural" and other programs. The rest could be directed toward government investments "to create new sources of wealth, income, and employment," as well as toward increases in credit possibilities for the private sector. While Cerro Colorado would create only 2,500 direct permanent jobs, support services for the mining operation would open up around 10,000 indirect jobs, making likely a new urban center of up to 40,000 people (CODEMIN 1976:16). In addition, the project would create a set of linked investment opportunities, including an explosives plant, factories to make replacement parts for the concentrator, industrial clothing manufacture, and food for so many workers and their families (CODEMIN 1979d:34; CODEMIN 1979a:30–31 listed twenty-six new investment opportunities).

Panama would feel the impact even before Cerro Colorado began producing copper. "[T]he four or five years of the construction period will [witness] a level of activity only comparable to the construction of the Panama Canal, although without reaching the numbers of jobs of that great work." Average employment would be 3500 people, with a peak of 7350. Five hundred million dollars, from wages, salaries, materials, contracts, and so on, would circulate within Panama.

That enormous inflow of money toward the country, that unprecedented level of economic activity with its indirect and multiplying effects, would without a doubt allow [us] to overcome the situation of economic stagnation which the country has suffered the last four

years, with its sequel of high indices of unemployment.
(CODEMIN 1979d:32–33)

Construction alone would turn the stagnant economy into a raging
torrent.

While noting that the estimates of Chase Manhattan's Department of Economic Investigations were "preliminary and tentative,"
CODEMIN used them to spell out the implications of Cerro Colorado's favorable impact on Panama's gross domestic product, imports,
exports, and balance of payments. In 1984, with Cerro Colorado, the
gross domestic product would increase by 26 percent over the projections without Cerro Colorado—more than a billion current dollars.
Gross exports of goods would increase by some $500–600 million,
doubling or even tripling the exports without Cerro Colorado; but
Cerro Colorado operations would only marginally increase the imports.
Panama could confront its chronic deficit in the current account of
balance of payments, while expanding its import capacity (CODEMIN
1979d:9, 33–34). For an "open economy" like Panama's, dependent on
imports for agricultural and industrial inputs and for consumer goods,
expansion of import capacity would be of "enormous importance."

> And much more than this. If we put into the perspectives the ten-
> dency for real prices of petroleum and its derivatives to keep in-
> creasing, and the implication of this tendency for the budget
> allocations that must be assigned here, the potential role of our
> copper in the expansion of import capacity is no longer just enor-
> mously important. It is, to put it crudely, simply vital for the very
> economic viability of the Nation. (CODEMIN 1979d:9.)

Cerro Colorado would diversify Panama's economic dependence on
canal-related activities, while geographically diversifying the domestic
development by positioning a strong pole of attraction in the western
part of the country—going so far as to produce a "radical change of
sign" in the rural-to-urban migration patterns (CODEMIN 1979d:9).
CODEMIN assured everyone that the economic benefits bore no
corresponding risks:

> Only profitable investments can pay for themselves and copper not
> only pays for itself, but also its obvious profitability as a purely
> Panamanian product in primary materials and exploitation is a pal-

pable promise of better days. Days where its profits contribute to the payment of our debts or to avoiding many future debts.

The financial institutions have confidence in the project and believe in the feasibility study. Thus, their loan to the mineral development company, for more than 1,100 million dollars, *without any guarantee from the State.* . . . Later studies calculate at 1 percent the probability of a low profitability in this operation. And at 85 percent the possibilities of great profits for the country. This is, in synthesis, the operation of copper. (CODEMIN 1979c; emphasis in original)

The economic risks, according to CODEMIN's official publications, would be minimal because predictions "prepared by prestigious firms specializing in such matters indicate that towards 1984" Cerro Colorado's copper production would be needed. Copper consumption should continue to grow, 3.5 percent to 4 percent yearly; from 1980 on, an additional 300,000 m.t. per year (more than 1-1/2 times Cerro Colorado's output) would be required. Prices should be strong: at least $1.47 per pound in 1984, with a more probable range of $1.47 to $1.67 per pound. The Export Development Corporation, the Canadian government agency for promotion and financing of exports, undertook "a very exacting evaluation of the Feasibility Study, concluding that the project was sufficiently trustworthy that an official offer of financing could be made," one that would be long term, at reasonable interest rates, with no requirement for Panamanian state underwriting (CODEMIN 1979d:26–27).

Cerro Colorado would employ the world's most modern technology, solving any potential ecological problems while allowing Panama to show its faith in progress. The ads headlined "Copper Indeed has Technological Solutions to the Problems of the Environment" and "Copper Production is Less Risky for the Environment than Oil Production." They continued:

Panama will exploit its copper with the most advanced technology. And with decision and faith in its progress.

Copper carries less ecological risk each day. Today's technology has marched at the rhythm of the demands of the most reputable ecologists of the World. When the Panamanian copper mines open their entrails to the commercial world, the gigantic mining-industrial complex—already, on the drawing board, the most modern in the World—will have added new techniques in all its different processes. Because today's Science does not stop working. . . .

For those of us who worry about the environment, the knowledge that the modern technology of copper exploitation is even less risky than that of oil is very encouraging. The great mining-industrial complex of Cerro Colorado, which collects the gases and takes economic advantage of them, and makes the waste harmless, is at one and the same time an additional source of jobs and the guarantee that copper is a natural resource which strengthens the country's economy, without adverse risks. (CODEMIN 1979c)

Modern technology and the condition of the project area itself together would take care of all potential ecological problems. In the immediate area of the deposit, mining activities would have little impact because "for many decades [human activity] has been bringing about the gradual deterioration of the area." Solid mining waste requires simple storage, the use of some land; this aspect "has no importance because the area is practically unpopulated and is not apt for agriculture." Whatever the decision about concentrator tailings, whether to transport them by river to the ocean or by pipelines to tailings reservoirs, they "will in no way be noxious for marine life." Any lands used will later be recovered and reforested (CODEMIN 1979b:23, 26–27). Deforestation near the mine will be minimal because most of the area has already been deforested; in fact, the mining project will help the area with a good reforestation plan (CODEMIN 1979d:32).

In sum, the Panamanian sponsors promised that Cerro Colorado would provide solutions to most of Panama's economic problems, through the short-range injection of $500 million during the construction period and the long-range income from the project—to the benefit of all. Financing would be risk-free. The world would need not only Cerro Colorado's copper, but much more besides; prices would be strong. Modern technology would ensure that Cerro Colorado would have no negative impact on the environment. Panama would use its natural resources, under Panamanian control, to solve Panamanian problems. To put it differently, in this view the transnational and national dynamics of the project coincided, to the benefit of the national dynamic.

CHAPTER 5

Limitations from the Transnational Dynamics

I n the Cerro Colorado project, Texasgulf found much that was attractive: the opportunity to continue its diversification; assured income with little risk; enhanced possibilities for obtaining financing; a major phosphoric acid plant; and even the chance to play an important role in the stability of the hemisphere.

Dr. Charles Fogarty became president of Texasgulf (1968) and later chairman of the board and chief executive officer (1973) with the mandate to continue the implementation of the corporate strategy he had drawn up to convince the board of directors to reject "an attractive merger proposal by a major oil and gas transmission company" in 1959. The key to this strategy was the diversification of Texasgulf from a sulfur company (at that time, Texas Gulf Sulphur Co.), to "a diversified natural resource company" involved with sulfur, oil, gas, base metals, potash, phosphate (Fogarty 1976:22–23). Even as a minority partner in the Cerro Colorado project, Texasgulf could substantially increase its market share of copper while it gained a valuable entry into and good experience with Latin America. The Cerro Colorado mine, with annual production of more than 185,000 metric tons of copper, would by itself account for around 2-1/2 percent to 3-1/2 percent of market economy country copper production. Association with one of the world's three or four biggest copper mines would give Texasgulf wide exposure to become a major force in the copper industry.[1]

TEXASGULF'S APPROACH

Kenneth Kutz, chief negotiator for Texasgulf, said that Texasgulf did not lay down conditions in its talks with Panama, but rather asked the Panamanians what they wanted in the contracts; then Texasgulf simply outlined what Panama would have to pay or give up in order to get what it wanted (E/MJ 1976:194). Mr. Kutz characterized this approach as "a lesson in the economics of life." This lesson included contractual provisions that minimized Texasgulf's economic risk while guaranteeing its income. Texasgulf obliged itself only to its contribution as owner of 20 percent of the operating company; its income would principally derive from guaranteed management fees. The joint operating company would pay Texasgulf, as administrator, $500,000 for supervising and carrying out the feasibility study, in addition to reimbursing its costs. During the construction period, Texasgulf as administrator would receive 1-1/2 percent (net) of "the design and construction costs of the Project including costs of highways, port facilities and other infrastructure . . . but excluding interest charges and other finance charges"; Texasgulf could also subcontract some phases of construction to itself. During the production period, Texasgulf would be entitled to two kinds of fees, a percentage of gross sales and a percentage of operating profits, in addition to its 20 percent share of net profits (Consejo de Legislación, Adm. VII).[2] With an equity participation of around $100 million, Texasgulf would be paid management fees of $69.5 million total during construction and the first five years of operations, whether the project paid for itself or showed huge losses.[3]

New major mining projects, beyond the financing capability of multinational mining corporations, involve complex arrangements of loans, supplier credits, and sales agreements. Mr. Kutz noted as an advantage the enhanced financing possibilities from participation in a joint venture with an LDC government, eligible for help unavailable to a multinational corporation. Panama could seek extensive development loans, since Cerro Colorado would in part be justified as a development project. The World Bank could be expected to finance infrastructure like the port and roads. The townsite and provision of electrical energy would not even fall under the Cerro Colorado project, but would be the responsibility of the government, which would seek development loans.[4]

Texasgulf also expected that Panama would realize increased revenues, available for Cerro Colorado, in conjunction with the Torrijos-Carter canal treaties. Even had the treaties failed to win Senate ratification, Mr. Kutz thought that the United States government would have a "moral obligation" to provide some sort of compensation; in early 1978, it was anticipated that Panama stood to receive increased United States development aid, whether directly or through U.S.-controlled multilateral institutions like the World Bank and the Inter-American Development Bank.[5] In addition, Texasgulf, a major producer of phosphate and fertilizer, found attractive the development of a plant to combine sulfuric acid (a smelter by-product) with imported phosphate to make phosphoric acid, a primary ingredient in some major fertilizers. This process would not only provide an economic solution to a critical ecological problem, the high sulfur content of Cerro Colorado's ore; it would also give Texasgulf an ideal base from which to make a strong bid for a large share of the fertilizer market anywhere in Latin America, taking advantage of Panama's location for easy shipping via either ocean. The contracts provided for the formation of a new operating company in which Texasgulf, again the manager, could permanently have 49 percent of the equity instead of its temporary 20 percent of the copper project (Consejo de Legislación, Assn. I.2). Texasgulf expected to sell phosphate to the project from its operations in North Carolina or in Mexico.[6]

Finally, in addition to the attractions discussed above, a high Texasgulf executive offered a political-cultural explanation for his company's partnership with Panama: Texasgulf sought to "save Panama." Texasgulf's fees were "trivial," the company would realize little profit from its 20 percent equity investment. But Panama was part of "our hemisphere," and Texasgulf wished to do its part "to keep Panama Christian and democratic." Panama belonged to the U.S. sphere of influence and should remain in that sphere: if Texasgulf didn't "save Panama, someone else would—Russia or Poland or Japan or Western Europe. We're only there to help."

This executive saw Torrijos' government as one which agreed that countries could best achieve economic progress through development of natural resources, not through handouts. Natural resource extraction, the starting place for economic growth, created basic wealth from nothing, as it were. A basic industry like mining provided work for the persons directly employed, plus another ten to twelve people per direct job: the workers' families, and the other businesses of the mining community (grocery stores, gas stations, automobile dealers, educators, and so on). All of this economic activity depended on the circulation of the basic wealth created by mining. Texasgulf realized that "the future of Panama rests on this mine," and was there to help guarantee that future. Texasgulf's contribution would be to approach the entire project from a free enterprise business vantage point, staying clear of politics.[7]

Texasgulf, then, could participate in the Cerro Colorado project with confidence that its activities both met corporate goals and carried a transcendental meaning, the salvation of Panama. Texasgulf might make less profit than it could elsewhere; but a different balance sheet would reflect the gains as Panama remained within the United States' sphere of influence.

Panama wanted recognition of its sovereignty and control of the mining project; Texasgulf wanted freedom from the threat of expropriation. The previously cited high Texasgulf official, arguing for a "new pragmatism," stated that "the days of the imperialist U.S. company are over"; mining companies that demanded fifty years of mineral rights in another country were unrealistic. Even if they were granted, it was unlikely they would be honored; countries all over the globe were expropriating or nationalizing mining projects. World public opinion supported the change, the United States government no longer supported the earlier manner of operating, and even a developed country like Canada was agitating for national control of minerals. It would have been "impractical" for Texasgulf to seek to own the Cerro Colorado project; new, more realistic approaches had to be worked out. Texasgulf seemingly satisfied Panama's objectives of sovereignty and control by accepting the minority equity share, granting Panama the majority of votes on the board of directors of the joint operating company, and agreeing to terms for Panama's buy-out of Texasgulf after some years of operation. Texasgulf hoped it had opened for itself the possibility of other rich agreements with LDCs while coming up with a formula that looked "expropriation-proof."[8]

Although Mr. Kutz denied it, it seemed that Texasgulf's new, "realistic" approach was to grant Panama's 80 percent ownership of the project but keep decision-making control while making its profits as administrator. The secure income from fees amounted to a high price tag on Texasgulf technology. As administrator and minority equity partner, Texasgulf would have virtually the same free hand in the project as if it had been principal owner. Texasgulf obtained control of major decisions affecting the project: veto power over decisions within the board of directors, and power to make and carry out other kinds of decisions. The major decisions of the board of directors of the operating company would be arrived at not through a favorable vote of the majority of the board, where Panama had five members to two for Texasgulf, but rather through the equal ratification of both Panama and Texasgulf. Included among these decisions were: approval of initial project specifications; selection of general contractors and major suppliers; major expansion of mining or processing capacity; a change in the independent accounting firm responsible for the audits; sales policies; and retention of dividends (Consejo de Legislación, Arts. V.8).[9]

The executive committee, composed of two Panamanian members and three Texasgulf members, would make other broad-ranging decisions by simple majority (Consejo de Legislación, Arts. VII). The administrator alone, when not in conflict with higher levels of decision and subject to other specified limits, would make normal operational decisions (Consejo de Legislación, Adm. XXIV, IV, V, VI).

Texasgulf also achieved a measure of control over Panamanian law; the contracts stipulated that the enterprise would be governed by the agreements themselves, and by Panamanian law only to the extent that there was no inconsistency with the contracts. "The parties concur in recognizing that all such inconsistencies are purposeful" (Consejo de Legislación, Assn. XL; cfr. Consejo de Legislación, Adm. XXXI); any new laws affecting the contracts could be a breach of the contracts by Panama.[10]

Although the clauses treating of labor policies specified that "applicable laws of the Nation" would be in effect and mandated preferential hiring of Panamanian personnel in all job classifications "under equal conditions with respect to qualification," the contracts left determination of qualification and hiring as the responsibility of the administrator, who would "inform the Board of Directors of [the joint operating company] periodically concerning the criteria upon which the personnel policies are based" (Consejo de Legislación, Adm. XVI).[11] Texasgulf also obtained exclusive responsibility for selection, hiring, and organization of all personnel, both for the design and construction

of the project and for production (Consejo de Legislación, Adm. IV.3.c
and IV.4.a). Texasgulf's supervisory responsibility with respect to engineering firms and contractors stated:

> The Administrator shall have the power to review the workmanship
> and the qualifications of personnel assigned by the contractors to
> the work, and may require replacement of employees if such action,
> in its judgment, is necessary or advisable for the proper execution
> of the work.[12] (Consejo de Legislación, Adm. IV.3.g.vi)

Texasgulf also won at least a symbolic victory in the contractual provisions for resolutions of disputes. Instead of following normal judicial
processes through which national court systems decide differences of
interpretation or questions of compliance with national laws, disputes
would be arbitrated by recourse to the Inter-American Commercial
Arbitration Commission (Consejo de Legislación, Assn. XXXVII and
Adm. XXVI). Even with this provision, Texasgulf retained the right of
diplomatic protest in the event of an undefined "denial of justice" (Consejo de Legislación, Assn. XVI and Adm. XXXII).

After the February 1976 signing of contracts that gave it the control
it sought over the mining project, Texasgulf began its work on the
$18-million feasibility study. Following standard procedures for "suc-
cessful companies," Texasgulf "essentially . . . duplicated the Canadian
Javelin work; [Texasgulf] wouldn't under any circumstances trust
someone else's exploratory work" (G. McBride, personal communication).[13]

The company brought in technical people from Canada to drill all
over the mountains, making their own estimates of the amount, grade,
and location of the ore.[14] Texasgulf's crews tunneled 400 meters into
the side of Cerro Colorado, sending several thousand tons of ore to the
Colorado School of Mines Research Institute, to test different methods
of milling (concentration) and smelting. They conducted hydrological
studies of potential sources of water for the concentration plant and
smelter: below Hato Chamí along the Cuvíbora River, north of Cerro
Colorado into Bocas del Toro, and near the Pacific Coast along the
Tabasará River. They looked for nearby valleys to fill with overburden
during mine construction and with "waste rock" during actual mining;
they studied alternative methods and sites for disposing of tailings from
the concentrator and slag from the smelter.

Texasgulf took over the Canadian Javelin facilities and equipment: closing the camp at Cuernavaca, adding a warehouse near San Félix and a new camp at Hato Chamí, expanding the camps at Escopeta and on Cerro Colorado itself. They upgraded the roads and put in new ones: from Hato Chamí to the top of Cerro Colorado (replacing Canadian Javelin's difficult-to-maintain road directly up the side of the mountain from Escopeta), from Hato Chamí to a point along the Cuvíbora River, from the top of Cerro Colorado for short distances north into Bocas del Toro, and later, from Hato Chamí all the way to Nancito, near the Pan-American Highway.[15]

Texasgulf contracted Brown and Root (Houston) and Seltrust Engineering (London), multinational engineering firms, to assist in the studies of the concentration mill, the smelter, the port, and other facilities. With their help, Texasgulf put together models of the copper deposits, mining plans, overall designs for processing the ore, flow charts, construction schedules, equipment needs, and a number of other studies, together comprising the overall concept of the mining project. Varying the size and complexity of the concept, Texasgulf put together different estimates of the costs of construction.

With consultants from the Toronto Dominion Bank, Lehman Brothers, and Chase Manhattan Bank, Texasgulf prepared complex computerized econometric models to forecast world economic trends during the life of the project. Using its own facilities and contracting further studies from Charles River Associates and Chase Econometrics, Texasgulf projected copper prices. Putting these variables together with the estimated construction costs, the company then prepared economic models for different scenarios, looking always to see both what copper price would be needed to pay the bills and what copper price could reasonably be expected. Finally, Texasgulf began the discussions with financial institutions which would have to provide almost all the capital for the construction of Cerro Colorado.

By May 1978, Texasgulf had completed its initial contractual obligation, turning over to CODEMIN some forty-eight volumes of economic, geological and engineering reports and summaries comprising the feasibility study. The contracts called for ninety days in which Texasgulf and CODEMIN would negotiate an agreement to proceed with the construction of the mine, "on the basis of the technical and financial recommendations made in the Feasibility Study" (Consejo de Legislación, Assn. VII).[16] But the two sponsors reached no agreement to proceed with the construction of Cerro Colorado; the overall price tag was too high, and the anticipated copper prices would never be sufficient to pay the bills.

The anticipated ninety days eventually stretched through all of 1979 and into 1980, as Texasgulf kept running new computer studies changing the variables, or contracting outside experts to develop independent projections. To lower construction costs, Texasgulf lopped off the phosphoric acid plant; then it discarded the smelter, planning to sell copper concentrates to European and Japanese smelters. It varied the size of the mine, to see whether smaller or larger tonnages would create economies of scale more in line with anticipated prices. It examined demand projections with great care, always concluding that demand should soon exceed mining capacity, so that during the 1980s the world "would require the equivalent of two Cerro Colorado's every year" (Dr. Fogarty in NM 1978).[17]

But the period was one of rampant inflation, hitting specialty items like major equipment and plants even harder than general consumer goods; even as Texasgulf sliced off hundreds of millions of dollars in discarding one part of the project, inflation increased the prices of the remainder. No change could bring the construction costs into line with any reasonable projection of copper prices; Texasgulf's efforts always concluded that Cerro Colorado would require a sustained price in the range of $1.50 a pound (so Dr. Fogarty in AMM 1979b).

> At that time, copper was selling for seventy cents a pound, and it had never been above a dollar except on some speculative basis on the London exchange. . . . It was just not thinkable to the managers and board of Texasgulf that copper price[s] would achieve those levels in the near term—"near term" meaning the next fifteen or twenty years. (G. McBride, personal communication)

Even if the gap between world demand and world availability developed as anticipated, prices would not rise to the needed levels. Why not?

> Generally the answer to that was, that at those prices, there will be substitution. Nobody's going to pay a dollar and a half a pound for copper when he can substitute glass or aluminum or plastic or this or that.[18] And so, in the end, we simply had to conclude [that] the

price of copper was not going to go to a dollar and a half within the economic life of the project. That's the rock on which the thing broke. (G. McBride, personal communication)

With considerable reluctance, Texasgulf finally recommended against going forward with Cerro Colorado. It told its shareholders:

> Efforts to finance the Cerro Colorado copper project in Panama continued throughout 1979, including efforts to find new equity participants. Since completion of the initial feasibility study by Texasgulf, the economics of the project have been heavily influenced by high rates of inflation worldwide. Texasgulf has advised the Panamanian corporation for the development of Cerro Colorado (CODEMIN) that it will not be presenting a proposal to proceed with the development of the Cerro Colorado copper project at this time.[19] (Texasgulf 1980:20–21)

As Dr. Fogarty put it, Cerro Colorado was a "fantastic potential operation. The problem is it's so damn expensive" (AMM 1979b).

FINANCING THE PROJECT: THE WORLD BANK AND THE EXPORT DEVELOPMENT CORPORATION

During the decision period Texasgulf, as obliged by contract (Consejo de Legislación, Assn. IX.2), cooperated in Panama's efforts to obtain financing for its share of the construction costs of Cerro Colorado; these efforts doubtless contributed substantially to Texasgulf's conclusion that Cerro Colorado could not be undertaken. Even though General Torrijos had obtained from the Canadian Export Development Corporation a commitment in principle to provide nearly half the capital needed for Cerro Colorado, the World Bank held the real key to Panama's success or failure.

The World Bank's importance to Cerro Colorado complied with a major policy shift toward increased involvement in nonfuel mineral projects in developing countries; the Bank intended to help "bridge the differences between producing countries and foreign mining concerns by providing an international 'presence' in mining ventures," since in recent years the perceptions of LDCs and multinational corporations tended "to diverge rather than come together." The Bank called its presence that of an "active catalyst," assisting the development of good chemistry in the interactions between mining projects and international financiers. To be that catalyst, the Bank announced it would

> help prepare projects and provide assistance at an early stage. Such preparation is needed, for mining projects, which typically involve a web of interrelated technical, financial, legal, and commercial arrangements, are among the most complex and costly in the world. (World Bank 1979:20-21)

The Bank would make its presence "effective" by contributing an average share of about 15 percent of total project costs. It would "bridge the differences" between LDCs and MNCs/other banks in two ways: by making its information and recommendations available to other potential lenders, saving them the expense of doing their own investigations; and by guaranteeing private investments through complicated cross-default provisions.[20]

The World Bank sent several missions to Panama to look over the work done there; its technical people went over all the Texasgulf studies, rechecked the conclusions, requested further work by the project sponsors, and did independent forecasts of copper demand and prices. The Bank also placed the Cerro Colorado project in the context both of Panama's overall economic situation and of the Western world economy. The Bank challenged the Texasgulf feasibility study projections of copper demand and prices as overly optimistic; it objected to omissions of major project costs from the proposed budgets. Leaving little of the project unquestioned, the Bank even disputed the aptness of the choice of Texasgulf to manage the project; one bank official privately asserted, in very strong terms, that Texasgulf had charged Panama substantially more than the real worth of its feasibility study. Finally, the Bank argued that Panama could not meet its increased debt obligations with Cerro Colorado; it insisted that Panama's already overwhelming indebtedness made its retention of 80 percent of project equity completely unrealistic.[21]

The World Bank people argued that the costs of constructing and operating Cerro Colorado would be considerably higher than those used in the Texasgulf feasibility study; they challenged some key omissions and low estimates in Texasgulf's work. For example, the Bank disapproved of the decision, embodied in the contracts (Consejo de Legislación, Adm. IV.3), to omit from project costs the planning, construction, and financing of the $50-$70 million townsite, left to CODEMIN or other agents of the Panamanian government (World Bank 1978:74).[22] They objected to the fact that Texasgulf, knowing it could not dispose of concentrator tailings by dumping them into the San Félix River to be carried to the Pacific Ocean, nonetheless did rot revise the budget to include the additional $140 million to build 70 km of slurry pipelines to mammoth tailings ponds along the coastal plain.[23] Texasgulf underestimated the costs of electricity for the project, budgeting only for the distribution system needed to plug into Panama's national network. IRHE, Panama's state electricity company, would not have the generating capacity to meet the mine's needs, equal to "all of Panama's 1977 electricity production" (World Bank 1978, 74); the mine would have to provide interim oil-burning power plants, generating more expensive electricity, while IRHE tried to finance the speeded-up development of the $150–200 million Changuinola I hydroelectric project in Bocas del Toro.[24] No budgets specified the costs of indemnification and relocation of people whose lands would be needed for the mining project; CODEMIN's president, Rodrigo González, simply asserted that "these costs are contemplated in the original cost" of the project (Cámara de Comercio 1979:69–70).[25] Finally, despite the fact that Cerro Colorado represented a mammoth five-year construction project, in an isolated, rainy tropical mountain environment, requiring custom-made supplies and materials from all over the globe, Texasgulf's cost estimates included only a low 7 percent annual inflation rate from 1977 to 1983, almost nothing for cost overruns, and included no completion guarantees.[26]

The altered assumptions of costs from the omissions of the feasibility study changed dramatically the projected overall price tag for Cerro Colorado: from $1,530.6 million to $3,400.8 million, plus $500 million for cost overruns and completion guarantees (see Tables 6 and 7).[27] Panama's equity would increase from $360 million to $936.2 million; accrued interest on this loan during construction would be $226.8 million, for a total new debt of $1,163 million, almost 50 percent of the outstanding public debt of 1978.[28]

The World Bank people also maintained that the mine would gen-

TABLE 6
Summary Characteristics of Cerro Colorado:
Deposit and Operating Characteristics and Capital Requirements

COPPER DEPOSIT CHARACTERISTICS

Mineral Inventory, 0.4% Cut-off Grade	1,380 mn m.t.
Years of Production at Planned Capacity	51.1 years
Average Grade at 0.4% Cut-off	0.78%
Months for Construction	60 months
Start-up	January 1, 1983

OPERATING CHARACTERISTICS

Ore Processed Per Year	27 mn m.t.
Annual Output of Blister Copper	182,500 m.t.
Annual Direct Cash Costs of Operation	$221.9 mn
(in 1983 dollars, before financing costs,	($0.56/lb)
depreciation, taxes and fees)	
Total Workforce at Capacity Operations	2,176 people

CAPITAL REQUIREMENTS *Millions U.S. $$*

Mine	$ 210.0
Concentrator	199.2
Smelter	181.7
Port	30.6
Roads	50.0
Water Supply	56.2
Ancillaries	$ 65.0
Total Unadjusted Capital Cost	$ 792.7
Inflation during Construction, 7% per year	240.0
Contingency at 15%	154.9
Contractor's and Administrator's Fees	45.5
Start-up	$ 80.2
Total Capital Costs[a]	$1,313.3
Interest during Construction[b]	$ 144.3
Total Costs	$1,457.6
Working Capital to Operate	$ 73.0
Total Financing Required	*$1,530.6*

[a] Excluding financing fees and related infrastructure investment by Panama for hydroelectric power conversion, permanent townsites, etc.

[b] Under medium financing assumption with 2:1 debt/equity ratio and attendant $449 million bank debt.

SOURCE: Texasgulf 1978:12–4 to 12–6 (Table 12–1).

TABLE 7
Cerro Colorado Capital Requirements:
Texasgulf Estimate Plus Omitted Costs

	Million $$
TEXASGULF ESTIMATES	
Mine	$ 210.0
Concentrator	199.2
Smelter	181.7
Port	30.6
Roads	50.0
Water Supply	56.2
Ancillaries	$ 65.0
Total Unadjusted Capital Cost	$ 792.7
(1977 dollars)	
PLUS OMITTED COSTS	
Tailings Disposal System	$ 140.0
Townsite	70.0
Hydroelectric Project	200.0
Environmental Impact Study (est.)	10.0
Compensation for Lands and Villages (guess)	$ 10.0
Total Unadjusted Omitted Costs	$ 430.0
(1977 dollars)	
New Total Unadjusted Capital Cost	*$1,222.7*
ADDED ESCALATION, FEES, CONTINGENCY	
Inflation during Construction, 10%/year, 6 years	$ 943.4
Contingency at 20%	433.2
Contractor's Fees (1.375%)	35.7
Administrator's Gross Fees (2.5%)	65.9
Start-up (Tg estimate + 3%/yr added inflation)	$ 95.8
Total Capital Costs	$2,796.7
(1983 dollars)	
Interest during Construction	$ 604.1
(includes fees and commissions)	
Total Financing Required by Project	*$3,400.8*
TOTAL BORROWING NEEDED	
Loans to joint operating company	$2,380.6
(including interest during construction, fees,	
commissions)—70% of total financing	
Panama equity loan	816.2
Interest during Construction on Panama equity loan	$ 197.7
Total borrowing needed	*$3,394.5*
Plus Texasgulf equity	204.0
Total Project Cost including Financing	*$3,598.5*

erate considerably less income than Texasgulf claimed; they argued that
copper demand would not increase to the extent Texasgulf said, that
copper prices would be lower, that the company would have difficulties
finding buyers for the copper, and that in the early years of the mine
Texasgulf could not produce the quantities of copper it promised. For
example, Texasgulf's original feasibility study predicted that the always-
volatile world copper market would soon enter into the recovery so
frequently predicted by industry analysts; with this recovery would
come a substantial steady increase in world (market economy country,
MEC) copper demand. The World Bank, using less optimistic forecasts,
projected smaller increases in demand; the substantial differences in the
anticipated demand for copper totaled three to five million metric tons
over the course of the 1980s, the equivalent of as much as twenty-five
years of Cerro Colorado's designed output.[29] If demand did not increase as forecast, copper prices would not rise as much as Texasgulf
predicted; the differing price predictions represented $48.4 million in
potential revenues to the project in 1983 alone.[30] Assuming its lower
demand projections, the World Bank disputed Texasgulf's marketing
studies; the Bank thought it would be difficult to find buyers for Cerro
Colorado's copper.[31] Finally, the World Bank did not believe that Cerro
Colorado would have as much copper to market as Texasgulf predicted;
the Bank disputed the Texasgulf "learning curve," the percent of designed mining capacity that could be brought on line in the early years
of production, as crews mastered the complex managerial, technological, and labor skills required (World Bank 1978:74). Texasgulf's learning curve of 50:95:100 projected operating the mine at virtually full
capacity by the end of the first complete year following construction;
the World Bank's curve of 25:66:87:100 meant 111,500 m.t. less copper
produced over the first four years, or approximately $365.3 million less
in revenue.[32]

The World Bank concluded that even without the added costs from
the omissions in the construction budgets, and even if Cerro Colorado
could find markets, project income would not allow Panama to keep
abreast of debt obligations incurred with the equity loans for the mining project. The Bank staff prepared sample income and cash flow
statements for the project, focusing on the crucial first years of production, when the grace period on loan repayment would end and overall
debt repayment obligations would be heaviest. Besides putting together

an example following Texasgulf's feasibility study, the Bank used its own projections and those of a consulting firm to alter some variables— mainly, copper prices—and ran three examples of its own; these four cases are summarized in Table 8. In the three World Bank cases, Cerro Colorado would not have generated enough income during the first six years of operations to cover all the debt obligations incurred; in the worst case, Cerro Colorado would be short nearly $1,000 million.

The "Net Operating Company Cash Flow" line summarized the money available after replacing equipment needed to keep the project functioning and after repayment of debts of the joint operating company; in two of the World Bank cases, Cerro Colorado would not generate enough income to keep up with the operating company's debt obligations. The "Pre-Tax and After Tax Income" line, negative in all four cases, estimated the income on which the operating company would pay 50 percent tax to the government of Panama (= "Pre-Tax") and from which dividends could be paid (= "After-Tax")[33]; it was negative even in the first two cases because of the 20 percent depreciation and amortization allowance agreed to in the contracts (Consejo de Legislación, Assn. XVI.1.b). With this allowance, "the highest priority is given to the cash flow, while at the same time corporate taxes and dividends are kept to a minimum" (World Bank Memorandum of 19 June 1979, in Posse 1980:21). For Panama, the disadvantage in this approach lay in the fact that its main income from the project would derive from taxes and dividends; its only other income would be the taxes on Texasgulf's management fees, equivalent to those fees themselves. So, even when the project operations generated enough income to cover Panama's own debt obligations from loans for its equity (the Texasgulf case only), that income would have been absorbed in the depreciation and amortization allowance, rather than being available for repayment of the government's debt.

The upshot was that even in the overly optimistic Texasgulf case, the government of Panama would have been short $367.5 million to pay its Cerro Colorado debts during the first six years of operations. In the other cases, Panama would have had to make up $435.3 million to $465.8 million. In all cases, it looked like the government would have to refinance its equity loans, that is, seek new loans to repay the old ones. This outcome hardly met the CODEMIN assurances of a self-supporting, risk-free investment.

TABLE 8

Cerro Colorado Income Statement and Cash Flow,
Totals for First Six Years of Production
Thousands of U.S. dollars, 1983 terms
Texasgulf (Tg) case: 1983–88;
World Bank (WB) cases: 1984–89

	Tg Case	WB-1	WB-2	WB-3
PRODUCTION	988,000	922,089	922,089	922,089
(m.t., 6 yr. totals)				
AVERAGE COPPER PRICE	1.46	1.59	1.31	1.18
($/lb., 1983 terms; weighted according to production)				
GROSS SALES	3,180,082	3,234,422	2,658,022	2,395,175
less Marketing and	−326,625	−304,834	−304,834	−304,834
Refining Costs				
plus Precious Metals and $H_2 SO_4$	77,094	71,951	71,951	71,951
NET SALES	2,930,551	3,001,539	2,425,139	2,162,292
less Operating Costs	−1,323,458	−1,466,926	−1,466,926	−1,466,926
OPERATING PROFIT	1,607,093	1,534,613	958,213	695,366
less Tg Management Fees	−87,570	−83,815	−63,767	−53,312
less Taxes on Management Fees	−87,570	−83,815	−63,767	−53,312
less Joint Company Interest Payments	−606,257	−702,400	−702,400	−702,400
less Depreciation and Amortization	−868,129	−746,070	−306,689	−82,216
PRE-TAX AND AFTER-TAX	−42,433	−81,487	−178,410	−195,874
INCOME				
plus Depreciation and Amortization	868,120	746,070	306,689	82,216
GROSS CASH FLOW	825,696	664,583	128,279	−113,658
less Replacement Investment	−37,080	−37,080	−37,080	−37,080
less Joint Company Loan Repayments	−284,000	−344,000	−344,000	−344,000
NET OPERATING COMPANY	504,616	283,503	−252,801	−494,738
CASH FLOW				
plus Taxes on Management Fees	87,570	83,815	63,767	53,312
less Panama Equity Loans	−455,100	−519,100	−519,100	−519,100
(repayment and interests)				
NET CASH FLOW	137,086	−151,782	−708,134	−960,526
including Equity Loans,				
excluding Direct Taxes				

SOURCE: Adapted from World Bank Memorandum, Industrial Products Department, June 1979, in Posse 1980: Annex I.

NOTE: The World Bank adjusted some of Texasgulf's feasibility study assumptions in putting together the income statement and cash flow. Listed in the continuation of the table (facing page) are the assumptions used.

TABLE 8 (CONTINUED)

	Texasgulf	World Bank
Total Financing Needed:	$1,530 mn	$1,760 mn. Includes $99 mn for delay in start of construction, $100 mn in additional expense for tailings disposal, and $31 mn extra interst during constr.
Financing Plans:	$750 mn loan at 9.5%, $320 mn loan at LIBOR + 1.5% = 12.5%, both for 21 years incl. 6.5 years grace	EDC loans of $1.1 bn consisting of $770 mn at 9.5%, $330 mn at LIBOR + 1.5% = 12.5%, both for 21 years incl. 6.5 yrs grace
Other Loans:	None	$130 mn at 10% for 16 years including 6.5 years grace
Equity:	Total equity of $460 mn (30% of $1,530 mn); Panama $360 mn (loan at 10% for 20 yrs incl. 5 yrs grace; Tg $100 mn	Total equity of $530 mn (30% of $1,760 mn); Panama $420 mn (loan at 10% for 20 yrs incl. 5 yrs grace); Tg $110 mn
Depreciation:	For tax purposes, 20% of undepreciated total capital expenditures to date; unused balance carried forward in line with 25 years accounting depreciation	
Production/Sales Capacity:	182,954 metric tons	Same
Learning Curve:	50:95:100	33:77:94:100

Inflation:

Base Cost:	1977	1977	
Rate:	7% per year	7% per year	

Copper prices[a]: ($/lb refined copper)	Texasgulf 1978	Texasgulf 1983	WB-1 1978	WB-1 1983	WB-2 1978	WB-2 1983	WB-3 1978	WB-3 1983
1983	1.04	1.46	1.07	1.50	0.80	1.12	1.26	1.77
1984	1.04	1.46	1.12	1.57	0.82	1.15	1.33	1.87
1985	1.04	1.46	1.13	1.58	0.91	1.28	1.15	1.61
1986	1.04	1.46	1.14	1.60	0.98	1.38	0.86	1.21
1987	1.04	1.46	1.15	1.61	0.98	1.38	0.70	0.98
1988	1.04	1.46	1.16	1.63	0.98	1.38	0.70	0.98

Marketing and Refining for both are from feasibility study.
Precious Metals Credit for both: $0.02 per metric ton
Sulfuric Acid for both: $8 per metric ton

Operating Cost:	From feasibility study	Same, plus 5% each to cover electricity, labor costs, supplies, recovery factors

[a]The "1978" and "1983" prices are the projected copper prices in dollars of 1978 and 1983, respectively, adjusted through inflation factors.

In the end, the World Bank concluded that the Cerro Colorado project, as conceived, was riskier and more expensive than Texasgulf's initial studies indicated. Nonetheless, throughout the discussions with the World Bank in 1978–79, the government publicly maintained that Cerro Colorado would go forward and would solve most of the nation's major problems. Perhaps Panama took the Bank's highly critical focus on Texasgulf's work as a glimmer of hope that the basic problem lay not in the costs and risks of Cerro Colorado itself, but in Texasgulf's conception of the project; after all, instead of concluding outright that the project was not viable, the Bank had only insisted that Panama reduce its equity.

Panama made changes of its own to adjust to the shifting dynamics of Cerro Colorado, insisting all the while that it remained firmly in control of the project. Already a number of observers questioned whether the government had any real power over the mining project; the government's new approach did nothing to alleviate those concerns.

Texasgulf announced it saw no way to go forward with the mining project. The World Bank challenged both the economic feasibility of the project and Panama's capacity to maintain a substantial interest in it. The government's own Council of Economic Advisors (*Consejo Consultivo de Economía*) urged a decrease in Panama's equity from 80 percent to no more than 60 percent. Nonetheless, CODEMIN and the government of Panama continued to promote Cerro Colorado, all the while diminishing their limited control as they sought major adjustments to the project's shifting dynamics. One suspects that the government of Panama countered these discouraging analyses with its own optimistic risk analysis and with the Canadian government's Export Development Corporation (EDC) offer of financing. However, these items, in different ways, seemed to offer less than met the eye.

Panama's Council of Economic Advisors, in addition to its suggestion about reducing Panama's equity, also pressed the government to contract further marketing and risk studies. To this end, in 1979 CODEMIN commissioned, for a million dollars, a risk analysis from Information for Investment Decision of Washington, D.C. The consulting firm, even while recommending a reduction in Panama's equity, calculated that Cerro Colorado was overwhelmingly likely to pay for itself, and very likely to earn substantial monies for Panama's public coffers from the outset. CODEMIN touted this study as proving that Cerro Colorado involved no risk for Panama.[34]

Not surprisingly, the problem of the risk analysis lay in the assumptions used for the computer-generated probability studies. The consulting firm's assumptions about the likely changes in the world copper market, based on econometric projections of Western world economic performance, looked very optimistic when they were made; and subsequent behavior of the economy and the copper markets suggested that Information for Investment Decision's experts were wildly wide of the target.

On July 20, 1978, Mr. R. H. Sumner, vice president of Export Development Corporation (EDC), wrote to Rodrigo González, president both of CODEMIN and of the joint operating company, with the only firm financing offer ever made known for the Cerro Colorado project. Mr. Sumner's letter confirmed

> that EDC is prepared in principle to consider taking a lead role in arranging total financing for the Cerro Colorado Project, provided all normal EDC financing and Canadian content criteria are met including the participation of Canadian financial institutions.[35] (Cited in Miller et al. 1978:17)

Both in Canada and in Panama, major questions about the EDC's largest-ever offer loomed ominously, and focused on the "normal EDC financing criteria," the "Canadian content criteria" and costs, and important domestic issues.

The "normal Canadian content criteria" meant that at least 80 percent of the EDC portion of the project financing had to be spent in Canada (LAWG 1980:28). "According to one World Bank estimate, Canadian equipment is relatively expensive—as much as 25 to 30 percent more costly than that which can be purchased in other countries" (LAWG 1980:29). Further, some Canadian analysts doubted that Canadian manufacturers could provide $600 million worth of construction and mining equipment, processing technology and plants, contracting, engineering, and technical services. "The *maximum* potential for Canadian content in exports of all kinds to the Cerro Colorado project is in the order of $400 million (1977 money terms)" (Miller et al. 1978:8; emphasis in original).[36] If the Canadian content requirement could not be fulfilled, "the EDC would convert some portion of its fixed interest rate loan to a floating loan rate that could be used as united money" with the other project financing (Posse 1980:16). This measure would, of course, make the financing even more expensive.

In Canada and in Panama, the EDC loans also became major domestic political issues. Canadian opponents saw the loan as a subsidy for foreign competitors whose very success would put Canadian copper producers at a disadvantage. EDC president John A. MacDonald defended the loan, arguing that it would result in "something in excess of a billion dollars [later revised to $742 million] of expenditures in Canada for Canadian equipment and for Canadian engineering designs" and "will provide something in the order of about 30,000 man-years of employment in Canada" (quoted in LAWG 1980:28–29). But besides questioning whether Canadian business could provide what Cerro Colorado needed, opponents noted that rather than enhancing Canadian exports, EDC loans often supported expansion of U.S. branch operations in Canada; the money would end up in the U.S. For the opponents, this loan would "facilitate new sources of copper supply, decrease prices and thus inhibit further growth of copper mining in Canada."

> Some Canadian mining companies—notably those which are Canadian-owned, of medium size and not part of the transnational corporate elite—have criticized the EDC for supporting a foreign competitor. They claim that the EDC gives state subsidies to foreign mining ventures which are unavailable for their own expansion plans in Canada.

The New Democratic Party saw the EDC offer as "a misguided strategy for developing Canadian manufacturing industries and one which will only subsidize the overseas profits of Texasgulf Inc." Mineworker union members pointed to EDC participation in the INCO, Ltd., nickel mine (EXMIBAL) in Guatemala, in support of their case that EDC financing of MNC mining projects helped neither third world nor Canadian workers.

> Instead, the EDC aids corporations in exploiting the Third World while forcing Canadian workers to accept lower wages and enabling the companies to extract more concessions from the Canadian state for their domestic operations.[37] (Quoted materials from LAWG 1980:27-29, 24)

The Panamanian domestic issue concerned whether the government would have to underwrite the EDC loans, made directly to the joint operating company. CODEMIN assured everyone that it was following the "clear indications of the National Government": project financing should have a flexible repayment schedule and should "fundamentally rest on the project's own economic merits, in such fashion that the financing not put pressure on the public finances" except for Panama's equity contribution (CODEMIN 1979d:27). But the EDC finance offer left the issue clouded. The EDC was under pressure to make sure the Panamanian government would underwrite or otherwise guarantee such a risky loan, especially with the political controversy surrounding it. Privately, an EDC official stated that the EDC had insisted from the outset on "some kind of undertaking on the part of the Panamanian government" to back up the loan (LAWG 1980:29); but CODEMIN maintained that the EDC did not require that the government of Panama underwrite the loan "in the strict sense" (CODEMIN 1979b:20/insert).[38]

The basic problem, of course, was what would happen if the project did not meet expectations of profitability, but lost money and could not repay its creditors. Who would pay? The government of Panama could not win public approval (or World Bank acceptance) of government-backed loans with so much at stake, on top of the already critical foreign debt. If the government had to underwrite in some fashion 80 percent of the project debt, the total new debt responsibilities (its own equity of $384 million plus 80 percent of the project's $1,120 million loan) would be $1,280 million, almost double its obligations as of year-end 1977. Politically, the government of Canada could not afford to subsidize a competing copper mine without some clear claim against the government of Panama in case of default. Both sides used self-protecting language in public statements, leaving the impression that the final negotiations for the loan package would involve very hard bargaining.

CHANGING PARTNERS: ENTER RIO TINTO-ZINC

Panama accepted the recommendations to reduce its equity in Cerro Colorado, deciding that 51 percent would be its minimum. As provided in the contracts (Consejo de Legislación, Assn. XII), Panama offered Texasgulf the right of first refusal to the shares it wanted to release; but this decision placed considerable "pressure on Texasgulf, minority partner, which would not be in condition to absorb the [added equity]." Instead, Texasgulf stated it would not stand in the way if the government wished to look for another partner (CODEMIN 1979d:7).

In May 1980, CODEMIN signed a "substitution agreement" (Consejo de Gabinete 1980) with the third transnational corporation to work on Cerro Colorado: the Rio Tinto-Zinc Corp. (RTZ), of London and the world. With this selection, Panama entered into partnership with one of the world's largest mining conglomerates,

> a holding company for an empire of subsidiary and associated companies—the RTZ Group—with interests in the mining and processing of almost every major metal and fuel, including aluminum and its products, borax, coal, copper, gold, industrial and agricultural chemicals, iron ore, lead, oil, silver, specialty steels, tin, uranium, and zinc. It is the second largest private producer of copper in the world, the largest producer of uranium, the monopolizer of world borax production, the fourth largest bauxite miner, and the fourth most important processor of zinc. . . . The Group's 1979 assets of $5.1 billion, sales of $5.5 billion, and before-tax profits of $992 million place it in the upper echelons of the global transnational corporate structure. . . . In addition to being one of the biggest and most diversified mining transnationals, Rio Tinto-Zinc is one of the most "international." Although British-based, over 88% of RTZ's assets and an equivalent proportion of its profits come from its overseas operations. Its London headquarters straddle a complex pyramid of subsidiary companies—over 600 in total— spanning 38 countries and employing over 56,000 people on every continent but Antarctica. . . . The CODEMIN-RTZ partnership weds . . . a relatively small state to a giant transnational corporation whose total group sales are [double] Panama's gross domestic product and whose pre-tax profits [exceed] Panama's total central government spending.[39] (Carty 1982:305–06, 304; translation from unpublished English draft)

The contemporary Rio Tinto-Zinc Corporation resulted from the successful post-1954 expansion of the original Rio Tinto Company, formed in 1873 to work the ancient Rio Tinto copper deposits in southwest Spain.[40] Trusting the shrewd foresight of chief executive Val Duncan, through the 1950s Rio Tinto expanded its explorations and investments in "safe" countries, building up rich uranium reserves and mines in Australia and Canada while developing the giant Palabora open pit copper and magnetite mine in South Africa. With the early-1960s merger of Rio Tinto and Consolidated Zinc Corp. (a British-owned mining company with interests primarily in Australia) to form Rio Tinto-Zinc, RTZ discovered the advantages of mergers and buy-outs for rapid expansion. RTZ tends to select already-defined resource deposits, avoiding tying up capital in lengthy exploration; its taste runs toward the massive projects—large-scale, low-grade, open pit—where its financial strength and technical expertise give it an edge over competitors. RTZ's London headquarters, firmly in control of the vast network of subsidiaries, offers them

> access to financial capital and powerful political connections. As RTZ itself explains, the most international, renowned and important of the services offered by its London Head Office "is the large-scale fund raising undertaken for new projects within the Group. Through its banking connections and its links with many international corporations, RTZ has arranged the financing of many of its major operations." (Carty 1982:319, quoting Rio Tinto-Zinc 1973; translation from unpublished English draft)

RTZ secures access to financial capital by maintaining links with major banking firms (including: Barclay's Bank, Midland Bank, Chemical Bank, Bank of America, Toronto Dominion Bank, Banque Rothschild) and by hiring bankers as chief executives—most recently, Sir Anthony Tuke, former chairman of Barclay's Bank.

Even with its great diversity, RTZ continued to be a copper company, moving to Panama as part of its strategy of expansion for the 1980s and beyond. With more than twenty known large copper deposits world-wide awaiting development, RTZ seemingly found several factors attracting it to Cerro Colorado and Panama. Politically, Cerro Colorado would enable RTZ to diversify and secure the supply of copper for itself and its patron government, England. The United Kingdom relies heavily on imports from Zambia and Zaire, focal points of political unrest and production stoppages; RTZ's Palabora operations in South Africa could suffer from political insurrection. Cerro Colorado would give RTZ a Latin American connection to match its Southeast Asian operations at Bougainville, Papua New Guinea,[41] further diversifying away from dependence on African sources; and Panama, alongside the major Third World copper-producing countries (Chile, Peru, Zambia, and Zaire), must have appeared to RTZ as stability itself.[42] Technically, the Cerro Colorado deposits, perhaps the world's largest, appealed to RTZ's expertise in large-scale low-grade operations; no other mining company has matched RTZ's record of reducing operating costs at such mines. Economically, RTZ must have expected recovery and substantial growth in copper demand and prices beginning by the mid-1980s.[43]

RTZ took over the Texasgulf contracts, altered to incorporate solutions to some of the principal difficulties with the Texasgulf project; the new clauses included the hydroelectric project and the townsite within the project's own parameters (Consejo de Gabinete 1980: Acuerdo Especial, Cl. VI), and gave RTZ the right to 49 percent equity in the project. RTZ also pledged up to $13 million to finance its own review and continuation of the Texasgulf studies, as well as to provide most of CODEMIN's operating budget for the year it would need for new studies.[44] As discussed above, in its corporate "resumé," RTZ, with its mammoth size and connections, listed two advantages over Texasgulf: its proven ability to get lending institutions to finance major new mines on a project basis, i.e., with minimal commitment of RTZ capital; and its vast experience in mining projects all over the world.

Using RTZ's vast experience in their quest for a "bankable document"—a proposal that would persuade financial institutions of the viability of Cerro Colorado—RTZ's project managers agreed with Texasgulf's plans to go to market with copper concentrates, dropping the hundreds of millions of dollars in costs for construction and start-up of a smelter; Bougainville had no smelter either. They continued Texasgulf's studies of the feasibility of removing the overburden hydraulically, i.e., using enormous quantities of water under high pressure to remove the top of the mountain.[45] They explored the possibility of cutting construction costs by moving the concentrator facilities from the rugged vicinity of Escopeta to a more level area on the small plain in the Guaymí community of Tebujo, about 15 miles south of Cerro Colorado; they considered the massive transport system needed to move ore from the open pit to the concentrator. And they hired the Fluor Corporation to carry out engineering, design, procurement, and construction of the project (AMM 1981).

But RTZ provided only one significant conceptual change for Cerro Colorado: "high-grading." RTZ had pioneered the design of mining plans for the removal of the highest grade ore from the ore body during the first years of operation of new facilities, to produce large quantities of marketable copper in relation to the ore mined.[46] The major drawback of high-grading—diminished profitability in the later life of the mine, when only lower grade ore remains—would fall most heavily on Panama, assuming full control of the entire operation after twenty years of extraction of the best ore; RTZ as project administrator would earn higher administrative fees, calculated on the basis of gross profits from the sale of copper. But Panama seemed willing to accept this trade-off as the only way to finance the construction of Cerro Colorado.

But high-grading, even in conjunction with other design changes, could not bring overall costs down enough to make the project viable. RTZ's only published estimates put a $3.2 billion price tag on Cerro Colorado (Rio Tinto Zinc 1981:16), requiring copper prices in the range of $1.50 to $2.00 a pound; the world copper market was no more likely to pay these prices for RTZ than it had been for Texasgulf. RTZ demonstrated that the problem of Cerro Colorado had not been Texasgulf's performance as administrator, but the combination of the high costs of needed infrastructure and the low prices of copper. As Dr. Fogarty said, "it's too damn expensive." As Dr. McBride said, copper prices in that range were "just not thinkable."

In fact, RTZ did not conclude its studies with the recommendation that Cerro Colorado not go forward. Rather, it proposed an interim stage, construction and operation of a $26 million pilot project to further test designs, engineering, concentrating processes, and other aspects of the project. On the basis of that proposal, RTZ and CODEMIN began negotiations of an agreement to proceed that would incorporate the fine-tuning of the arrangements between RTZ and Panama. These negotiations proceeded fairly smoothly until they hit three major sticking points: labor legislation governing the mine's workers, the location of the townsite, and control of the hydroelectric facilities.

Seemingly, RTZ wanted legal assurances that Cerro Colorado's workers would not strike during construction and early operations; the Panamanian government apparently was uncertain it could accept these provisions without major political problems. The workers themselves would have objected strenuously to the removal of one of labor's principal weapons in its negotiating arsenal; and Panamanian capitalists would have demanded the same government backing in their own battles with labor.

RTZ offered three arguments for its contention that the townsite had to be located in the vicinity of the mining project itself: the need to have vital personnel in the immediate vicinity in case of emergencies; the increased insurance costs to cover the daily two-hour round-trip commute for 3500 workers; and the fear that workers would demand compensation for their forced commute. Given its long and difficult experience with the Canal Zone and the United Fruit Company banana plantations, Panama wanted no more enclaves within its territory; it wanted an accessible city near the Pacific Coast. Also, in conversations with Guaymí leaders, the government had made only one firm promise: that it would not allow construction of a latino city within the Guaymí area unless the Guaymíes themselves wanted it. They did not.

RTZ was willing to include the Changuinola I hydroelectric project within Cerro Colorado's specifications and budgets, but insisted on control of the management of the project as well as the right to set the tariffs for electricity—both to Cerro Colorado and for sale to IRHE for national distribution. Panama, again with experience of foreign corporate control of its utilities, wanted Changuinola I under IRHE, with rates to be set according to national norms.

While CODEMIN and RTZ were still struggling to find acceptable compromises on these points, CODEMIN's general manager, Rubén Darío Herrera, died, leaving CODEMIN's management without one of its most experienced people. Then General Omar Torrijos died in a plane crash. Although negotiations continued, in the jockeying for power to fill the vacuum in Panama it soon became apparent that no person or faction had the control to make and carry out an agreement on the controversial Cerro Colorado project. In frustration, RTZ invoked its contractual right to oblige CODEMIN to pay its full share of the continuing costs (maintenance and further studies) of the project. Panama, already strapped and seeking ways to roll over its burdensome foreign debt, could not continue; in November 1981, Panama and RTZ put the Cerro Colorado project in mothballs.[47]

CHAPTER 6

The World Copper Industry in Control

Throughout the eleven years of activity concerning Cerro Colorado, one basic question received contradictory answers: who is in charge? The contradictions and the reasons for them revealed the complex dynamics of Panama's attempts to become a major western-world copper producer.

In its successful dealings with the Canadian Javelin Company, Panama had adopted a relatively inflexible position: it insisted on sovereignty and control over the mining project through major equity participation and a limited-term contract with its multinational partners. When Canadian Javelin refused to accept Panama's terms, the government terminated negotiations, indemnifying the company with only 20 percent of the compensation that Canadian Javelin had demanded. Even so, other multinational corporations—including Noranda, an important member of Canadian Javelin's consortium—remained interested in the Cerro Colorado project; Panama, still needing assistance from multinational mining enterprises, had not frightened them off.

PANAMA'S INABILITY TO CONTROL THE PROJECT

The Panamanian government may have misinterpreted its own success, concluding that Panama had real power in its dealings with multinational corporations. In reality, factors beyond Panama's control contributed to the resolution of its problems with Canadian Javelin. Even though John Doyle had initially announced that Canadian Javelin would undertake the Cerro Colorado project by itself, his company was too small and inexperienced for such a major undertaking. Financial institutions would never have provided the capital; any other possibility of Canadian Javelin's raising the necessary capital died under the avalanche of disastrous publicity when the Securities and Exchange Commission (SEC) accused Doyle of stock fraud and suspended trading in his company's shares. Doyle successfully organized a powerful consortium for Cerro Colorado. But his company, the smallest and most vulnerable member of the consortium, could only contribute its first right to negotiate an exploitation agreement; it had no concession. Since Doyle needed a quick agreement with Panama in order to strengthen his position both with the SEC and with the other members of the consortium, Panama could afford to take its time. Presumably, the other members of the consortium appreciated that their chances alone were at least as good as their chances in partnership with Canadian Javelin.

With its contracts with Texasgulf, Panama discovered the complexities of a major modern mining project, receiving some harsh lessons in "the economics of life" as a debt-ridden LDC seeking to become one of the world's major copper exporters. Panama's claims about its relationship with Texasgulf hardly squared with the results of a careful reading of the CODEMIN-Texasgulf contracts, to say nothing of the actual unfolding of that relationship in practice.

Panama, focusing on its ownership of the copper deposits, claimed to have won recognition of its sovereignty; but the contracts denied Panama's rights to pass laws, and removed from Panamanian courts the power to settle disputes in interpretations of the contracts—themselves part of Panama's laws.[1] With its 80 percent equity in the joint operating company, Panama claimed to have control of the mining project; but the contracts gave Texasgulf either outright control or at least veto power in all the major decisions concerning the project (CEASPA 1979a; Zorn 1977).

Panama learned that the price of its own control of the mining project would have been the project itself; international financial institutions would not participate unless a reputable major corporation participated in and had control over the running of the project.[2] Panama even defended decisions to cut out parts of the project, in hopes of bringing construction costs down to something feasible, despite the fact that the loss of smelting and refining capacity virtually eliminated the nation's hope of using forward linkages from copper production as the impetus for further industrialization.

Perhaps the promised billions of dollars in new income from the mining project would have compensated Panama's losses of sovereignty and control; but here too, Panama learned that sovereign ownership of massive amounts of copper, and 80 percent equity in the company exploiting that copper, did not necessarily result in major economic gains. Any financing agreement would have put Panama's claims at the end of a long line of institutions clamoring for money.[3] Even Panama's multinational partner would be ahead of Panama in line; in exchange for the transfer of technology, Panama had traded the high cost of Texasgulf's no-risk fees.[4] No international lender would finance Cerro Colorado only with the collateral of the mining project itself; lenders would require that loans be underwritten by the project sponsors, at least in accord with the equity ratio.

In exchange for control of its energy resources, Panama had to finance the 200–300-million dollar hurry-up expansion of its hydro-electric facilities, a massive (but denied) state subsidy for a project that was supposed to pay for itself.[5] To eliminate the possible formation of yet another enclave within its borders, Panama would build the town and set the wage scale for workers; but as a trade-off it saddled itself with at least $100 million in added expenses and yet gave Texasgulf considerable power in setting labor policies.[6]

Dependent Panama sought help from multinational mining companies precisely because the nation did not have the finances, technology, or experienced people to put together the mining project.[7] CODEMIN, not equipped to conduct independent research using its own nationals, received all information relevant to Cerro Colorado from its multinational corporate partners. Furthermore, the country had to rely on them (or other foreign actors) for the interpretation of that information. Most likely, the information and interpretations CODEMIN received included Texasgulf's increasingly negative assessment of the prospects for Cerro Colorado; certainly they included the World Bank's cogent arguments about the risks of the project. Yet

Panama consistently denied any problems with the project itself. CODEMIN management's insistence that the project could not possibly fail itself underlined the difficulties inherent in drawing proper conclusions from the complicated data available. Texasgulf, dedicated to maximizing its own income, declined the invitation to make more money by increasing its equity participation; but CODEMIN seemingly interpreted Texasgulf's actions differently. The World Bank couched some of its arguments concerning the risks of the project in language that implied that the basic problems lay not in the world copper market, but in the performance of Texasgulf; in the process, some World Bank officials probably contributed to CODEMIN's misinterpretation of the prospects for Cerro Colorado.[8] CODEMIN also contracted another foreign group, Information for Investment Decisions, to do an "independent" risk analysis of the project; but the assumptions used by the consulting firm were by no means independent, and CODEMIN never seemed to challenge those assumptions. Finally, when Texasgulf decided to back away, Panama decided that the solution was to change multinational corporate partners.

In its partnership with Rio Tinto-Zinc, Panama found itself without even a semblance of control over Cerro Colorado. CODEMIN, after spending several years singing the praises of its 80 percent equity in Cerro Colorado, acceded to domestic and international pressure and reduced its equity to 51 percent. After arguing the benefits that would accrue to the nation by excluding the cost of the townsite and a new hydroelectric project from the budget, CODEMIN signed a new agreement putting these items into the project. At the same time, CODEMIN achieved no favorable adjustments in those contractual provisions which had been so roundly criticized in Panama and elsewhere.[9] Panama moved from Texasgulf, a relatively small, relatively inexperienced multinational corporation, to partnership with RTZ, one of the world's truly giant mineral corporations—one with a history of dominating nations much larger and more powerful than Panama.[10]

But even having Rio Tinto-Zinc in charge could not create favorable conditions for the development of Cerro Colorado; even RTZ, with its technical and financial resources, could not change the situation of the world copper market. The conclusions that Texasgulf had drawn—that the immense copper deposits made Cerro Colorado a very attractive prospect, but that prices would not rise enough to pay for its exploitation—remained in force for RTZ. Although the British company proposed a pilot project as a continuation of work on Cerro Colorado, it was unlikely that further efforts could have made the mining enterprise viable. The dominant dynamics in charge of Cerro Colorado rested certainly not with Panama, nor even with RTZ, but with the world copper industry and markets, themselves under the ultimate control of the Western world economic system.

Ironically, the same Panamanian government that ceaselessly insisted it was in complete control of the overall dynamics and decisions of the Cerro Colorado project, seemed unable even to control its own national copper company. Cerro Colorado involved a wide range of domestic political and economic interests; those who controlled the project held enormous power. The contracts named CODEMIN the principal, if not exclusive, agent of the state for the Cerro Colorado project, making it guardian of the nation's interests, business partner of a foreign transnational corporation, and party and judge with respect to compliance with Panamanian laws.[11]

The power of CODEMIN, with its built-in conflicts of interest, made it unlikely that this state agency could reliably excercise the primary responsibility of promoting Panama's national interest in the mining project.[12] On paper, CODEMIN responded to the nation's executive. In fact, the company seemed more the private preserve of General Torrijos and CODEMIN president Rodrigo (Rory) González; it paid relatively little attention to the executive.[13] CODEMIN did not submit its annual financial reports to the Comptroller of the Republic, as required by law; repeated official requests brought no responses. Contrary to its claims of making all information about the project available to anyone who wanted to see it, CODEMIN did not even keep Dr. Aristides Royo, the Panamanian president, accurately informed of major aspects of the project; even after the World Bank's criticisms, after RTZ had replaced Texasgulf, President Royo seemed genuinely surprised that anyone might question any of CODEMIN's optimistic projections of risk-free benefits for Panama from the development of Cerro Colorado. During the 1981 negotiations between CODEMIN and Rio Tinto-Zinc, expatriate financial consultants to the executive obtained less outdated versions of items on the bargaining table than did President Royo, who asked the consultants for copies of materials they had only gotten from CODEMIN with great difficulty; the consultants, even though armed with written authorizations from vice president (later president) Ricardo de la Espriella, could not get current information from CODEMIN.[14]

So much power with so little effective accountability is open to abuse; never absent from considerations of Panama's dynamics in the Cerro Colorado project was the fear of official corruption, the fear that General Torrijos and CODEMIN president González made decisions to enhance their personal gain from the project rather than to advance the best interests of the nation. In placing Rodrigo González at the head of CODEMIN, Torrijos chose a man whom many regarded as Torrijos' closest, most powerful ally, the same person who managed Torrijos' own financial affairs; many people in Panama believed that González looked out only for himself and for Torrijos. People assumed González enjoyed the direct protection of the highest real power of the state; when González spoke, people heard Torrijos.[15]

From the outset, CODEMIN took a highly politicized approach to what became a highly politicized project; the state mining company consistently came forward with optimistic public statements that backed Torrijos' statements about the project. CODEMIN's publications and announcements indicated that, in the opinion of its top management, Cerro Colorado could not help but provide thousands of jobs, improve Panama's foreign exchange earnings, and diversify its economic dependency; these assertions headed the lists of reasons to proceed immediately with the project. No matter what was happening on other fronts, the tone never changed.

Some of the CODEMIN staff worked hard in the sincere belief that the project had the importance and the potential for the republic that their publicity stated. The field members of the original Panamanian Copper Commission had begun their work with common bonds of enthusiasm and dedication; they were caught up in the excitement of their close association with a project of such importance for Panama. They threw themselves into the project, tried to master the studies left by Canadian Javelin, read what they could about the Guaymíes, and worked hard to assess and compensate damages caused by the construction of the Canadian Javelin road.

However, when the Commission became installed as the CODEMIN bureaucracy, the common bonds seemed to give way to power struggles, jealousies, suspicions of political persuasions, and doubts about old friends. Rodrigo González held virtually absolute power within CODEMIN. People believed that economist Rubén Darío Herrera, general manager of CODEMIN, received his job because his affiliation with the Party of the People (Panama's communist party) would be useful to keep that party behind the mining project.[16] Roquebert, named technical manager of CODEMIN, was generally considered to be an honest, unpoliticized, incorruptible, and nationalistic engineer whose principal limitation was his technocratic view of the world and of the social problems associated with Cerro Colorado; rumors circulated that Roquebert was excluded at times from information and decision-making in which he should have been involved. Some of his decisions were reported to have been reversed without his consultation.

The staff of the Department of Social Development was a mixed lot. It included people whose concerns largely were limited to job security; others had political ambitions, or were window-dressing, to appease one or another group. Some employees were looked upon with suspicion by their co-workers. Overall, no one appeared to have much power within the overall structure of CODEMIN. One department member apparently saw no conflict in maintaining divided loyalties between work concerns and personal ties to General Torrijos; at the same time the member criticized a colleague who retained ties to old friends who questioned the project. Another, apparently in conjunction with a growing relationship to the National Guard, moved away from accountability to the Department to more direct work with the Guaymí Indians. The two Guaymíes who worked in the Panama City offices seemed to be there chiefly for their own convenience; their principal concerns were to finish their university degrees and live well in the capital. León Palacios, who did public relations work in Chiriquí for the Department, seemed to use his position to advance his aspirations within the Party of the People.

Different aspects of the project required cooperation among a variety of government ministries. People in other ministries, such as the Ministry of Planning and Political Economy, complained that they could not get information they needed from CODEMIN. CODEMIN and other ministries (for example, the Ministry of Housing) seemed mutually worried about which agency might get credit for common projects, and they were suspicious that any other agency might encroach on their turf. Because CODEMIN was not responsible to these agencies, and because they were not responsible to CODEMIN, the stage was set for a high degree of bureaucratic infighting as different interests came to the fore. Each agency was keenly aware of the need for self-protection in the event of any major problem that might arise, yet desirous of increased shares of the credit in the event of any successes. People saw Cerro Colorado as an enormous pie; many hungered for a larger slice.

THE WORLD COPPER INDUSTRY

In its quest to develop Cerro Colorado, Panama thought to contribute to production of a metal of considerable versatility and importance in the industrial world. Copper has high electrical and thermal conductivity; it is very malleable and is easily soldered. It has good tensile strength, resists corrosion, and enters well into alloys. The electrical and telecommunication fields use about half of today's copper output; the remainder is used in other aspects of the building industry, in general engineering (such as the construction of water turbines, power station equipment, heat exchangers, chemical plants, and machine tools), and in transportation.[17]

Panama wanted to market its copper in the European Economic Community and Japan, countries that use 55 to 60 percent of market-economy country copper. In the nineteenth century, as these countries industrialized, they depleted their own deposits. The European- and Japanese-owned mining houses found copper in distant places; Africa, Latin America, Asia, and Oceania became important supply areas. But the mining houses usually maintained and operated processing facilities in their home countries, near their markets—traditional home-country corporations that used copper in manufactures; the source areas did not develop their own industries based on copper.[18]

From the outset, the developed countries that relied on imported copper dominated their political relationships with the exporting countries. Some of these relationships were established as direct colonial ties, as in Africa (Belgium in Zaire, the United Kingdom in Zambia and Zimbabwe); others were an elaboration of neocolonial policies in politically independent nations (Great Britain and the United States in Chile and Peru). Major mining corporations, like the trading companies that preceded or accompanied them (see Wolf 1982), generally maintained close ties with their host governments, which in turn were generally willing to "protect the investments" of these corporations through various expediencies at different times and places: military intervention, manipulation of "free trade," differential import-export tariffs, unequal treaties, and so on.[19]

Meanwhile, early in the twentieth century, western U.S. producers began mining low-grade porphyry deposits, usually with less than 2 percent contained copper; a typical porphyry deposit now is less than 1.0 percent contained copper. With this change to a lower grade, producers used technological innovations to develop economies of scale, to compensate for the need to move and process more material. Large open-pit mines increasingly replaced underground operations, and the size and efficiency of transport and processing facilities grew by leaps and bounds to accommodate the increased quantities. These technological changes were capital intensive, and greatly reduced the direct labor force of mining operations.[20] These moves toward more capital-intensive mining further concentrated essential controls in the already powerful hands of the countries and multinational corporations that created, owned, and manufactured the capital goods in which the technologies were incorporated: mammoth dump trucks and corresponding mining equipment, blasting materials and techniques, manufactures of processing facilities, and creation and ownership (through patents and licenses) of the processes themselves.

Beginning in the 1960s and picking up momentum in the early 1970s, LDC host governments sought ways to change the balance of power in their relationships with the developed countries and the multinational corporations. Zaire and Zambia achieved independence from Belgium and England under the auspices of nationalist movements that wanted not only their own national flag, but also recognition of their sovereignty over their natural resources and of their right, as independent nations, to legislate controls governing the activities of major foreign investors. Chile and Peru, long independent but in fact subject to control from outside, wanted both the symbols and the substance of recognition that their copper was part of their national patrimony, rather than the patrimony of the multinational corporations that controlled its extraction and marketing. These countries negotiated new relationships with mining companies, seeking greater control of their mineral wealth, even resorting to expropriation and nationalization when they found no other way to achieve what they thought was rightly theirs.[21] In 1967, these same countries formed the Intergovernmental Council of Copper-Exporting Countries or CIPEC, to be a force for the stabilization of wildly fluctuating copper prices.[22]

CIPEC governments, along with other LDC mineral producers, usually developed five general objectives for mining projects:

(i) revenue and foreign exchange benefits; (ii) objectives relating to ownership and control of the mining project; (iii) objectives concerning the transfer of technology, employment, and training of nationals and diminution of the country's dependence on foreign expertise; (iv) objectives concerning linkages between the mining project and the rest of the national economy, including requirements for local purchasing, local processing, and other indirect linkages; and (v) what might be called political-legal objectives, dealing with such issues as assertion of sovereignty over natural resources, paramountcy of national law and procedures for settling disputes between the government and multinational corporations.[23] (Zorn 1980:215)

If CIPEC governments had their agendas for mining projects within their countries, MNCs also had conditions they considered crucial for their own participation in these projects. Mikesell listed twelve items for the "ideal" demands of a foreign investor:

(1) majority equity ownership; (2) full control over production, employment, investment, purchases of materials and equipment, marketing and distribution of earnings; (3) tax provisions that will enable the foreign investor to earn and repatriate the capitalized value of the investment, including the repayment of external indebtedness, within a relatively short period of time, and a corporate tax rate that does not exceed that imposed by the home country of the parent company; (4) foreign-exchange arrangements that permit the foreign investor to hold sufficient export proceeds abroad to meet all external obligations, including those arising from current foreign purchases, and to remit dividends and authorized capital repatriation; (5) freedom to make payments to the parent company, or to other foreign firms, for technical services and the use of pat-

ented processes and to import equipment and materials from any
source so long as the prices and quality are competitive; (6) exemp-
tion from import duties on equipment and materials employed in
construction and operations; (7) no export or production taxes or
royalties, and guarantees against the imposition of new taxes or
other legislation or regulations that would affect the operation and
profitability of the investment that did not exist at the time of the
investment agreement, or were not specified in it; (8) guarantees
against expropriation or contract renegotiation during the life of
the agreement; (9) negotiation of an agreement covering exploration, production, and operations before any substantial exploration
outlays; (10) a minimum tenure of the life of the mine, often at
least 30 years after the initiation of commercial production; (11) in
the event of expropriation, a guarantee of full compensation based
on replacement cost of assets or present value of projected earnings;
(12) arbitration of disputes arising in the implementation of the
contract by an independent arbitration agency such as the International Chamber of Commerce Court of Arbitration or the World
Bank International Center for the Settlement of Investment Disputes.[24] (Mikesell 1979b:50)

By the mid-1970s, following some initial turmoil as CIPEC countries
briefly succeeded in their challenge to the foreign interests that controlled their copper production, the balance of power had shifted back
in favor of developed countries and their MNCs. CIPEC had little
possibility of becoming the major force sought by its members; exploitable copper was too abundant worldwide, and too many substitutes
were available.[25]

Developed countries and their MNCs, determined to maintain
both secure supplies of copper and their hegemony in LDC producing
areas, adjusted rapidly to the growing assertions of nationalism in
mineral-rich LDCs. These adjustments, carried out through the exercise
of advantages enjoyed by those who for so long had controlled mineral
production, took four main forms: radical shifts in exploration, notice-
able changes in the share of copper produced in "safe" countries and in
LDCs, changes in processing and new technology, and more sophisti-
cated financing of expansions and new construction.

Transnational mining firms radically shifted the focus of exploration for new reserves; in the early 1970s, major multinational mining

corporations allocated 85 percent of their exploration expenditures for efforts in DCs and only 15 percent for LDCs, "despite the generally higher exploration costs and greater exploration saturation in the developed countries" (Bosson and Varon 1977:31). They concentrated about 80 percent of all exploration expenditure in four countries whose investment climates they regarded as "safe": Canada, the United States, South Africa (including Namibia), and Australia (then including Papua New Guinea).[26] From 1960 to 1975, new exploration added 234 percent to the available reserves in "safe" countries (including the Philippines under Ferdinand Marcos), while proven CIPEC reserves increased by only 44 percent (Tilton 1977:44). As Mikesell (1979b:12) noted,

> "Political risk analysis" came to supplement—and in many cases was now conceived to surpass in importance—the usual "economic risk analysis" involved in making new investment decisions.[27]

The skewed exploration soon resulted in shifts in the regional shares of copper production itself. In the critical "unstable" period of 1965–75, CIPEC production grew by 2.2 percent per year, while production in Canada, the United States, South Africa, Australia, and the Philippines grew by 3.9 percent per year. CIPEC annually accounted for about 42 percent of market-economy country mine production from 1955 to 1968; from 1969 to 1972, the CIPEC share dropped to 38.9 percent, and from 1973 to 1976 dropped even more, to 37.6 percent. The "safe" LDCs (including Papua New Guinea) increased their annual share from 7.2 percent in 1969 to 12 percent throughout the 1970s.[28]

The production of copper ordinarily includes: extraction of the ore, frequently less than 1.0 percent contained copper; milling and concentration of the ore to yield a concentrate of about 25 percent copper; smelting, which results in blister copper of approximately 98 to 99 percent purity; refining of blister copper to form cathodes of 99.8 percent (or more) purity; and casting of the industrially pure copper as semimanufactured wirebars and other forms suitable for further manufacture into final uses. Each stage of production adds value; but the initial stages, extraction and concentration, create the majority of the added value (Mezger 1980:75).

In contrast to other LDC metal producers, copper-producing countries have historically smelted and refined a good percentage of their ore in their own country. CIPEC members smelt around 93 percent of their own copper; and they increased their share of refining from 54 percent in the early 1960s to a record 71 percent in 1980.[29] The developed-country share of processing has declined over the past thirty years.[30] Even so, DCs and MNCs have retained sufficient volume of smelting and refining to ensure their control over the copper industry; and the final stage of processing, casting the refined copper into wirebars and other forms for the use of manufacturers, has remained a DC monopoly.

In recent years, European and Japanese custom smelters and refiners have expanded their facilities and encouraged substantial increases in the production and sale of copper concentrates; copper's relatively high value means that transportation costs do not add significantly to overall production costs (Mezger 1980:74).[31] Through the early 1980s, several important new LDC copper producers—Papua New Guinea, Indonesia, Malaysia—had no smelters or refineries, exporting only copper concentrates; from 1976 to 1980, their mines produced almost 9 percent of market-economy country copper each year. The expansion of capital-intensive developed country processing facilities has created more difficult economies of scale that work against less developed countries.

In addition to expanding their processing facilities, DC multinational corporations increase their control through technological innovations in the processing itself. In the 1970s "continuous casting" became an important process for making wires needed for the electro-industries, which account for about half of all copper use. Wire manufacturers formerly worked with wirebars cast from cathodes, usually at the refineries. With continuous casting, however, semimanufacture and part of refining are combined into one continuous process, eliminating the production of wirebars, thus cutting both labor and energy costs. The product of continuous casting is superior to wirebars for the electro-industry and commands a premium price.[32] Continuous casting adds to the concentration of capital and power in the copper industry; continuous-casting plants "require heavier capital investments per unit of output" than do conventional plants, favoring the largest corporations that can raise the capital for integrated production. Makers of continuous-cast copper, to retain their competitive edge, use very high-grade cathodes; this need encourages backwards integration into refining and even smelting. Since the high-grade copper must be used immediately for further production, continuous casting plants must be located near plants involved in the next stage of manufacture (Mezger 1975:71–74; 1980:65 ff). The technological change to continuous casting guarantees that a significant part of copper processing must be undertaken by MNCs and in DCs, and cannot be undertaken in LDCs, which have no capital to invest and virtually no facilities for the manufacture of copper products.[33]

Mezger (1975:74) summarized the effects of technological changes:

> In sum, since copper nationalizations and demands for higher shares in profits by the [LDCs] lessen the profit rate in production, multinational corporations in copper have found a new method of securing profitability, extracting surplus value via . . . expensive technology, creating thus, at the same time, a new form of dependency. In many ways, this counterbalances, or more than outweighs, the controls the underdeveloped copper-exporting countries have so far gained via partial or total nationalizations of copper mines and organization into CIPEC.

Multinational mining firms (sometimes backed by their home governments) have successfully used reallocation of exploration and new investments, as well as processing innovations, to reassert their control over world copper production. In addition, shocks to the world economic system, such as the petroleum crisis of the early 1970s, brought about greater sophistication in the complex mechanisms of financing new projects, giving MNCs increased leverage in their relationships with LDCs. In the 1970s, inflation enormously increased the costs of bringing new projects into production; economies of scale in new low-grade copper projects, which (so sponsors are convinced) must be gigantic in order to be profitable on a cost-per-unit basis, have pushed overall start-up costs out of sight—precisely the situation of Cerro Colorado. Whereas MNCs used to finance new mines or the expansion of existing capacity through retained earnings and their own borrowing, MNCs by themselves can no longer finance major new projects or even major expansions of existing facilities.[34]

Financing problems of multinational mining corporations pale alongside those of LDCs, trying to manage very burdensome foreign debt before even considering huge expenditures for new mining facilities. And LDCs like Panama, struggling to break into the world of mining, face even more overwhelming problems because costs are further driven up by the absence of needed infrastructure, already available in DCs and in copper-producing LDCs. Infrastructure requirements include major production of electrical energy, industrial roads, ports, and even towns or cities. Since the areas where mineral deposits are located tend to be isolated from the already somewhat-developed regions of these countries, this infrastructure has the further peculiarity of being almost exclusively useful for the mining project. It is perhaps redundant to observe that development of infrastructure on this scale is also highly capital-intensive, which requires major DC inputs. To these costs must be added the inherent risks in developing a new mining project (which project may or may not begin production at a time when world copper prices are high enough to bring a profit), and it is even more readily apparent that such projects cannot be financed either from already insufficient LDC government revenues or from MNC corporate coffers.

New facilities are financed through highly complex loan arrangements that increasingly involve a consortium of many major international banking firms; the arrangements envisioned for financing the Cerro Colorado project were typical of these patterns. Banks will not make these loans unless experienced, reputable international mining firms have complete control of the operations of the mining project. Bankers also seek the added security provided by the presence of multilateral lending agencies like the World Bank and regional development banks, guaranteeing through their major shareholders—the DC governments—that LDCs will be slow to change the rules once the game is in progress.[35]

Copper corporations, financial institutions, and developed countries have efficaciously reasserted their hegemony in the face of LDC nationalism. However, they did so by revising their strategies in such manner as to emphasize and take advantage of their traditional strengths.

> It should be made clear these "patterns" of copper corporations are in no case the outcome of a worldwide conspiracy against poor underdeveloped countries. Rather they are the result of the inherent logic of profit making and securing existing relations of production. (Mezger 1975:74)

As Panama discovered, a contemporary copper mine is the visible part of a mystifying web of global economic and political relationships. While LDCs possess within their borders the majority of the world's known copper reserves, they do not control its exploitation and marketing. Rather, copper is produced in the interest of and under the control of the major DCs, whose agents of interest and control are the principal transnational mining corporations and financial institutions. The interest served is the continued capitalist economic growth of the DCs, and through this means their continued economic and political hegemony of the western world. The controls are maintained through such factors as size, technology, financing, pricing, and marketing. Clearly, as the case of Cerro Colorado and the general observations about world copper production indicate, LDCs have relatively little power to influence the benefits they derive from the extraction of their own natural resources.

But as the Cerro Colorado case also demonstrates, not even MNCs and DCs can, by themselves, make the world copper market behave as they wish. Copper prices rise and fall rapidly, according to perceptions of world supply and demand. No single group of corporations or countries has control over the world's economic system; no single group of western corporations or countries can force copper prices up or down.

Although the abundance of copper and the availability of substitutes have kept CIPEC members (and other LDC producers) from gaining significant control of world copper production and marketing, their control over their own copper operations gives them a sometimes self-defeating influence over supply and prices. Countries that depend on copper for foreign exchange and for export earnings often cannot afford not to produce and sell their commodity, even should they suffer some losses when oversupply pushes prices below production costs. As prices fall, profit-oriented MNCs cut back on production; but highly indebted LDCs have little alternative but to continue production and watch prices remain weak.

Most large mining corporations are sufficiently diversified that they can survive a relatively extended period of low profits in one or two major areas of their operations. Since some MNCs successfully represent themselves as the principal guarantees of uninterrupted supplies of vital raw materials for their home countries, they may be able to count on help from their home governments if their circumstances become truly dire. But LDCs, in general, have neither the diversification nor the outside backing to confront their problems in like manner; they must keep returning to the DC-controlled bargaining tables, accepting IMF economic measures in order to refinance oppressive debts, taking on new loans that mortgage the very problematic present to the completely unknown future. In light of the experiences of other copper-producing LDCs, Panama's inability to find a way to develop the Cerro Colorado mining project did not look so unambiguously damaging to Panama's future economic well-being.

PART 3

Opposition to Cerro Colorado

The struggles discussed in Part 2 took place in CODEMIN's offices in the Banco Nacional tower in Panama City, in Texasgulf's headquarters in Stamford, Connecticut, in Rio Tinto-Zinc's headquarters in London, in the edifice housing the World Bank in Washington, D.C., and in other major corporate and financial power centers of the western world. Like theater people opening a new show out of town, the sponsors went about their parts with an eye toward their reviews in New York or London.

Meanwhile, in Panama, others fought with the main performers, wanting if not to rewrite the script, at least to expand their roles. As proponents of the Cerro Colorado project claimed, the mammoth project would have consequences extending to every sector of Panamanian life. Such a project could not help but provoke a variety of responses, and could not avoid generating controversy.

Several groups in Panama voiced opposition to the mining project, focusing their grievances on aspects of the proposals that they believed threatened their interests and prerogatives. Their political styles governed the methods they used to express their disagreements. In response, CODEMIN's and the government's presentations of the proposals to different audiences sometimes acknowledged the controversies, and sometimes included overt attacks on the opposition.

To gain United States Senate ratification of the Torrijos–Carter canal treaties, General Torrijos allowed the resuscitation of political parties and the expression of some public opposition to government plans and programs. Although his government controlled the news- papers and television stations, radio, the main popular medium of com- munication for most Panamanians, enjoyed considerable freedom of expression.[1] The immensity of the Cerro Colorado project provided ample ammunition for Torrijos' critics.

The most extreme critics offered wild scenarios of widespread eco- logical and human disaster from the development of the mining project. Among their more virulent attacks, they maintained that the smelter, to be located on the Pacific Coast near the port, would emit noxious gases that would destroy all vegetation within a wide radius—cattle pastures, commercial crops, peasant subsistence products, and forests, all would disappear. They raised the specter of the same gases rendering people sterile and causing everyone's hair to fall out. They insisted that other waste from the mine would destroy all the fish in the rivers and wipe out the rich marine life in the Gulf of Chiriquí.

For the most part, radio opponents of Cerro Colorado absolved themselves from the tedious work of doing research on the mining project. Frequently they cited a dated study of possible ecological haz- ards of the smelter, weaving the report's careful projections of negative environmental consequences into their own scenarios of a science- fiction wasteland. They painted vivid word-pictures of the areas sur- rounding major mining projects in other parts of the world, pictures that generally went far beyond even the most devastating effects of ecological irresponsibility. Occasionally they interviewed people they described as foreign environmental experts, interpreting relatively care- ful statements as proof that their worst fears would be realized. Having prejudged the matter, they made no attempt to look into the environ- mental safeguards built into the smelting technology actually under consideration.

These hostile radio personalities seemed interested more in using Cerro Colorado to create opposition to the government than in engag- ing in the much-needed debate about the merits of the project for the different sectors of Panama. Even when affiliations went unannounced, most Panamanians knew what parties or political/ideological tenden- cies the major radio commentators represented. In many cases their opposition masked the fear that, on the heels of the generally popular gains of the canal treaties, a successful start for the Cerro Colorado project would translate into a long tenure in power for Torrijos and his backers, once Panama returned to electing its presidents and legislators.[2]

This opposition, and CODEMIN's and the government's responses, turned the debate about Cerro Colorado into an informal plebiscite on the popularity of the government itself. Through 1979, relying still on Torrijos' popularity, the government denied the claims of the opponents, characterizing them all as mouthpieces for the old oligarchy, still stinging from the reforms of the revolution. Opponents of the mine, said CODEMIN, wanted to return to the days of yore when the government served only the interests of the wealthy elite while the majority poor and lower middle class paid the costs. The issue became one of political loyalty—pro-government meant pro-mine, anti-mine meant anti-government.

In many respects, the government itself benefited most from the extreme, self-interested opponents to Cerro Colorado. CODEMIN easily dismissed their exaggerated, unfounded claims; in addition, the sponsors of the mine lumped almost all questioning of the project into the same heap as the attacks of this self-interested opposition. Inadvertently, these opponents helped the government achieve its goal of avoiding a serious, open debate on the merits of the project itself.

More subtle in its approach than the radio commentators was the Panamanian Chamber of Commerce. Instead of opposing the project, it raised questions on matters of "grave concern," especially seeking assurances that the government of Panama would not be required to provide its own guarantees of the loans needed for the construction of the mining project. After preliminary skirmishes via paid newspaper advertisements, the Chamber of Commerce invited CODEMIN to participate in a nationally broadcast forum on the Cerro Colorado project; CODEMIN accepted. The Chamber of Commerce invited its members nationally to submit their questions for CODEMIN and its panel of experts, who received written copies of all questions some days prior to the forum.[3]

But, instead of using the broadcast as an opportunity to clarify issues of substance, the lengthy forum dedicated much of its limited time to relatively arcane aspects of the contracts between Texasgulf and CODEMIN. The Chamber of Commerce appeared to be trying to get CODEMIN to admit that its 80 percent ownership of the mining project yielded 50 percent (or less) of the decision-making power as well as serious problems for national sovereignty. CODEMIN maintained it was in control, or at least in sufficient control, to take care of the issue of sovereignty and the legitimate interests of the nation (Cámara de Comercio 1979:22–50).[4] The remainder of the forum included some confusing exchanges concerning the sources of, and financing for, electricity for the project, some discussion of ecological concerns, and an occasional question relating to other aspects of the project. The Chamber of Commerce, from beginning to end, maintained that it only sought the best solutions to national problems; for its part, CODEMIN expressed appreciation for the opportunity to continue its efforts to provide the fullest possible information on all aspects of the mining project, in the interest of letting everyone see exactly what was going on. The Chamber of Commerce did not substantiate nor even allude to its basic premise, announced in its newspaper advertisements, that Cerro Colorado was a "marginal, controversial, [and] risky" billion-dollar investment.

The Chamber of Commerce probably had several underlying concerns governing its questioning of the Cerro Colorado project. Undoubtedly, some of its members feared that CODEMIN, behind its public façade of free exchange of all relevant information concerning the project, its plans, and negotiations in process, might secretly commit the nation to a series of agreements that would compromise the future of the country. Also, it seems likely that some Chamber members were anxious to find a way to exert some influence on the project, to make sure that the private sector got its share of the promised bonanza. And, given that the Chamber of Commerce was the principal instance of economic organization for the main powers in Panama's traditional political parties, one might assume that the Chamber opposed the project because it feared that successful development of Cerro Colorado would fairly guarantee another generation of Torrijos-style government.

The forum resulted in some important assurances from CODEMIN president Rodrigo González: that the government would not have to provide guarantees for loans to the joint operating company; that the decision to proceed with construction would not be taken without the support of the executive's economic consultants; that no decision to proceed with the project would be taken until careful environmental-impact studies were completed; that the government and the people of Panama would not have to pay for Cerro Colorado's energy needs; and that project revenues would cover the major loans (Cámara de Comercio 1979:62, 56, 42, 44).[5]

However, some of the misinformation given out in the forum cast doubts on the credibility of these assurances. González obfuscated the question of the importance of the Canada Development Corporation (CDC) as principal stockholder of Texasgulf, and maintained that CDC and the Export Development Corporation (EDC), the principal financing source for Cerro Colorado, had no connection with each other (Cámara de Comercio 1979:41). In fact, public records showed that the CDC controlled some seats on the board of directors of Texasgulf, and two representatives of Canadian government ministries sat on the boards of directors of both the EDC and the CDC; on the face of it, it was extremely unlikely that the EDC had no connection with Texasgulf (LAWG 1980:30). On close analysis, González' discussion of the possibility of the Panamanian government's underwriting of EDC loans made to the joint operating company did not meet the principal question being raised (Cámara de Comercio 1979:42–45). CODEMIN and IRHE, the national electricity company, seemed to go to some lengths to avoid giving direct answers to questions concerning the financing of Cerro Colorado's energy needs; their responses at best conflicted with the conclusions of an internal study undertaken by IRHE that was fairly widely distributed (Cámara de Comercio 1979:55–58, 70–72; IRHE 1979b). Close investigation of the project disclosed that when González pointed to careful environmental and social impact studies, he was in fact pointing at nothing at all.[6]

Powerful rural interests from Chiriquí, who comprised a rural elite long opposed to the Torrijos government (and to a number of its predecessors), chose a different tack for their opposition to Cerro Colorado. Quickly created and suddenly active environmental groups (such as *Sociedad Amigos de la Naturaleza de Chiriquí* and *Sociedad Amigos del Arbo*) united with the leadership of key business associations to form a committee dedicated to the "integral defense of Chiriquí" *(Comité Pro Defensa Integral de Chiriquí)*. Under the guise of concern for the ecology and the health of the people of the region, the committee tried to create popular opposition to the government through opposition to the mining project. While the substance of their claims differed only accidentally from those of the extremist radio commentators discussed above, their approach sounded far more measured and less shrill (see Comité Pro Defensa de Chiriquí 1979).

CODEMIN took two approaches in response to this kind of opposition. On the one side, seemingly respecting the fact that many people had fears about the environmental consequences of Cerro Colorado, CODEMIN both continued its repeated assurances that modern technology rendered all these concerns non-problems, and published a pamphlet of Rubén Darío Herrera, the general manager (CODEMIN 1980a). However, Herrera's pamphlet, in slightly dressed-up language, in essence presented the statements that CODEMIN had been making all along. It offered only one new piece of information, in the form of references to a United Nations review of the environmental questions raised by the mining project (CODEMIN 1980a:4).[7]

For their part, CODEMIN's public relations people, usually in meetings and conversations that were unlikely to be reported nationally, offered a different analysis of the source of the concerns of the opposition group from Chiriquí. With Cerro Colorado, they maintained, the poor of Chiriquí would find ready employment for good wages, whether directly with the mining company or indirectly through related services. They argued that the principals of the Chiriquí committee depended on seasonal low-wage laborers in their businesses; with Cerro Colorado, campesinos and Guaymíes would be unwilling to work under the same conditions and for the same low wages as previously. This opposition to the mining project, then, as CODEMIN portrayed it, masked crass self-interest in the continued exploitation of the poor of Chiriquí.

While proponents and opponents of the project vied for public attention, the consultants and employees of the mining enterprise continued their studies and work at the mine site itself, in the mountains of eastern Chiriquí. No one, whether for or against the project, took much notice of another audience for their views, the Guaymí Indians. When called upon, supporters of the mine made the obligatory remarks bemoaning the abject poverty of this backward audience, prefatory to the obligatory assurances that the mining project would bring the Guaymíes into the twentieth century and could only solve their problems of hunger, illness, and ignorance. For sure, there would be some discomfort and disruption; but in the long run, the authorized scenario called only for happy endings and satisfied citizens. Few, if any, of the spokespersons for or against the project knew or cared about whether the Guaymíes had any concerns about the impact Cerro Colorado might have on their lives.

In fact, whereas the sponsors could only hope and guess about other effects of the mining project, its actual effects on the Guaymíes could be observed from the arrival of Canadian Javelin's first crew. And, despite the disclaimers of the sponsors, its future effects could be only too realistically predicted with some confidence by analysis of the Guaymí region and circumstances, by projection from the effects of the exploratory activities, and by reference to parallel experiences in other mining areas of the world.

Part 3 presents the impact on the Guaymíes of the Cerro Colorado mining project—the anticipated impact had the mine been constructed, and the actual impact from the years of exploratory work. But the principal concern of Part 3 is the discussion of responses to these impacts. For the Guaymíes, although they might have begun as a fairly passive, fairly receptive audience, worked to change the situation into one that included their active participation. In this movement, they were accompanied and assisted by others who, more often than not, came together under the umbrella of the Panamanian Catholic Church. These others, including some priests, expressed their concerns for the Guaymíes and other poor of Panama through a close scrutiny of all aspects of the project, through participation with the Guaymíes in educational activities, and through direct involvement in national and international solidarity efforts on behalf of the Guaymíes.[8]

CHAPTER 7

Impact of the Cerro Colorado Project on the Guaymíes

The ten years of studies and exploration of the Cerro Colorado copper deposits had their impact, especially among the people of the immediate area under study. For the local Guaymíes, the tens of millions of dollars in exploration created significant problems; the sponsors' proposals pointed to even more sweeping problems had conditions permitted the multibillion-dollar construction and operation of the copper mine.

The sponsors made little attempt to pull together information about the kinds and degrees of disruptions to Guaymí communities that would arise from the construction and operation of the mining project. But they published sufficiently detailed plans to allow others to project what communities would be affected—through complete loss of lands and relocation, through partial loss of lands and disruption of lifeways from roads and pipelines, or from hazards and inconveniences caused by the project's demands on water supplies.[1]

PROJECTED IMPACT ON THE GUAYMIES

Cerro Colorado's impact on the Guaymíes would have resulted from the construction and operation of mine facilities and infrastructure within the Guaymí area. Estimates indicated that the Guaymíes might have lost around 300 km² of land to the mine; the loss of this land, almost all in Chiriquí Province, would have exacerbated the already critical land situation. The joint operating company, Cerro Colorado Copper Corporation, received a concession area of 720 km² in which to continue exploration for seven years, adding parts of the concession area to the project area as desired. The concession area included 150 Guaymí communities, with an estimated 1980 population of 6,250.

Mining project land needs would have required the relocation of some Guaymí communities. At least five communities in the immediate vicinity of the mine would have lost almost everything; seven more communities would have been moved to accommodate the construction camp; and three communities (at the Cerro Laguna site) would have lost everything to the dam and reservoir. The estimated 1980 population of these fifteen communities was 824. Because of the intricacies of Guaymí land tenure and use rights, it would have proven extremely difficult to devise relocation formulas to guarantee that the Guaymíes affected could secure their subsistence in the same way as before the arrival of the mining project.

The road from the mine to the port might have passed through a total of twelve Guaymí communities (excluding those likely to have disappeared) with an estimated 1980 population of 1,410 people, and ten campesino communities with an estimated 1980 population of 550.[2] A variety of physical environmental problems would occur as a result of road building, because of the rugged topography of the area (CSMRI 1977:II–2, No. 6). Rugged mountainous terrain combined with the tropical rains to make landslides a constant threat; to avoid slides, the builders would have to make the cuts along the road at very flat angles, just as earlier builders discovered in the construction of the Corte de Culebra of the Panama Canal. CODEMIN estimated that the roads would require an average of 50 meters of land on each side of the route (Cámara de Comercio 1979:67–68), but the average could have been much higher. The road would have removed some land from Guaymí and campesino use and restricted movement from one side to the other. The accompanying slurry pipelines could rupture "with attendant damage [from] the slurry spilled." Also, "a few dump ponds are usually provided along the line for discharge of the pipe in the event of plugging" (CSMRI 1977:XI–Annex 21). "The operation of the proposed mine will probably influence three major river basins, the San Félix and

[Cuvíbora-] Tabasará on the Pacific Ocean, and the Cricamola on the Atlantic Ocean" (CSMRI 1977:XI–1). Throughout the construction period, major surface water systems would become so silty that they could not be utilized in the customary ways. This problem would be especially grave in the Chiriquí dry season when many of the streams dried up and people were more dependent upon the rivers; this area had fewer year-round streams than other parts of the Guaymí area of Chiriquí. The San Félix and Cuvíbora river systems would be permanently affected by construction and mine runoff, even if these rivers were not used for tailings disposal. Between the proposed dam site on the Cuvíbora River and the confluence of the Cuvíbora with the Tabasará, there were twenty communities with an estimated 1980 population of 2,405 people. These would have been adversely affected by the contamination of the Cuvíbora during the dry season, as well as by the permanent reduced flow below the dam (Alvarado 1979). In addition, the mine and related construction would probably have affected the subterranean water system by altering the distribution pattern of the water, as well as by contaminating the waters of the natural springs that provided drinking water for the majority of the Guaymíes (Alvarado 1979). The Cerro Colorado planners overlooked the water needs of these Guaymí communities, stating that "[a]dequate supplies of fresh water are available for use by the Cerro Colorado Project and little or no present competition exists for the use of this water" (CSMRI 1977:II–1, No. 5).[3]

If the dam and reservoir had been built on the Bocas del Toro (Caribbean) side of the Continental Divide, the effects could have been felt along the entire Cricamola drainage, which included 68 communities with an estimated 1980 population of 2,640. These communities probably would not have suffered shortages of water, for there is no dry season on the Atlantic side. However, the Bocas del Toro Guaymíes supplemented their diets with fishing; and several large communities along the wide coastal plain depended upon the Cricamola for drinking water, as well as for bathing and laundry. These villages would have been affected immediately by any contamination that occurred.

The 2,000 Guaymí residents of Valle de Riscó in the Changuinola area of Bocas del Toro would have been displaced by the lake formed by the Changuinola I hydroelectric project. The relatives of these Guaymíes, the residents of the corregimientos of Mununi and Piedra Roja just north of Cerro Colorado, worried that many of the people of

Valle de Riscó might try to reactivate lapsed land claims (J. Bort, personal communication). The hydroelectric project would have tied up more than 28,000 hectares: 5,300 hectares for the reservoir and 23,000 hectares for a zone of protection, a catchment area of forest to ensure adequate rainfall for the hydroelectric project (IRHE 1979a). Of the total, the 5,300 hectares of Valle de Riscó and about half of the zone of protection had been cleared and were in use for agriculture and pasture; that is, over 60 percent of this area was already occupied.[4] At the beginning of 1981, studies began for an alternative hydroelectric project in eastern Chiriquí, along the lower Tabasará River; preliminary information indicated that the lake formed here would displace a number of campesino and Guaymí communities along the Chiriquí–Veraguas border.

ACTUAL IMPACT OF THE PROJECT ON THE GUAYMIES

The actual impact of the Cerro Colorado and Teribe-Changuinola projects on the Guaymíes was small in comparison with what could have been expected had the projects gone forward; but even this was significant. Study of the impact caused by the preparation for the projects serves three purposes: it provides some idea of what the projects brought to the lives of the people affected; it gives concrete indication of how the mining project itself became the most effective vehicle to raise Guaymí consciousness; and it prepares the way for later discussion of the varied responses to the projects.

The most visible impact of the Cerro Colorado project work was the construction and use, in the heart of the Guaymí area, of various facilities needed for the technical and commercial evaluation of the ore deposits. Beginning in 1970, Canadian Javelin erected drilling platforms and the camps of Escopeta and Cerro Colorado; only after 3–4 years did Canadian Javelin add the road from San Félix to the mine area. By the time the project was suspended, the facilities included the main road from San Félix to Hato Chamí, thence in one direction to Escopeta and in the other to Cerro Colorado itself; the test road from Hato Chamí to a point on the Cuvíbora River, later extended to Nancito; hundreds of small concrete drilling platforms all over Cerro Colorado and the immediate surrounding area; three or four small stations to gather weather and water data; and the camps built at the bridge crossing the San Félix River, at Hato Chamí, at Cuernavaca, at Escopeta, and on Cerro Colorado. These camps included various facilities: a parts shop, storage sheds, earth-moving equipment, and fuel tanks at the San Félix bridge; earth-moving equipment, a repair shop, fuel storage, dormitory buildings, a kitchen and dining room, and a health clinic at Hato Chamí; test-ore storage, testing equipment facilities, a dormitory building, a kitchen and dining room, and a health clinic at Escopeta; drilling equipment storage, a test tunnel, a dormitory, and a kitchen and a dining room associated with the Cerro Colorado camp. All of the camps had diesel-fueled electric generators. The Cuernavaca camp sat empty and stripped (except for occasional use for meetings) after Texasgulf finished its major drilling work and cut back its crews in 1977. During 1978 to 1980, the total on-site work force, distributed among the camps, was around 100 men. Associated with these facilities, another major impact of the Cerro Colorado project on the Guaymíes was the constant flow of traffic on the roads, and activities necessary to maintain the roads themselves (see Figure 3 in Chapter 1).

No Guaymí communities in the Cerro Colorado impact area had to relocate; none lost more than a small percentage of its lands. The roads passed through three Guaymí communities, with an estimated 1980 population of 2,000. Ten communities were located along the sides of the principal mine road (San Félix, Hato Chamí–Escopeta and Hato Chamí–Cerro Colorado), five of these within a radius of 4 to 5 km of Cerro Colorado itself. These communities were subjected to the noise and dust of mine traffic, but, over time, they became accustomed to these changes, and the tendency to build up communities along the sides of the roads suggested that they thought the benefits outweighed the difficulties.

All construction activities connected with Cerro Colorado at some time or other muddied the waters of local streams and rivers. Regular landslides along the principal mine access roads kept the maintenance crews active pushing more dirt down the embankments and cutting new terraces above the roads in hopes of preventing future slides. Some communities complained that such activities dirtied their stream for two or three months at a time.

Mine crews cut several short penetration roads to the north of

Cerro Colorado, crossing the Continental Divide, to allow hydrology studies and drilling, and to seek tailings and waste-rock disposal areas. Early attempts to install measuring instruments along the Flores and Coralia Rivers (upper Cricamola drainage, Bocas del Toro Province) ran into hostility in some of the communities there. In the dry season of 1980, Texasgulf cut a penetration road to Nancito; this road caused the most concern on the part of the Guaymíes, probably because it came without warning at a time when they were considerably more aware of the potential negative aspects of Cerro Colorado. This road became impassable with the first rains of May; Rio Tinto-Zinc, which initiated field studies for another route, left it to collapse.

These vehicles, physical installations, and the men who accompanied them made up the tangible parts of the mining project for the Guaymíes. In and of themselves the camps, neat and clean in appearance, occupied relatively little territory, generated little garbage not taken care of by the people themselves, and did not blight the surroundings. The vehicles made noise that at times could be heard from quite a distance; but the noise was not excessive nor particularly disturbing. The roads themselves, and the work needed to maintain them, dirtied the water, removed some land from production, increased erosion, and forced some Guaymíes to do a lot of work to undo some of the damage; CODEMIN paid more than $100,000 in indemnification to Guaymíes for losses to "improvements" on lands taken over for the Cerro Colorado installations.[5]

But these effects were generally quite localized, except for those emanating from work on the mountain itself, which muddied the waters of the San Félix River along its entire length. By and large the workers kept to themselves; in their direct interactions with the Guaymíes, they tended to be polite and, ordinarily, respectful. The issue was not that the mining project destroyed the land base or otherwise directly threatened the physical existence of the Guaymí people.

Rather, the overall impact lay in the fact that the mining project simply did not fit in the Guaymí area. It was completely foreign, it operated on completely foreign mindsets, it served completely foreign goals. It was an intrusion whose impact made day-to-day life more complicated and, generally, rendered the Guaymíes powerless and incompetent in their own territory—powerless to initiate changes on their own behalf, powerless to comprehend what was happening in their world, powerless in the face of constant rumors and anxieties, powerless to seek legal remedies or to withstand the overwhelming technological superiority of the mining project. The mining project introduced into the Guaymí area a foreign world, a "latino" world. Guaymíes now acted at home as they characteristically did when visiting "foreign" turf: passively and incompetently shuffling about like "dumb Indians." And many Guaymíes therefore came to resent the project.

The Case at Tebujo

Project planners had no idea of the actual impact that work on the mining project would have; they thought that their presence represented expanded opportunities for the Guaymíes, the beginnings of real "progress." When they opened a test road from Hato Chamí to Nancito during the dry season of 1980 (January to March), they defended their work as one that gave the Guaymíes of the area a better trail for their business and shopping trips to latino towns. They were unaware that most Guaymíes of the area affected had to do their business and preferred to do their shopping in Tolé, the district seat. Smaller Nancito, in Remedios District, had no government offices; and with less competition, the one major store had higher prices than its counterparts in Tolé.

In building the road, the sponsors knew nothing of the damage that went uncompensated. Tractors cut a short stretch of this road, 200 to 300 meters, into a slope on the property of the Rodríguez family of Tebujo, a Guaymí community of the corregimiento of Maraca, Tolé District. This bit of roadbed, averaging five meters in width, covered a total area of approximately 1000 to 1500m², or 0.1 to 0.15 hectares. But the consequences of opening up this stretch of road, neither foreseen nor recognized after the fact by mine or CODEMIN supervisors, were typical of problems caused by the mining project.

In the area affected, the Rodríguez family lost very little that was indemnified by cash payments: exhaust fumes from a tractor damaged one of their six orange trees, tractors uprooted two or three mango trees and destroyed about half of the family's 100 pineapple plants (Figure 4, feature A). No seasonal crops (rice, corn, or beans) awaited harvest when the tractors arrived. Workmen took down the fences that, in two places, crossed the route of the road; they left the barbed wire

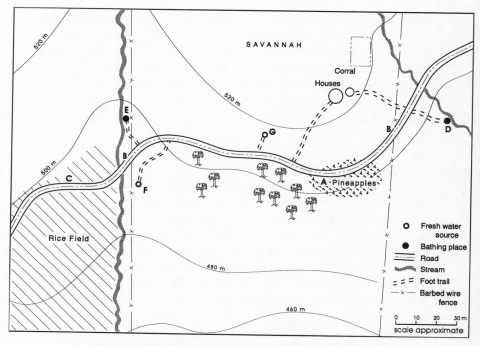

Figure 4. Penetration road, Tebujo: Rodríguez family lands

with the family, who lost two or three fenceposts (Figure 4, feature B). CODEMIN paid indemnification only for these damages.

But the family suffered other losses. First, they lost arable land (Figure 4, feature C). Besides the strip of land removed from production, the cultivated land immediately below the road became less productive. Construction of the road removed a strip of vegetation with its root systems, increasing erosion along the road. Runoff from the tropical rains deposited clay from the road bank on the cultivated land below. The strip of road also altered the previous runoff patterns; new streamlets caused additional inroads of erosion below the road. Moreover, in 1980 the family cultivated the affected land after only five years of fallow, far short of the ideal 25 years; further reduction of productivity came in the face of an already difficult situation.

Over the previous ten years, like many other Guaymíes, the Rodríguez family had been engaged in a land dispute with their neighbors. The disputed piece of land was not much larger than the piece lost to the road. Young estimated that at best, 50 percent of Guaymí land was arable (Young 1980b), but in Tebujo, 35 percent was a closer estimate. Most of the remaining land, impoverished by sun, wind, and rains, had little topsoil over the hard clay; this savannah grassland served for pasture in the rainy season only. The loss of scarce arable land exacerbated the land problem. The 1980 census, reporting a 16.5 percent population decline in the area from 1970 to 1980 instead of the 30 percent growth characteristic of the Guaymí area, suggested the scope of the problem (Table 9); population fluctuations of the past 20 years indicated considerable movement as Guaymíes sought to resolve problems of land scarcity.

The Rodríguez family received no indemnification for the land lost. By Panamanian government definition, the entire Guaymí area was national land *(tierra nacional),* meaning that the government considered itself the owner. Compensation in such cases included only the "improvements," that is, the cash equivalents of crops destroyed; fallow land was "unimproved national land," and was not indemnified (Lobo 1980a, 1980b). The Rodríguez family—husband, three wives, three married sons and their families, a married daughter and her family, and the younger children—all depended on this land for subsistence.

The piece of road, which crossed two small streams, affected the Rodríguez family water supplies. The stream nearer the house formed two or three small pools just below the road (Figure 4, feature D); for years, these pools were the principal bath and laundry sites for the Rodríguez family. The muddy runoff from the road filled these pools

TABLE 9

Population Density: Corregimiento of Maraca (Tolé)
(Area = 50.1 km²)

	Population	Persons/km²	% Change
1960	848	16.9	
1970	1,241	24.8	46.3
1980	1,036	20.7	(−16.5)

SOURCE: Estadística y Censo, various years.

with dirty water during most of the rainy season, rendering them useless to the family.

Along the other stream, the family used rocks to dam up a small pool as a new bathing and laundering place (Figure 4, feature E). But this pool lay just off the road, which became the principal trail of the area. With people passing by, the new pool lacked the privacy that the family wanted for baths. Displaced soil from the construction of the road blocked the natural channel of this stream on its way to the river below. Work crews installed a metal conduit under the roadbed; but the first rains washed down months of accumulated leaves and branches, which plugged the conduit. The backed-up water formed a stagnant pool, adding slippery mud and mosquitoes to the entrance to the bathing spot.

The Rodríguez family, like all the Guaymíes of the area, obtained water for drinking and cooking from a series of underground springs. To ensure nearby sources of drinking water, they carefully cleaned and drained the small pools that formed where the springs broke to the surface. The construction of the road included the "side-casting of superficial materials" (in the phrase of CSMRI 1977:xi–26) down the bank above one of these pools; the dirt all but destroyed the family's crucial dry-season reserve spring, and the muddy runoff kept the water constantly dirty (Figure 4, feature F). Similar side-casting blocked the drainage of the main spring; another pool of stagnant water, much closer to the house, slowly expanded (Figure 4, feature G). The rains turned the bank into mud several inches deep, narrowing the new entrance trail and making it more hazardous to obtain water. Although the Mineral Resources Code of Panama stated that "the concessionaires [of a mining project] may not . . . contaminate the sources of water in prejudice to villages, towns, or cities . . . " (Ministerio de Comercio e Industria 1975: Art. 128), no provisions or precedents encouraged the Rodríguez family to expect compensation for their water-supply problems.

As noted earlier, in two places the road builders removed three strands of barbed wire fence—a total of only 30 meters of barbed wire. Removal of these fences allowed the Rodríguez family's eight cattle to roam freely, creating a host of problems; the road provided the cattle with an unobstructed superhighway on which to seek greener pastures. Some cattle broke into a patch of the family's sugar cane and ate most of it before they were discovered. Another time, local authorities called the Rodríguez family head to answer for the fact that two of his cows entered a patch of sweet manioc *(yuca)* several kilometers below their home; the family had to pay the irate farmer for the damages. Another cow got into the newly sprouted rice of the neighbor who disputed some land claims of the Rodríguez family. The neighbor tied the cow to a tree behind his house and left it there for three days, without food or water, until the family found it. The neighbor claimed he did not know who the owner was and therefore could not notify him.

The family experimented with letting the cattle run loose in the mornings, while people working in their fields could watch out for them. Then, in the afternoons, the family rounded them up and tied them to trees in the small corral near the house. This difficult and time-consuming procedure created new problems. The cattle, accustomed to roaming in the pastures, resisted confinement; the family only used the flimsy corral every few weeks, when they gave their cattle treatments against infections.

Several cows in heat attracted the attention not only of the Rodríguez family's bulls, but also those of their neighbors. The bulls came running, bawling and snorting, down the hillside; they broke down the corral fence. The cows, tied to trees, panicked and tried to break free. Dogs yapped, and children and grandchildren threw rocks, while Señor Rodríguez and his older sons worked to reinforce the corral; the wives and their nursing infants provided an amused audience for the matinee. After a long day's work in the fields, family members spent another two or three hours (often in the rain) playing their parts in this performance.

Had a tractor killed a cow, the government would have paid compensation. But no officials acknowledged the problems and extra work the road brought with it. When the workmen cut the road, the local Guaymíes were beginning the busy time of the agricultural cycle, when they burned the fields to plant them as the first rains came. Following almost immediately, the Guaymíes began the arduous and time-consuming first round of weeding. This work involved reciprocal obligations with relatives and neighbors, important chores that left little time for fence-building. Juan, one of Señor Rodríguez' adult sons, when he had finished most of his own weeding, neglected work owed to others. It took three days to cut fence posts, drive them into the

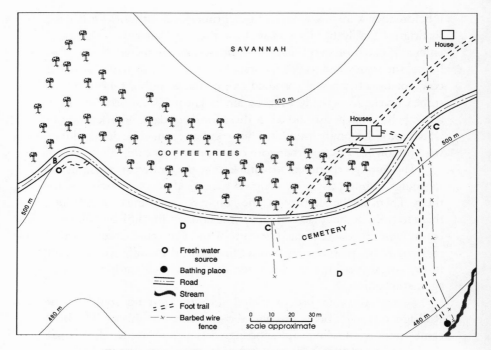

SAVANNAH

520 m

Houses

House

COFFEE TREES

500 m

C

A

500 m

B

O

D

C

CEMETERY

D

500 m

480 m

480 m

O	Fresh water source
●	Bathing place
═══	Road
∿	Stream
= = =	Foot trail
—×—	Barbed wire fence

0   10   20   30 m
scale approximate

Figure 5. Penetration road, Tebujo: Aparicio family lands

ground, and string barbed wire along the edge of the road to enclose a
section of pasture below the house.

Some Tebujo neighbors of the Rodríguez family, the Aparicio family, had built up their coffee holdings to about a thousand plants by the
time the mining people decided to construct the road; an operator
aimed his bulldozer to cut the road through the center of the coffee
patch. When Señor Aparicio put up strong resistance, the operator
detoured and left the coffee intact (Figure 5, feature A). But the dirt
pushed aside from the detour covered part of a small cemetery and
buried the Aparicio's fresh-water spring (Figure 5, feature B). A new
spring, just below the road, filled with muddy water with each rain; this
water supply lay about 20 minutes away. When the workmen removed
the Aparicio's fences (Figure 5, feature C), cattle roamed freely in the
cemetery and among the coffee trees, where they knocked off immature
beans.

The Aparicio family home and lands began at the edge of the large plain used by several Tebujo families for open grazing. With cattle wandering around, Señor Aparicio abandoned, at least for that season, his plans to plant bananas and plantains, both permanent crops, just below the road (Figure 5, feature D). Since he did not know whether the mining project intended to use the road, he thought it unwise to put his fences up again until the rainy season made the road impassable for vehicles. Although it became clear that the mining company had no intention of maintaining the road that year, rumors circulated that they would return in the following dry season. He feared that, even with fences to keep the cattle out, he would still have to contend with the bulldozers if he went ahead with his planting.

These examples from a mining project "study" of road engineering show some ways the mining project forced Guaymíes to react to changes over which they had no control. Rather than bringing "progress," the mining project brought greater complications to their daily lives. Despite the assertions of project planners that the road would benefit the Guaymíes, the Guaymíes recognized that no one took them and their interests into account; the planners built the road in their own interests only.

The Guaymíes of Tebujo had no legal grounds to resist the building of the road; the mining people had all the legal power. Although the road took only a small amount of land, the loss of arable land was critical; since the government regarded itself as legal owner of all indigenous lands, it paid no indemnification for land lost to the road, to say nothing of land lost to rumors and fears. The meager compensation payments made for loss of "improvements" added insult to injury; the official formula for payment had not been revised since 1965, and it was hopelessly outdated. CODEMIN, when challenged, made clear that the only choice for the Guaymíes was to accept or reject the payments offered; the amounts were not negotiable.[6] Inevitable bureaucratic delays in approving payments meant that affected Guaymíes did not receive money in time to buy food to replace what was lost; when families ran short of food, they looked for salaried work outside the Guaymí area.

No one provided them with straight answers about whether the mining company would return the following season to do more road-building; everyone heard rumors that they would be back for more "study." The rumors created further uncertainties; local Guaymíes were reluctant to use some other lands for fear that their work and their seeds would be wasted when the mining people returned.

Although a few young men spoke of taking up arms against the project, all were aware that the mining company, owned by the government, would have called in the National Guard to ensure that the project could proceed without any resistance on their part. Even had there been some doubt about the Guaymíes' legal standing, no one in the area had legal authority to take any action; by the time any legal procedure originated outside the area could have taken effect, the mining company, with its technology, would already have gotten its way. The local Guaymíes, with no comparable technology, could hardly have tried to block the movement of the bulldozers.

The people of Tebujo did not understand the purpose of building the road through their area. They were told it was a study—the same answer they received earlier when they asked what the survey crews were doing putting up stakes all through their area, marking the path later followed by the bulldozers. They wondered what kind of study was done with bulldozers instead of books, pencils, and paper. The only kind of study they understood was what their schoolchildren did with their lessons. When the company made no attempt to maintain the road, they were even more confused. Why build the road only to let it fall to pieces with the first rains? They felt they were being toyed with.

Nowhere along its the entire 44-kilometer journey through the Guaymí and campesino area did this road pass through unused lands; engineers would have been hard pressed to find a less destructive alternative route. No one could predict the precise impact of this (or any other) major technological industrial project. At times, apparently slight local harm masked more profound local or distant damage. In the context of Guaymí subsistence, what to engineers was an unimportant "short-term" negative impact sometimes translated into hunger, months of contaminated water supplies, and burdensome extra work for the local residents.

Other Cases: Further Encroachment

Long before the mining project put its road through Tebujo, the Guaymíes of upper Remedios District experienced their own powerlessness in the face of the intrusions of these powerful and radically foreign elements into their world. In 1970 the first workers from Canadian Javelin wandered up the Guaymí trails to set up their exploratory operation; they simply arrived and went to work, without ever seeking permission from the Guaymíes of the corregimiento of Hato Chamí.

Canadian Javelin undertook its work on a small scale. Until late in their stay, when they began the road from San Félix to Cerro Colorado, the Canadian Javelin people limited their activity to the immediate area of Cerro Colorado itself. Texasgulf, from its arrival in early 1976, considerably widened the scope of Cerro Colorado work—and its local impact—by upgrading and using the principal road, and by building the camp, with equipment storage and repair facilities, in Hato Chamí. Texasgulf also built several penetration roads as part of its research on different aspects of the mining project.

But to a visitor arriving for the first time after the Cerro Colorado infrastructure was already in place, the intrusions were difficult to perceive, for the changes showed up in subtle, ambiguous ways: in opportunistic responses to the possibility of more money from the sale of woven bags called *chácaras;* in hopes that Cerro Colorado would open new agricultural markets; in schools indebted to outsiders; and in mixed signals, rumors, and generalized anxiety about the future.[7]

For example, as in many places in the Guaymí area, some women of Hato Chamí had *chácaras* they wanted to sell. But around Hato Chamí, the prices for bargaining began several times higher than in other parts of the Guaymí area; women were ready to pass up the sale rather than come down to prices comparable to elsewhere. They were holding out for the return of "Mr. Williams," who once or twice had paid high prices for *chácaras.*[8]

Some Guaymíes complained that they could not afford *chácaras* because the women would no longer bargain. All Guaymí men and women used *chácaras* to carry everything or to store things in their homes. And Guaymíes delighted as much as anyone else in a richly designed, beautifully colored thread *chácara.* Mr. Williams might have enjoyed these interesting indigenous handicrafts, might have wished to give some money to poor Guaymí women, might have wanted to gain some good will. But the effect of his purchases was to create manufacturers' hopes of further windfalls and Guaymí consumers' resentment of high local prices.[9]

Some Guaymíes saw in the road and the mining company vehicles the opportunity to engage in agricultural production for the market in David, the capital of Chiriquí Province. One large family planted extra *yuca* (sweet manioc) on their farm lands. But they were unprepared to handle the complaints of family members who wanted free *yuca* or of neighbors who could not afford the prices of the David market. Transportation from the mining project, essential to the venture, was not subject to Guaymí control; when transportation was denied them, they ended up with an abundance of *yuca,* but no access to a market.

When CODEMIN's roving ethnologist brought in trucks to transport Guaymí coffee beans for marketing in western Chiriquí, at considerably higher prices than those paid in San Félix, Guaymíes with the possibility of getting their coffee to the mine road increased their production as much as possible. These marketing arrangements, never under Guaymí control, brought a host of added problems, complaints, and suspicions to the Guaymíes who took part in them. People waited for days when the ethnologist did not arrive with the trucks on the scheduled date; her scales reported lower weights than theirs; they had to return later, with more days of waiting, for her return with the payments; and many were paid less than they expected.

Some Guaymíes of upper San Félix District also engaged in production for market, but they integrated the new approaches with traditional Guaymí practices of distribution of excess production, and they produced for a Guaymí market at prices affordable to Guaymíes. Bort (1976), for example, described in detail how the owner of a small sugarcane mill in Cerro Otoe established his business, arranged for purchase of sugar cane, and adjusted what he understood of business and technical practices to what was acceptable to the people around him, working on different strategies to get and keep community support for his venture. His business did not depend on non-Guaymí elements for its success or failure.

The people of Cerro Otoe, who formed a cooperative store, arrived at their consensus decisions slowly, Guaymí-style. They collected money at the pace they could afford, and they bought materials for the construction of their co-op house in San Félix as money became available. The process took place at a snail's pace; but it remained a Guaymí process, established on a solid foundation. These Guaymíes made essential decisions in their own interests; when these interests conflicted with those of their neighbors, they looked at the wider interests and adjusted their own (Bort 1976). The changes introduced in the upper San Félix area tended to be the results of choices of individual Guaymíes or of Guaymí communities or families. Even though these changes came with a certain amount of tension, overall they remained under the control of the Guaymíes themselves.

In contrast, the basic impetus for changes in Hato Chamí came from outside, from the mining interests. Some Guaymíes capitalized on the new possibilities; but they always depended on elements outside their control. The process had its ambiguities and created more tension and conflict than was the case in the upper San Félix area.

Many Guaymí caseríos wanted a school. Usually someone took the lead in promoting it at the local level, gaining the support of others in the community, making contact with appropriate government authorities, and so on; community involvement in the project of getting a school often provided the occasion for the discovery of new methods of community organization. Once an official school was established, the assigned teachers usually worked with the community to obtain government appropriations for a permanent building and better facilities. In Hato Chamí, thanks to the mining project's access road, a new, well-constructed school came easily. The appropriate government agencies transported the materials and work crews necessary to give the people a major school and, later, a small health center.[10] Guaymí parents supported the school, but various complaints seemed to indicate a feeling (vague, to be sure) that the school was not theirs. Rather, it was much more the work of the latina principal.

In contrast, concerned parents of Cerro Otoe and Hato Pilón, encouraged and sometimes cajoled by the teachers, gave schools to their children. The schools provided some focus for organization and unity in the community. Community members transported on their backs or on horseback the building and school materials—cinder blocks, bags of cement, sheets of corrugated roofing material, school desks—several hours up the mountain trails from San Félix.[11] In Hato Pilón, a local committee worked with the elected representative to hire a Guaymí with some training in masonry to build the school. The parents' organization provided the only instance of meetings that attracted people from different factions of the local conflicts of Hato Pilón.

But in Hato Chamí, the school did not occasion community organization. The principal and the Guaymí-elected representative did not get along well. She considered the school part of the realization of her dream of bringing to the Guaymí area the "progress" she proudly proclaimed she favored.[12] She analyzed her problems and disagreements with the representative as stemming from his being a traditionalist follower of the Chiriquí cacique, and thus opposed to progress.

For his part, the representative had earlier worked to organize a bilingual school with volunteer Guaymí teachers in Hato Chamí, about the time the principal arrived to start the government school.[13] The representative, still something of a Mama Chi traditionalist, had been less than an enthusiastic supporter of the establishment of the government school. But it seems likely that his problems had less to do with being "anti-progress" than with his (correct) perception that the school, established under the principal's control and at her instigation, was not in fact a community project, and was a challenge to his growing authority in the community. In addition, the representative had been pressured to cede the land for the school from his family lands in Hato Chamí, without any participation in the decisions and without any recognition of his disputed land claims in the caserío (e.g., his rights over some of the lands occupied by people moving their houses to be nearer the school).[14]

The Hato Chamí school did not help the community organize itself. The principal and the other teachers, to an even greater extent than their counterparts of Hato Pilón and Cerro Otoe, dominated the parents' club. They controlled the agenda for meetings, then privately complained about the low level of parental interest. They made little effort to actively involve the parents in considering the various aspects of life in the Hato Chamí area as these impinged upon the education of their children. Most meetings dealt with narrow school topics such as parent participation in teacher-organized civic presentations by the students, fund-raising for specific school purposes, or the distribution of remaining U.S. Agency for International Development products at the end of the school year. Although three of the five teachers were themselves Guaymíes, there was no discussion of putting together a pilot project for bilingual education.

But the school did occasion the expansion of the caserío of Hato Chamí; several families built second homes near the mine road and the school to shorten their children's travel time. Concentration of houses in some Guaymí communities responded to the urging of Guaymí leaders like the Chiriquí cacique. But in Hato Chamí, agglutination came about from individual family decisions to take advantage of government- and mine-sponsored initiatives. Such initiatives, however, were commonly responses to non-Guaymí interests rather than those of the Guaymíes.[15] In the absence of community consensus for building up the caserío of Hato Chamí, those with claims on the lands occupied by new houses expressed apprehension that the new residents would soon take even more land for pastures and local gardens, once they tired of the frequent treks back and forth to their caseríos of origin to check on their animals and to bring back food. Those with older local land claims resented these infringements, but seemed powerless to do anything about them in the face of CODEMIN urging of expansion and agglutination of settlements as a means of better delivery of services.[16]

Rumors and the Sense of Powerlessness

Constant rumors among the Guaymíes accompanied the activities and presence of the mining operation. These rumors increased the residents' levels of anxiety. Representatives from CODEMIN tried to dispel the rumors, but only fed the growing Guaymí sense of incompetence and powerlessness. For example, throughout the period 1978–80, rumors flew back and forth about the impending relocation of Guaymí communities—Hato Rincón was slated to be the dumping ground for the overburden from Cerro Colorado; the area from Hato Chamí to Boca del Monte would be the likely site of housing and other facilities for the 3,500 or more workers of the construction period; Escopeta would become the principal industrial area, the site of the concentrator and the stockpile for the ore awaiting processing; Cerro Laguna would be flooded by the damming of the Cuvíbora River. Communities along the San Félix River would be lost if the river's course had been changed to move concentrator tailings to the Pacific. Other communities would be in the way of new roads or other facilities. The rumors in the Guaymí area gained strength with the frequent government announcements, during the same period, that the decision to proceed with the mining project was imminent.

Hato Rincón sat alongside the Hato Chamí–Escopeta road, below the Hato Chamí–Cerro Colorado road, about a 20–30 minute walk south of Escopeta and perhaps an hour or so north of Hato Chamí (see

Figure 3 in Chapter 1). Although, ominously, the design for the mine included the use of Hato Rincón as the waste dump for Cerro Colorado overburden, the residents received mixed signals about their future from the mining enterprise. They had heard they had to move, but nevertheless personnel of the mining project helped them build their community's cinder-block school. No one could imagine putting a permanent school, so rare in the Guaymí area, in a community that would be destroyed. The residents believed that mining personnel would not have played such an active role in the school's construction if they knew that it would only be wiped out along with the community itself.[17]

The people of Hato Rincón worried about where they would go, what lands they would farm, how they would keep in contact with their extended families. They knew, as did all Guaymíes, that there were no free lands anywhere near Hato Rincón. They also knew what various mine and government officials said about the Guaymí area. Some officials, speaking to latino or foreign audiences, emphasized that the area to be affected was unusable by humans, and in any case was virtually uninhabited. CODEMIN president Rodrigo González gestured across the horizon as he assured journalists, taken to Escopeta to see the dimensions of the project, that they could see for themselves that no one lived there; he was standing about 200 meters from a little cluster of Guaymí houses, hidden behind some trees. President Aristides Royo told a foreign journalist that no one lived within a radius of 30 kilometers of Cerro Colorado (FT 1979); such a radius in fact included all the nearby latino towns on the Pacific Coast as well as thousands of Guaymíes on both sides of the Cordillera. These statements, widely quoted on radio shows, found their way back to the Guaymíes, who had good reason to fear that these people believed their own statements that relocation would be no problem.

Whenever possible, they asked mine and CODEMIN people about their relocation. CODEMIN personnel said that such matters were still under study, that any relocation would include new and better houses, and that CODEMIN and the government could be relied upon to compensate any Guaymí losses and, in general, to take care of Guaymí interests in these matters. The people of Hato Rincón, talking among themselves, often said:

> Houses are fine, but we can't eat houses. Money is fine; but in no
> time, it's gone. We need land. Land never goes away. You can't

plant money. You can't grow money. You can't eat money. Only
land assures us of food.

Other communities heard similar rumors about what would happen to
them; their responses were similar to those of the people of Hato
Rincón.[18] In the CODEMIN-sponsored seminar of December 1978,
Guaymíes raised questions about the communities already affected.
CODEMIN personnel skirted the questions, repeating the assurances
that the government of General Torrijos would never go back on its
concern for the indigenous people of Panama.

Within this climate of growing unease and uncertainty, any incident took on great significance for the Guaymíes. A couple of members
of the National Guard, stationed at Escopeta, became involved with a
couple of Guaymí women. Although the circumstances seemed unclear,
many Guaymíes were incensed.[19] Guaymí men insisted that Guaymíes
should only live with Guaymíes.[20] People voiced concern for the importance of preserving this value; Guaymíes saw the whole affair as the
introduction of prostitution into their area. News about this incident
travelled fast through much of the area, both north and south of Cerro
Colorado, provoking comments, jokes, criticism, and, along with everything else, fear.

When Guaymí leaders met with project sponsors in the
CODEMIN seminar held in Hato Chamí and Cuernavaca in December
of 1978, they repeatedly voiced their fears that the Cerro Colorado
project would bring prostitution into their area. Guaymí men saw their
women as almost powerless in the face of the blandishments of latino
men offering them money, food, and other things not readily obtain-
able locally. Arguing from their experience in latino towns, they found
the mixture of an all-male work force and alcohol to be even more
threatening.[21] Project sponsors insisted that no such problems would
occur. Rules barring alcohol and barring relationships between mine
employees and Guaymí women would be enforced strictly. But the
sponsors did not say what the Guaymíes most wanted to hear—that no
men from the outside would be living in the Guaymí area—so the
Guaymíes remained unconvinced about CODEMIN assurances.[22]

Changes brought about in Hato Chamí (and, in general, in upper
Remedios District), even changes that benefited people, came about
more in response to initiatives taken by the government and mining
project than as a result of Guaymí efforts, planning, and consensus. As a

result, the people lost important elements of a sense of control of their lives and world. Those who thought themselves victimized by some of the changes had little motivation to try to resolve their conflicts and tensions with their neighbors. Instead of aiding in organizing and unifying Guaymí groups at the local level, many of the changes increased divisions and tensions in Guaymí communities.

The rumors contributed to the perception that the Guaymíes were powerless over major aspects of their lives if the mining project went forward. They were anxious over the possibility of being told where to live and where to farm; they were apprehensive over the prospect of being invaded and enticed into prostitution. The project sponsors, who seemed to make light of Guaymí concerns, gave responses that only increased Guaymí anxiety while underlining the perception of Guaymí incompetence or powerlessness. The Guaymíes had no experience that enabled them to understand the scope of the mining project; their inexperience contributed to their powerlessness.[23]

Co-opting Local Leadership

The elected representative of Hato Chamí was an astute Guaymí leader in local matters; but he was completely out of his element concerning the mining project. He became convinced that he had the ear of the appropriate people of CODEMIN, of the joint operating company, of the National Guard, and of the government; he thought he could personally resolve any problems brought about by the mining project. He saw himself both as the highest local official of the national government—a questionable perception in the best of cases—and as the local authority of the cacique.

The way different officials curried his favor contributed to his exaggerated belief in his own power. The representative had risen to some local prominence as the jefe inmediato of the Chiriquí cacique; with the cacique's backing and with active campaign help from CODEMIN's ethnologist, he ran for office and was elected representative in 1978.[24] The ethnologist, as godmother, arranged for the arrival, by helicopter, of a National Guard colonel to be godfather for the baptism of one of the representative's children.[25] The representative expected that his *compadre* (literally "cofather," the godfather of his child), the colonel, was going to provide him with materials to build a good house of concrete blocks and a metal roof; and he often asserted he could solve this or that problem simply by getting in touch with his *comadre* ("comother," the godmother of his child), the ethnologist from CODEMIN.

The representative thought his authority even extended to the mining project. David Ruiz Williams, vice president (and local head) of Texasgulf Panama, called on him several times in the course of visits to the mine area; the representative referred to Williams as a personal friend. The representative claimed special privileges from the joint operating company, which he thought obliged to bring a bulldozer to level the area where he wanted to build his new house, as well as to transport him to and from Hato Chamí, along with merchandise for the little store he started (using some of his $300 per month salary as elected representative), whenever he wanted a ride.

But events indicated that he had little power; most of what he believed he had been promised did not take place. He used his own money to buy materials for the construction of his new house; his *compadre* added a few sheets of roofing material. The mining company finally sent a bulldozer to level the land, but when he was unsatisfied with their work, they refused to do it over. He often had to make excuses when his *comadre* did not show up for meetings he had scheduled with her and members of the community; eventually, he began to complain about her behavior.

The mining company did provide him with rides to and from Hato Chamí, contrary to their established policies. But he spent many hours waiting impatiently for the next vehicle, grumbling that they were supposed to provide him with rides immediately upon demand. Late one night he arrived drunk at the guard house beside the bridge, outside San Félix, and belligerently threatened the watchman; the mining company cancelled his rides altogether.

When rumors persisted that the mining company wanted to build another road, the representative insisted that he could stop them if he chose, simply by telling them that he and the community had decided that the existing roads were sufficient for their purposes. Following numerous complaints about damages from mine-related work, representatives of the joint operating company and of CODEMIN established with him a commission of Guaymíes who would be informed beforehand of plans for new construction that would affect any Guaymíes. The commission was to survey the terrain to foresee local damage, discuss the matter with the Guaymíes concerned, and reach prior preliminary agreements concerning compensation.

Early in 1980, shortly after the commission was established, Texasgulf did not notify this commission when the mining company began construction of the test road from Hato Chamí to Nancito (discussed in the Tebujo examples above); the snarl of tractor motors provided the first warnings of the invasion. One Guaymí commissioner went along a few days behind the tractors, talking with people who had lost crops or otherwise suffered damages; for his efforts, he earned the criticism of the people affected and the accusation that he was just another employee of CODEMIN.

Constraints on Guaymí Perceptions

The Guaymíes measured the project in terms of their own reality as they sought to decipher what went on and how it mattered to them. People of the caserío of Cerro Laguna, about 45 minutes' walk south of Hato Chamí along the Cuvíbora River, heard rumors that the mine intended to dam the river just below them (Figure 3). They heard that the backed-up waters would flood the plain where they lived and farmed, and that they would have to be relocated. But they saw no reason to dam the river. After all, they reasoned, the mine already had a good road to the river (a single-lane road built to facilitate hydrology tests), and the mine had trucks. They thought the mine could haul all the water needed from the river to the mine area. Their reasoning mechanized their own process of providing water for household needs. They could not imagine that the mine might require all the water available from the entire river.

CODEMIN personnel—their ethnologist was, for a while, a frequent visitor—told the people of Cerro Laguna that the whole matter was under study, that there was as yet no plan to dam the river and flood their area, and that in any case CODEMIN would provide them with everything they needed in the event of relocation.[26]

A basic difference between the Guaymíes of upper Remedios District and those of upper San Félix District provided a measure of geographic variation in the Guaymí response to the project. Residents of the mine area (upper Remedios District) were more likely to exhibit behavior usually shown only by Guaymíes in latino towns rather than by Guaymíes on their own turf. On their own turf, the Guaymíes were ordinary, competent people—alert, attentive, knowing what they were doing and how to do it. They bantered back and forth with each other and with outsiders they came to trust. They laughed and carried on like anyone else. They got angry with each other and showed it in a variety of ways. Their show of affection and concern for their children was noted by any outsider who spent much time with them on their own terms; mothers, fathers, other adult relatives, and older siblings often played with the infants, carried them around, consoled them, and took good care of them. When they had problems, they knew what resources were available and how well those resources were likely to work. They knew when and where to plant, and when to harvest. They knew how to get from here to there. They had remedies to try when someone became ill. They knew how to relax with each other, how to be sociable, and how to visit.

In the towns, Guaymíes were more likely to look out of place and incompetent—the latinos' stereotypical "dumb Indians." Women tended to group around the entrance to a store, peering in while the men shopped. When the women went in with the men, they tended to trail them, occasionally speaking quietly in Ngawbere about some item or other, their faces impassive. If someone complimented them on their children or their clothing, they seemed not to hear. Parents showed little affection for their children in the presence of latinos, tending only to correct them when needed. While the men were somewhat more responsive in latino settings, they shared such basic behavior with the women. Latinos might insult them with derogatory comments in their hearing; some latino men laughed as they commented on the good fortune of Guaymí men who had several wives, could have sex all day and all night, and never had to do any work. The Guaymíes would not acknowledge that they had heard.[27]

In the mine area, the Guaymíes were more likely to exhibit similar behavior—not all the time, of course, but when around people from or facilities of the mining project. Sometimes mothers and their children, looking all poor and bedraggled, begged for food outside the kitchen of the Hato Chamí camp. The cook, obliged by policy to throw out extra food, felt guilty and angry; he complained that the Guaymíes were lazy, looking only for handouts.[28] Sometimes little groups of Guaymíes gathered at the door of the building that housed the workers' television set, trying to catch occasional glimpses. They sat or stood passively watching dominos or ping-pong, just like the Guaymíes who gathered around the door of the latino stores in San Félix. The workers occasionally made derogatory remarks, but no one responded.

The mining project, with its varied messages of Guaymí powerlessness, brought forth the Guaymí passivity and seeming incompetence that was frequently manifest in Guaymí dealings with latinos on latino turf. But now it was not on latino turf, but on the Guaymíes' own turf. It seemed that the Guaymíes accepted the messages that they were incompetent and powerless.

The underlying Guaymí experience with the mining project demonstrated the root powerlessness from which the above instances took on reality. Legally, the Guaymíes had no rights. From the arrival of Canadian Javelin, no one asked any Guaymí permission for anything to do with the mining project. If any Guaymí complained, the project sponsors had only to refer to their legal rights to do what they saw necessary anywhere in the concession area.[29]

Aside from legally backed power, the project sponsors also demonstrated another kind of power against which the Guaymíes had nothing to compare: the power of industrial technology. The very ease with which the mining project effected major alterations in the landscape had to call into question Guaymí perceptions of the stability of the very world in which they lived; what had always been stable and fixed in their universe was no longer so. No one had ever before put a major road into the Guaymí area; no one had ever before demonstrated to them that the mechanization which many of them knew from work outside their territory could also take place within their territory—that hills could be leveled, a small town could be built, and that the landscape itself could be radically altered.

Without warning, tractors arrived, narrowly skirting Guaymí homes and passing through pastures and cultivated lands, ruining water supplies and doing damage that the Guaymíes could not have done with their largest work party; fifteen minutes of bulldozing created fifteen days of makeshift repair work for the people affected. In Hato Chamí, almost overnight bulldozers leveled the hilly area occupied by a family and construction workers put up the buildings—an instant modern small town. From the mining company's unpublicized (and later denied) decision to test the carrying capacity of the San Félix River, for weeks the waters of the river ran muddy during the dry season along their entire course, from origin to Pacific Ocean, a feat otherwise accomplished only by the intense rains of the height of the wet season; because of the project, not even the seasons were set.

All this technological power merely supported a study for a project whose real beginning would have brought the complete destruction of one major river (the San Félix), the damming and diversion of another (the Cuvíbora), and the leveling of one of the larger mountains in the Guaymí area. Backed by their power, the sponsors casually discussed using all the water from major rivers and cutting away the top half of Cerro Colorado itself to create an open-pit mine. If the Guaymíes doubted the possibility of such a future, they needed only reflect on the smaller changes to nature that they had already witnessed.

Summary—Powerless to Manage One's Own Life

The preceding discussion of the impact of the mining project shows how the work of a small number of mining people brought about changes in Guaymí life, outlook, and approaches. While some of the changes might have brought benefits to individual Guaymíes, the basic impetus for change came from outside, served other interests, and excluded consultation with the people affected. From the mining project, the Guaymíes received an underlying message: they were powerless to improve their own lives, or even to know what improvements were needed. In contrast, the changes introduced in the upper San Félix area resulted from choices of individuals, families, or communities. Even when these changes came with a certain amount of tension, they remained under the control of the Guaymíes themselves. The underlying message was one of the ability (power) of local people to improve their own lives.

The Guaymíes were powerless to comprehend the scope and significance of the mining project; they could only measure it through their own reality. Project sponsors abetted the miscomprehension of the reality, as in the case of the elected representative's exaggerated sense of his own authority. Explanations offered to the Guaymíes were partial, self-serving, misleading, and accompanied by the message that others would take care of everything, so the Guaymíes ought not to worry.

The movement of the mining project kept challenging the Guaymí understanding of things, bringing more confusion.

The activities and presence of the mining operation were accompanied by constant rumors that contributed to the Guaymí perception that they were powerless over major aspects of their lives if the mining project went forward. They were anxious about the possibility of being told where to live and where to farm; they were apprehensive over the prospects of being invaded and enticed into prostitution.

They knew that the government did not understand Guaymí life. The project sponsors, who seemed to make light of Guaymí concerns, failed to dispel the rumors or calm the anxieties; as before, the message to the Guaymíes was always that others knew everything important, would make all the decisions, and would take good care of the Guaymíes.

All these areas of powerlessness were founded in the reality of the mining project itself, one which brought into the Guaymí area a totally alien world, a world in which others had all the power and competence, the Guaymíes little or none. The underlying Guaymí powerlessness was in contrast to the power of people who legally had all the rights, and who technologically had the power to radically alter the landscape and even nature itself.

CHAPTER 8

Early Guaymí Opposition
to Cerro Colorado

While the opponents of the government launched their attacks on the mining project, the Guaymíes did not (in the phrase of one of them) "sit back and wait for the bulldozers to run over them." Tentatively at first, then more openly, then quite vociferously, they mounted their own opposition to the Cerro Colorado and Teribe-Changuinola projects; with the collaboration of non-Guaymí allies, the Guaymíes worked to organize themselves, to demand that they and their interests be taken into account in the planning for Cerro Colorado. Unable or unwilling to believe that the Guaymíes could mount a response in their own interests, the sponsors accused "outside agitators" of creating problems among the Guaymíes; but the attitudes and activities of the sponsors themselves made the greatest contribution to raising Guaymí consciousness about the effects of the projects and the outside interests being served.

This discussion of Guaymí responses focuses on the movements that opposed these projects. The clarity of this discussion is possible only after the fact, and only then by leaving out some of the complexities. Among the 50,000 or more Guaymíes, there were people who knew virtually nothing about the project and who cared very little about what happened; there were others who supported the mining project, and still others who thought the whole question too complex for them to sort out.[1] Some people's views changed several times: Guaymíes who at one time or in some circumstances supported the project, or at least saw advantages to its development, at another time or under other circumstances opposed it; people who at one time professed ignorance of and indifference to the mining project, at another time took part in congresses and voted unanimously against it.

All this may seem confusing and filled with contradictions, but confusion and contradictions were two of the major effects of the intrusion of the projects into the Guaymí area. The Guaymí people, with limited resources and very little experience to help them, had to struggle with the significance of these projects for their lives. For an abjectly poor people, part of this struggle was the attempt to evaluate ways in which individuals, families, and communities might profit from the presence of the mining operation. While people were concerned with long-term possibilities and effects, of necessity they looked also to short-term consequences; as a result, many Guaymíes who had serious objections to the project and no confidence at all in its long-range benefits for them, only too readily took any job that the mining company offered them. Despite possible misgivings, they had to eat, and they had to feed their children.

THE BEGINNING OF GUAYMÍ OPPOSITION

The Suitche Incident

In mid-1978, in Suitche, an isolated Guaymí community of upper Bocas del Toro Province just over the Continental Divide from Cerro Colorado, trouble broke out. Some community members destroyed equipment that had been placed in the river by project hydrologists to test its suitability as a water source for the mine. The community feared that the mining project would disrupt their lives. CODEMIN dispatched the head of its Department of Social Development to solve the problems. In negotiations with Cacique José Mónico Cruz and with local leaders, the CODEMIN representative promised scholarships to an agricultural school for several young men of the community, help with seeds and fertilizer, and assistance in obtaining materials for a school and a health center; in exchange, the community allowed hydrologists to install new measuring devices. All of this was carried out with minimum publicity. CODEMIN's rapid response to the community's opposition may have indicated that the project sponsors felt vulnerable to Guaymí discontent; the company moved quickly to buy the community's good will with a demonstration that the mining project was beneficial. The community profited, albeit briefly.[2]

Hato Chamí Seminar

In Panama City, during the meetings of the National Assembly in October 1978, CODEMIN presented to Guaymí elected representatives and other Guaymí leaders its vision of the mining project and its benefits. Several of these leaders visited CODEMIN offices; in different ways, they informed CODEMIN of their discontent with the lack of information and discussion concerning the impact of the project. Under pressure from these Guaymíes, CODEMIN organized a one-day seminar for Guaymí leaders, held in December 1978 in the empty Cuernavaca camp; the company provided transportation, and food and lodging in the Hato Chamí camp, for the Guaymí participants. CODEMIN's representation included all its major officials: the president (also president of the joint operating company), the general manager, the technical manager, the head of the Department of Social Development, and other staff and consultants. Even General Torrijos was on hand.[3]

CODEMIN, although it advertised the seminar as a dialogue, filled the agenda with presentations on the benefits of the mining project for Panama's and the Guaymíes' future, the latter guaranteed by the oft-mentioned ways that the Torrijos Revolution had always taken care of the Guaymíes. Little time was allotted for questions. CODEMIN did not come to discuss and negotiate with the one hundred or so Guaymíes present; at no point did CODEMIN ask the Guaymíes to indicate their concerns. CODEMIN asked the Guaymíes to decide only one matter related to the mining project: whether the Guaymíes hired for construction work would prefer to live in the same camp with latinos, or would want a separate camp for Guaymíes only. No choice was offered about having these settlements in the Guaymí area.

The evening before the seminar, most of the Guaymí participants met until late into the night in the Hato Chamí dining room, working to establish common criteria for the next day's discussions. A number of those present argued that the meeting had come about because of Guaymí pressure; they insisted that the Guaymíes should take over the seminar with their own agenda. But the Guaymíes reached no consensus. Some said that they owed it to CODEMIN to listen to what it had to say, since the Guaymíes had too little information on which to base a position; others, recounting various instances of damage inflicted on local communities, urged outright opposition to the project. Although they failed to unite around one approach, they brought to the fore enough problems and questions that most agreed they had to force CODEMIN to alter the agenda. Some of the arguments of that night reappeared months later as elements of a Guaymí position on the projects.

In the following day's meeting, the Guaymíes forced CODEMIN to hear their concerns. They repeatedly voiced fears that the 3,500 latino men who would come to build Cerro Colorado would bring drugs, alcohol, and prostitution into their area. They requested specifics on promises of jobs, improved health care, and markets for their crops. They worried about the rumored relocation of communities. They wondered about government plans with respect to their comarca. And they opened the topic of direct Guaymí participation in the revenues of the project.

CODEMIN's vague responses repeated earlier promises of benefits or stated that some of these matters were under study and could not yet be discussed. CODEMIN insisted that everything was under control, that there would be no problems, and that the Guaymíes should trust them. After all, this was the government that uniquely in Panama's history had shown its concern for indigenous people; it had only their interests at heart. CODEMIN's approach was at the same time patronizing and adversarial; its officials did not seem to grasp that Guaymí repetition of the same questions and concerns throughout the course of the day meant that they did not find CODEMIN's responses credible. General Torrijos, seated in the audience for part of the meeting, suddenly walked out, muttering under his breath; the Guaymíes laughed later, saying that he was angry over their continued distrust of CODEMIN, distrust which he took personally.

CODEMIN had sponsored this seminar in hopes of gaining Guaymí endorsement for Cerro Colorado. Ironically, the significant outcome of the meeting was that CODEMIN presented to the Guaymíes their first opportunity to meet among themselves and discuss their concerns about the mining project. The Guaymíes began to appreciate the size and scope of the project, and to recognize that what they saw around them was only a faint glimpse of what was to come; even so, they heard many local people talk about the disruptions already suffered. They pooled their rumors and concerns about the future. On the other side, CODEMIN's evasive replies fueled the very concerns they sought to allay; the calls for loyalty to a government that took care of the people reminded the Guaymíes of years of promises without action on their comarca.

OPEN GUAYMI OPPOSITION

The Cerro Colorado mining project continued to dominate national news in Panama through much of 1979; the Roman Catholic hierarchy entered the public discussion with two publications, one on the specific concerns of the Guaymíes (Núñez y Consejo 1979) and one on the national concerns raised by the project (CEP 1979).[4] In the Guaymí area, more and more individuals and communities became concerned. Communities held meetings, and some Guaymí leaders discussed aspects of the project in Panama City, seeking information and trying to determine its advantages and disadvantages.

The Canquintú Congress

To increase grassroots participation in the formulation of specific proposals for the comarca and the carta orgánica, Guaymí leaders organized the First General Guaymí Congress, scheduled for September 18–21, 1979, in Canquintú, a large Guaymí settlement of Bocas del Toro. Although the congress agenda emphasized the comarca and carta orgánica, the organizers also included the Cerro Colorado mining project and the Teribe-Changuinola hydroelectric project. With this congress, the growing Guaymí opposition to Cerro Colorado came into the open.

To prepare themselves for the congress' discussion of these projects, some communities held special meetings. In the Remedios corregimiento of Cerro Iglesias, four communities (Cerro Balsa, Quebrada

Guabo, Cerro Iglesias Cabecera, and Orema) united to hold a series of meetings to discuss Cerro Colorado. They recounted their experiences when the mining companies arrived in the early 1970s, what had happened with the building of the road through their corregimiento, what the prospects for getting jobs had been, and what it seemed the future would hold for them. They noted that the project sponsors, who had never consulted with them, still showed no signs of considering them important in the planning of the project. They recognized that no Guaymíes learned to operate vehicles or to do mechanical work; the company hired them only to clear brush with machetes, to carry things on their backs or, in a couple of cases, to sweep floors or help the cooks in the camps. Seven hundred people signed a letter, read at the congress of Canquintú, protesting the likely destruction of the San Félix River and expressing their concern that the project was located not in an unpopulated area, as the sponsors claimed, but "in the midst of a number of communities and inhabitants, that is, Cerro Colorado is in the heart of the Guaymí Comarca." They concluded their letter:

> Not only for these reasons do we reject the exploitation of Cerro Colorado, but also [because of] many other problems and injustices that the mining corporation has committed.[5] (Congresos Guaymíes 1980:93)

Cacique José Mónico Cruz and his Bocas del Toro supporters, hosts of the congress, were the principals among the many people who worked on the organization of the Canquintú congress. A couple of months before the congress, the cacique, with Ricardo Smith and Miguel Cruz, two of his Panama City collaborators, asked CEASPA to assist the Guaymíes in the preparation of a background document on the likely effects on the Guaymíes of the mining project; the document would be distributed and discussed during the Canquintú congress. They wanted Guaymí participation in the preparation of the document; they wanted also to take advantage of the work done by sympathetic non-Guaymíes concerning the project.[6]

CEASPA met with Mónico and his advisors, in Changuinola and in Panama City, to clarify Guaymí concerns regarding the projects and to find out specifically what they wanted the document to do. The Guaymíes did not want CEASPA to recommend a stance for them with respect to the projects. Rather, they wanted a solid analysis of the project from the point of view of their concerns and misgivings, so that they could discuss and decide their posture among themselves.[7] Smith and Cruz worked on all the drafts of the document; the cacique and the other advisors discussed the document in detail as it was written.

This document summarized the mining project, discussed its potential impact in the areas of Guaymí economy, ecology and health, culture and society, and politics and legal standing; it then offered brief conclusions from the analyses presented. Several appendices listed ways in which different communities might be affected by the project; it named the communities that lay within the concession area, and it included texts from the Panamanian constitution of 1972, the Mineral Code, and the contracts with Texasgulf.

Since the Guaymíes had little image of a major mining project, the team working on the document decided to complement it with a slide and tape show, to be given its premiere at the congress and then to be reproduced and made available for Guaymí community meetings.[8] The slides included a variety of views of Guaymí life, reproductions from magazines to show large-scale mining and its equipment, and pictures of different aspects of the Cerro Colorado project itself. The text, taped in Spanish and Ngawbere, discussed the main areas of impact of the mining project, raising a series of questions for discussion among the Guaymíes.

The residents of Canquintú built a special meeting place for the congress, a large area of rough benches covered by a tin roof. The local priests wired the hall to hook up lighting, for night sessions, powered by Canquintú's diesel generators; meetings went late into the night, with breaks for meals. People wandered in and out as they wished. The atmosphere in general was happy; rarely did so many Guaymíes gather in one place.[9] The Guaymíes welcomed a number of observers who arrived for the congress; the non-Guaymíes included people who worked with the Guaymíes of Changuinola and several priests from Tolé, Remedios, and Canquintú, all of them invited by delegates.

The meeting opened with the election of the officers responsible for running the congress; although the overwhelming majority of delegates were from Bocas del Toro, the people elected officers from each of the three provinces (Bocas del Toro, Chiriquí, and Veraguas). Ricardo Smith and Miguel Cruz, the associates of Cacique Mónico who had worked on the document analyzing the mining and hydroelectric projects, emerged as president and secretary, respectively. Martín Manteca, a Chiriquí Guaymí whose political loyalties were more ambivalent, was named vice-president. Then the congress approved its agenda and began a lengthy discussion, point by point, of the draft proposals for the carta orgánica and for the law to delimit the comarca. For the most part, as business progressed, it included extensive readings and repetitions of prepared documents, translations into Ngawbere and Sabanero (the language of the Guaymíes from Veraguas), and discussions of the significance of and alternatives to the proposals.

Knowing that the mining project was on the agenda, CODEMIN sent members from the Department of Social Development: León Palacios, its principal fieldworker; Marcelo Bruno, a Guaymí; and a latina social worker (the latter two from its Panama City offices). Palacios and Bruno, working closely with Manteca and another Guaymí, Federico Santos,[10] soon discovered that the basis for the discussion of the project would be a document that they had never seen. They were thwarted when they tried to get an advance copy; Smith, Cruz, and others responsible for the document kept all copies until the congress decided whether it wanted the document or not.

The CODEMIN people pressured the congress principals, especially Smith, to put a presentation by Palacios on the agenda, to explain the mining project to the congress. In private, they made two arguments: that the congress ought not discuss the mining project because there had been insufficient preparation; and that CODEMIN be invited to address the congress, in order to provide the needed preparation. They maintained that whatever the mysterious Guaymí document said, it could not be a sufficient basis for the important deliberations of the congress; the congress could not possibly discuss the project without prior input from CODEMIN, the government agency responsible for it. Smith, with support from Cruz, held out; he said they could not address the congress unless the congress decided to hear them.

Late in the afternoon of the final full day of the congress, the officers proposed the discussion of Cerro Colorado. They announced that a Guaymí commission mandated by the Bocas del Toro cacique, with technical assistance, had prepared a document; did the congress delegates want to discuss the document? Many speakers expressed satisfaction that Guaymíes had prepared a study of the mining project; they appreciated the prospect of a discussion that depended on their own resources instead of one dominated by other interests. The people were curious to see the document.

Very smoothly, Manteca represented CODEMIN. He argued that, since no one had seen the "Guaymí" document, it was impossible to determine whether it could provide an adequate foundation for the consideration of such an important issue. He continued by observing that the congress was honored by the presence of representatives of CODEMIN, who would be happy to take part in a full and open discussion of Cerro Colorado, and he announced that these representatives had brought their own document.[11] Who better, he added, could explain the project to the Guaymíes? If CODEMIN were not heard first, then the discussion could hardly be called open and free.

Although the topic on the floor of the congress was how to proceed, many delegates spoke about their experiences of and concerns with the projects themselves. When Manteca or his companions objected that the remarks were out of order, Smith, an excellent debater, noted that the discussion fit Manteca's agenda: the testimony of the delegates demonstrated that the Guaymíes could discuss the projects without prior input from the project sponsors. People talked about losses of lands for agriculture, about dirty water, about inadequate compensation for damages, about rumors of relocation, and about fears of "vices" imported by latino workers. Someone read the letter from 700 people of the corregimiento of Cerro Iglesias in Remedios and another letter from a group in Tolé; these readings included the request that the congress of Canquintú go on record opposing the projects. The delegation from Valle de Riscó managed to present most of its case against the hydroelectric project. Guaymí women usually did not actively participate at meetings, but sat listening in silence; however, several women spoke out, receiving ovations from the congress. In all the specific discussion about the projects, only Manteca and his companions found anything positive to say.

As the discussion proceeded, it was clear to everyone that the sentiment of the delegates was to move to the reading and discussion of what was now being called "the Guaymí document." But Manteca and two or three others kept the congress tied up in procedural matters until they broke for a late supper. During the break, CODEMIN again pressured Smith, this time arguing that they should be allowed to show their slides, since the other slide show was scheduled. Alone against Palacios, Bruno, Manteca and Santos, Smith could not hold out; he said they could present their slide show. Palacios then assumed that his could precede the Guaymí slide show. However, just before the congress reconvened, hurried discussions with Smith brought a change that would turn out to be decisive: the Guaymí slide show would be presented ahead of CODEMIN's. When the delegates returned from supper, Manteca picked up where he had left off. By now it was after 9:00 p.m.; the delegates decided to view the slide shows, then return to the earlier discussion.[12]

The Guaymí slide show went first. People who had wandered off, hurriedly returned; the meeting area was never so crowded as that night. People delighted to see pictures of themselves and their neighbors; many could recognize the Guaymíes on the screen. The taped commentary, in Spanish and Ngawbere, brought further approval. Throughout the half-hour presentation, the meeting area was alive with the murmurings of the viewers. When the show ended, many wanted to see it again, immediately.

After some delay to set things up, Palacios and Bruno took over with CODEMIN's presentation. Palacios had brought a couple of dozen slides, ordinarily used in presentations to local business groups around the country. Denied permission to explain the project to the delegates, Palacios used the slide show to achieve his purpose. On the opening slide alone, a title slide saying "Cerro Colorado and the Future of Panama," he spoke for nearly half an hour, pausing after every sentence or so for Bruno to translate. He had no slides of Guaymíes and no slides of the Guaymí area, but only slides of graphs, mock-ups of the project, maps, and actual installations.

Having started around 10:00 p.m., Palacios did not conclude his presentation until around 1:30 a.m. Shortly into his presentation, people began talking with each other. But the tone around the area was very different from the tone during the earlier show; people chatted in normal voices about things that had nothing to do with the presentation. People fell asleep or left; by the end, the meeting area was half-empty.

When Palacios finally finished, the remaining delegates returned to the discussion of whether to take up the Guaymí document. Even though the discussion continued for another hour or so, it was clear to all that the point was now moot; there no longer was time for a full discussion. The next morning's agenda was already overcrowded; the congress had to finish its proceedings in preparation for the arrival of government officials who would hear the results of their deliberations and make some response. CODEMIN therefore succeeded in keeping the Canquintú congress from engaging in a formal discussion of Cerro Colorado.

Heightened Opposition

Just as CODEMIN's seminar in Hato Chamí inadvertently provided Guaymí leaders with their first opportunity to meet and discuss common concerns about the mining project, so also CODEMIN's success in preventing the Canquintú congress from discussing the project had the unintended result of heightening Guaymí opposition to the project. As part of the last morning's business, the delegates passed resolutions on the two projects. These resolutions formed Guaymí commissions to study the projects and to report, with recommendations, to an "Extraordinary General Congress" (called for April 1980 in Soloy, Chiriquí) whose only agenda would be these projects. The Guaymíes were determined to discuss the projects.

Although the resolutions only mandated the formation of the commissions, the "Considerations" expressed clear judgments on the projects (and, in context, on the events of the night before). The congress stated that CODEMIN intended to use a great deal of Guaymí land, had never consulted with the Guaymíes, and would not specify anything concerning plans to attend to Guaymí needs and interests with regard to the project.

> There are diverse types of CODEMIN propaganda for the indigenous population, in which is not found any type of real message concerning the present and future problems of the indigenous community.
> Given that the Project is located in the very heart of the Guaymí Comarca, the indigenous Guaymí people have the right to demand more information concerning the exploitation of Cerro Colorado.[13] (Congresos Guaymíes 1980:91, Considerations 4 and 6)

Clusters of delegates buzzed with critical comments on CODEMIN's manipulation of the congress; no one had been deceived into believing that the lengthy procedural discussion had been anything other than a coarse attempt to prevent the people from talking about the projects. Many people laughed as they observed that the multimillion dollar mining company was afraid of the poor Guaymíes, afraid to let them air their views, afraid to allow them to discuss a document prepared by their own people.

The delegates were also angry; the manipulation of their congress further persuaded them that CODEMIN, IRHE, and the government could not be trusted, and that the assurances they were receiving that the projects would benefit them were as empty as they had feared. They were more skeptical than ever about whose interests would be served by the projects.

As many as could got copies of the Guaymí document to study with their communities; arrangements were made to print and distribute more copies after the congress. Even before the congress ended, some had looked at it; their comments increased the interest of others. CODEMIN also distributed its booklet; those who glanced at it simply expressed their puzzlement at receiving a document that made no sense to them.

The First Guaymí General Congress of Canquintú represented the first Guaymí-controlled open discussion of the mega-projects the government planned to carry out within the proposed comarca. Although CODEMIN kept the discussion of the Guaymí document from going forward, its work at sabotage backfired; people left the congress more skeptical than before about the credibility of government promises regarding Cerro Colorado and Teribe-Changuinola, and more determined than before to carry out their own analyses of the advantages and disadvantages the projects would entail.

However, this skepticism did not yet encompass other issues that Guaymíes were discussing with the government. The Minister of Government and Justice, Adolfo Ahumada, addressing the closing session of the congress, received a standing ovation when he said: "Carry this message with you in your hearts—this government indeed is going to grant the comarca" (Congresos Guaymíes 1980:90).

The wrong turns of CODEMIN's delegation at the congress greatly damaged CODEMIN's own attempts to win over the Guaymíes. When Jaime Roquebert, CODEMIN's technical manager, addressed the closing session of the congress, he echoed Ahumada's satisfaction that the congress had put together a commission to study the projects, and pledged full cooperation from CODEMIN. He acknowledged that it was appropriate for the Guaymíes to do their own analysis of the projects and their interests, and assured them that CODEMIN wanted the results of this analysis in order to better plan for the delivery of the benefits of the projects. But the technical manager, unaware of the maneuvering of Palacios and the others from the Department of Social Development, had no way of knowing how unbelievable his statements were.[14]

Hato Rincón Community Meetings

Even before the Canquintú congress, several Guaymí communities had attempted to discuss their concerns with CODEMIN; their experiences helped them delineate positions that brought into the open more Guaymí opposition to Cerro Colorado. The people of Hato Rincón, whose location alongside the road near Escopeta gave them frequent contact with mining company personnel and bosses, were disturbed by the mixed signals they received about the permanence of their community (see Chapter 7). Several meetings with CODEMIN left them frustrated. They felt they were unable to get credible answers to their questions. They doubted CODEMIN's assurances that they had nothing to worry about, but they did not know how to follow up with further questions. They wanted another meeting with CODEMIN, but this time they were determined to prepare themselves well. Their approach illustrates how some Guaymíes evaluated the project's impact on them, clarified their own interests, and figured out strategies and tactics to defend those interests.

The people of Hato Rincón knew and had confidence in the priests of Remedios; they asked for help to prepare for a meeting with CODEMIN. For these preparatory sessions, perhaps three in all, a priest used CODEMIN's publications, Bishop Núñez' pastoral letter (Núñez y Consejo 1979), the slide show prepared for Canquintú, the Guaymí document of Canquintú, and a large colored map the priests had made.[15]

The sessions, held in the local schoolhouse, began with the slide and tape show, using a battery-powered projector. First, those who gathered went through the slide show without interruptions, so that everyone could get an overview of the dimensions of the mining project; then they went back through it more slowly without the cassette. The people talked about the different aspects of their lives depicted in the slides. When they reached the slides of the mines and equipment for mining, they engaged in lengthy conversations to try to imagine the sheer size of the project—the open pit, 4 km by 5 km, the 16-cubic meter shovels, and the 166-metric-ton dump trucks. No one had ever imagined vehicles so large; one picture depicted a man dwarfed alongside a tire of a dump truck, another a woman standing on the cab at the top of the 10-foot ladder. The images were sobering.

The evenings continued with a recreational viewing of slides of the Guaymíes of upper Remedios, concentrating on slides of the people of Hato Rincón. People laughed as they saw themselves or others, made comments about what was going on or the mood of people pictured, and especially laughed about the generally serious expressions on people's faces.

After showing the slides, the priest brought out the large colored map of the three districts of eastern Chiriquí (Tolé, Remedios, and San Félix). Except for some of the students, few people had looked closely at a map; however, in a short time people could visualize the relationship between the two-dimensional map and the geography they knew so well. With the map, they saw the area included in the project in its various dimensions: the size of the open-pit mine, the area around the mine that CODEMIN projected would have to be vacated, the concession area, the locations and sizes of the workers' living areas, the reservoir, and the routes of roads, pipelines, and electricity lines (see Figure 3). For the first time, the people of Hato Rincón saw that the project was truly immense. Before the meetings they had imagined it as comparable to the small "towns" built in Escopeta and Hato Chamí, the road that ran along the edge of Hato Rincón, the other road above their caserío, and the dirty water in the stream that ran through the caserío. They had little trouble relating to what other communities already experienced from the mining project; their free-floating anxieties about the likely effects of the project quickly became specific concerns for themselves and for many others of the Guaymí area.

They went over the map numerous times, returning to ask again what this or that symbol represented. One teenager asserted that he had learned the whole map; the others demanded a demonstration. He went through all the features without a mistake, and repeated his performance at a later meeting. His effort gave the others confidence, and some of the adults also came forward to explain the location of all the parts of the mining project.

When the residents were confident they had a good sense of the overall scope of the mining project, the meetings turned to discussion of their specific concerns and preparation for their meeting with CODEMIN. Based on their understanding, they now began to ask what was going to happen to them and to the other Guaymíes of the areas affected. One of the students used a cassette recorder as they went around the room raising all their questions and concerns. These focused on the loss of lands, on relocation, compensation, and the general impact on the Guaymíes of so many foreign males living in their area.

They had been through much of this before, albeit with less understanding of what they were up against. But now their old fears returned:

> If we ask our questions, CODEMIN will just tell us everything is
> fine, everything is taken care of. We know this isn't so; but we
> don't know how to keep the conversation going.

They decided they needed practice.

The priest took the part of CODEMIN; the people asked their questions, and he gave CODEMIN's answers. For example, they asked: "Is it true that Hato Rincón will be relocated?" The answer from the priest came back: "We don't know. The entire project is under study." As they suspected, once the answers came back, they were stuck. The priest discussed their concerns with them, helping them to focus their uneasiness with the responses. They talked among themselves in Ngawbere, asked questions in Spanish of the priest, returned to their consultations, and by trial and error worked out the further questions they wanted to ask. For example, they asked:

> What do you mean, "it's under study"? Who is doing the study?
> Why haven't we seen anyone from CODEMIN coming around to
> look at our lives, our work, our families, to get some idea of how
> we live and what we want? Your experts only mention Hato Rin-
> cón as the site for depositing the waste rock when the mine pit is

opened up; what other site is being considered? And what involvement do we have in any of the decisions about our future? What
criteria are being used in looking at these questions?

As they went along, they tried out their questions; the priest did what
he could to provide responses representative of CODEMIN. Each time,
as the people returned to their discussions, they developed greater confidence in their ability to elaborate their more specific concerns and
devise ways of continuing to raise questions without simply saying "We
don't believe you" to CODEMIN.

One of the students wrote down the questions and their sequence.
Different people took turns asking the questions, listening to the different answers, and following them up with further questions on the same
topic, always stopping for discussion among all present. From this
practice, the people selected delegates who would be responsible for
the different lines of questions and follow-up; these people practiced
and practically memorized their parts. They always sought to pin
CODEMIN down, to get specific statements, information, or commitments they could work with. Then, in the light of these, they wished to
make known their responses.

When they discussed relocation, the priest repeated CODEMIN's
promises that any relocation would be carried out justly and humanely,
that they would have new lands as good as or better than the ones they
had at present, that they would have help in putting up houses, and that
they would have help in agricultural techniques to improve their yields.
In their discussion, they talked about whether they wanted to move or
to stay, and why. The elder of the community said he didn't want to
move, but could not think of any argument against having to move; he
was very frustrated. Why didn't he want to move? He said:

> I'm *from* here. I was born here, I grew up here. My parents were
> from here, my grandparents were from here; they are buried here. I
> can't go somewhere else; I'm from *here*.

As they discussed his statements, they slowly realized that they contained the fundamental argument against relocation. In his own way,
the elder had stated that his rights were historical, preceding the creation of the government or the Republic of Panama; part of his very

identity was that he was not just somebody from anywhere, but this person from Hato Rincón.

The statement "I'm from here" summarized a number of attachments to living in Hato Rincón. The residents were all related; their complex ties were inextricably social, economic, cultural, and political. These ties depended upon occupying the same lands. Each family could almost be said to live in several houses: they dropped in on each other, exchanged gossip and opinions, commented on things heard on the radio, did chores together, passed food back and forth, and allowed their children to play and sleep in each other's houses.

The people of Hato Rincón also had complex ties with other communities. Some residents had married people from Cerro Otoe, several hours' walk from Hato Rincón; a family from Cerro Otoe exercised inherited rights to plant crops in Hato Rincón, but had no house. Others married into families from the Bocas del Toro side of the cordillera, several hours' walk away, and farmed there as well as in Hato Rincón. One man, in addition to his wife and children in Hato Rincón, had a second wife in another caserío 2–3 hours away; he lived and farmed in both places. If Hato Rincón were relocated to the Changuinola area of Bocas del Toro, several days away, he would have to make some very difficult choices.[16]

Family ties also included regular visits with one's family of origin— to keep up with the development of siblings and nieces and nephews, to tend to elderly kin, and so on. The people of Hato Rincón did not want to be relocated so far away that their visits would require several days of walking and part of their limited resources for bus fare. Like anyone else, they had no desire to be uprooted and put down in an area with which they were unfamiliar, where they had no friends or relatives, where they had no knowledge of the geography or the specifics of the climate and weather; they were from Hato Rincón.[17]

Although the principal concern of the people of Hato Rincón was that of their rumored relocation, they spent some time discussing other concerns. They talked over in detail the problems created for them by the road above their caserío (the Hato Chamí-Cerro Colorado road). During the rainy season, the runoff from the road made the creek that flowed through the caserío dirtier than usual. The creek would stay dirty for days on end. Occasional slides on the road meant extensive repair work by the mining company, which in turn meant more dirt in their creek—their bathing and laundry place. Erosion also had its effects on the crops they planted below the road. As they discussed these matters, they became all the more concerned over various prospects for ecological damage from the project throughout the Guaymí area.

They also talked about taking jobs with the mine. Several men from Hato Rincón worked for the mine during the Canadian Javelin era; later, only one man found somewhat regular employment with the mine. The people of Hato Rincón heard the constant assurances that the mine would provide them with lots of jobs; they wanted to know when this employment would begin, what kind of jobs would be offered, and why they received no preference when the company was hiring. In these discussions, they saw that no one from Hato Rincón (and virtually no one from elsewhere in the comarca) had the background or training to aspire to any kind of job with the mine other than work with machetes, axes, or shovels—the only kinds of jobs any of them had ever obtained with the project. They knew that Texasgulf wanted a ninth-grade education as a minimum for job training; no adult from Hato Rincón had more than a third-grade education.

Finally, they talked about the CODEMIN people with whom they wanted to meet. They talked about the three mining company managers they knew, regular visitors in Hato Rincón: the security chief, the head of the crews in Hato Chamí, and the Cuban-American on-site manager for Texasgulf; they had no interest in meeting with any of them.[18] They had had unsatisfactory meetings with the head of the Department of Social Development; she seemed unaware of the real problems they were concerned with, and she clearly had no decision-making power within the corporate structure.[19] So, they decided to insist on meetings with the top management of CODEMIN. They decided how to go about arranging the meeting, accepting the security chief's frequently made offer to serve as go-between.

These discussions followed the same format as their discussion of relocation: asking their questions, stopping for a while to talk things over, figuring out their real concerns, working out follow-up questions, writing everything down, and appointing a spokesperson.

When they were confident that they were prepared to meet with CODEMIN, they decided to set up the meetings; they asked the security chief to let the heads of CODEMIN know they wanted a meet-

ing. The people of Hato Rincón insisted on having a part in working
out the date and time of the meeting; they disliked the usual pattern of
simply being informed, with little notice, of appointments to meet with
CODEMIN or other government people. Also, they hoped that setting
a meeting time by common agreement would prevent the repetition of
the common Guaymí experience of showing up for meetings only to
find that those who had called the meeting were unable to come because of some unanticipated, and unexplained, change in schedule.

The chief said he would arrange the meeting as they requested;
however, a few days later he sent word announcing that the head of the
Department of Social Development would arrive on such-and-such day
to meet with them. The people of Hato Rincón were angry; but they
had prepared for this possibility, and knew what they would do. When
the department head showed up for the meeting, a couple of people
informed her that they could not meet with her; the meeting time had
not been worked out by mutual consent, and the moment was incon-
venient—they had too much other work to do. They also informed her
that they wanted a meeting with someone with decision-making power
at CODEMIN, not with her. Although the people were careful to tell
her that they had nothing against her personally, she left very angry
because she had come all the way from Panama City for nothing.[20]

After a few more attempts to have the security chief arrange a
meeting for them with CODEMIN's management, the people of Hato
Rincón sent in their own request for the time and date of the meeting.
They received no reply and decided to assume that the time was acceptable.[21] They showed up, but no one from CODEMIN did. So far as
anyone could tell, no one ever paid any attention to their request to
meet with someone higher than the head of the Department of Social
Development.

The people of Hato Rincón spent several weeks studying the mining project, preparing for a meeting with CODEMIN, and then talking
over their reactions when no meeting took place. In the process, fears
and concerns that had been topics of occasional private conversations
and anecdotes became matters for open discussion and for growing
consensus. They discovered that, despite the many assurances received
from people associated with the mine or the government, they counted
for nothing in the planning of the mining project. They concluded that
the mining people had no tolerance for discussions with Guaymíes who

prepared themselves for meetings; CODEMIN sent the one they heard the mine workers call *la niña* (the little girl) from the Department of Social Development instead of anyone who had real power.

The people of Hato Rincón had good memories of the early stages of the mining project; but the activities and attitudes of Texasgulf and CODEMIN brought them to question both the project itself and the credibility of project spokespersons. CODEMIN blamed the priests of Remedios, whom they called "outside agitators," for stirring up the people of Hato Rincón. In fact, the priests assisted them with information, materials, and discussion, to help them realize the full scope of the mining project. But the initial doubts and worries arose from the people's experiences, and became more focused in the give and take of their preparatory meetings. More than the priests' activities, the mining activities themselves heightened the consciousness of the people of Hato Rincón. The residents of Hato Rincón went from being a mild, non-politicized community to one committed to working to get answers to their questions and to be taken seriously in the plans of the mining project.

Even though CODEMIN and some government people publicly stated that no Guaymí community could oppose or question the project on its own, without being manipulated by outside agitators, the people of Hato Rincón were convinced that they themselves were responsible for their views of the project. They saw, in their relationships with the project and its personnel, that words did not mean what they seemed to mean, that promises were empty, and that if Guaymí interests were to be protected, then Guaymíes themselves had to define and protect them.

Tolé Responses: Effects of the Penetration Road

Chapter 7 provided a description of the effects of a small stretch of the penetration road built by the joint operating company in the dry season of 1980. When similar effects occurred along most of the length of this 44-km road in Tolé, people had new questions and devised new responses to the mining project and, on a wider level, questioned the government itself; as in Hato Rincón, the principal consciousness-raiser was the mining project. Three instances in Tolé illustrate Guaymí responses to the project: the efforts organized by people of Tebujo (the "Cerro Puerco" resolution); the activities of the Mama Chi devotees of Cangrejo; and the extraordinary overtures to the Guaymíes made by some campesinos of Tolé.

The Cerro Puerco Resolution. While the penetration road was still under construction, some Guaymíes—mainly catechists who worked with the Catholic parish of Tolé—began organizing Guaymí responses; Juan Rodríguez of Tebujo played a key role as organizer and secretary.[22] They held meetings among themselves, complained about what the road had already done and what it was likely to do once the rains came, and decided to try to include more people in their discussions. In February 1980, in the corregimiento of Cerro Puerco, their efforts resulted in a gathering of people representing at least eight caseríos.

The people who took part in this meeting were angry. They talked about the specific effects of the construction of the road through their lands; some of the participants read parts of Bishop Núñez' pastoral letter, thereby helping the others gain a sense of the wider implications of the project. They complained about the attitudes of the workers who did the construction. They were deeply offended by what they considered the high-handed approach that made them people without rights on their own lands. They mocked the statements they had heard that the road was for them. "Are we millionaires? Who could ever buy a car? Anyway [they chuckled bitterly], only the women will know how to drive!" (The people joked that the mine workers were offering driving lessons to the women, because mine workers sometimes let women ride in the cabs of their pickups while they sent men to the back.)

The participants narrowed their possible responses to three: to request a meeting with CODEMIN; to put themselves in the way of the equipment; or to write a denunciation for publication in the national press. Some of them had taken part in meetings with CODEMIN, and most of them had heard of such meetings; they agreed that a meeting with CODEMIN would be a waste of time, since it would only result, in their view, in more lies and empty promises. Although a few of the young men urged planting themselves in front of the machinery, most of the people were not ready to do something that would move their opposition to a new, unknown level of resistance. So they decided on a public denunciation.

The commission that drafted the denunciation, following the accepted form, began with a series of "considerations" leading to the "resolutions." Reflecting the mood of the participants, it did not confine itself to the mining project or the road; the "considerations" sketched a Guaymí view of their recent history.

> [S]ince the arrival of the Spaniards, the Indian has been and continues to be outraged, oppressed, maltreated by the landowners, traders, bar owners, intermediaries, politicians, and large companies. Every government since the independence of our republic has failed to protect Indian peoples and has not even enforced the few laws concerning Indians that protect our human rights.[23]

After a series of more specific "considerations" concerning the negative effects of the road, the document resolved to denounce the centuries of exploitation, denounce the unjust laws, and denounce all projects carried out by outsiders. Only at the end did they

> demand an immediate halt to the road that CODEMIN is building until the Indian people, fully convinced, give their positive reply [and] reject the mining project indefinitely as it does not bring any benefit to the Indian people.

This resolution, published in the business-oriented newspaper *La Estrella de Panamá* (March 8, 1980), was supported by 497 Guaymí signatures, each with its corresponding identity card number. The public denunciation represented the first time a group of Guaymíes had taken its case to the public of Panama.[24]

Mama Chi Opposition. Perhaps the most extraordinary Guaymí opposition to the mining project came from a small band of devotees of the Mama Chi revivalist religious movement of the caserío of Cangrejo, a short walk north of Tebujo. Characteristically, the Mama Chis isolated themselves from other Guaymíes and from all outsiders. But when the penetration road went through the middle of Cangrejo, they adopted new tactics. Using their capacity to work in organized fashion, the Mama Chis met to discuss this new threat to their welfare. They quickly recognized that they were too few to confront the threat by themselves; they sought support. One of their number asked the priests of Tolé for help; he came away with copies of

Bishop Núñez' pastoral letter, which he carefully and laboriously studied. Then he helped other Mama Chis from Cangrejo to organize meetings both among themselves and with other Guaymíes; with his minimal reading skills, he read to others the pastoral letter and urged them
to discuss the impact of the road and of the mining project in general.

At these meetings, the Mama Chis asked people to make statements concerning the mining project; a young man with a notebook
summarized these discussions. Those who could, signed their names;
others sat for hours writing the names of the majority who could not do
it for themselves. These pages, referring to meetings in a number of
communities over a period of several weeks, contained summary statements attributed to more than 2,000 Guaymíes whose names and communities were recorded. Some excerpts:

> This project was begun and carried forward without the consent of
> the Guaymí Indian population; the construction has caused the loss
> of much labor of the traditional Guaymí Indian. . . . This road is
> no benefit for us, the poor Guaymí Indians who are here. The head
> of the company comes around saying that the exploitation of Cerro
> Colorado is beneficial to make the Guaymí Indian wealthy. We In-
> dians could have millions of dollars but we are not going to eat this
> money; rather, we maintain ourselves with the products we plant
> and grow in our traditional way. . . . We live poor and we do not
> want to be wealthy.

> The exploitation of the mine is no benefit, but rather is pure mal-
> treatment and ruin and damage for us poor Indians. For these rea-
> sons no one wants or permits the exploitation of Cerro Colorado
> among the Indian population. We are poor naturals[25] living natu-
> rally poor as God Jesus Christ[26] left us to live . . . and we do
> not desire any kind of wealth or benefit from the state or from
> landowners.

> Let it be communicated to the head of the company that we must
> be respected; it is prohibited to go forward with the installation of
> Cerro Colorado. No worldly government can countermand this
> order, which comes from the celestial government of God Jesus
> Christ the most powerful. No human beings, no matter their scien-
> tific qualifications, can fabricate a world. . . . The poor Indian pop-
> ulation speaks and swears before God Jesus Christ that we want to
> live tranquilly and in peace and asks with all respect pardon of the

national government. We are not speaking against the government; rather we are asking for respect and consideration and pardon for the Guaymí Indian population, poor among the poor. But the order of things must be fulfilled and can only be regulated before God Jesus Christ because we are all human persons but there cannot be only one race, but all have our rights not to be maltreated, all have our rights to live naturally and traditionally.[27] (Excerpts from meeting of 27 May 1980 in Sabana Grande)

. . . We poor Guaymí Indians do not need the exploitation of this project. Please, this project must be prohibited and there must be respect for the residence of the poor humble natural Indian, the property of a poor person, because we do not have land available to live on and we do not have water to bathe in and we do not have water to drink and we do not have water for our cattle and horses and animals.

This communication will be given to the head of the mining corporation, that he might leave us Guaymí Indians to live apart from everyone else, poor, humble. We don't need any kind of mining benefit because we are not in agreement with this damage or destruction or maltreatment which in fact this mining project is bringing about. The machinery comes through and causes us to lose our land and the produce of our trees and plants. (Excerpts from meeting of 25 May 1980 in Río Santiago)

. . . No Guaymí Indian wants the mining project. The mine and its road can no longer utilize our lands; we Guaymí Indians only need that the project be prohibited because there is no land available even for us. If they are going to do away with the poor Indian, then it is better that God Jesus Christ come to do away with the Republic [of Panama] whole and entire.[28] Excerpts from meeting of 20 April 1980 in Cangrejo)

The Mama Chis also sent a delegation to try to make peace with an old opponent, Cacique Lorenzo Rodríguez of Chiriquí Province.[29] They offered to work with him for the comarca, and urged him to oppose the mining project. The cacique was noncommittal.

Campesino Involvement. If the Mama Chis formed the most extraordinary Guaymí opposition to the mining project, the activities of another group of Tolé must be seen as equally

extraordinary: the campesinos of a newly formed cooperative who decided to actively support the Guaymí struggle. In Guaymí discussions
of the comarca, a major unresolved issue was the status of poor campesinos who lived within the area claimed by the Guaymíes. These
campesinos were, for the most part, descendants of people who had
homesteaded in the area around 100 years ago; they knew no other
home. Generally, their farming methods, overall economy, and lifestyle
were indistinguishable from those of the Guaymíes; the campesinos
spoke Spanish instead of Ngawbere (although some were learning
Ngawbere) and the campesino women did not wear the dresses typical
of Guaymí women. The landowners of Tolé, who ordinarily exploited
campesinos and Guaymíes indiscriminately, held a number of meetings
with the campesinos to rally them around a banner of common race
against the comarca, which sought to expropriate the lands unlawfully
titled by Tolé cattlemen.[30] Some of the campesinos, led by a couple of
catechists who were good friends with some Guaymí catechists, began
to see through these efforts of the cattlemen; they recognized that they
had a potentially better future as non-Guaymíes within the Guaymí
comarca than subject to the continued depredations of the pasture-
hungry cattlemen. They formed an association that supported the comarca, and began to look into the mining project and its effects. In the
process, they discovered that the mining project offered them the same
things it did the Guaymíes.

This group sent a delegation to begin conversations with Cacique
Lorenzo, assuring him of their support for the comarca and trying to
get some sense from him of his attitude toward the campesino presence
within it.[31] They also sent observers to Guaymí meetings, including the
congress of Soloy, to support the Guaymí cause.

SUMMARY: OPPOSITION FLARE-UPS

With the First General Congress of Can-
quintú, the Guaymíes took an active role in analyzing the mining project, examining the promises made and the reassurances given, and
drawing their own conclusions. At Canquintú, CODEMIN's attempt at
sabotaging the Guaymí discussions almost guaranteed a critical, even
hostile, Guaymí examination of the project and its likely effects. People
could not help but wonder why CODEMIN was so afraid to have the

Guaymíes look at a document their own people had helped prepare; they decided that there must be some substance to it.

The mining project itself, carried out in ways that showed no concern for the people affected, served as the most significant force to elevate Guaymí awareness. The people of Hato Rincón, initially friendly to the project and enthused to see the activities so nearby, became disillusioned not only with the project, but with the government itself, sponsor of the project. Again, the reluctance of CODEMIN to engage in open and frank conversations with Guaymíes who had prepared their case was a major contribution to the changed evaluation of the project.

The penetration road built in Tolé, accompanied by the complete failure of the mechanisms worked out in agreement between CODEMIN and the Guaymí-elected representative of Hato Chamí, contributed even more to bringing into the open the growing opposition to the mining project. In Tolé, Guaymíes for the first time issued a public denunciation of the government. Guaymíes who by ideology isolated themselves from all who were not coreligionists, under the threat represented by the road, sought cooperation with others, even showing themselves willing to compromise what earlier had been non-negotiable parts of their creed. Campesinos, despite the uncertainties of life as a minority under the government of the majority Guaymíes, organized to support the comarca and join the Guaymíes in opposing the mining project.

The Department of Social Development of CODEMIN, assigned the task of representing the project to all these groups, had no strategy equal to the challenge. CODEMIN could not take part in open discussions of the implications of the project because despite its claims, it had done no research on the effects, and had not begun to draft policies for relocation, compensation, preservation of Guaymí values, or guarantees of job possibilities. While the top management continued to claim that no one lived in the area of the project, the people of the Department of Social Development continued in their offices in Panama City, leaving Palacios to represent them in the Guaymí area without any supervision.[32] Their only consistent approach to the mounting problem with the Guaymíes was to maintain that there was no problem other than that brought on by outside agitators, specifically the Catholic clergy of eastern Chiriquí.

CHAPTER 9

Guaymí Opposition Coalesces
and Gains Outside Support

Guaymí questioning of the mining project began tentatively and quietly; CODEMIN and government reactions provided impetus for the questioning to become opposition. But, as the First Guaymí General Congress of Canquintú had carefully observed, there was as yet no Guaymí consensus regarding the projects. The minutes of the congress stated: "It is explicitly noted that this Congress, given that it did not analyze the projects, has not [adopted] a posture in relation to the projects" (Congresos Guaymíes 1980:89).

Although CODEMIN's manipulations prevented the Canquintú congress from formally discussing the Cerro Colorado and Teribe-Changuinola projects, the delegates elaborated measures to enable the Guaymíes to analyze the projects; they formed a study commission to report to an extraordinary congress. Furthermore, people continued informal discussions of the projects in the light of Guaymí interests and experiences, even though CODEMIN showed itself incapable of entering into a dialogue with them. The various engagements between the Guaymíes and CODEMIN fostered growing skepticism, which in turn helped the Guaymíes recognize they had to prepare themselves better for future encounters, and had to rely on themselves if their interests were to be protected.

DEVELOPING A GUAYMI CONSENSUS

The Extraordinary Guaymí General Congress of Soloy

The congress of Canquintú scheduled an-other congress with the express agenda of carrying out the Guaymí analysis of the Cerro Colorado and Teribe-Changuinola projects. This Extraordinary Guaymí General Congress met April 17–19, 1980, in the caserío of Soloy, San Lorenzo District, Chiriquí Province. The congress involved a series of preparatory steps, some behind-the-scenes maneu-vers, and lengthy discussions. It had serious repercussions not only in the Guaymí area, but across Panama and internationally.

Despite their mandate from Canquintú and CODEMIN's pledges of support, the twelve Guaymí commissioners sent out to study the mining and hydroelectric projects did not meet together. From their homes, spread throughout the Guaymí area of Veraguas, Chiriquí, and Bocas del Toro, they could not establish effective communications and coordination of their efforts; and they had no budget to enable them to move around or meet together (see Congresos Guaymíes 1980:12). Some commissioners took part in a meeting or two with CODEMIN and IRHE, and some of them visited with residents of Valle de Riscó.[1]

As the date of the Soloy congress neared, some of the commis-sioners talked things over, concerned that they were likely to show up empty-handed. One of these, Miguel Cruz, did more than express his concern; he wrote an analysis of the projects.[2] In it, Cruz took advan-tage of the fieldwork he did along the route of the penetration road in Tolé—his conversations with people affected by the road, his discus-sions with the Mama Chis of Cangrejo, and his first-hand observations; he had also worked diligently on the "Guaymí document," whose pre-sentation in Canquintú had been prevented by CODEMIN. Cruz pre-sumed the earlier work of the Guaymí document, even though this document had not been formally considered by the Canquintú con-gress. He set himself the task of providing an updated analysis, con-centrating on events of the half year between the two congresses. Be-sides his own work, he had access to the continuing investigations and analyses by CEASPA and others.

Obviously, Cruz was motivated by more than concern for his image should he and the other commissioners arrive in Soloy with nothing done; he was determined to give the people their opportunity to carry out a thorough discussion of the projects. He knew from experience that the one who arrives at a meeting with something in writing has considerable say in the agenda for the meeting; others end up reacting to the document, even if they decide to reject it. If no Guaymí document were available, the field would be open for the commission members (including Manteca), who wanted to turn this discussion over to CODEMIN and IRHE.

Cruz finished his document on the eve of the opening of the congress. He debated whether to hurry to David to make a few photocopies; but the recollection of the problems in Canquintú, trying to control distribution of copies of the Guaymí document until the congress had its say, led him to the decision to go to Soloy with only one copy. No one would be able to sneak a look in order to prepare another sabotage.

Manteca and Santos assumed responsibility for most of the arrangements for the congress; the Guaymí mayor *(alcalde)* of San Félix District, working with them, handled the finances.[3] They were supposed to obtain the promised budget from the government, get National Guard buses to transport people, and arrange for food. The three organizers made big promises, and clearly intended to continue in charge through the congress itself. But they ran into a number of problems, and arrived for the congress without the widespread support they had expected.[4]

During the Canquintú congress, some Guaymí leaders had learned an important lesson: the necessity of keeping some debates off the floor of the congress itself. Before the Soloy congress opened, two preparatory meetings strongly influenced the outcome. One of these dealt with deciding who would run the congress. Manteca and his associates, more favorably disposed toward CODEMIN, urged holding new elections of officers; Smith and his group argued that the present congress was a continuation of Canquintú, and that the officers elected there should continue.[5] They finally decided to take the question to the opening session of the congress. But the transportation delays meant that Santos, Manteca's ally, and his contingent from Chiriquí failed to arrive for the opening session; the majority of those present were from Bocas del

Toro. Although Manteca moved to postpone the election of officers until later, he was too late; the congress confirmed that Soloy was a continuation of Canquintú.

In another meeting before the congress opened, Cruz apprised the other commissioners of the report he had written. Reactions were mixed: some, like Manteca and the San Félix mayor, opposed the presentation of a report that none of them had seen; others were delighted that something was available for the congress to discuss. Manteca argued that each commissioner should present a brief oral report, explaining to the congress that the issues were very complex and that they had had little time to do their work. After some discussion, Cruz presented the group with two alternatives: either accept his report as their own, or watch him take to the congress the fact that he, alone, had prepared a report and wondered if the congress wished to consider it. All were aware that the latter approach would leave them looking very bad; the various excuses for the non-functioning of the commission looked flimsy alongside Cruz' fifty typed pages. The other commissioners, including Manteca and the mayor, accepted Cruz' report as the work of the Canquintú commission.[6]

Manteca and his associates, planning to be in control of the congress, had invited CODEMIN and IRHE to lead the discussions of their respective projects. However, after first losing the chance to run the congress, and then agreeing to commission support for the Cruz report, they were in a potentially embarrassing position. They could not credibly argue against the Canquintú commission report because, as commissioners, they were supposedly coauthors. Yet they wanted to preserve their credibility with the government agencies, to whom they had promised to deliver the congress. After their success in stalling a full discussion of the projects at Canquintú, they apparently had concluded that they could easily manipulate their fellow Guaymíes, whom they looked down upon as country bumpkins. But other Guaymíes had also learned lessons from the Canquintú experience, and came to Soloy much better prepared.

After various preliminaries, around noon on April 17, the congress began its consideration of the projects. Cruz, as delegate for the Canquintú commission, read the lengthy Cerro Colorado part of his document, pausing frequently for translation into Ngawbere and Sabanero. The minutes of the congress noted that the study was "somewhat extensive" *[un poco extenso]*, covering "the impact of this project on the Guaymí people and region" and concluding

> with concrete evidence that this project in virtually no way what-
> soever favors *[no favorece en casi nada]* the Ngawbe people. Rather,
> in the phase of primary development of the project, grave injustices
> have been committed against the affected communities; Cerro Col-
> orado does not guarantee any real benefit for the indigenous popu-
> lation. (Congresos Guaymíes 1980:45)

After the reading, the delegates opened a lengthy and sometimes heated discussion of the mining project. Most speakers denounced the project, adding their own complaints to those mentioned in the study. Typical criticisms of the projects included:

> Among the people, there is unease and fear with respect to Cerro
> Colorado. CODEMIN follows a policy of confusion; its publica-
> tions only talk about the good things. But in the communities af-
> fected, the people ask that the project be suspended and that they
> receive greater consideration. We are ignored; they go right over
> the top of us, we are worse off than animals. (University student
> from Veraguas, leader of Frente de Liberación Guaymí)

> In the United States, they have to talk with the caciques before
> they build a mining project on a comarca; shouldn't it be the same
> here? In the Constitution it says that they must provide us with
> schools and other benefits; it is a lie to maintain [with
> CODEMIN] that these things come from Cerro Colorado. (Stu-
> dent from Soloy)

> This project brings us discord—it's already happening, it divides us.
> The problem is to take care of our family tomorrow and for the fu-
> ture. This project will bring the disappearance of our culture, our
> way of life, our race. We must say no to the project. (Leader from
> Valle de Riscó)

> CODEMIN promises benefits; until they get down to specifics, we
> must say no to them. I am the elected representative of Cerro Igle-
> sias. When they exploit the mine, they are not going to take us into
> account. None of the work of the mining company has been con-

sulted with the people, even less with the elected representatives. If the road goes through a cemetery, we must demand that they first remove the bones of our grandparents. (Elected representative of Cerro Iglesias, Remedios District)

The conclusion we must draw is to say to the government that it must halt the projects. A boss from CODEMIN talked with me about 100 scholarships for Guaymíes. But as our study indicated, there are lots of promises. We are not little children, unable to make decisions. We are not here to create divisions; the projects create the divisions. Our policy must be: first, the comarca, and suspend the projects until we have the comarca.[7] (Leader from Tolé)

Some few suggested that the project was good and the objections were based on outside manipulation; one speaker blamed the Catholic priests for the Guaymí opposition to Cerro Colorado.[8] But most of the participants dismissed these objections as unfounded, and saw in them a revelation of the objectors' loyalties:

a handful of individuals of well-known orientation wanted to discredit the Commission's Study with the argument that the Study wasn't the work of the Commission, but rather of interlopers [personas ajenas] . . . seeking to undermine the indigenous movement. The truth is that [these objections] contributed to the identification of the indigenous elements who are unconditional defenders of the Cerro Colorado project. (Acta de Soloy, Congresos Guaymíes 1980:45)

Participants shouted down several speakers who tried to defend the project and attack the study. Late in the night, when the discussion ended, by clear consensus the congress opposed the exploitation of the mining project without prior legal approbation of the Guaymí comarca; this consensus formed the basis for the Soloy resolution on Cerro Colorado.

During the long consideration of Cerro Colorado, although people moved in and out of the meeting area, for the most part the several thousand delegates sat and listened. Some few took notes; others taped the entire reading, planning to play the tapes for their communities when they returned home.

On April 18th, the congress repeated the process of the 17th, this time giving its attention to the Teribe-Changuinola hydroelectric project. Once again Cruz read the appropriate part of the study, with translations. A well-prepared delegation from Valle de Riscó took the lead in the ensuing discussion as different spokespersons addressed various concerns; delegates from other parts of the Guaymí area added their words of support.

> Since IRHE began its study of the hydroelectric project, it has paid no attention to the communities which will be flooded. We do not believe IRHE's promises of scholarships and jobs; for years now the indigenous people have been demanding the comarca, and nothing has happened. Now we are going to lose our only resources. (Female leader from Valle de Riscó)

> Even if they offer us a horse made of gold, we do not have to accept; we have food every day from our own labors. The people unanimously reject the hydroelectric project. The government says that the people must be heard; and the people say this project is bad for them. This is not the opinion of one leader, but of the people. I went to Bayano to get information. Government functionaries said that the people there live well, were well indemnified. I said I wouldn't believe it unless I saw it for myself. I asked the people; they said no, it was a lie, the government didn't pay them correctly but just messed them up. When I arrived in Panama City, they took me to the offices of the head of IRHE; he tried to get me to accept his views. I told him I was not there to negotiate but to be a messenger for the others; he walked out. While the government says it's important to talk with the masses, it tries to use us leaders as instruments just as before they used us to haul gold. I ask your help—this Congress speaks with authority. We can say no to the project. (Male leader from Valle de Riscó)

> After we named our commissioners in Canquintú and some of them went to Valle de Riscó, IRHE claimed it conducted another investigation, polling the commissioners for their positions on Teribe-Changuinola. Then IRHE published a flyer stating that we of Riscó were aware of the project and in agreement with IRHE, as were the commissioners and the cacique. IRHE said the area was unpopulated jungle.

We have to state that the Indian lives from the light of the sun and the moon, not from light made by humans – a light that would destroy our culture. We are indigenous people; we do not want the situation of Coclé, where there are no longer indigenous people. We are from here.[9] (Male leader from Valle de Riscó)

[The IRHE project] is already having an impact. The people who live in the area have sent a delegation and resolutions to the congress, asking that the congress not accept this project; we delegates have to do something for them. If they themselves are doing what they can, we have to support them; it would be different if they themselves did nothing. Be careful; they try to move these projects in wherever they find a flat spot. If they promise a little school, they do so in exchange for the project. They say that without the project, we will get nothing; but if we fight, we can get everything. (Male student from Chiriquí)

The government is playing games with our race. We hold a general congress, we hold a regional congress, we hold a local congress; the government says "yes, we're going to give you your comarca," and we go home content, happy. And nothing. The Indian has no right to land, to a house—and is going to be left without women. (Male local leader from Veraguas)

My concern is that the masses say no to the projects, while a handful [of leaders] say yes to them. We must pay attention to the masses. I went to the U.S. and saw a [mining] project in Pennsylvania. In that place the grass does not live; almost nothing grows. But in Valle de Riscó and in Chiriquí we live by means of natural resources and not by other things. We live from what our great-grandparents left us; we live from our crops. They must be defended. (Elected representative from corregimiento of Piedra Roja, Bocas del Toro)

We must unite ourselves with the communities affected. The projects are not for our benefit; the only ones to benefit will be those who already hold the advantage. If we do not maintain ourselves firmly united, our only benefit will be to pay others' electricity bills. (Student from Veraguas)

Standing before 4,500 people in Canquintú, General Torrijos clearly stated he would give us the comarca. Nothing. We have 45,000 people who accept the comarca and the carta orgánica; but still we don't have them. They want to open up a road to bring cattle into Bocas del Toro; Urracá fought against these invasions. In different countries of Latin America they kill thousands of Indians; people die of malaria and other illnesses. The same will happen to us. But our problems are our own fault—we go get drunk. Now our young people are getting a good foundation, and they ought to unite. But no; they get jealous because one has a beard or another a nice shirt, and divisions arise. Our whole problem is our divisions; the government isn't to blame, we are.

I went to see the new minister [of Government and Justice]; for four months he's been too busy to see me—he has to read his newspaper. But when it's time for politicking, the Indian looks very pretty to them—later, nothing. They say: we need more investigation—they investigate the horse, they investigate the cat, but nothing happens. They think we are brutes, that we don't know anything. I told the minister: I'm not a comedian, I'm like Urracá. President Royo promised me the comarca. Who's in charge? Royo? General Torrijos? the minister? Tomorrow they have to answer us; they can't just give us candy. For us: first the comarca; then, if the people want, the projects. We are not against anyone; we just want our rights. (Cacique José Mónico Cruz of Bocas del Toro Province)

They narrated numerous unpleasant encounters and attempted encounters with personnel both from IRHE and from the National Guard; they related their perceptions of attempts to manipulate them, and their strong rejection of the hydroelectric projects. The people of Valle de Riscó made a stronger case than those from the area of Cerro Colorado. They had some contact with indigenous people affected by the Bayano hydroelectric project, already several years old; they challenged IRHE and the government to prove the credibility of their promise to take care of everything, by first resolving the problems created in the Bayano area.[10] Virtually every speaker concluded the same way: first the government should grant the comarca, and then the matter of the projects could be addressed; no one spoke in favor of the government view. This discussion, finished by early afternoon, resulted in the same consensus as that of the mining project—that the Guaymí people would oppose the development of the projects until the government passed laws establishing the Guaymí comarca (see the *Acta de Soloy,* Congresos Guaymíes 1980:46).

The congress then named several commissions to draft resolutions, principally on the Cerro Colorado and Teribe- Changuinola projects; Marcelo Bruno of CODEMIN joined the commission on Cerro Colorado.[11] Since he could read and write better than anyone else on the commission, he was named secretary. Apparently hoping his education would give him some advantage, he proposed that the commission begin its work by having each participant go off alone and write up a draft of the resolution; most members could scarcely read or write. When they reconvened a while later, Bruno read his version, which acknowledged the congress' serious objections to the mining project, then urged further study of the project and more conversations with CODEMIN. In their turn, some very traditional Guaymíes, for whom the entire process must have been completely foreign, pulled out small scraps of paper and read their proposed drafts: "No to Cerro Colorado" or "The Guaymí People Reject Cerro Colorado" or "Comarca First." Period. Bruno smiled in recognition of his defeat, and the commission wrote up its resolution condemning Cerro Colorado.

In the morning session of April 19, the commissions reported the drafts of the resolutions; the process was interrupted by the arrival of the delegation from the government and had to be postponed until late in the afternoon. Marcelo Bruno presented the resolution on Cerro Colorado; after a few minor changes, the congress unanimously approved it.[12] The "Considerations" included explicit reference to the "Study presented by the Commission" created in Canquintú, in order to provide that study with official status (Congresos Guaymíes 1980:50). This study itself referred to the earlier Guaymí document as "an essential part of the present study" (Congresos Guaymíes 1980:13); in this fashion, the congress of Soloy made official the document that CODEMIN had managed to exclude from the congress of Canquintú—a bit roundabout, but effective.

Whereas the "Considerations" of the Canquintú resolutions tended to complain about lack of specific information, those of Soloy clearly stated the congress' negative perceptions of Cerro Colorado, noting the grave threats to their lands, the damage already done, the absence of concern for the "physical, moral, and spiritual destruction" involved, the promises in place of acceptable responses, the only occasional and partial reports, and, in all aspects of the project, the total absence of consultation with the Guaymíes. The congress resolved

TO DEMAND THE SUSPENSION OF THE CERRO COL-
ORADO PROJECT UNTIL THE GUAYMI COMARCA BE
DEFINED [and to urge President Royo to give] a prompt re-
sponse to the DELIMITATION OF THE GUAYMI COMARCA,
AND AFTER THAT TO NEGOTIATE ABOUT THE CERRO
COLORADO PROJECT. (Congresos Guaymíes 1980:50; capitals
in original)

The congress also unanimously rejected the Teribe-Changuinola hydroelectric projects, again linking the prior definition of the comarca to any
further discussion of the projects:

> The Guaymí people, meeting in the Extraordinary General Con-
> gress celebrated in Soloy, maintain their well-defined criteria:
> WHILE THERE IS NO COMARCA, WE SHALL NOT PER-
> MIT ANY PROJECT IN THE INDIGENOUS AREA [capitals in
> original].

This resolution expressly based the Guaymí skepticism on the government's handling of the Bayano project:

> The Guaymí people cannot accept the carrying out of the Teribe-
> Changuinola Project, because we do not know [*ignoramos,* we don't
> know and don't trust] of benefits based on promises, as we have
> sufficient experience, for example the case of our indigenous com-
> panions of Bayano, who were given many promises that have not
> been kept.[13] (Congresos Guaymíes 1980:51)

CODEMIN fared poorly at Soloy; after providing the portable sound
system for the congress to use, CODEMIN personnel never used it.
Rodrigo González, president of CODEMIN and of the joint operating
company, arrived about the time the congress opened; he asked to meet
alone with the caciques. During a recess, a militant group of delegates
met privately with him. Despite the insistence of Manteca and his
associates, the delegates remained firm: González could meet with a
properly representative delegation of Guaymí leaders after the congress,
with ample preparation; but there would be no private meeting with
the caciques. Like everyone else, he could also sit in on the congress as
an observer; but he could only have the floor as part of the government

delegation on the final day. Neither he nor anyone else representing CODEMIN could participate in the discussion of the mining project; the congress was Guaymí, and would remain so. González, already angered by having to wait to meet with the delegation, left the meeting and returned to Panama City. The IRHE representatives fared no better; they too were excluded from addressing the congress.[14]

While the congress was considering the resolutions, the government delegation arrived to hear the results of the congress and to begin the official response. As for any major Guaymí meeting, the president of Panama was invited to lead the government delegation; during the congress, many people had expressed the sentiment that President Royo himself had to show up or they would no longer believe that he was serious in his assurances that the government was negotiating in good faith with the Guaymíes concerning the comarca. Ricardo Rodríguez, the new minister of Government and Justice, headed the government delegation; President Royo sent his regrets. Minister Rodríguez, already briefed by some of the government people observing the congress, knew that the resolutions would link the prior negotiation of the comarca to any Guaymí cooperation on the projects.[15]

Rodríguez' response to the congress began with the one predictable statement inevitably used for such occasions: the current government, he assured them, continuing the Torrijos revolution, had more than any government in the history of the republic concerned itself for the indigenous people of Panama. "We of the National Government are going to give you the Comarca" (Congresos Guaymíes 1980:47). But, he went on, as government spokespersons always did, the people had to be patient; the legal questions involved were complex, and the government needed to study everything carefully. He said that he had a commission engaged in that study, and he was waiting for their report.

As a sign of continued government concern for the Guaymíes, Rodríguez presented them with some gifts: two or three wheelbarrows, a few sacks of fertilizer, some shovels and hoes, and other odds and ends. He told them the government was considering the feasibility of putting in two-way radios in different Guaymí caseríos, aware that communications were difficult in the Guaymí area. With these radios, he thought, the Guaymíes would have quick access to health care by calling on the National Guard to send a helicopter to transport critically ill people to health facilities.[16] The response of the delegates even to the assurances about the comarca was not nearly so enthusiastic as had been their response to the same assurances from Adolfo Ahumada, Rodríguez' predecessor who came to the closing of the Canquintú congress.

Shortly into his impromptu address, Rodríguez started criticizing the congress. He accused it of "blackmail" and of marching under an ill-advised "political banner" (i.e., playing politics) in linking the comarca with the mega-projects. He attributed these actions to the delegates' being confused by "people with old mental structures" and people who "believe they know everything while in fact they know nothing." He lamented that the congress had been led down the primrose path, in his opinion, by outside agitators, non-Guaymíes who sought their own interest at the expense of what was clearly to the advantage of the Guaymíes in their close relationship with the government. The Guaymíes should support Cerro Colorado because it would solve all their problems (quotes and summary from *Acta de Soloy,* Congresos Guaymíes 1980:47–48). No one present misunderstood him; even though he did not specify to whom he was referring, people took him to be talking about Catholic bishops and priests.

To Minister Rodríguez' shock, after his speech the congress officials invited several Guaymíes to give their reactions. As succinctly summarized in the minutes of the congress:

> People of the Congress responded, refuting all the accusations made by the Minister, with solid arguments which left clear that the Guaymí people are not being manipulated; that the Guaymí position with respect to Cerro Colorado and the Hydroelectric Projects is based on problems and concrete facts and not a simple political banner, much less blackmail; that the Guaymí people want progress and development but not in the form which the State and Government [sic] wants to impose, via huge projects that guarantee no real benefit and which only proceed in detriment of the Guaymí people; and that the National Government is accustomed to defraud the indigenous people, toying with them via promises. (Congresos Guaymíes 1980:48)

An articulate delegate from Veraguas, in his challenge to the minister's remarks, made explicit what the minister had left implicit: that he was referring to efforts by agents of the Catholic Church, thought to be manipulating the Guaymíes into opposition to the projects. The delegate thanked Bishop Núñez, seated near Rodríguez on the platform, for his pastoral letter; but he had not read Núñez' pastoral letter, and, he observed, during the discussion of Cerro Colorado, no one had mentioned it. He noted that he was from an area of Veraguas that was never visited by priests, and that he knew no priests or bishops. Although several priests were attending the congress, he had not met them. The priests had not asked to address the congress, and, so far as he was aware, different from government observers, the priests had made no attempt to influence the congress. According to his friends, the priests were there only to show their support for the Guaymí people. This delegate could assure the minister that his own negative evaluation of the Cerro Colorado project had nothing to do with the Catholic Church. If the minister did not mean the church when he referred to outsiders who were manipulating the Guaymíes into politicizing the mining project, he went on, then perhaps he had in mind opposition political parties. But no representatives of opposition parties came to the congress, and no delegates spoke about any of the parties. So, he asked the minister, if we are being manipulated, who is doing it? The only outsiders not from the church were representatives of different government agencies, including CODEMIN and IRHE.

In arriving at his evaluation of the projects, he continued, he had heard a document written by a Guaymí commission, then had listened as many delegates from Chiriquí and Bocas del Toro spoke of their experiences of the mining and hydroelectric projects, of the damage to their regions, of their numerous meetings with project sponsors, of the many promises they heard, of the failure by those responsible to keep any of the promises, and of their all-around displeasure with the projects. On that basis, he joined the other delegates in passing the resolutions to which the minister objected. He suspected that the minister found it difficult to believe that the Guaymí people, based on their own experience and intelligence, could see clearly what was going on with these projects.

Several others underscored the approach taken in this delegate's remarks to the minister, always insisting that the Guaymí people made their own decisions and were not victims of the manipulations of outsiders. They also questioned the assurances of the minister regarding government work on the comarca and the government's concern for the welfare of the Guaymíes. They observed that whenever the conversations with the government seemed to be progressing, the government would require further "study." But no one ever heard more about these studies; and every change of ministers brought the same message. What happened to all these studies? They implied that the gifts, too little to do anything worthwhile in the Guaymí area, were like trying to distract hungry children with a few pieces of candy; they demanded something more substantive.

Some noted that Minister Rodríguez had yet to meet with the Guaymí representatives concerning the comarca; he always seemed to have something else to do. One person recounted Cacique Mónico's experience of going to Rodríguez' office, hoping for an appointment, and being told that the minister was too busy to see him; then he saw the minister sitting at his desk reading a newspaper. Mónico went home with the impression that for the minister, reading the newspaper had priority over a meeting with Guaymíes and a settlement of the long overdue question of the comarca.

Rodríguez asked to speak again. He hurriedly apologized to Bishop Núñez, assuring him that he had never for a moment intended to cast doubts on the noble work of the Catholic Church. He vigorously denied that he had the church in mind when he spoke of manipulation. He also expressed his shock that anyone could have thought that he had anything other than the highest respect for the intelligence of the Guaymí people; he did not know what could have led anyone to interpret his remarks in that fashion.

He again assured them that the government was laboring in good faith to work out the complex questions regarding the comarca. He told them that he had carefully reviewed the record of dealings between the Guaymíes and his ministry, and knew of the various times the government had said it needed to study this or that question.[17] He knew that whenever the Guaymíes had been asked to bring more information, they had done so.

Then came his most revealing statement of all: he acknowledged that, despite what they had been told for several years, the government had yet to do any studies whatsoever to take care of its side of the bargaining process. However, he promised, his own assurances of government action were true; he now had a budget and personnel from several ministries to work on these questions.

He also assured them that he wanted to work with their representatives, as the government had promised, but had been very busy and had not had time. He would see them any time. A couple of delegates, taking him at his word, named a date and time that the Guaymí commission for the comarca would see him in his office. Rodríguez had clearly not expected this response; he stumbled around, mumbled a couple of incoherent phrases, then said that he could not see them at that time because of other engagements. Fine, they said: when shall we see you? After a bit of going back and forth, they pressured him into getting out his calendar and making an appointment to renew discussions with the Guaymíes concerning the comarca.

After the government delegation left, the congress reconvened around 4:00 p.m. to conclude its business. As the first item, they asked that Bishop Núñez address them. The bishop, briefed by the priests observing the congress, spoke briefly and simply: he was delighted to be present for the closing of this amazing congress, he shared the concerns of the Guaymíes, and he pledged the support of the church in Chiriquí for the Guaymí comarca, which he recognized as essential for their future. He referred to his pastoral letter on the copper mine, noting that the church did not oppose the project, but only that the church saw that the project did not seem to take the Guaymíes into account. The church, he maintained, had no independent interest in these matters; rather, the church was in solidarity with the Guaymíes in their struggle to achieve for themselves the rights they were guaranteed both by their dignity as human persons and by the Panamanian constitution. The delegates gave him a standing ovation.

Aftermath of the Congress

The Extraordinary Guaymí General Congress of Soloy marked an important shift in the approach of the Guaymíes. The Guaymí people remained loyal to Torrijos and his government for a long time, doing everything asked to move forward the negotiations for the comarca. When the copper project first entered their area, even those adversely affected tended to give the sponsors the benefit of any doubts they had regarding the advantages to the Guaymíes of the project. But the continuing problems created by the project, and the frustration of the Guaymíes as they sought information and answers, raised doubts about the merits of the project and gave rise to opposition. The opposition, at first guarded and localized, became more open until, at Soloy, thousands of Guaymíes met to analyze and condemn the projects.

The resolutions, which captured well the lengthy discussions of the congress, articulated the growing Guaymí consensus: as long as the comarca and the carta orgánica remained dreams or promises from the government, the Guaymíes could not assume they would receive legal protection when faced with the major problems and dislocations brought on by the mega-projects. Experience of the work on the projects showed them that whatever the sponsors said, in fact no one consulted with the Guaymíes, and apparently no one intended to.

The government's and project sponsors' reactions to questions about the projects only served to harden Guaymí opposition. During the recess following the departure of the government representatives, little groups of delegates made their commentaries as they milled around the area. They were proud that they had stood up to Minister Rodríguez, and that they had spoken clearly. They were impressed that they had forced him to back off, effectively to take back virtually everything he had said in his main address. They laughed as they recalled that he had stumbled around for words, in effect saying that when he had earlier said "no," he was amazed that anyone had taken that to mean "no"—he clearly meant "yes." They understood well how important it had been for him to be able to "clarify these misunderstandings!"

They were indignant that Rodríguez had accused them of falling victim to the manipulations of church people. They did not agree that the church's efforts had played a major role in their own analysis of the projects. In addition, they thought his approach was condescending; he spoke to the Guaymíes as though they were little children who could be "bribed with candy" (as a number of Guaymíes expressed it) instead of as adults who were capable of judging for themselves what was going on in their world.

From Soloy, many Guaymíes carried back to their caseríos the message that the government could not be trusted, and that the promises of a comarca were only words. As a result of the minister's statement about the absence of often mentioned government studies regarding the comarca, for the first time some of those responsible for negotiating began to question whether the government was in fact working in good faith. They had previously believed that all the delays were really explained by the government's claims of complexity, budget restrictions, and the need for more information; they did not miss the significance of the minister's remark, made under the pressure of the moment, that in effect the government had done nothing to move forward the process of defining the Guaymí comarca. It had not even done any of the work it said it was doing.

The Extraordinary Guaymí Congress of Soloy seemed to mark a watershed; Guaymí meetings after the Soloy congress took on a more aggressive tone. Many Guaymíes now realized that they could not rely on government promises, that the people would get what they demanded only if they organized and applied pressure. Guaymí leaders met in August 1980 in Alto de Jesús, Las Palmas District, Veraguas Province, where they unanimously adopted an open letter to Panama's president, Dr. Aristides Royo. They protested the government's failure to respond to the Guaymíes, referring specifically of the lack of attention to the resolutions of the Soloy congress. They characterized the Cerro Colorado and Teribe-Changuinola projects as ones that "totally ignore our people's land rights and guarantee no benefits whatsoever for the Guaymí people." And in their conclusion they hinted, for the first time, of the possibility of violence (Dirigentes Guaymíes 1980:2).

A disturbed President Royo[18] ordered a meeting with Guaymí leaders in October 1980. He came with a proposal for the partial definition of the comarca, conceding to the Guaymíes the eastern part of Bocas del Toro Province; however, by asking for an immediate reply, he tried to make it an all-or-nothing decision. To his surprise, the Guaymíes responded that since they had received no advance copies of this proposal, they needed time to go over it carefully and to consult with the people. Later they rejected the proposal; they saw the government's move as an attempt to divide the Guaymíes so that those with the most at stake could not count on the support of the rest.

OUTSIDE SUPPORT FOR THE GUAYMI POSITION

The Soloy congress also marked a growing awareness on the part of a number of Guaymí leaders that the Guaymíes could not succeed alone; they were too few and too isolated to be able to force the government to take them seriously. They needed the active support of non-Guaymíes: resources and skills to transmit their message (the resolutions) to groups within and outside Panama, and alliances in Panama with other people who would also be adversely affected, albeit less directly, by the development of the Cerro Colorado project.[19] At the same time, with the resolutions of the Soloy congress, the Guaymíes themselves had for the first time adopted a public position that outside groups could publicize and support.

The publicity generated around Bishop Núñez' and the Panamanian Bishops' Conference's pastoral letters, published in April and May of 1979, had laid the groundwork for national and international attention to the Guaymí case.[20] In October 1980, Catholic clergy and religious women working with the Guaymíes, led by the bishops of Chiriquí and of Bocas del Toro, gathered in Canquintú for their first meeting together, to discuss wide-ranging aspects of their work with the Guaymíes. The participants, joined later by the bishop of Veraguas, signed an open letter (published in the Panamanian press and widely distributed elsewhere) uniting the church "with the cry of the Guaymí people" heard in Soloy and other Guaymí meetings. This cry: that the government keep its oft-repeated promise promptly to delineate the Guaymí comarca, and that it do so before proceeding with the major projects planned for the Guaymí area. The open letter called upon the Christian communities of Panama to unite themselves in solidarity with the Guaymíes.[21] Many grassroots communities met to discuss the project, its impact on the Guaymíes and its impact on them, and to issue statements for the Guaymíes and against the projects.

Survival International (and others) in London, and the International Work Group on Indigenous Affairs (IWGIA) in Copenhagen, brought the Guaymí case to the attention of the organizers of the Fourth Russell Tribunal, whose November 1980 meeting in Rotterdam focused on the rights of the Indians of the Americas. The Russell Tribunal in turn issued a late invitation to the Guaymíes to present their case; Miguel Cruz flew to London and Rotterdam. The panel of international jurists declared in their judgment

> that the Government of Panama violates . . . international rights, because it is facilitating the execution of mining and hydroelectric projects, by national and transnational corporations, without recognizing the rights of the Guaymí Indians to their lands. (Russell Tribunal 1980)

Groups in Canada made effective use of the Guaymí statement of position in conjunction with other materials concerning the Cerro Colorado project, launching a campaign to raise national consciousness of the relationship between indigenous problems in Canada and indigenous problems elsewhere, in the context of economic policies in Canada and their impact outside. Several Canadian organizations had earlier combined to send a delegation to Panama in January 1980; their on-site investigation (DeRoo et al. 1980) was an important element in the decision to feature Cerro Colorado in the 1981 Lenten discussions sponsored by several denominations across Canada.

In London and in the United States, people presented shareholders' resolutions to the directors of RTZ and to the Fluor Corporation, the U.S. engineering firm hired to construct Cerro Colorado.[22] These resolutions supported the Guaymí position enunciated in the Resolutions of the Soloy congress: first the comarca, then negotiations regarding Cerro Colorado. From these and other efforts within and outside Panama, Guaymí leaders, Panamanian government officials, and executives of CODEMIN received telegrams and letters supporting the resolutions of the Soloy congress.

The Guaymíes, encouraged in their stance by the widespread publicity and support, continued their meetings and attempts to organize themselves.[23] In March 1981, with the help of non-Guaymí supporters in Panama, they presented the week-long forum on the Guaymí people and their future (published as CEASPA y Comité 1982). With this forum, they succeeded in taking their case from the remote mountains of western Panama to downtown Panama City, generating for the first time in Panama considerable coverage in the newspapers, and on radio and television. The Guaymí forum, besides creating considerable publicity within Panama for the Guaymí cause, also brought about the formation of an ecumenical solidarity committee to promote the Guaymí stance.

CHAPTER 10

"Outside Agitators": The Catholic Church and Cerro Colorado

I t made sense that the Guaymíes turned for support to people and groups who, for them, seemed lumped together as representatives of the Catholic Church: the bishops, various Catholic clergy working directly among the Guaymíes, and CEASPA. Guaymí leaders were only too aware that, despite occasional moves to co-opt Guaymíes and campesinos who would be affected by Cerro Colorado, the vocal non-Guaymí opponents of the project showed little or no concern for Panamanian workers, campesinos, other poor, or the Guaymí Indians. Although these opponents, in raising their questions, maintained that they sought only the best interests of all Panamanians, they reduced these interests to the business and political objectives of Panama's traditional power elites.

The government, CODEMIN, and IRHE said that the Cerro Colorado mining project and the Teribe-Changuinola hydroelectric project would help all Panamanians, especially the poor; they said the projects would have no significant negative impact in the mountains of eastern Chiriquí or western Bocas del Toro. None of the non-Guaymí opponents of the projects challenged these statements. The Guaymíes were not fooled into thinking they could look to the traditional elites for the support they needed.

However, as some Guaymí leaders knew, even before the non-Guaymí opposition to Cerro Colorado came into the open, a small group of different outsiders had formed to gather information, discuss possibilities, clarify analyses, and review changing developments as these moved from their beginnings to heightened levels of political activism and polarization. This group of outsiders noted that the supposed principal beneficiaries of the projects, the Guaymí Indians and the Panamanian nation, were simply foils, cleverly used in the speeches of the proponents of the projects. Generally working under the umbrella of the Catholic Church, this group willingly cooperated with the Guaymíes.[1]

PASTORAL LETTERS AND CHURCH ACTIVITIES

In his speech at the Soloy Congress, the Minister of Government and Justice, Ricardo Rodríguez, had accused "outside agitators" of manipulating the Guaymíes, of filling their heads with exaggerations and distortions about Cerro Colorado and Teribe-Changuinola, and of inciting them to opposition to the government. He had scarcely disguised his conviction that on their own, the Guaymíes could only agree both that these mega-projects represented progress for them as well as for Panama as a whole, and that the government he represented was clearly committed to taking care of the needs and interests of the Guaymíes. Despite his hasty denials after the Soloy delegates roundly refuted his insinuations, the Minister was unmistakably accusing Catholic bishops and priests of being these outside agitators; he was making reference to two pastoral letters concerning Cerro Colorado (Núñez y Consejo 1979; CEP 1979), and to church-sponsored activities launched by these letters.[2]

The writing and publication of these pastoral letters, and the follow-up activities related to their dissemination, represented major steps that fostered cooperation between the Church-sponsored investigative team and the Guaymíes at the local level. Furthermore, at the level of national dynamics, the bishops raised questions about the effects of greatly adding to the foreign debt in order to dedicate a major part of the nation's resources to a highly risky project over which the government sponsors had little control. In empathy with the poor and powerless of Panama, they articulated a position that found few supporters among the traditional elites, or the political and military blocs that ran the country. To put these events in their proper context, it is necessary to back up again to the December 1978 CODEMIN-sponsored seminar for Guaymí leaders at Hato Chamí.

CODEMIN's seminar in Hato Chamí had produced the unintended outcome of providing the Guaymíes with their first opportunity to raise their questions, and to hear the government's inadequate responses. The same seminar produced other unintended results because of the impact it had on the Catholic Church personnel of Chiriquí Province. Daniel Núñez, Bishop of Chiriquí, attended the seminar as one of CODEMIN's handful of invited observers.[3] In what he regarded as his special concern for the Guaymíes and their problems, he had for some years looked for clergy and religious to work with them, and he wanted to hear about and support projects that would help the Guaymíes improve their own situation. Earlier that year, Núñez had accepted a CODEMIN invitation to tour the mine facilities; in his public letter of thanks, he became a problem for CODEMIN when he raised questions about the impact of the mining project on the Guaymíes and about CODEMIN's planning with respect to this impact (Núñez 1978).[4] During the December seminar, Núñez heard for himself the concerns of the Guaymíes and the inadequacy of CODEMIN's responses. All of this troubled him. He asked members of the investigative group to monitor mining project developments and their relationship to the Guaymíes, to keep him informed, and to discuss with him other ways the church might try to ensure proper attention to Guaymí interests.

By March of 1979, the people working on the interdisciplinary investigation of Cerro Colorado had gathered sufficient information and analysis to conclude that the project, as then conceived, would almost surely be disastrous for the Guaymíes. They recognized that CODEMIN's approach at the Hato Chamí seminar was typical: despite claims to be providing full information on the project to the Guaymíes, CODEMIN was in fact doing public relations promotion of the project, assuring the Guaymíes that Cerro Colorado could only benefit them. CODEMIN's efforts contributed to Guaymí confusion about the scope and impact of the project; Guaymí understanding was extraordinarily limited and Guaymí opinion accordingly very mixed. The Guaymí people not only lacked accurate information; they had not developed social and political organization adequate to define and defend their own interests in this major project.[5]

Other information indicated that the Department of Social Development of CODEMIN had no understanding of the Guaymí situation and had undertaken no studies that could form the basis of plans to mitigate the negative impact of the projects. For example, some Department personnel had only begun to realize that Guaymíes occupied caseríos all along the San Félix River, and would suffer serious problems if the river were used for tailings disposal. Given this evaluation, the investigators feared that the supposedly imminent development of the Cerro Colorado project might mean the end of the Guaymí people— not through genocide (as in Guatemala in the late 1970s and early 1980s) but through ethnocide as an unplanned side effect of the introduction of a multibillion-dollar advanced industrial project into the midst of their living space.[6]

In addition to studying the project's implications for the Guaymíes, the investigators also had analyzed the CODEMIN-Texasgulf contracts (CEASPA 1979a), the current situation of the world copper industry and markets, some experiences of other copper-exporting LDCs, and some of Panama's prospects. These analyses indicated not only that the Cerro Colorado project looked very risky for Panama, but also that Panama did not have the control of the project that CODEMIN's and the government's spokespersons said was theirs. The project not only boded disaster for the Guaymíes; it also looked like a very high-risk mortgage of the economic future of Panama itself.

Bishop Núñez decided to publicize the concerns raised by the investigative team, and to commit his diocese to solidarity with the Guaymíes, the people most directly affected. He hoped not only to put pressure on the project sponsors to take Guaymí interests seriously, but also to enable his own pastoral agents to respond to Guaymí requests for help in sorting out the complexities of the mining project. On April 19, 1979—the annual Day of Indigenous Peoples in Panama—Bishop Núñez and his Presbyteral Council published a pastoral letter called "The Guaymí Indians and Cerro Colorado" (Núñez y Consejo 1979).[7]

The bishop grounded his concern for the plight of the Guaymí Indians mainly in Catholic social teachings: CELAM (1970–Medellín, 1979–Puebla), and encyclical letters and other statements of recent popes. He made clear his commitment to the "preferential option for the poor" and his desire to be the voice of the voiceless Guaymíes, the "poorest of the poor" (CELAM 1979: nn. 31, 34, 1134–65; Núñez y Consejo 1979:2, 15). He argued that the mining project could only bring true development to Panama and to eastern Chiriquí if its sponsors committed themselves to "integral development" along the lines of the social encyclicals of recent popes; he summarized his point of view with the statement that "the mine ought to be at the service of people and not people at the service of the mine" (Núñez y Consejo 1979:2, 3–5, 13–15).

The heart of the pastoral letter, Part Three, raised detailed questions about how the sponsors proposed to handle the impact that published plans for the project represented for different aspects of Guaymí life: threats to land and water, plans for relocation and compensation, protection from outsiders and from forced changes in values and social relationships, assurance of job-training and employment, encouragement of Guaymí participation in decision-making, and a direct share of the profits from the mine. The pastoral letter summarized important aspects of Guaymí life, such as the interrelationships and interdependencies of the inhabitants of Guaymí communities, and outlined major aspects of the proposed project as presented by CODEMIN (for example, the possibility of using the San Félix River for disposal of tailings from the concentrator). Each section concluded with specific requests for information on the impact of the matters discussed, on background studies undertaken by CODEMIN, on plans for the mitigation of negative consequences, and on consultations with the Guaymíes affected (Núñez y Consejo 1979:6–12). Aware that the project sponsors had yet to begin the promised studies of the Guaymí situation and disturbed that they were not consulting the Guaymíes, Núñez provided the basic questions for a comprehensive assessment of the social impact of the mining project and insisted on Guaymí participation. But he presented no accusations or definitive judgments.[8]

Núñez' pastoral letter preceded action on the part of the Panamanian Bishops' Conference, which had kept itself informed on the national prospects for Cerro Colorado's impact. On May 11, 1979, the Conference, while joining many other Panamanian religious groups rallying around Núñez, published its own pastoral letter widening the scope of the questions to include the desires, needs, and interests of all Panamanians (CEP 1979). Adopting the same stance of the preferential option for the poor, the bishops looked at the national and transnational dynamics of the mining project. They concluded that the transnational dynamics of the copper industry would far outweigh the national dynamics in vital project decisions that would affect the nation. Within the national dynamics, they questioned Panama's ability to finance its share of the project, called for more clarity and debate about the trade-offs should the project force the government into hard choices about the allocation of scarce funds, and indirectly brought into the open the widespread but unpublicized concerns about the integrity of the Panamanian management of the project. The Conference endorsed Núñez' insistence on the fulfillment of government promises concerning the Guaymí comarca and the full participation of the Guaymíes in decisions that would affect them. It also urged the elaboration of a popularly based national development plan that would include broad consultation with all Panamanians, and some decisions about the allocation of the millions of dollars of anticipated government revenue from the projects. Like Núñez, the Conference made clear it did not oppose the project, but advocated open national debate on its merits, to ensure that Cerro Colorado would become a project of and for the people of Panama.

In the highly politicized arena created by the opposition's virulent attacks and the government's calls for unquestioning loyalty, the bishops tried to carve out space for national discussion of the impact of the mining project. The bishops said that they relied on their own standing as moral leaders watching out for the interests of those least likely on their own to be able to influence the project.

Both these pastoral letters received wide dissemination throughout Panama. The texts were published as pamphlets and in Panamanian newspapers; they were read in their entirety on radio programs. Newspaper and radio commentators interviewed church representatives and offered interpretations of the themes presented, usually according to their own persuasions with respect to the Torrijos government and the mining project. Even if few people in Panama grappled directly with the texts and arguments of the bishops, almost everyone was aware that the church had spoken on Cerro Colorado, raising serious questions about its viability and its impact. The bishops succeeded, to some degree at least, in creating some space for open discussion of Cerro Colorado, discussion that at times transcended the politically partisan charges and countercharges of the debate until then.[9]

Catholic pastoral workers across Panama organized readings and discussion of the pastoral letters, inviting congregations, students, and fledgling grassroots Christian communities to analyze the Cerro Colorado project's likely impact on the Guaymíes and on the other poor sectors of Panama. Bishop Núñez' letter, more lively in style and more narrowly focused on the needs and aspirations of a concrete group of people, was the more accessible of the pastoral letters. For Catholic pastoral workers, it served to begin building a sense of solidarity with the Guaymíes, who until then had remained pretty much an unknown people from an unfamiliar part of the country. The Conference letter, less inspirational and more analytical in tone, treated themes that were rather more abstract and subtle, despite the national concerns it addressed. As a result, the popular responses were more subdued.[10]

In Chiriquí, Bishop Núñez frequently discussed the themes of his letter, both on his weekly radio program in David and in his visits to different groups in his diocese. The Veraguas diocesan radio station, widely listened to in the Guaymí and campesino areas of Veraguas and eastern Chiriquí, broadcast the entire letter several times, sometimes with simultaneous translation into Ngawbere and Sabanero; it interviewed Núñez and others, and presented several panel discussions on the theme.

In eastern Chiriquí, dissemination and discussion of the pastoral letters provided the means for church participation in educational work with the Guaymíes. Armed with and protected by both pastoral letters, the priests could now respond openly to Guaymí requests for information concerning the mining project and its likely impact. Furthermore, as pastoral agents working under Bishop Núñez, part of their responsibility was the dissemination of his and the Conference's pastoral letters. The booklet version of Núñez' letter had numerous photographs of Guaymíes; many people wanted copies as *recuerdos* (keepsakes), and the parishes provided them.[11] Priests of Tolé and Remedios answered requests to take part in discussions of the impact of the project with Guaymí and campesino communities, mainly based on Part Three of the pastoral letter.[12] The priests took to the communities not only copies of the pastoral letters, but also their adaptation of a government map of the communities of the districts of San Félix, Remedios and Tolé. The large multicolored map, encased in clear plastic because of the rains, depicted the location of the principal installations of the mining project: the mine itself, deposits for waste rock, concentrator, roads, pipelines, electrical transmission lines, tailings disposal, and smelter.[13] The map proved to be an effective educational tool to help local communities appreciate the magnitude of the mining project; although many people had never seen a map before, they quickly saw the relationship between the map and the area and communities with which they were familiar.

In these meetings, the people talked about what they had heard about the mining project and its possible effects; some communities already had several years' experience of living with the mine road and its effects, and this could be discussed. Invariably the conversations included fears of sterilization and death from the poisonous smoke from the smelter, concerns fostered by the exaggerations of national radio commentators opposed to the government; the priests tried to dispel these exaggerations. In these meetings, the priests had two objectives: to provide people with accurate information about the project itself (its location, its plans, its scope and magnitude, and its possible effects), and to assure the participants of the church's support in their own attempts to minimize the negative aspects of the project while maximizing the benefits it might bring them. Included among the effects were discussions of CODEMIN's promises of ways the project would benefit the Guaymíes. The priests tried to use educational methods that respected Guaymí ways of learning and discussing these matters. They also recognized that the Guaymíes themselves had to sift through the information as best they could, analyze and evaluate its implications, and arrive at their own positions to support the project, to question it, to fight it, or even to do nothing about it. The priests, at one time or another, encountered all these responses.

RESPONSES TO CHURCH ACTIVITIES

Through careful wording of their criteria and questions, Bishop Núñez and the Panamanian Bishops' Conference tried to avoid direct confrontation between the Catholic Church and the government. They succeeded, inasmuch as there were no public outcries, threats, or denunciations. But the stakes were too high, the project too controversial, the sponsors too secretive about the project's prospects and problems, and the bishops too visible for matters to remain there. The sponsors responded publicly from their Panama City offices, and privately or semiprivately from their offices and from the field in Chiriquí.

From its Panama City offices, CODEMIN publicly embraced the

church's support for its own preoccupations with the future of the Guaymíes and for the important national issues raised by the project. CODEMIN president Rodrigo González claimed that the questions concerning the Guaymíes, raised in some form or other at the Hato Chamí seminar, had been studied and that CODEMIN had the answers—there would be no problems. But instead of directly addressing the principal issues raised in the bishops' letter, CODEMIN launched a public relations campaign that simply repeated the sponsors' unstinting optimism about Cerro Colorado. The unprecedented deluge of catchy advertisements (CODEMIN, 1979c), press conferences, trips to the mine area, and other activities of CODEMIN through the middle months of 1979 were probably, in good part, a response to the Conference pastoral.[14] To the bishops' questions, CODEMIN simply responded that all was well. Less directly, the sponsors fanned the flames of enthusiasm for Torrijos as an antidote to problems in the mining project; government spokespersons implied that the bishops' questioning of the project made common cause with the disloyal, anti-popular opponents of the government.[15]

In private, representatives of CODEMIN's management strongly protested the bishops' subtle insinuations regarding their honesty. Of all the issues raised in the Conference pastoral letter, CODEMIN management found most deeply disturbing the bishops' insistence that project management be closely and openly accountable to the nation. Nevertheless, the top managers took measures that cast further doubts on their own probity. Although they insisted over and over that nothing about the project was secret, and that anyone could look over the Texasgulf studies or any other documents pertinent to the public debate, they permitted only very restricted outside access to these documents, took part principally in carefully controlled public meetings, and looked for other ways to control the flow of information.

Within CODEMIN, some employees were denied access to information germane to their areas of responsibility, for fear they would pass it on to others outside the company. The Ministry of Planning and Political Economy, which was charged with overall implementation of the government's long-range development plans, was only able to obtain limited information from CODEMIN for its intragovernmental analyses of the benefits and risks of Cerro Colorado. The Comptroller of the Republic could not coax budgets and expenditures from

CODEMIN, even though Panamanian law required their submission. During the CODEMIN-RTZ negotiations on an agreement to proceed with the next phase of the project (1980), even President Royo could not obtain current drafts of Panama's proposals or find out what major issues remained unresolved. Coming at a time when CODEMIN's top management was publicly denying the existence of the project's major problems, the church's questioning of Cerro Colorado was used to create a climate of suspicion within the corporation. The coincidence of church questioning and doubts raised by the World Bank and other financial agencies promoted the feeling that someone was leaking confidential information, even though the only people in CODEMIN with access to that information were those who promoted the suspicions.

But investigators needed no information from leaks to know that Cerro Colorado was in trouble, and to figure out what the major problems were. By carefully studying CODEMIN publications, by following closely the ups and downs of the world copper market, by finding relevant articles in U.S. publications and doing independent fieldwork, and by exchanging information and ideas with others outside of Panama, the investigative team analyzed the overall dynamics and most of the problems created or faced by the mining project. Just the fact that "firm" dates for beginning construction came and went without comment indicated that something was amiss, namely, that the bottom had dropped out of the world copper market, and that the sponsors had not obtained the necessary financing for the project. Over time, CODEMIN confirmed these suspicions in the guarded language of its official pronouncements.[16]

Also away from public hearing, representatives of the Department of Social Development acknowledged that CODEMIN had done no studies in the Guaymí area. Still, they protested that Núñez' pastoral letter prematurely raised public questions that no one could answer. They contended that the bishop's approach would only create unfounded fears among the Guaymíes, making it more difficult for CODEMIN to help them see that the mining project would be to their benefit; to the Department it appeared that the church sought to stir up trouble among the Guaymíes. They maintained that the questions raised by the clerics were unanswerable because of the major uncertainties of the design of the mining project itself. They depended on Texasgulf for research, analysis, and other basic information; yet, for Texasgulf, all aspects of the project remained "alternatives" until final decisions were made. When members of the Department of Social Development tried to organize preliminary social impact studies, Texasgulf quickly deflated them by presenting six or eight possible routes for the mine road, three or four possible locations for dams, three port sites, and four major alternatives that included dozens of subalternatives for concentrator-tailings disposal.[17] In all studies, the only part of the project that remained geographically fixed was the mountain. Anyway, they asserted, the five-year construction period of the mining project would allow ample time for them to carry out social impact studies and mitigations; at that time, all the major decisions about location of project facilities would be firm, and they would know what to study.

They also complained that Núñez' questions were unanswerable because the Department of Social Development had too many responsibilities given their available personnel, no budget to carry out needed studies, no advance knowledge of decisions that would affect the Guaymíes, and, above all, no power within CODEMIN. The Department, aside from its responsibilities for CODEMIN's relations with the Guaymíes, also oversaw some of the special education and training programs that were part of the development of Cerro Colorado, such as the training of heavy-equipment mechanics, carpenters, and masons. It was supposed to arrange government scholarships to allow future Panamanian mining engineers, geologists, mining economists, and other specialists to study at foreign universities. To a certain degree, the Department also functioned as a public relations unit, explaining the project and its benefits to different groups in Panama. However, the Department had virtually no weight within CODEMIN; it was marginal both in decision-making and in budgeting. CODEMIN concerned itself more with the financial and engineering aspects of Cerro Colorado than with social concerns.[18]

While no one denied that the Department depended on Texasgulf for information and had little power within CODEMIN, it was still difficult to accept these explanations as satisfactory. Even though Texasgulf proposed several alternatives for some major features of the overall project design, field surveys usually indicated that the differences among them represented only minor variations, small technical changes that would have little effect on the overall social impact. In contrast, the investigative group, with fewer personnel and a far smaller budget,

had used published information to do fieldwork. It was able to survey the likely alternatives for the major mining project installations, to
make lists of the communities most likely to be affected, and to talk to
many Guaymíes about their understanding of the project and their
desires. Long after the work of the investigative group was underway,
CODEMIN had yet to place any of its trained personnel in the field to
look over the Guaymí situation, and report back a body of useful data.
Instead, the principals of the Department of Social Development remained in their offices in Panama City while the Department's small,
untrained field staff engaged in public relations efforts among the
Guaymíes, trying to persuade them that the mining project was good
for them. The fact that the Department, after a period of almost three
years, was still unable to provide any answers to the social questions
posed by the project led directly to the public questioning embodied in
the pastoral letters.[19]

The Department of Social Development of CODEMIN accepted
Texasgulf's contention that no social impact studies of the Guaymí area
need be undertaken until final decisions had been made about the
mining project itself—that is, until mine construction began. Therefore, despite the Department's excuses for its own shortcomings, they
also claimed that they had plenty of time during the five years of mine
construction to carry out any studies needed in the Guaymí area.

The Texasgulf argument, echoed within CODEMIN, had several
parts. The anticipated five years of construction would allow more than
enough time for the sponsors to discover and resolve the problems the
project might create for the Guaymíes. The sponsors would choose
among the alternative sites for the project facilities as part of the decision to proceed. Until then, studies in the Guaymí area could not be
properly focused. Texasgulf argued that going into the communities to
do questionnaires on people's lives and habits, goods, and necessities,
would only serve to arouse fears of the unknown and unwarranted
expectations. The fears of the unknown could not be countered and
expectations could not be fulfilled until major decisions concerning the
project were made. In Texasgulf's view, it would be better to postpone
the studies until all the pieces of the puzzle were in place and the overall
pattern was clear. In the end, if the sponsors decided they could not
develop Cerro Colorado, they would have wasted no time and money
on social impact studies.[20]

Texasgulf had little incentive to concern itself over the social impact of Cerro Colorado. The company bore no liability; the contracts shielded Texasgulf from responsibility for adverse social effects arising from its operations in Panama, and enabled it to keep a low profile before the Panamanian public. Texasgulf had only to comply with the prevailing national laws and its contracts; questions of social welfare were the responsibility of the state (E. A. Wieselmann, in conversation with Canadian delegation; see DeRoo et al. 1980).[21]

The transnational partner had no desire to add the interests or needs of the Guaymíes to the already monumental technical problems of design and engineering. For example, engineers working on the 65-km road from the port to the mine sought a route which required the fewest bridges and curves, involved the lowest angle of ascent, and minimized the risk of constant landslides. If to these criteria Texasgulf added considerations of Guaymí farmland, pasture, households, water supplies, and the host of other details of survival in the Guaymí area, it would have regarded the "technical" problems of road construction as overwhelming. Texasgulf went to Panama to design, build, and operate a copper mine; it viewed other factors in the light of those priorities. Rather than take potential negative social impact into account in the design of the project, Texasgulf made decisions based on engineering and economics; it could worry about the mitigation of negative social impact once construction was underway. At that time, project sponsors would still have four to five years to do studies and make all necessary arrangements for the affected population.[22]

For a variety of reasons, Texasgulf's arguments found a willing audience among the people of CODEMIN. CODEMIN approached Cerro Colorado as a business venture, seeking to maximize the gains for Panama while minimizing the risks. When faced with its built-in conflict of interest as the nation's principal agent overseeing all aspects of the mining project, CODEMIN's top management emphasized profits from the mining enterprise over solutions to social problems (see CEASPA 1979a). Already feeling pressure from the government as they spent borrowed money without producing a viable mining project, the managers of CODEMIN had little interest in funding studies that might not have had immediate utility. None of the workers in the Department of Social Development had any experience in anticipating, preparing for, and coping with the social impact of a large-scale project among indigenous people. Perhaps more attuned to office work and bureaucratic struggles, and lacking first-hand experience of the minimal necessities of life for someone doing fieldwork with the Guaymíes, they did not seem to realize that they could do at least preliminary social impact studies without any special budget.[23]

CODEMIN, the state's representative as business partner in the joint operating company and the only state agency charged with oversight of the mining project, should not also have been in charge of the social impact assessment. CODEMIN saw itself as an agent of the Torrijos government; as the Guaymíes came to oppose the project and CODEMIN, their opposition extended to include the government itself. By establishing another state agency for the social impact work, Panama might have tried to build a structure more credible to the Guaymíes and their supporters.[24] As it was, Panama replicated the experiences of other nations: once the state became a partner in a project, the indigenous people tended to see the state as the one making all the decisions that affected them; the state became the agent of the multinational corporation.[25]

Neither the Guaymíes nor those who worked with them could convince the sponsors that delaying the study of the social impact of Cerro Colorado until construction began meant that the sponsors had already decided that Guaymí interests and concerns would have no influence on the project. If the studies of the Guaymí situation were undertaken as part of the feasibility studies, the sponsors could try to incorporate solutions to the conflicting technical and social problems into the very design of the project. In the absence of plans to mitigate likely problems, serious problems would arise for the Guaymíes once construction began.

Significantly, even if the sponsors were able to foresee some of these problems in time to consider alternatives, any design changes to accommodate the Guaymíes would bring about delays at the most critical stage of the entire project, when capital was being expended at a phenomenal rate without immediate return. Delay of any kind would increase the risk that the grace period on loan repayment would end before the mine was operating at sufficient capacity to generate the income to repay the loans. Even with considerable good will, the sponsors would nonetheless come up against tremendous financial pressure to leave the design alone. Thus, any social impact study that might have influenced the design of the mining project would have had to have been undertaken as part of the feasibility studies. If the partners were serious in their promises to incorporate the results of social impact studies into the design of the project, this whole process would be less expensive if done while basic design features were still under discussion.[26]

While the sponsors' responses from Panama City manifested public support of the church's questions along with behind-the-scenes maneuvering, in eastern Chiriquí representatives of the sponsors went on the attack, trying to discredit the church and to harass local priests. CODEMIN's field personnel and two or three on-site managers of the joint operating company, apparently persuaded that the church's work with the Guaymíes posed a threat, adopted directly confrontational tactics in response to the bishops' letters and church activities. Although they sometimes admitted that the mining project would cause some dislocations and inconveniences to the Guaymíes, the field personnel insisted that Núñez and the priests really advocated keeping the Guaymíes as a "living anthropological museum," poor and miserable, in contrast to the revolutionary government's goals of providing the Guaymíes with basic advances in health, nutrition, education, and economic security. They maintained that the church, under the guise of concern for the Guaymíes, had an interest in keeping them impoverished and ignorant.[27]

They accused the priests of advocating, at Guaymí meetings, the wildly exaggerated claims of the virulent opposition, specifically that the Cerro Colorado project would bring widespread sterility and death to residents of eastern Chiriquí. They claimed to have a cassette recording of a priest making such statements.[28] For them, the church had decided to join the traditional elite opposed to Cerro Colorado, apparently as a tactic to oppose the Torrijos revolution.

Most workers in the mining camps received these stories as true, and the atmosphere changed accordingly. Whereas the workers had earlier received the priests warmly, offered them rides in company vehicles, and invited them to eat with the workers and sleep in the camps, after the publication of the pastoral letters many workers no longer offered rides, no longer stopped to chat, and scarcely said a civil word of greeting. Two irate field managers drafted a statement, signed by almost all the workers, denouncing what they saw as the misinformed statements of the bishops and urging the people of Panama to back the mining project as a source of jobs, national development, and advancement for the Guaymíes. One of these field managers also wrote a "Guaymí" petition endorsing the development of Cerro Colorado; but he failed to persuade the Guaymí elected representative of Hato Chamí to take it around for Guaymí signatures.[29]

One incident indicated well the climate of growing hostility to the priests, the tactics of the mining company, the information from which they operated, and the responses of the Guaymíes. Local priests, with written permission from CODEMIN in Panama City, drove their jeep on the mine access road, one of two or three rough roads that went into the Guaymí area of Chiriquí, and the only one that went all the way to the Continental Divide. Priests from Tolé arrived one day at the guard shack just outside the town of San Félix. They were on their way to meet some Guaymíes from a distant community who were coming to pick up coffee plants as part of a parish-aided self-help project. Unexpectedly, the watchman would not let the priests pass. He had received new orders from a local mining company boss barring the priests from using the road without explicit approval each time; the approval had to come from one of four bosses who resided in the Escopeta camp, at the foot of Cerro Colorado, twelve to fourteen hours' walk from the guard house. The watchman said he did not know the reason for the change, but thought it might have something to do with the danger of slides blocking the road.[30]

Some priests tried several times to talk with a CODEMIN manager in Panama City, to discover where these orders had come from and why the earlier permission had been revoked, but no manager was ever available. A CODEMIN engineer, certain that there was some misunderstanding, went to clear it up—but returned to his office to affirm that the order was indeed legitimate, and that he could find out nothing more. The priests were given to understand that the decision came "from the highest level," but could find no one to take responsibility for it or to discuss the basis of the problem.

On a rainy afternoon some weeks later, two priests crossed the Continental Divide above Cerro Colorado from Bocas del Toro Province, en route to Remedios; at the invitation of Cacique Mónico of Bocas del Toro, they had accompanied him to a Guaymí regional meeting in a remote community a few hours north of Cerro Colorado. The on-site boss who had signed the order barring use of the road to the priests gave them a ride in his pickup. Obviously very angry, he accused them of deliberately stirring up unfounded Guaymí opposition to the mining project; he said that León Palacios, the CODEMIN representative at the regional meeting, had told him that the priests manipulated the Guaymíes to continue their opposition, filling them with horror stories of what the mining project would do.[31] Eventually he wrote his memo cancelling the permission to use the mine road. He said he had done so because the priests only went to Guaymí communities to tell lies about the mining project, and he would not let them use the road to make their wrongheaded task easier. When they asked him where he obtained his information, he referred to the cassette recording and to conversations with CODEMIN's field people. The priests expressed surprise that someone whose daily work relied on fairly scientific methods would accept such an unscientific basis on which to condemn them, and they urged him to go talk to Guaymíes himself, to hear what they said the priests were doing. But he saw no need to do this.[32]

These tactics backfired for the mine sponsors. When the Tolé priests could not attend their meeting to deliver coffee plants, they followed the normal practice for communicating with remote communities: they had a radio station announce that the meeting was called off because the mining company would not allow them to use the road. The Guaymíes were furious that they had to journey fourteen hours down to Tolé, then carry the plants back to their community. Counting the lost day because of the cancelled meeting, the new arrangements cost them three days (plus some time to rest from their travels) instead of four hours. The story spread quickly; angry Guaymíes saw through the mining company's efforts, and this enhanced the credibility of the priests. The Guaymíes enjoyed telling the story of CODEMIN's fear of the priests and of the Guaymíes as well.

The head of security for the project and León Palacios of CODEMIN's field staff also argued that the church and the mining project ought to join forces on behalf of the Guaymíes. They proposed that the local priests serve as mediators between the mining operation and the local Guaymí communities; they offered the priests an office in the Hato Chamí camp, a CODEMIN-sponsored base of operations. In CODEMIN's view, if the church truly desired the good of the Guaymíes, it would accept the offer.

The priests recognized the proposal as a brilliant stroke on the part of CODEMIN. CODEMIN had nothing to lose and everything to gain; the priests had nothing to gain and everything to lose. If the priests accepted, CODEMIN could reap the public relations benefits of its good-faith efforts to do all possible to protect Guaymí interests while muzzling the priests, who would be employees of the project. Meanwhile, the Guaymíes would have seen the church working for and supporting the project, no matter what anyone said; the church would have no credibility as an independent ally of the Guaymíes. And if the priests declined the offer, CODEMIN could raise questions about the church's seriousness in seeking real solutions to Guaymí problems, adding to its contention that the church sought only to stir up problems. The priests decided to manifest openness to the proposal, and asked for meetings and concrete proposals, in the hope that CODEMIN was merely posturing. In the event, although the two men brought up their idea several more times, CODEMIN scheduled no meetings and tabled no proposals.

INTERPRETING RESPONSES TO CHURCH ACTIVITIES

Without candid admissions from some principals, one cannot determine whether the CODEMIN and Texasgulf managements in Panama City ordered, approved, or even were aware of their Chiriquí representatives' harassment of church workers. As already noted, CODEMIN's top management withheld from its own personnel (and from the nation) important information that would have made it clear that the church represented only one voice, and not the most powerful one, questioning the viability of the project. It seemed probable that CODEMIN's management, perhaps even its president, at least supported after the fact the decision to deny the priests the use of the mine road. But, in general, there were enough indications of poor communication among the different levels of the sponsors' people involved with the Guaymíes to leave doubt concerning home-office support of many local actions. Department of Social Development representatives in Panama City complained they had no control over the activities of León Palacios and other field staff; their complaint was believable, given the cross-purposes at which the Panama City and Chiriquí staffs at times worked.

Whatever the degree of coordination of the Panama City and Chiriquí responses to church's activities may have been, the approach of those in the field and those in Panama city showed some underlying similarities and some differences. All the sponsors' representatives seemed convinced that there was no "Indian problem" connected with Cerro Colorado. Judging from their statements, they viewed the Guaymíes as poor, ignorant, and backward, like children who needed to trust that the adults in their lives knew what was best for them. To the sponsors, the Guaymíes had "nowhere to go but up" (DeRoo et al 1980:4, quoting the project planners); any changes brought about by the mining project could not help but better their lives. And even should the mining project have been problematic for the Guaymíes, they were incapable of noticing. Within CODEMIN and the government, there was little interest in making provision for the relative autonomy of the Guaymíes, for the protection of what remained of their territorial base, or for their right to be active participants in shaping their own future (see Lobo 1980a, 1980b).[33]

Consequently, when the Guaymíes voiced their concerns and, later, held meetings to denounce the project, the sponsors hunted for "outside agitators" who manipulated them; they found the church workers easy and available targets. The sponsors claimed that the priests sought to persuade the Guaymíes to go against their own best interests. They insisted that the priests must have been acting from hidden motives— perhaps they were naive, perhaps they were reactionary opponents of the government. Whatever the case, according to the sponsors, the motives of the church workers assuredly were different from those presented in the pastoral letters.[34]

The sponsors' uncritical acceptance of western capitalist notions of progress reinforced their views of the Guaymíes; a major modern industrial complex could only be a step forward for everyone involved. The mere fact that Panama (and the Guaymíes) would receive the latest mining technology was in itself an unquestionable step forward—not only in the expected economic benefits, but in the very introduction of "modernity." If a modern mine was itself progress, all the more so could it only be progress for people as backward as the Guaymíes.

As a corollary of this view of progress, the sponsors believed that any difficulties encountered along the way were merely technical problems, all solvable through technical means. And technical problems could only be solved by people with technical training; the Guaymíes could not be expected to understand the real nature of the problems themselves, nor to make serious contributions to their solutions. This attitude could not admit of unsolvable problems or of irreconcilable clashes of values; the overriding fundamental value was progress, and any other value paled by comparison.

A great deal of effort on the part of the Guaymíes and their collaborators went toward trying to argue their right to be taken seriously in the development of the project. But for the project planners,

> the Guaymí [were] another of a series of technical problems—such as how to dispose of waste materials from the mine—needing technocratic solutions. . . . Governments and corporations define the indigenous question as simply one of "integrating" and "incorporating" native peoples into a development model in which they have little or no say. (DeRoo et al. 1980:4)

The attitudes of the project sponsors were like those of their counterparts developing similar projects in indigenous areas around the world. Among proponents of large-scale industrial projects,

> there is a strong tendency to underestimate and to understate social impact and social costs, and there is a tendency to believe that, whatever the problems may be, they can be overcome. . . . No one asks for proof that the problems anticipated really can be ameliorated in a significant way—the assumption is that they can be . . . and I think this assumption is demonstrably false. (Berger 1977:143)

> The results [of this approach to indigenous questions] are almost uniformly disastrous. The introduction of a new and dominant industrial economy (with its non-native work force, wage labor, and related economic consequences) thoroughly disrupts the indigenous way of life and alienates native peoples from their own systems of economic, political, and social organization. (DeRoo et al. 1980:4)

The project sponsors simply could not grasp that the Cerro Colorado mining project as then conceived would set in motion dynamics which could well destroy the ability of the Guaymíes to exercise some control over their own lives. Given their belief that the project could only help the Guaymíes, and given their conviction that the Guaymíes were like children, incapable of deciding for themselves what kind of life was most in their own interest, they saw themselves as presenting the Guaymíes with a unique chance for betterment under the auspices of a concerned government and its development project.

Since CODEMIN had undertaken no studies to determine the social impact of the Cerro Colorado project, its personnel had nothing of their own with which to challenge these perceptions, convictions, and biases. For them, no right-minded person or group could entertain doubts about the virtues of industrial development. The Catholic Church's admission of doubt raised for them suspicions of a different sort: that the church had some other motive (wrongheaded, even if sincere) for opposing the mining project. Those most friendly to church people interpreted their motives as misguided attempts to keep the Guaymíes in some state of primitive isolation, even though (they were convinced) such isolation would only guarantee to the Guaymíes continued poverty, backwardness, sickness, and so on. Others, less friendly, interpreted their motives as thinly disguised support for the reactionary political opposition to the Torrijos revolution.

But the most fundamental difference of perception between the church workers and CODEMIN revolved around an appreciation of the capacities of the Guaymíes themselves. None of the CODEMIN people believed that the Guaymíes were capable of arriving at an assessment of the mining project other than the one that CODEMIN presented; they thought the Guaymíes incompetent to perceive their own best interests and to move to defend them. Consequently, when Guaymí opposition increased, they took this as proof of the extraordinary ability of a small band of priests to manipulate a large group of Guaymíes. The stage was set for them to respond not to the issues raised, but to their interpretation of what lay behind the raising of the issues: the manipulation of the Guaymíes by outside agitators.

With its arrival in 1980, Rio Tinto-Zinc promoted studies of the Guaymíes affected by the mining project; the company budgeted part of its prefeasibility fund for this purpose.[35] RTZ managers in Panama stated that their corporation would act in the same socially responsible way in Panama that it did everywhere else in the world. They pointed to their Bougainville project as an example of their good work with indigenous people. They noted their support for preferential hiring practices, for model credit unions, and for other forward-looking instances of company policies. However, in its operations in South Africa, Namibia, Bougainville, and Australia, RTZ worked within indigenous or aboriginal peoples' territories, and provoked storms of national and international protests by the people affected, by social scientists and activists who studied the cases, and even by the United Nations. RTZ weathered these storms without making any serious concessions in its operational procedures.[36]

While the responses of the sponsors, whether those from Panama City or those working in Chiriquí, showed underlying similar attitudes, the responses also showed some marked differences. Whereas the Panama City responses tended to remain polite, with even the disagreements expressed privately rather than publicly, the Chiriquí responses, as discussed, became openly aggressive and harassing.

While church people in Chiriquí were trying to deal with the responses of the sponsors, CODEMIN senior management must have been working to salvage the project itself. In retrospect, it is likely that the questioners who principally concerned them were not the church groups, but powerful banking and corporate interests: the World Bank, fundamental to financing the project; Texasgulf, unwilling to go forward with the project and unable to increase its equity; and RTZ, negotiating the terms required for rescue of the project at a time of world recession, low copper prices, and little demand.

In Chiriquí, the local-level management (and even more, the workers) had a day-to-day stake in the mining project; for them, a decision to proceed with Cerro Colorado meant secure jobs and good pay, well into the future. Senior management concealed from them the reasons why the project kept being delayed; they felt threatened, and looked for the source of the threats. For them, the church's questioning, which they saw as opposition to Cerro Colorado, seemed to be the most visible, dangerous threat to the future of the project.[37] The local priests, known to be working with the Guaymíes, were the most readily available representatives of that threat.

In this climate of uncertainty and project delay, some of the behavior of the priests was probably interpreted in a manner that fueled the suspicions of the workers and their local bosses. The priests sought close contact with the Guaymíes. Hence, instead of accepting the invitations to eat and sleep in the camp of Hato Chamí, enjoying the amenities of plentiful food, electricity, running water, dominos and television in the evening, and real beds, the priests chose to camp either in a room of the schoolhouse or with Guaymí families. Instead of having frequent and leisurely encounters that would naturally have included conversations about what the priests did with their time, the workers saw the priests only occasionally, often heading up or down a Guaymí trail toward communities not accessible by road. Instead of hearing reports of religious services such as those frequently conducted by the decidedly conservative foreign evangelical Protestants from Las Lajas, the workers got vague responses from Guaymíes about what the priests were up to—just sitting around visiting, asking questions, and talking about a variety of things.[38]

The priests made no attempt to publicly challenge the aggressive tactics of the sponsors' Chiriquí workers. The priests feared that making their grievances public would only escalate the confrontation without bringing an end to the harassment. Since the real power lay with the sponsors, the priests calculated that they had nothing to gain and much to lose in a more public confrontation.[39]

In any case, the priests were convinced that the sponsors' real problems were with the Guaymíes, not with the church; and making the struggle with the church public would likely serve to further distract from the real issues. The priests recognized that they themselves had no direct stake in the debate about Cerro Colorado; rather, the Guaymíes had to take responsibility for their own interests. In the process, to the degree the Guaymíes organized to insist on their own point of view, the Guaymíes themselves could provide some protection for the priests against the harassment. That is, while it did not seem wise for the priests to denounce the project sponsors, the Guaymíes could do so with greater reason—and with more impunity. So, the priests hoped that the Guaymíes themselves would come to appreciate more and more what the sponsors were doing, and act on their own conclusions. The fact that the obviously articulate priests did not complain publicly may have persuaded those responsible for the aggressive tactics that they could attack without fear, confident that their opponents were weak.

At the time, the local priests themselves did not fully grasp the fact that the real battle had less to do just with the Guaymíes and more to do with the future of the project itself. The priests tended to interpret

CODEMIN harassment at the local level as having to do with the Guaymíes and their work with them. The attacks also had to do with the perceptions of a national church threat to the project, and with the priests' (and the Guaymíes') availability as targets for the fears and frustrations of the local workers.

The local-level harassment by people associated with the Cerro Colorado project was a counter-productive response to misinterpretations of what the church workers were doing; the people principally responsible for these attacks could, with little effort, have corrected these interpretations. But it is also true that, during this entire period, CODEMIN's top management concealed from everyone the fact that the project had encountered major problems that turned out to be insuperable. Had CODEMIN fulfilled its pledges to disclose all relevant information, perhaps its workers would have arrived at different evaluations of the significance of the church's activities; and the church personnel could have better evaluated the Guaymí part of the Cerro Colorado equation.

CHAPTER 11

Assessments of the Guaymí-centered Opposition to Cerro Colorado

The efforts of the Guaymíes and of their allies invite assessment. One assessment could examine the immediate results of these efforts, using criteria of effectiveness in achieving goals; another could use wider criteria or other goals, whether these explicitly informed the activities or not.

IMMEDIATE RESULTS OF EFFORTS

For several years, the Torrijos government kept the nation poised awaiting the unveiling of its two most important policy initiatives: the Panama Canal treaties, and the Cerro Colorado mining project. The government promised that, once completed, both would be sources of pride and security for Panamanians for generations to come. As people grew restless, bogged down in the dreary everyday life of rising inflation and prices, increased unemployment, a stagnant economy, and monotonous politics, the regime stirred them up with glimpses of a brighter future, counseling patience and continued confidence in the revolution.

The Torrijos-Carter canal treaties were ratified in 1978. In 1979, when the treaties went into effect, the Panamanian government sponsored public ceremonies to mark the occasion. People gathered from across the nation. Many of them strolled in small groups along the roads and across the manicured lawns of the administrative area of the Canal Zone, across the street from Panama City, enjoying the freedom to wander around the grounds that for decades had been off limits to Panamanian nationals.

No one saw General Torrijos among the heads of state and other dignitaries gathered to congratulate Panama on its accomplishments; he sent a cryptic message from "somewhere in Panama." Informed sources let out the word that he was in one of his rural residences, boycotting the ceremonies in anger over the late changes injected into the treaties well after he and Carter had signed them. In the ratification debates of the United States Senate, Arizona Senator Dennis DeConcini succeeded in imposing a "condition" that gave the United States the unilateral right, in the event of interference with the operations of the Canal, to "the use of military force in the Republic of Panama" after the year 2000, when the Canal was scheduled to come under full Panamanian control. And the House of Representatives reneged on the substantial grants and loans promised to Torrijos in exchange for accepting these amendments to the treaties (see LaFeber 1979:228–54, 281). Despite all the fanfare, the treaties fell far short of fulfilling the government's promises to the citizens of Panama.

Attention turned to the other major government initiative, the Cerro Colorado project. The sponsors claimed that they had created a fail-proof design based on state-of-the-art technology that would resolve all potential problems, whether technical, financial, or ecological. But co-sponsor Texasgulf withdrew when its analysts concluded that the project was too large, too expensive, and too risky.

The arrival of Rio Tinto-Zinc rekindled the hopes that Panama would become a major copper producer. But the combination of Panama's scaled-down equity interest and Rio Tinto-Zinc's new concepts proved insufficient to overcome the obstacles to the development of Cerro Colorado: the absence of necessary infrastructure in Chiriquí, Panama's financial insolvency, worldwide inflation, and exceedingly low copper prices. In the end, the "new concepts" brought by RTZ produced a design that looked depressingly similar to many other copper projects in many other developing countries.

At first, few critics in Panama dared raise questions about the copper project. Gradually, however, many voices filled the air, including those of the Panamanian bishops and their associates. These church-backed groups, because of their analyses and their ability to persuade some key people to look at their work, forced at least some consideration of a number of major issues concerning the copper project. These issues included the dynamics of the project and their implications for Panama, the real costs of the project, the risks of the project, the implications of Panama's proposed increased indebtedness, and contractual arrangements that left Panama without real power. The church-backed groups and their allies also analyzed threats to the natural environment posed by the project, and raised questions about the technology to be employed. And they questioned the use of revenues expected from the project, examined the implications of the project for popular sectors of Panama, and assessed the impact of the project on the Guaymí Indians.

Some of these contributions paralleled similar efforts by others. From the beginning, church people publicized concerns about the risks of the project, about Panama's indebtedness, and the rising costs of Cerro Colorado; others, like the World Bank, the International Monetary Fund, and Panama's *Consejo Consultivo de Economía*, independently raised similar questions. While church groups challenged the optimistic forecasts concerning the social and environmental impact of the project, others from within CODEMIN quietly complained of the failure of the project's sponsors to undertake serious studies of the likely impact. While church people worked to expose the "salvation-through-technology" mindset of the sponsors, the World Bank revealed that the smelting process was unproven on such a large scale, and would be unlikely to perform as well as the sponsors said.

In other areas, church people were virtually the sole agents who raised crucial questions. The Panamanian bishops, CEASPA, and the Canadian associates challenged the very dynamics of the project, pointing to the fact that the national dynamics were at the mercy of the transnational dynamics. The Panamanian bishops and CEASPA raised serious questions about the financing, risk, and allocation of revenues from the project, noting that the increased indebtedness would have its most severe impact on the poorest sectors of Panama. These groups therefore urged the development of a popularly based plan for Panama's future; no one else in Panama provided this kind of analysis of the Cerro Colorado project.

Whereas the bishops and CEASPA expressed concern about the national implications of Cerro Colorado, the Guaymí Indians and their local supporters added other notes. While others worried about how they could cash in on the anticipated bonanza of the mining project, the Guaymíes worried about how they could survive the radical rearrangement of their living space and the onslaught of thousands of foreigners. They objected to the new technologies, the alien ways, and values in conflict with the lifeways they had developed over the centuries.

CODEMIN's representatives went to some lengths to keep the Guaymíes from seeing what was coming or talking about their own desires and needs; the angry Guaymíes looked elsewhere for information and support. They demanded that the government keep its promises to grant them their comarca and carta orgánica, tools that would provide them legal backing to negotiate concerning the project. When they learned that these promises had given rise to no government actions, they found ways to make their case before national and international groups, and looked for support for their cause.

CODEMIN, arguing that it would take care of all legitimate Guaymí interests and convinced that the Guaymíes could not independently raise their voices against the project, attributed their efforts to outside agitators, who, CODEMIN claimed, pretended that the drab reality of everyday Guaymí life offered the model for the future. Instead of attending to the questions raised by the Guaymíes and the clerics, CODEMIN's representatives denied the substance of their arguments and, at times, attacked the questioners. Although the project sponsors succeeded in making things uncomfortable for a number of people, few people on the scene were taken in by their maneuvers. Until well after the arrival of Rio Tinto-Zinc, of all the non-Indian groups, only Bishop Núñez, the Canadians, and CEASPA could speak authoritatively about the situation of the Guaymí Indians, because only they could base their statements on serious investigation at the local level.

Nonetheless, there was no evidence that CODEMIN and the government ever took the Guaymíes or their supporters all that seriously; CODEMIN's top management treated the questions and criticisms as public relations issues. The various activities failed to bring about the inclusion of the Guaymíes as active participants in the Cerro Colorado project. No design changes took account of the concerns being voiced; the only changes were those prompted by the quest for a less expensive, more cost-effective copper mine, to counter inflation and interest rates that pushed the costs beyond what the sponsors could finance in the absence of the often-predicted recovery of the world copper market.

Eventually it emerged that CODEMIN had other major concerns: the conduct of negotiations with Rio Tinto-Zinc for an agreement to proceed with the next phase of Cerro Colorado. As noted in Part 2, no such agreement came about; Panama's immediate hope of becoming a major copper producer were buried with General Torrijos in 1981. Also buried was the government's incentive to work out an acceptable agreement with the Guaymí Indians regarding their comarca. Rumors circulated for a time, occasional meetings took place, but nothing happened. The Guaymíes still have no comarca.[1]

ASSESSMENTS BASED ON OTHER CRITERIA

Guaymí Organization

Young and Bort (1979) argued that for the Guaymíes to successfully confront the major challenges facing them, they had to create efficacious political organization that transcended the limitations of their traditional kin organization and consensus decision-making. In the 1960s, the Mama Chi religious revivalist movement swept the Guaymí area, giving the Guaymíes a sense of unity and purpose that went far beyond the confines of a caserío or a kin group. However, when the prophesied end of the world did not arrive, and when some people attempted to give the movement a political orientation to agitate for Guaymí rights, the movement lost most of its adherents.[2]

The activities associated with the Cerro Colorado and Teribe-Changuinola projects, especially the congresses of Canquintú and Soloy, represented extraordinary new Guaymí efforts to create for themselves a political organization able both to unite the community and to represent it before the non-Guaymí world. However, these activities failed to gain what the Guaymíes wanted: the comarca, and an active voice in the major projects planned for their territory. In this sense, these activities ran into the same obstacle in the political arena that the Mama Chi movement encountered in the religious sphere: leaders promised but could not deliver.

As the projects themselves diminished in immediacy, and as the government backed away from its feeble efforts regarding the comarca, the Guaymíes themselves tended to return to life as before. As happened following the Mama Chi movement, individual Guaymíes continued their efforts to organize, to establish groups and movements, and to struggle for leadership. But their followers, whose commitment had never been as firm as the leaders wanted to believe, drifted away.

The Mama Chi movement and the activities concerned with Cerro Colorado drew on approaches traditional to the Guaymíes, combined with elements borrowed, consciously or not, from others. Even though the congresses seemed to be imitations of Cuna organizations, and some of the debate imitations of latino styles, one might also see in these activities something akin to earlier Guaymí organization in response to external threats. Historically, Guaymí caseríos and kin groups united under temporary leaders when they had to engage in warfare either to advance their own interests or to defend themselves. Perhaps the thousands of Guaymíes who involved themselves in major activities around the Cerro Colorado and Teribe-Changuinola projects echoed these earlier ways of transcending the organizational limits of kinship.[3]

The Catholic Church's efforts with and on behalf of the Guaymíes marked the Cerro Colorado struggle as different in kind from earlier Guaymí attempts at organizing. Besides the internal pressures to create an organization able to confront their new problems, the Guaymíes also had significant support from the outside, from non-Guaymíes. Before the publication of Núñez' pastoral letter, negotiations for the comarca were on-again, off-again, low-level, almost private affairs that involved a handful of Guaymíes and never more than a few government officials. There was virtually no Guaymí activity concerning the mining project prior to the pastoral letters and the arrival of the church-backed groups in Guaymí districts.

Supported by the activities of the bishops and various church people of Panama, the Guaymíes themselves became much more active on their own behalf. Communities held their first independent meetings to discuss the mining project; they concluded that they needed the protection of the comarca before they could have any security about their future. Guaymíes who had done little other than pass on various rumors about the mining project became more actively interested, struggled through Bishop Núñez' pastoral letter and the CEASPA-Guaymí analysis of the projects, and looked for opportunities to organize their communities and to force CODEMIN to take them seriously. Guaymíes organized several congresses, learned from the ways they were manipulated, and passed resolutions condemning the projects and demanding the comarca; the analyses that helped them see the extent of the dangers emanated at least indirectly from church work.

The efforts of the Catholic Church on behalf of the Guaymíes clearly made a difference; the educational work of bishops and priests contributed to the Guaymíes' analyses of the Cerro Colorado and Teribe-Changuinola projects, and the public support of the hierarchy put added pressure on the government to take the Guaymíes more seriously than before, in the negotiations for the comarca and carta orgánica. But the Catholic Church did not initiate or control the Guaymí organizational efforts. Throughout the period of the events discussed in the preceding chapters, Catholic priests had no standing in Guaymí communities to enable them to convoke meetings; the various meetings discussed in this book took place only because Guaymí local leaders organized them. Whenever Guaymí participants wished to work out some point among themselves, they spoke for some while in Ngawbere, a language that none of the priests had succeeded in learning. Guaymíes worked out their own objectives, strategies, and tactics, at times arriving at positions that seemed ill-advised to the priests.

Far from entrusting the elaboration of the objectives and tactics to outsiders, Guaymí leaders remained at least somewhat suspicious. These suspicions arose from several factors: their history, ethnic viewpoints, and internal power struggles. Presumably, Guaymí awareness of centuries of exploitation at the hands of the "Spanish," as they called most non-Guaymíes (except for when they used the Ngawbere epithet *suliá,* "cockroach"), fostered considerable skepticism of the real intentions of outsiders. Although in some conversations Guaymí leaders recognized that the Guaymíes could not achieve their goals without active, sympathetic allies, more often they tried to work alone; leaders rarely consulted with the outsiders, rarely talked things over, and rarely provided full answers about their end of questions of mutual concern. At times, they interpreted suggestions from outsiders as thinly disguised attempts to force the Guaymíes to serve the hidden interests of non-Guaymíes.[4]

In common with many ethnic (or other) groups, particularly those with a history of exploitation by outsiders, the Guaymíes have a strong "us-them" way of defining themselves; part of their identification is that they are, quite consciously, not members of some other group. For their survival as an ethnic group, the Guaymíes have lived in some isolation from outsiders, and have maintained at least some measure of control over their contacts with non-Guaymíes. Consequently, they have generally defined the world and their own problems in their own terms, and according to their own viewpoints; they have had little experience of, and little sympathy for, other points of view that purported to be more comprehensive. Thus, for example, they looked at the Cerro Colorado project, saw that it ran against their interests, and opposed it. Their leaders gave little serious consideration to the Torrijos government's investment (in various senses) in the project, and to the likelihood that the government would write them off as uninformed, backward opponents.[5] They did not strive to find ways of coordinating their viewpoint with that of others, including their outside associates; rather, they expected their allies fully to accept and affirm their viewpoint.

Guaymíes caught up in the power struggles of creating new organizations also had their suspicions of outsiders. Not infrequently, they interpreted a lack of unconditional support for their own group as a mark of support for their opponents. Outsiders could not help but feel the effects of these power struggles, even though they tried to avoid identification with any particular faction. It was impossible to cooperate effectively with "the Guaymíes"; one could only work with particular Guaymí individuals and groups.[6]

The Guaymíes themselves, as they strive to forge adequate responses to the challenges that continue to arise from the dynamics of their lives as a poor ethnic minority in Panama, will provide the definitive assessment of the significance of the activities described in this book. If they succeed in forming themselves into a viably united people, the Mama Chi movement and the later Cerro Colorado activities will have been important early experiences of organization that transcended kin groups. But the Guaymíes may never develop effective non-kin political organization except in the face of some imminent threat, when their efforts will face the added pressure of having to respond too rapidly to complex threats from the outside.

Church Involvement

The Catholic hierarchy in Panama and in Canada openly tried to influence the Cerro Colorado project, to en-

hance the possibilities of benefits for Panama as a whole and for the
Guaymí Indians in particular. In their work together within their national conferences, the bishops overcame the tendency for each to emphasize his own prerogatives in his diocese, to the detriment of for-
mulating a national response to an issue. And the cooperation between
the Panamanian and Canadian conferences was a rare occurrence in a
church structure whose normal international efforts are sponsored by
or mediated through the Vatican in Rome. Bishops of both conferences
invited individuals and groups from outside their ranks to provide them
with information, analyses, and suggestions. The Canadians, accustomed to ecumenical cooperation, persuaded the Panamanian bishops
to establish working ties with Protestant groups in Panama, where
ecumenical endeavors were more out of the ordinary.

The Panamanian episcopal conference pastoral letter on Cerro Colorado marked a significant, unified voice applying Catholic social teaching to a complex socio-politico-economic reality of Panama. But the
reality transcended the boundaries of Panama; the international episcopal cooperation extended the approach to the quest for a unified voice
addressing the issue in both countries.[7] This collaboration was decisive
in the injection of the bishops' viewpoint and questions into the international debate on the mining project; the visit to Panama of the Canadian representatives and the publication of their report (DeRoo et al.
1980) were important moments in this process. In all these activities, the
bishops sought to focus international attention on an international
issue with major ramifications for Panama. The bishops had no power
to control or change the mining project; but they could try to mobilize
public opinion and so try to influence the project.

The Panamanian hierarchy's uncharacteristically unambiguous support for the "preferential option for the poor" and its willingness to
take a stand on a controversial set of issues facing the country encouraged many church personnel working in poor sectors of Panama. In the
midst of the uncertainties about what the CELAM bishops really intended at Puebla in adopting this preferential option,[8] the authoritative
stances of Bishop Núñez and the episcopal conference encouraged
church personnel to form grassroots Christian communities in Panama
allied to the cause of the Guaymíes. Supported by the pastoral letters,
these local communities saw that the mining project was not the bonanza promised by its sponsors, and that it had serious negative im-

plications for all popular sectors of Panama. These communities formed the nucleus of Panamanians in solidarity with the Guaymíes. And from these experiences, the same communities moved to reflect on other aspects of Panamanian reality as they experienced it.

The unusually consistent efforts of representatives of the Catholic Church came about because these bishops and priests looked beyond their more parochial concerns like the administration of sacraments, the qualifications for the ordination of the church's ministers, or the preservation of their place in society. Instead, as the Second Vatican Council had urged, they looked to the needs of the disadvantaged in the world in which the church lives (see *Gaudium et Spes*, No. 1 and 4, in Abbot 1966:199–200, 201–02).

Solidarity Efforts

Those who worked with the bishops on their Cerro Colorado efforts had to arrive at some basic agreement among themselves on the likely benefits and risks of the mining project. This very diverse group, people of different backgrounds and formation working in different locations (see Preface), began its work together with quite diverse perceptions of Cerro Colorado. Some thought that the mining project would greatly benefit Panama as an LDC through the creation of new jobs, the immediate stimulus to the stagnant economy, and the injection of massive foreign exchange; the only major concern lay in questions about the integrity of the top Panamanian administrators of the project. Others considered the Guaymíes to be an unorganized working class, without much awareness of their ethnicity, and thought the project would provide them the necessary stimulus to develop class consciousness and class-based alliances with other groups in Panama.[9]

Further study and conversation helped; but only in putting together a written analysis, at the request of the bishops' conference, did group members develop a common appreciation of the full scope of the Cerro Colorado project, including the risks involved and the problems it could create on all levels in Panama. This analysis (CEASPA 1979b) became the basis for the substantial agreement needed among the members of the investigative team in order to continue working together closely.[10]

Once united, this group sought solidarity linkages both for Panama as an LDC and for the Guaymí Indians. From these contacts came information not readily available otherwise, experiences of other people, and possibilities for including the Cerro Colorado project and the situation of the Guaymí Indians on the agenda of several international meetings concerned with development and marginalized peoples: the Russell Tribunal in Rotterdam, a Cornell University meeting on the social impact assessment of large-scale resource development projects, a Washington, D.C. seminar on native rights and transnational corporations, and others.

Organizations in many countries call attention to the activities of transnational corporations and the growing threats to indigenous peoples worldwide. Given proper information and contacts, these organizations energetically publicize, educate, protest, lobby, and submit shareholders' resolutions, as expressions of their solidarity with peoples unable to get a hearing on their own. The group working on the Cerro Colorado project exchanged information with many organizations and people: in Denmark, the late Helge Kleivan and the International Work Group on Indigenous Affairs (IWGIA); in Australia and New Zealand, International Development Action (IDA) and individual researchers; in England, Survival International, the Catholic Institute for International Relations (CIIR), and PARTiZANS, a group that critically monitors Rio-Tinto Zinc activities; in Canada, the Latin America Working Group (LAWG), the Task Force for Churches and Corporate Responsibility (TCCR), and Project North, a group supporting native peoples in northern Canada; and in the United States, Shelton Davis and the Anthropology Resource Center (ARC), Cultural Survival, Al Gedicks and the Center for Alternative Mining Development Policy, and the Interchurch Center on Corporate Responsibility (ICCR).

The approach developed in the church group, discussed in the Preface, fit well the realities of Panama and the Cerro Colorado project. By extending its concern from the needs of the Guaymíes to the issue of Panama as an LDC, its members were able to shed light on various levels of the impact of the project, and to avoid the pitfalls of a narrowly "indigenistic" approach that would have found little sympathy in the country if people were convinced that the interests of the minority Guaymíes ran counter to those of the nation at large.

However, despite attempts to organize solidarity efforts to include both aspects of Panamanian concern, international public attention and energy focused primarily on the plight of the Guaymíes. Except for Canadian groups linked around LAWG, solidarity organizations tended to analyze the Cerro Colorado project from the more limited perspective of the Guaymíes, rather than including the Guaymíes themselves within the framework of a wider analysis; even in Canada, public attention focused primarily on the Guaymíes.[11]

People anywhere could readily imagine and empathize with the Guaymí case: a poor minority ethnic population struggling for survival, threatened by transnational corporations and the national government, and denied even the right to an opinion about its own future. Both the Guaymí delegates to the Soloy Congress and those who supported the Guaymíes nationally and internationally might almost have had in mind the conclusions that Douglas Sanders reached in a 1975 report[12] on the legal situation of the Guaymíes in the face of Cerro Colorado:

> Indian groups [and their supporters] are often seen as opposed to progress because they resist development projects. The projects resisted are planned by outsiders and are designed to serve outside interests. Whatever local benefits they have are side effects, not primary goals of the project. The projects are seen by the native group as involving a threat to their way of life. . . . It must be remembered that reserves [or comarcas] are seen by Indians [and their supporters] as affording some cultural protection against the culturally aggressive national population. The development projects can seriously undercut that cultural protection. The Cerro Colorado mine in the heart of the Guaymí territory could compromise the reserve in all the ways that the Canal Zone compromises the life of Panama. (Sanders 1975:40-41)

However, people abroad were not as readily able to imagine and empathize with the more complex Panamanian case. This case too involved a poor population (a world minority) struggling for survival, threatened by transnational corporations and the national government, and denied the right to an opinion about its future. But the discussion of the effects of the Cerro Colorado project on this population involved abstract what-ifs that had to do with national indebtedness and future government measures to pay the bills, instead of concrete images of destroyed lands and crops and of unusable water supplies. And it might

have happened that the project sponsors' promises of a national bonanza would, after all, have been fulfilled. One could readily grasp that
the Cerro Colorado mine would compromise the Guaymí comarca, in
all the ways the Canal Zone compromised the life of Panama; perhaps
not so obvious was the conclusion that the Cerro Colorado mine would
equally compromise the life of Panama.

It is particularly difficult to organize effective international solidarity efforts on behalf of the people of LDCs. In cases where majority
poor populations of given countries face well-documented repression,
such as in Nicaragua under the Somozas, in El Salvador and Guatemala
under military and right-wing elites, or in South Africa under the rule
of apartheid, then people in Europe, North America, and Australasia
begin to mobilize and agitate for changes in these loathsome conditions. If, in addition, repressive regimes receive support from developed-country governments, more often than not the United States—as
has been the case with the decades-long support given the Somozas,
President Reagan's support for the Nicaraguan contras, and for the
Salvadoran and Guatemalan military, and his lukewarm objections to
the racist regime of South Africa—then people in the developed countries may agitate all the more forcefully against such connivance in the
repression of others. But even these solidarity campaigns usually rest on
a handful of people who wage an uphill battle against widespread ignorance and indifference or effective official misinformation.

As in the case of Panama in confrontation with the developed
world, the task of mobilizing international solidarity efforts on behalf
of people who face the constant, ever-present problems of the poor is
even more difficult. The populations of less-developed countries commonly face national governments and wealthy elites who are allied with
foreign interests; they live in states dependent on transnational corporations for technology, expertise, financing, and marketing. Their countries are minor partners in a global economy whose controls, always
difficult to find, clearly lie outside the borders of the LDCs. Few people
in the developed world pressure for radical changes in the basic relationships between developed and less-developed countries, including
particularly, changes in the direction of greater equality and more self-
determination on the part of the peoples of most of the world.

In the LDCs, as in the DCs, native peoples usually form minority
ethnic groups. While they are frequently threatened, now probably

more than ever before, the threats to them are perhaps no greater than the threats to others who share the same socio-economic class characteristics in the same countries. Probably, the most effective strategy to collaborate with native peoples for their own survival would be one that works with them and others to form alliances that transcend the narrower, more ambiguous organizational principles of ethnicity and that include class relations. A class-based strategy would be more likely to set goals that demand more radical structural changes. At the same time, it would be more likely to avoid the pitfalls encountered when using ethnicity as a base, particularly the risk of confrontation between peoples of different ethnic groups (e.g., native peoples, campesinos, or workers) whose overall class interests are at bottom the same.

NOTES

Chapter 1: Overview of the Cerro Colorado Project

1. The Extraordinary Guaymí General Congress of Soloy is more fully discussed below, in Chapter 9.

2. Only at the end of a second edition did CODEMIN 1979a, a document used to promote the mining project, include two pages titled "Social Aspects of the Project"; the original version made no mention of the Guaymíes. The context of Guaymí life and problems will be given in Chapter 3; the varied impact of the mining project on the Guaymíes, along with Guaymí responses, will be taken up in detail in Part 3.

3. In the Guaymí *caserío* (village or settlement) of Hato Pilón, District of San Félix, southwest of Cerro Colorado, average annual rainfall from September 1971 to November 1978, as measured by one of the residents under contract with the Panamanian electric company IRHE, was 4900 mm (almost 193 inches). On average, 65 percent of the rainless days occurred during the dry season months of December through April.

4. In 1865, Bidwell reported "there are copper mines near San Feles [San Félix?], and near the road going from Boca [*sic*] del Toro to David" (Bidwell 1865:336).

5. A Japanese mining firm obtained exploration rights for Petaquilla, and did some exploration; but it made no proposal to develop the site.

6. During these years, the Cerro Colorado project changed sponsors, plans, and costs several times. This opening summary relies on CODEMIN announcements of 1978 and 1979 (especially CODEMIN 1979a) to present the

main aspects of the Texasgulf-CODEMIN proposal; the major parts of the project did not change much under Rio Tinto-Zinc. Part 2 will present a discussion of the sponsors, the changes, the costs, and other variations of the project, as appropriate.

7. The metals that interested the project sponsors were unevenly distributed throughout the Cerro Colorado deposits. Therefore, the studies included estimates of the lowest percent of contained metal (called the "cut-off grade") that could economically be extracted and processed before the processing costs would exceed the probable income from the sale of the metal. Using the cut-off grade, the sponsors then calculated the overall average copper content of the deposits. From these calculations, the sponsors estimated the total reserves of the deposits.

The Cerro Colorado sponsors adopted a cut-off grade of 0.40 percent copper; from this, they calculated that the overall deposits averaged 0.78 percent copper and totalled 1,380 million metric tons. Everything below the cut-off grade was categorized as "waste rock"; the "waste-to-ore" ratio was 3.18. With a cut-off grade of 0.001 percent copper, the average dropped to 0.39 percent but the reserves increased to 4,110 million metric tons (see CODEMIN 1979a:8).

8. Part 2 will discuss the financing of the project in detail, the demand and price projections, and other matters related to the analysis and criticism of the proposed arrangements.

9. These camps were like small towns; each was composed of several cinder-block buildings with metal roofs, and included diesel-powered electrical generators, hot and cold running water, kitchens and dining rooms, bedrooms, communication equipment, and some recreational facilities.

Chapter 2: The Torrijos Years, 1968–1981

1. This overthrow brought to three Arnulfo Arias' uncompleted terms as president; he had also become president in 1940 and in 1949, and was ousted each time. His supporters claimed that the 81-year-old Arias again won the presidency in the elections of 1984; but after long delays, the electoral commission declared his opponent, Nicolás Ardito Barletta, the victor.

2. Property in land solidified political and economic ties of the merchant elite. The suburban cattle ranches, lying up to 38 km east and west of Panama City, also included some fruit orchards and grains (mainly maize). By 1607, officials counted 53,000 head of cattle on 54 ranches *(hatos)* in this area (Sauer 1969:287). The merchants also controlled the temporary housing and

warehouses in the unoccupied Atlantic terminal of Portobelo (which replaced Nombre de Dios, burned by pirates in 1596), as well as most of the real estate in Panama City.

3. After the abolition of Spanish Crown grants *(encomiendas)* in 1558, Natá's residents, struggling to survive, mixed with the surrounding Indians and other less-fortunate newcomers (e.g., soldiers who abandoned ranks on their transit through Panama for the Indian wars in Chile [Castillero C. 1967:69–71]), and established the basic pattern of small- and medium-holders, working the land and selling excess production as they could. The brief boom of providing foodstuffs for the Concepción gold mine in northern Veragua (ca. 1559–90) encouraged their dispersion through the Azuero Peninsula and into present-day Coclé and Veraguas provinces (Gudeman 1978:15); when mining declined, these farmers and ranchers, prohibited from sending their surplus cattle and maize to the oversupplied transit area, had to cut back by 50 percent on their production (Castillero C. 1967:75–77).

4. These towns, in addition to provisioning the overland trade, engaged in shipbuilding and lumbering (Castillero R. 1968:7). When the Spanish arrived, they probably entered a land of about one million inhabitants (Bennett 1968:37). Within two or three decades, thanks principally to the devastations of Pedro Arias de Avila (Pedrarias Dávila), only a few thousand Indians remained; most of these had become hostile to the Spanish, and did all possible to avoid contact with them. The isthmus thus could not provide the "animal power" needed for the transit; by 1520 the Spanish were importing Negro slaves from Africa (Guzmán 1956:18), and in the 1530s and 1540s they enslaved 200,000 Indians from Nicaragua for Panama and Peru (MacLeod 1973:52).

5. Although the Treaty of Utrecht allowed the English to send only one ship per year to Panama, in effect it was a legal concession of "rights" already won by pirates and privateers who appeared in the late sixteenth century and harassed the trade routes through most of the seventeenth century, working as "informal" representatives of the British, French, and Dutch interests in breaking up the Spanish monopoly. Privateers established alternative isthmian crossings to move European contraband goods outside the Spanish monopoly.

Spanish-controlled trade across the isthmus fluctuated throughout the seventeenth century and well into the eighteenth century; the annual Portobelo Fair, principal event for the movement of Spanish goods to South America, had declined from forty days to only two weeks by 1637 (Mack 1944:59), and was suppressed altogether in 1739. From the earlier periods of yearly arrivals of large fleets, which guarded the Spanish monopoly, came gaps of two to three years without ships by the end of the seventeenth century, and the abolition of the Spanish convoys in 1748 (Mack 1944:60). By the mid-eighteenth century, Spain was principally using the transit area as a crossing for troops, trying to quell separatist movements in South America, and as a resting and staging area; the economy of the period is well-named one of "quarters" or barracks by Jaén S. (1973:12—13), since there were few other than soldiers who required the attention of the commercial elite.

6. The latifundistas formed a tight-knit group of families who dominated local rural politics and succeeded in subjugating the surrounding Indian caseríos. The latifundias were almost exclusively dedicated to cattle-raising, which was land-extensive but did not require a continual input of labor. Ownership of land and cattle determined membership in the rural elite, who by the mid-nineteenth century controlled the administrative, bureaucratic, political, military and religious offices. The Indians and mestizos, engaged in subsistence agriculture and pushed to the less arable mountainous regions, remained powerless (Figueroa N. 1978:102—105).

7. The railroad eliminated the jobs of laborers who worked the old river-and-trail crossing: native guides, muleteers, and boatmen. The small inns on the Atlantic and along the old transit route closed. Foreign laborers brought in for the construction project were thrown out of work once the railroad opened.

8. Notes LaFeber (1979:12):

> During the fourteen years after the line opened in 1855, 600,000 travelers used it and as much as $750 million in gold bullion moved from California to the eastern United States along the Panama Railroad. Through 1905 it paid nearly $38 million in dividends to the owners.

9. In 1863, a Panamanian merchant headed the list of the eighteen wealthiest individuals. In 1872, eight foreigners had surpassed him; by 1875, twenty of the top twenty-four merchants in Panama were foreigners (Jaén S. 1973:29). Toward the end of the nineteenth century, the United Fruit Company established its first banana plantations in Panama, on the western Caribbean coast (present-day Bocas del Toro Province), relying principally on Negro labor brought in for the construction of the railroad and, later, for the failed French canal. By 1913, the United Fruit Company owned property valued at seven or eight million dollars, about 25 percent of the total private property in Panama (LaFeber 1979:76).

10. United States interest in the area began early in the nineteenth century, when U.S. shippers, in the midst of an embargo on trade with Europe

brought about to avoid entanglement in the Napoleonic Wars, sought a shorter route for their growing trade with China. The Monroe Doctrine, following closely on the achievement of independence by most Latin American nations, announced U. S. intentions to keep the Western Hemisphere for its own interests.

11. Often the United States exercised sovereignty by sending troops to the isthmus, as Farnsworth and McKenney (1983:15) noted:

> During the period from 1846 to 1903, the United States landed troops on the Panamanian isthmus seven times at the invitation of the government of New Granada or its successor, Colombia. Each of these landings complied with the provisions of the Treaty of 1846 whereby the United States had agreed to guarantee the sovereignty of Colombia against other claimants. The duration of these troop landings varied from a few hours to several weeks.

12. Castillero C. (1973:40) well summarized the overall impact of the railroad from the perspective of Panama:

> The supposed opulence which the California flood had brought, with its hundreds of thousands of emigrants, with its railroad, with its gold . . . , only six years after its beginning, left in Panama only unemployment, bankruptcies, internal wars, and a burdensome international commitment brought about by the North American demand for indemnification for the incident of the Watermelon Slice.

The "Watermelon Slice" *(Tajada de Sandía)* refers to the riots of 1856, sparked by the refusal of a North American to pay for a slice of watermelon taken from a local vendor. The riots were an explosion of popular Panamanian reaction to the frustrations of having to bear the insulting attitudes and actions of thousands of insensitive North Americans who despised Panamanian culture and traditions. In one of the ironies of United States–Panamanian relations, the U.S. government forced the Colombian government to pay more than $400,000 in compensation for damages which all European diplomats testified were provoked by U.S. citizens (see Rippy 1931:73–74; Castillero C. 1973).

13. Technically, the U.S. assisted the Panamanian rebels through a self-serving interpretation of its obligations under the 1846 treaty. In the name of keeping the railroad open and operating, U.S. troops and gunships prevented Colombian troops from landing in Colón and crossing the isthmus to put down the rebels. Then the U.S. government hastened to recognize the new, independent government of Panama. See McCullough (1977), LaFeber (1979).

14. The period 1956–1966 was one of gradual restabilization.

15. The local commercial sector now formed an oligarchy: a group of families who governed the country largely for their own, rather than the public, interest. The principal twenty families fell into three groups: (1) those families with deep roots in Panama, whose wealth came from large landholdings, commercial activities, and real estate, and who had been involved in gaining independence from Colombia; (2) European immigrant families who came during the canal construction, establishing small construction and service-dependent industries; (3) a few Jewish families who arrived soon after the canal was completed, and established export-import businesses. By the 1930s, these three groups formed an interlocking set connected by commercial, social, and kinship ties; by 1968, they controlled 99 of the top 120 companies in Panama (Gandásegui 1974:151–68).

16. From early on, Panamanian legislation favored foreign investment. In 1917, the Panama Power and Light Company received a monopoly over electric services in Panama City and Colón. In 1957, the government freed foreign companies from most taxes, especially on imports, and from customs inspections. By early 1964, the government exonerated from taxes virtually any company that asked, and by 1965, 173 companies had signed special contracts, while a total of 404 firms had some sort of special arrangement with the government (see Gandásegui 1974:134–36).

17. The Arias Madrid brothers, Harmodio and Arnulfo, took over the leadership of the movement in 1931. Harmodio, elected president in 1932, renegotiated the canal treaty in 1936, strengthening Panama's rights in the Canal Zone and removing the U.S. right to intervene in Panamanian affairs; Arnulfo, elected to succeed him, resisted the further establishment of U.S. military bases on the eve of World War II (LaFeber 1979, Soler 1976).

18. The labor force faced divisions imposed by its differing sectors and by its geography. Workers within the enclave economy of the canal, an area not open to free access by other Panamanians, had difficulty perceiving their common interests with the laborers of the weak industrial sector or the disproportionately large service sector beyond the enclave. Workers on the United Fruit Co. banana plantations in the western provinces of Chiriquí and Bocas del Toro had little contact with people from the transit area. Trade unions began to form in the early 1920s, and received stimulus to increase during two short periods of industrial expansion: after 1936, when treaty renegotiation created more favorable conditions for local industry, and during World War II, when Panama had to become self-reliant in certain manufactured goods (see Gandásegui et al. 1980).

19. Between 1961 and 1963, the U.S. gave $41 million yearly in economic as-
sistance to Panama, a six-fold increase over the yearly average of $7 million
from 1951 to 1961 (LaFeber 1979:133).

20. The 1966 per capita income was $531, but 5 percent of the population
controlled 33 percent of the total, while 50 percent of the employed population were small farmers mostly earning less than $100 per year. Panama had
the population and resources to be a net exporter of food, but "the country
spent $12 million in 1968 to import staples" because of a "lack of transporta-
tion in the interior, inequitable land holdings, and archaic agricultural methods." Of more than 2,000 manufacturing firms, only 60 (many owned by
foreigners) employed more than 50 workers; these accounted for 61 percent
(in value) of all manufactured products. The government, favoring people of
"oligarchical or skilled middle-class background who chose the right side in
the presidential elections," was the largest employer (30,000). Next came the
Panama Canal Company (13,000) whose "employment had dropped steadily
since 1945." Third was the United Fruit Co. (11,000), "so large and powerful
. . . that the Panamanian government could not control it." In 1966, unemployment had reached 25 percent of the labor force "congregated in the already congested slums of Panama City and Colón" (LaFeber 1979:150–51).

21. Torrijos managed to keep discontent within the National Guard either
from becoming organized or from creating threats to his control, even when
some of the higher ranking officers became disgruntled because there was no
further room for promotion—the top echelons were all filled, and no one
was retiring. In part, he achieved this by looking the other way as various officers used their positions to enrich themselves through corruption: selling
off contraband wood products from the Bayano, dealing in contraband imports through the Colón Free Zone, getting on the payroll of corporations
that had major government contracts. If, as was rumored, Torrijos himself
was among the wealthiest people in all of Latin America at the time of his
death in 1981, it was also the case that a number of colonels (including the
then-head of military intelligence, Manuel Noriega) had managed to acquire
fancy homes in sections of Panama City traditionally occupied only by
rabiblancos (a Panamanian popular term literally meaning "white tails"), while
imitating their commander-in-chief himself in having second and third
homes in other parts of the country such as the beaches of Coclé or the cool
mountains of western Chiriquí.

22. Panama's major student movements had, historically, opposed the National Guard, since the Guard was the instrument called out to put down
their protests. But Torrijos managed to gain the support even of the Panamanian Student Federation, long opponents of the U.S. role in Panama and

foes of the oligarchy's stranglehold on domestic politics and economics (see NACLA 1979:24). Besides advocating some of the same reforms they agitated for, and by succeeding in making himself the popular representative of the workers and campesinos they supported, Torrijos also won the backing of some key leaders of Panama's Communist party, the Party of the People *(Partido del Pueblo)*, with which many students and some workers' organizations sympathized. Early on, Torrijos sought and won the backing of the major leaders of this party, convincing them that he sought many of the same things they did and giving them government posts that they had never obtained under the previous "democracies" (see NACLA 1979:24).

The small, Moscow-aligned Party of the People—Communist in name more than in anything else—was little threat to Torrijos or even to his predecessors. Many Panamanian leftists were convinced that the Party was the most infiltrated in the Americas, knowingly or unknowingly manipulated by the U.S. government. Critics argued that Torrijos did not really make concessions to them, but rather managed very effectively to co-opt them.

23. Some opposition was allowed, but there were limits; when some radio commentators exceeded the limits, Torrijos found ways to suspend their licenses.

24. The Assembly could not write or amend legislation; it could only approve or disapprove, and it had no voice in budgetary matters. During the remainder of the year, the government itself enacted legislation.

25. Northville Industries of Long Island, N.Y., built and operated the petroleum transshipment facility located near Puerto Armuelles in western Chiriquí. Supertankers brought Alaskan oil to the off-shore pipeline; the oil was unloaded into on-shore storage tanks, whence it was reloaded into smaller tankers that could transit the canal's locks. In 1981–82, oil companies financed construction of a Northville Industries pipeline from near Puerto Armuelles in western Chiriquí to Laguna de Chiriquí in Bocas del Toro, allowing the direct movement of oil across the isthmus from supertanker to supertanker.

26. With the 1970 legislation, according to LaFeber (1979:176),

> banks could be established with minimal requirements and funds whipped in and out of the country with no questions asked. The government helpfully imposed a lid on the interest rate paid domestic savings, but allowed other rates (for example, bank lending) to be determined by the vagaries of the marketplace. The 1970 law, combined with Panama's currency being interchangeable with the dollar, the country's excellent location, its foreign communications (which some bankers believed superior to London's), and its political stability made the Isthmus a banker's paradise.

27. The Colón Free Zone (established in 1953), an area where companies could import goods duty-free for reexport, became the major shopping center for many Latin American business people, because they were able to look over a variety of goods without having to travel to the products' countries of origin. In 1971, 154 establishments registered $270 million in sales; in 1978, 1,000 companies did $2.8 billion in trade.

28. Another important influence in Torrijos' good relations with the international business community, one that is impossible to evaluate with any precision, was the fact that corporate and government representatives found Torrijos both very accessible and enjoyable company. Torrijos had a reputation as a high-living, hard-drinking man who liked to rub elbows with the powers of the international business community. For their part, a number of corporate and government emissaries presumably found that relaxed parties with a nation's leader added to their own sense of prestige and importance.

29. The oil bill doubled from 1973 to 1974, on 4 percent fewer barrels. In 1979, the quantity of oil imported was only 45 percent of the high reached in 1972, but the price was more than 360 percent higher.

30. In 1968, the foreign debt was $109.8 million, 52.9 percent of the total public debt of $207.6 million and 14.2 percent of the gross domestic product of $771.2 million (figures expressed in constant 1960 dollars). In 1978, the foreign debt was $1,813.3 million, 76.1 percent of the total public debt of $2,383.5 million and 78.6 percent of the gross domestic product of $2,306.1 million (figures expressed in 1978 dollars). (Because Panama is an international finance center and since Panama's currency is the U.S. dollar, a certain portion of the foreign debt is disguised as internal debt; therefore the actual numbers would be higher.) The 1968 public debt represented 26.9 percent of the gross domestic product; the 1978 public debt represented 103.4 percent of the gross domestic product. In 1968, the gross domestic product per capita was $541.00, the public debt per capita $145.60; by 1978, these figures were $1,617.90 and $1,732.50 respectively. As Panama's indebtedness increased, lending agencies insisted on interest rates that were less like those of development loans and more like commercial loans: interest payments in 1978 were $190 million, 8.2 percent of the gross domestic product. (All calculations are based on information from *Panamá en cifras*.)

31. Earlier, few had voiced concerns that this leading area of the economic boom was itself non-productive, i.e., was not one that produced new industries that could continue to grow, and in turn spawn other industries and guarantee revenues for years to come. The economic crisis made it obvious that the boom had not been solid; it had been sustained principally by con-

struction and by services, neither of which generated further production or related growth.

32. Payer (1974) discusses the ways that the International Monetary Fund forces debtor countries to cancel programs that benefit the poor sectors of the population: workers, peasants, and the under- and unemployed.

33. In 1974–75, sugar sold for $0.33 per pound; by 1976–77, when the Panamanian government began to produce exportable sugar with its new sugar mills (ingenios), the price had fallen to $0.095 per pound. When the bottom dropped out of the international sugar market, the U.S., to protect its sugar-beet growers, reduced import quotas; Panama, already selling at a loss, also lost some of its market.

34. In 1973 and 1974, direct foreign investment in Panama reached more than $30 million per year; from 1975 to 1978, the total investment was $7.1 million. In 1979, with the Torrijos-Carter treaties in place and Panama's "stability" supposedly guaranteed by the legalized U.S. military presence at least until the year 2000, foreign investment rose to $40 million (see Gjording 1981b).

35. Torrijos took advantage of the emphasis on national unity to quietly squelch attempts to form popularly based organizations that might have pushed his government toward a different "revolution." For example, he fired Dr. Renán Esquivel as Minister of Health and backed away from his earlier support of local health committees which, under Esquivel, had been organized around the premise that the basic health problem of Panama was inadequate nutrition caused by the unequal distribution of resources.

36. For example, while he spoke against the illegal use of the Southern Command's School of the Americas as the training ground for fighting insurgents throughout Latin America, he enjoyed visiting his alma mater, making friends of the U.S. military personnel who ran the school, and giving them rides here and there in his helicopter (see LaFeber 1979:168–69).

37. See Part 2 of this book for a full discussion of the question of control vs. equity.

The deepening of foreign control over Panama in the 1970s, using economic matters and the private sector as agents, illustrated only too well the efficacy of the approach of the Trilateral Commission, which sought to move away from reliance on gunboat diplomacy in favor of more subtle, but no less effective, economic diplomacy. See Sklar 1980.

38. The original treaties gave the U.S. even more control over affairs on the isthmus than had been the case under the Bidlack-Mallorino Treaty between the U.S. and Colombia.

39. Under pressure from U.S. senators, Torrijos accepted amendments that allowed the U.S. the unilateral right to intervene militarily "for the security of the canal" after the year 2000; but he received promises of substantial revenues (both grants and loans). These payments hinged in large part on the Carter Administration's agreement that the canal operations could easily have produced much greater revenues through the century, and that Panama had never received anything approaching just compensation for the use of its territory. The House ignored the 75 years of subsidies to U.S. shipping (through artificially low tolls) and threatened to make Panama pay for the never-amortized construction costs. President Carter, never very adept in his relations with the Congress, failed to turn things around; and Panama no longer enjoyed the strong international backing it had gained at the beginning of the negotiations in 1973. See LaFeber 1979:228–54 for discussion of some of these questions.

40. Shortly after its creation, the Democratic Revolutionary Party applied for membership in the Socialist International, the alliance of the major socialist parties of Western Europe. However, the Party's attempts to accommodate the contradictory interests of Panama's classes and factions produced such a mishmash of ideology and platforms that the Socialist International rejected the application.

Contrary to the claims of the U.S. right wing and of the Panamanian opposition, the Torrijos revolution was far from "socialist." LaFeber (1979:167ff) characterized Torrijos' reforms as "School of the Americas Radicalism":

> The inspiration for Torrijos's reforms . . . was not Cuban. Nothing provided a better key to the General's politics than to understand that his program was inspired by that anti-Castro, counter-insurgency institution in the Canal Zone, the School of the Americas.

41. The traditional parties, disbanded while still in the disarray that had given the 1968 presidential elections to Arnulfo Arias, had been unable to mount effective popular protests because they had never worked to develop themselves into organizations representative of the interests of the majority of the people of Panama; their popular support depended more on their ability to buy votes at election time than on their platforms and performances. Most Panamanians did not miss them. Arnulfo Arias' Panameñista Party did have popular backing among many people; but Torrijos' effective moves to claim for himself the role of representative of the broad masses of Panamanians left many Panameñistas with divided loyalties as they recognized that Torrijos, no less than Arnulfo, was their leader.

42. The Catholic Bishops also questioned the Cerro Colorado project through the publication of two pastoral letters (discussed in Part 3), one raising concerns about the projected impact of the mine on the Guaymí Indians, the other trying to elevate the acrimonious national debate to a serious discussion of the overall issues raised by the mining project (see Núñez y Consejo 1979, CEP 1979).

Torrijos was never able to win the support of the Roman Catholic hierarchy. In 1969, under circumstances never officially investigated, Héctor Gallego, a priest working in the rural areas of Veraguas Province, disappeared, never to be seen again. All believed that he was kidnapped and killed by members of the National Guard, protecting the interests of some local business people, reputedly relatives of Torrijos, whose exploitation of the campesinos had made them a target of Gallego and his church-backed campesino organization. Mark McGrath, then bishop of Veraguas, worked very effectively to gain solidarity for the church's fight on behalf of Gallego, but Torrijos stonewalled. McGrath later became archbishop of Panama City and head of the Panamanian Bishops' Conference; although McGrath never spoke of it publicly, all believed that he viewed the developments of the Torrijos revolution through the optic of the Gallego case and his deep distrust of Torrijos.

43. The government's campaign for the Cerro Colorado project, at least as transmitted to local communities, included claims as exaggerated as those of the opposition: all campesinos and Guaymíes would find permanent employment with the mine; all small farmers could increase their production manyfold, because they would sell to the mine; the mine would solve all Panama's economic and social problems.

44. During and after the 1979 strike, as well as the 1978 strike, I spoke with a number of public educators in rural schools of western Panama. In 1978, a number of teachers praised the educational reforms, contrasting them with the inadequacies of the previous curriculum; a year later, they angrily denounced the reforms as "communist" and demanded a return to the previous curriculum. They admitted, however, that they had never read or discussed the publications that accompanied the new curriculum, and that their only personal complaints reflected not "communism," but government inefficiency in getting them the tools they needed to teach the new courses; nor had they read or discussed the studies critical of aspects of the reforms.

The private sector help for the educators was essential because Panamanian teachers supported themselves on their salaries; the union had no strike fund to provide food for its members. Thanks to the outside backing, teachers in provincial capitals lined up at distribution centers where they received food, clothing, and some cash; they were thus able to stay on strike for nearly two months. Rural teachers, without the same access to outside help, went to their families.

In Panama, as throughout Central America, the political right often employed the term "communist" as an extreme characterization meaning "enemy" or "opponent," using the overtones of repressive states and "Godless atheism" to help fan the popular flames. Few thought to look for substantive indications of Marxist, Russian, Cuban, or Chinese influences.

45. Although the teachers fairly begged for support of the organized working class of Panama, leaders of the labor movements were only too mindful of the repeated failure of the teachers' organizations to take any interest in the problems of workers; while the teachers presented themselves as "workers" during this strike, in general they considered themselves "professionals," a decided cut above the working class. Many labor movement leaders looked for ways to keep their constituencies from taking part in these demonstrations, considering them manipulations by the right wing; but the grievances of the rank and file were too many, and the opportunities to voice these complaints too few. The demonstrations were massive.

The private schools, mainly Catholic, joined the strike in solidarity with their public school colleagues, despite the fact that none of the strike issues (including the educational reforms) affected them. Some government officials claimed that Archbishop McGrath gave them private assurances that he would stay out of the fight, only to throw the hierarchy's support behind a Roman Catholic commission that claimed that the educational reforms were in some measure communist-inspired.

46. The Party, depending on Torrijos himself for its unity, could not escape the tensions of divisions and factions in Panama. When Torrijos died in 1981, the tensions broke into the open. The divisions and factions within the National Guard, kept submerged through the shrewd efforts of Torrijos himself, came forth as high-ranking officers fought to take the place of their fallen leader. In quick succession, the Guard underwent several changes of commander-in-chief; the Party backed and unbacked various candidates for the presidency; and the Guard removed the president, and later his replacement, both Torrijos appointees. In the presidential elections of 1984, it seemed that only through resorting to the time-tested methods of lengthy delays in announcing the vote-count could the Guard, again firmly in control of the country, hand the presidency to Party candidate Nicolás Ardito Barletta, opposed principally by an old, tired, weak, muddled, but still popular Arnulfo Arias.

47. Representatives of densely populated *corregimientos* (political divisions

similar to voting districts) could organize highly publicized and embarrassing demonstrations to pressure the government to improve local services.

48. Even the occasional perceptions of arbitrary or unjust actions by members of the National Guard somehow were not taken as reflections on the commander; people thought that if Torrijos knew, he would make sure the abuses stopped.

Chapter 3: Dynamics of the Guaymí Region

1. The wealthiest cattle ranchers live in Panama City and occasionally commute by private airplane to their extensive holdings in eastern Chiriquí.

2. Young (1971:12–18) provides a more detailed description of Guaymí dress and adornment. In the 1980s, expensive dresses, fairly closely patterned on the traditional women's wear of the Guaymíes, had begun to appear in stores in Panama City; out on the streets, they became a folkloric alternative to the slavish imitation of the latest U.S. fads.

3. Between San Félix (at about 100 meters above sea level) and Hato Pilón (at about 600 meters), a walk of three or four hours, the trail descends and ascends ten or twelve times to cross creeks.

4. Young (1971:107–25, including 15 pages of photographs) provides detailed descriptions of houses and caseríos.

5. The reader interested in knowing more about Guaymí swidden agriculture will find an excellent detailed description in Young (1971:60–72), including plant inventories, average yields, planting and harvesting cycles, differences in elevation, preferred types of bananas, etc. The discussion in the text provides only a brief summary of Young's work. At the end of his discussion, Young notes that "there are no basic differences in crop inventory and method of land utilization between the [Guaymí] and latino subsistence farmers of Chiriquí Province" (1971:69–70).

6. "Single kin-group *caseríos* are the largest multi-function corporate groups in [Guaymí] society, but membership in these groups is determined not by descent but by locality and bilateral filiation" (Young 1971:125). The Guaymí (male?) ideal of establishing post-marital residence on lands of the husband's kin had to yield in practice to demographic and economic factors (Young 1971:125ff).

7. Young's (1971:160–68) discussion of reciprocal cooperative labor includes nuances of who owes return labor to whom within kin circles, good reflections on the efficiency of exchange labor, and some discussion of the threats

posed to the continuation of reciprocal labor from increased Guaymí involvement in a cash economy and wage labor.

8. See Young (1971:226), Bort (1976:55), and Young and Bort (1976a, 1979). The Guaymíes' bilateral inheritance of rights to use of lands theoretically meant that a significant number of individuals could bring forward equally strong claims to the same plot; residence on and actual use of kin lands were two factors that usually modified claims in individual cases. However, "[t]raditionally no precise set of rules applies to inheritance of use rights to land. . . . The hamlet [caserío] without at least one land claim dispute pending is rare and every hamlet has the threat of land disputes hanging over it continuously" (Bort 1976:55–56). Guaymí difficulties in finding lasting resolutions to these disputes bore out Young's statement at the beginning of his "tentative" discussion of Guaymí land rights: "It appears that the [Guaymí] themselves are frequently hard pressed to resolve questions of priority of land rights" (1971:149).

9. Guaymí men practiced polygynous marriage; they maintained that they usually had fewer household fights when they married sisters, but they gained access to wider land rights (and labor obligations) when they didn't.

> Marriage in [Guaymí] society is not simply the union of man and woman; it is also the basis of alliance between the kin groups. . . . Each time a marriage (or divorce) occurs, there is a shift in residence of individuals and a change in access to the use of sections of land, in labor commitments, in the personnel of productive and consumptive units, and in the network of social relations in general of numerous people. (Young 1971:172)

10. John Bort documented the years-long process of arriving at the necessary consensus decisions for the establishment of the Cerro Otoe cooperative with its store in Cerro Otoe and its house in San Félix (see Bort 1976). Although the process was very slow, it was sure; the cooperative was much more successful than most other Guaymí business ventures.

11. Guaymí predecessors enjoyed this abundance of land and resources because of the devastation of the Spanish conquest; when the Spaniards arrived, the peoples of western Panama were apparently engaged in fairly frequent wars and raids for land. See Young 1980b.

12. Some Guaymíes have recently revived the celebrations known as the *chichería* and the *balsería*. I heard of several *balserías,* although I was never able to observe one; I took part in a *chichería* and heard of others.

13. Cabarrús (1979:45–46) reported that very few Guaymíes in Bocas del Toro still knew of older rites and customs. The Mama Chi movement has

prohibited them; later, access to education brought with it a new sophistication that labeled these practices "superstitious" or "backward." Consequently,
those few who held onto older rites and customs, practiced them in secret.

14. Reported Young:

> On the whole, attempts to Christianize the Guaymí and to convert them to
> town life met with little success. . . . Some Guaymí did become Chris-
> tianized and latinoized; others, after apparently brief and unhappy stays in
> the towns, fled back into the farther reaches of the mountains of Veraguas
> and Chiriquí where there have been no active attempts to proselytize since
> the end of the first half of the seventeenth century. Nevertheless, these back-
> sliders [sic] apparently carried with them some knowledge of Catholicism
> which gradually combined with elements of native religious belief to form a
> kind of folk Christianity. . . .
>   The reluctance of the Ngawbe [Guaymí] to accept the teachings of
> Protestantism bears little relation to their knowledge and strength of belief
> in Catholicism. Their Catholicism is a folk variety built around a basic belief
> in God and the Blessed Virgin and incorporating a series of supernatural
> beliefs quite similar to those recorded in the earliest documents relating to
> Guaymí customs. As Catholics, the Guaymí are nonparticipants. There are
> no churches in the Indian territory, no circuit-riding priests visit the area,
> and there are no resident priests in most of the towns bordering the terri-
> tory. The only Ngawbe I encountered who had been baptized as Catholics
> had had this rite performed when, as children, they had lived with latino
> families; yet almost all profess to be Catholics. (1971:53–54)

Perhaps an exception to Young's note on Guaymí reluctance to accept the
teachings of Protestantism would be the Guaymíes of the Valiente Peninsula
in Bocas del Toro, where the Reverend Ephraim S. Alphonse worked as a
Wesleyan Methodist missionary from 1917 to 1938 and from 1948 into the
1960s (a total of 37 years) when he retired to Panama City, where, with great
energy and marvelous good humor, he continued his ministerial work into
his eighties and occasionally gave classes in Guaymí at the national university.
Rev. Alphonse, who spoke the local dialect of Ngawbere fluently, worked out
his own version of a Guaymí grammar (Alphonse 1956, 1980) and a massive,
still unpublished dictionary that the priests of Remedios–San Félix tried to
expand and to adapt to the dialect of Chiriquí Province.

By the late 1970s, when I worked in Panama, a number of religious
groups sought converts among the Guaymíes, including the Ba'hai faith, the
Summer Institute of Linguistics (SIL), and U.S.-based protestant fundamentalist evangelical groups including the "New Tribes Mission." Some Guaymí
activists complained vociferously about the SIL, claiming they were CIA
agents in disguise, etc.; the government of Panama eventually revoked their

contract, although I think the reasons had more to do with disputes about deliveries of studies than Guaymí complaints (whose basis I could never understand anyway since, to my knowledge, the SIL's work was only linguistic and, in comparison with other sources of problems for the Guaymíes, fairly unobtrusive). Our few contacts with the Protestant fundamentalist groups working in the area were generally disagreeable; their aggressive style seemed to include seeking open fights with representatives of the Catholic Church.

15. Cabarrús (1979) argued that the Catholic Church in Bocas del Toro provided an important source of power for Cacique José Mónico Cruz through its fairly unquestioning support of him, even when the United Fruit Co. was manipulating him against the interests of Guaymíes working the banana plantations. Cacique Mónico lived in Canquintú, an uncharacteristically large settlement (perhaps sixty Guaymí houses) built up, with his encouragement, in large part through the efforts of the local priests.

16. With respect to self-help projects, Catholic agents (like everyone else) had to work by trial and error in the attempt to discover what kinds of projects could really benefit the Guaymíes in the principal areas of concern: better nutrition, indigenous management, and promotion of autochthonous organization. Projects like those of Canquintú, for example, begun in the 1950s, seemed from the perspective of the late 1970s to be too big and too complicated technically for the Guaymíes to have much possibility of taking them over and keeping them going; in this sense they might be labeled "paternalistic." Projects begun much later, as in Tolé and Remedios–San Félix, tended to be very smallscale, and from the outset placed considerable emphasis on the need for local (Guaymí) control and management. This emphasis showed itself, for example, in the fact that more money went to salaries of Guaymí staff (promotors, specialists in cooperatives, agronomists) and to sponsoring ongoing short courses and seminars on how to run a cooperative store (and in the process build local organization) than into the small counterpart loans (average $200) to the groups setting up the store. Counterpart loans to communities to set up small fish ponds averaged about $35. The relatively few government projects in the Guaymí area seemed designed in a vacuum of knowledge of Guaymí reality and promoted either no organization or highly dependent ones; these projects seemed very paternalistic in orientation.

17. Besides those baptized while living with latino families, as Young mentioned (see note 14 above), over the years a number of Guaymíes had joined the hundreds of latinos who lined up for baptisms on the annual occasion of the visit of a priest to celebrate the feast days of the small towns bordering

their territory. So, it didn't seem too surprising that almost anywhere we went, Guaymíes with otherwise little or no experience of priests, knew at least that we should baptize, and repeatedly asked us to baptize their children and numbers of adults. On two widely separate occasions, in Hato Pilón and in Hato Rincón, after considerable discussion and consultation with my fellow Jesuits in Remedios–San Félix, I baptized groups of Guaymíes. My only other ministerial work among the Guaymíes consisted in doing the best I could to answer questions in informal conversations.

18. A number of Guaymíes spoke this way to me and to other priests. I recognized that these statements could have been made in (unconscious) hopes of telling us something they thought we might want to hear, although they could also have arisen from people's desires to deepen their relationship with God.

19. In general, all the groups of priests discussed in the text were attracted to the Guaymíes within the framework of Latin American theology of liberation, with its special emphasis on the poor as the primary recipients of the liberating message preached by Jesus Christ, a message summarized in the Christian gospels as the "Kingdom of God." The theological support of these different groups of priests and nuns has been and continues to be the subject of numerous writings and analyses from virtually every imaginable perspective. Gutiérrez (1973) is one of the earliest widely known introductions to the main lines of liberation theology; in the context of Central America, Berryman (1984) offers a good discussion of activities motivated by this theology.

In a slow, patient process of evangelization, they sought to discover, with the Guaymíes, ways in which the Catholic faith could be enculturated, that is, adapted to Guaymí history, culture, and values instead of representing an imposition of a completely foreign mindset. In these efforts, aside from strong arguments for the necessity of this kind of approach, they could find little written that provided them either with experiences with indigenous groups elsewhere or with concrete suggestions of how to proceed. After a couple of false starts, only toward the end of 1980 was it possible to organize a meeting of most of the church people working with the Guaymíes, to share common problems, compare approaches and experiences, and begin work toward some unity of criteria.

Not surprisingly, the specific orientation of any given group of Catholic priests or nuns depended on a variety of factors, including the culture, personalities, and convictions of the different religious orders and individuals. In Bocas del Toro, the priests, Augustinians from Spain, had arrived around the 1950s to replace the earlier priests, Vincentians from the United States.

Another branch of Augustinians, also from Spain, worked in Tolé. In San Félix–Remedios we Jesuits were mostly Panamanians, but included one Spaniard, and me from the United States. In the 1970s, the nuns in Canquintú and Tolé were members of the religious congregation Missionaries of Mary Immaculate and St. Catherine, from Colombia. Thus it is very difficult to present a general summary that would fairly represent the nuances of different approaches at different times and places. Given this major qualification, and given that my own experience was mostly in Chiriquí with one group of priests, what I wrote in the text seems to me a fairly accurate set of generalizations. I am unaware of any Catholic missionaries among the Guaymíes engaging in harangues against any aspects of normal Guaymí practices, or in attempts to convince Guaymíes of the "need" to be baptized or otherwise converted to Catholicism. The basic approach was one of going slow, trying to understand Guaymí ways, and from there trying to discover what elements of Christianity might complement these ways.

In any case, to my knowledge the priests and nuns were well aware that whatever their personal preferences might have been with respect to the evangelization of the Guaymíes, they had little "power of convocation," that is, little possibility of organizing, on their own, any kinds of activities in the Guaymí area. Only by spending time getting to know people, through many visits to the same caseríos, could they begin to gain acceptance as outsiders who had not come to exploit the Guaymíes, but had come for some other purpose.

20. The problem was less severe in Bocas del Toro, which still had large tracts of virgin forest available for Guaymí expansion, despite disputes over the Guaymíes' rights to make use of these areas. Young (1971:6) maintained that the soil on the Caribbean side was "somewhat less hospitable to farming"; but Cabarrús (1979:45) thought that Bocas del Toro had an abundance of good land underutilized because of the absence of good communications.

21. Young (1971:50) concluded that the majority of the contemporary campesinos of western Veraguas and the coast of Chiriquí were descendants of Indians, perhaps Guaymíes, who had settled and remained in towns formed by the early missionaries. References to a large group who burned their town houses and fled to where they could live according to their own traditions (Young 1971:53), and to Indian raids of latino towns (e.g., Tolé and even David) well into the eighteenth century (Castillero R. 1968:21–24), suggest that the Indians did not passively accept these intrusions of regional dynamics.

In the nineteenth century, U.S. explorers studied Chiriquí–Bocas del Toro routes for a transisthmian canal, discussed the feasibility of mining coal in western Panama, proposed transisthmian highways and railroads in the same area, planned the construction of U.S. naval bases in Bocas del Toro to keep watch on the British along the Mosquitia Coast of Nicaragua and Honduras, and even persuaded President Lincoln to give serious consideration to the voluntary or forced shipping of freed slaves to "unoccupied" Bocas del Toro (see Mack 1944:272–77; Rippy 1931:44–45; Bidwell 1865:343; Castillero R. 1968:63–69).

22. Later, after flooding destroyed plantations and railroad bridges along the Cricamola, the United Fruit Company moved its Bocas del Toro operations to their present location in the western part of the province, letting what remained of the plantations and railroad beds be reclaimed by the jungles, the Guaymíes, and a handful of families of black Caribbean origin.

23. See below in Chapter 3 for discussion of the Guaymí Comarca and legal situation.

24. Sarsanedas (1978:94 note 27) cites an informant who said that in 1930, permission was given (by the government?) that anyone who wanted could take lands within the Guaymí reserve; the same note gives four examples of latino purchases between 1930 and 1943.

25. Sarsanedas (1978:32), in a study of numerous cases in only two or three communities in Tolé District, lists the presumably illegal alienation of some 330 hectares entirely within the Guaymí zone, and another 650 hectares partially in Guaymí territory, all by ranchers who live in the town of Tolé. This study, with data up to 1975, does not offer any information about the extent of similar losses in other parts of Tolé. In some corregimientos of Tolé District the definition of lands that probably should belong to the Guaymíes is complicated by the presence of poor campesino families who have lived in the same area with the Guaymíes for some one hundred years. But the Guaymíes tended to accept the presence of those who lived on and from the land, whereas they opposed those who were absentee owners.

I made no field study of the alienation of Guaymí lands. In the San Félix and Remedios districts of eastern Chiriquí, I knew of two or three cases of Guaymíes who rented pasture land to latino ranchers, and I knew of some complaints of their kin/neighbors who feared that these rentals would be a step toward alienation of the lands.

26. General Omar Torrijos, in a speech to Guaymíes some years after her death, maintained that the visionary Mama Chi had not died from fever, as everyone believed, but had been killed by

> the hounding of the alcaldes [mayors] of Tolé, of Horconcitos [San Lorenzo District], and Remedios, because persecution also kills. She was

harassed as though she had been a criminal, because they didn't understand
that she was performing good works; she wanted to unite the Indians. . . .
(Torrijos 1973:55–56)

27. See Sarsanedas (1978:25–26, 92). Young (1971, 1976a, and 1978) provides
excellent discussions of the Mama Chi movement.

28. General Torrijos recounted how he, then a Major in command of the
National Guard in Chiriquí, went with fifty men to Soloy to arrest Samuel
González, the "cacique" of the Mama Chi movement, because Samuel

wanted respect for Indians, because Samuel didn't want whites to come into
the Indian Reserve to harm the Indians. . . . I stayed several days in the
mountains because I wanted to befriend Samuel. When I became his friend,
he explained to me why the Indians were fighting, what they were struggling for, and I, instead of taking him prisoner to David [the provincial
capital], became his ally. (Torrijos 1973:55)

29. Guaymíes said that 200 of them, unarmed, went to Tolé to see about the
release of Cacique Lorenzo; latinos claimed that 700 armed Guaymíes
showed up, and the residents of Tolé feared the Guaymíes were ready to take
the town by force (Sarsanedas 1978:48).

30. Young (1971:108) stated:

A few [Guaymí] have purchased sheets of corrugated zinc to use as roofing
material. This practice seems to be a display of wealth more than anything
else, since, in a practical sense, houses with thatched roofs are much better
suited to present conditions of technology and environment. A thatched
roof allows the smoke from the cooking fire to escape, and it keeps the
house relatively cool during the day and relatively warm at night. A metal
roof appears to have none of these advantages.

I agree with Young's reflection on the practicality of thatched roofing, and
would add that good thatched roofs tend to last longer—up to thirty
years—than the zinc, which corrodes and sprouts leaks.

However, in parts of Chiriquí, by the late 1970s the scarcity of good materials for thatching turned zinc roofing into more of a necessity than a luxury, despite its expense and the problems of transport. Guaymíes complained
of having to walk three or four days to the nearest good growths of
thatching grass. Since one roof required many loads of grass, roofers either
had to contract large caravans of men and horses, or make many journeys.

31. While optimal fallow varies among micro-environments, about twenty-
five years would be necessary for relatively complete recovery of soil fertility
in Chiriquí and southern Veraguas. I assume that the soils on the Caribbean
side would require at least a similar period of fallow.

Young (1971:77–81) made estimates of Guaymí land needs using a formula devised by Carneiro (1960). According to this formula, in order to allow twenty-five years of fallow, supposing with Young that 50 percent of their land was arable, the present population of 50,000 would require more than 11,470 km² of land; my estimate of the actual territory occupied by the Guaymíes was about 6,800 km². Although Carneiro's formula does not take into account the variability of the subsistence system and various mitigating factors (including out-migration), it does give a general picture of the overall situation.

32. Bort (1976) includes the study of other "non-traditional" Guaymí economic strategies, the ways that these were incorporated into traditional Guaymí patterns, and some problems that were created.

33. The Guaymí labor force in Puerto Armuelles dropped from around 2000 to about 300 (Young 1971:100).

34. Young (1971:99ff.) and Bort (1976:56ff.) provide more detailed information about Guaymí wage laborers and about those who lived and worked outside the area for longer periods of time, then returned permanently.

35. As will be discussed later, the reservoir needed for the first phase of the Teribe–Changuinola hydroelectric project would submerge the Valle de Riscó, flooding the area occupied by these Guaymíes.

36. This group suffered harassment from relatively affluent latinos of the Río Sereno township, who tried to move onto the lands that the Guaymíes had laboriously cleared and planted. The latinos sought to take advantage of, in effect, free labor to clear virgin tropical forest for their own use as cattle pastures.

37. Bort (1976:42–49) worked with census data up to 1970 to argue that considerable migration was occurring within the Guaymí area, from higher elevations to lower, i.e., from corregimientos nearer the Continental Divide to corregimientos nearer the border area with latinos. He noted that, were subsistence agriculture the primary consideration, the reverse would have been expected, since the higher elevations were less densely populated. His explanation was that "[p]eople are apparently moving from the higher, more remote areas to the areas bordering on *latino* lands allowing them easier access to areas in which they can secure employment" (1976:48). In the corregimientos he defined as bordering dominantly latino areas in Chiriquí, the 1960–70 population increase was 30.8 percent, but in the corregimientos he defined as bordering the Continental Divide, the increase was only 9.0 percent. However, the 1970–80 increases did not continue the 1960–70 trends:

the increases were 32.9 percent in the high areas, 23.4 percent in the low. These later census data could be seen either as raising questions about Bort's argument, or (were the argument to be confirmed through fieldwork) perhaps as indicative of a change in strategy when people did not find the jobs they sought.

In making this argument, Bort was struggling to explain the marked difference between the expected and the recorded population increase, in the absence of any available systematic study of Guaymí migration, whether internal or to outside the Guaymí area. He accounted for part of the apparent decline in population growth through out-migration, in line with "informant accounts [that] indicate heavy migration to areas outside of those held by the Guaymí" (1976:48). I heard many similar accounts. As he noted, the Panamanian census did not count as indigenous people anyone who was outside the indigenous areas on census day, so that it would be difficult to know how many Guaymíes had opted for permanent moves away.

But census tables might provide the basis for an enlightened guess. Putting together the following: the assumption, with Young (1971:80) that since Guaymí population tended to increase around 30 percent every decade from 1930 to 1960 (see table below), it should continue at about that rate; the fact that in the last thirty or forty years no one knows of any factors (e.g., epidemics or knowledge of contraception) that would cause a decline in the rate of increase; the impression that access to health care has improved for them; and the census information that from 1960 to 1980 their population increase did not maintain itself at 30 percent per decade; from all these, one might conclude that the "missing people" left the area. The number of Guaymíes "missing" in this fashion might be around 8,000, or about 16 percent of their recorded population.

Indigenous Population Increase per Decade, 1930–80, Western Panama

1930–40[a]	1940–50	1950–60	1930–60	1960–70	1970–80[b]
24.1%	21.2%	41.0%	30.6%	19.5%	20.6%

[a] 1940 population revised in line with Young (1971:80, 48).
[b] 1980 population estimate adapted from 1980 census.
SOURCES: Calculated from Young (1971:80, Table 10) and Estadística y Censo.

38. In Chiriquí, Guaymíes working for the Chiriquí Land Company donated funds to build twelve schools, and the government agreed to provide teachers; by 1964–65 only four of these schools were functioning (Young 1971:20). In the corregimiento of Cerro Iglesias, a Protestant group had built and staffed a small school, which had been operating since the 1930s.

39. Since teachers received their assignments by seniority, most teachers in the Guaymí area were young. Teachers received no extra compensation for food, travel, or hardship for their work in the remote areas of the country. Almost all these teachers put in requests for transfers at least to more accessible Guaymí communities if not to latino towns. Teachers in Cerro Otoe worked at a distance of six to eight hours' rugged walk from the town of San Félix, the nearest town served by a road. Teachers in Hato Pilón were a couple of hours closer, while those in Hato Julí were about an hour from San Félix. Teachers in remote areas held extra classes and combined their days off each month to have time to travel to their homes.

40. The teachers I spoke with were unaware of the incongruity of presenting as the norm a kind of life they themselves had never seen.

41. Given the difficulties of understanding and supporting the educational process in the first place, it is easier to appreciate the devastating effect in the Guaymí area of the teachers' strikes in 1978 and again in 1979. Both strikes came around August (the school year ends in early December). In 1978, the teachers went on a kind of strike that required them to remain in their places but not to offer classes—ready to return to work at a moment's notice. The teachers had no more idea than anyone else when the strike would be settled; so they asked the children to check in each day, to see if there would be classes. The strike lasted 3 or 4 weeks. The whole procedure made some sense in a town, where students and teachers lived a short distance from school. But in the Guaymí area, teachers could not return to their homes because they would be unable to go back to work as soon as word arrived by radio that the strike had ended. And many students lived 45–60 minutes away. Neither parents nor students understood why the teachers, who were there anyway, did not just go ahead and offer classes. Teachers, for their part, were angry at their perception that the parents did not back their strike, which seemed to them so clearly justified. Parents did not back the teachers' wage demands because they regarded the teachers as wealthy, since their income so far exceeded any Guaymí incomes. In the longer 1979 strike, teachers left the area completely; so at least parents and students did not have the confusion of seeing the teachers there, but not having classes.

But in both years the effect in the Guaymí area was the same: many parents, not really understanding what was going on and in any case not very sympathetic, did not send their children back to school once the strikes ended. In the handful of schools where I was able to check, enrollment after the strikes dropped by about one-half to two-thirds. Between the time lost to the strikes and the failure to return for the final weeks of school, many students lost two complete years of schooling.

42. A government study (LAWG 1980:15, translating CEASPA y Comisión 1979 and referring to Comisión Interagencial para el Estudio de la Población Guaymí 1978) brought out some bleak statistics.

> In a survey completed [in 1978], it was found that 20% of the population suffered from tuberculosis, that 60% of the children suffer from malnutrition, and that 60% of the population have tapeworms. Also, over one quarter of all pregnancies result in a stillborn child or a child who does not live past five years of age. . . . According to the same survey, only 35% of the people had been vaccinated against TB, 21% against whooping cough, and 18% against measles.

43. Most Guaymíes had little understanding of what was going on in the centers. No one spoke to them in Ngawbere, and even the men usually did not understand Spanish sufficiently to engage in technical conversations with the medical people; women looked very discouraged if they had to come alone with a child. The doctors, frequently recent graduates from medical school, often provided hurried, impatient explanations using esoteric vocabulary; latinos could not understand them either. Sometimes the medical personnel would berate Guaymí parents for neglecting to bring in a sick child sooner, or for not knowing how to take good care of their children; their frustration and criticism would increase as they met the seemingly passive, uncomprehending faces of the objects of their dressing down. Few Guaymíes were confident of their comprehension of the ways health centers operated, decided on courses of treatment, charged for services, and so on.

The government also sponsored a program of rural health assistants equipped with small subcenters in local communities; but it did little to adapt this program to the realities of the Guaymí area, where it had little impact. Roman Catholic nuns provided local health care through their permanent stations in Llano Ñopo (Tolé District, Chiriquí Province) and Canquintú (Bocas del Toro Province); for a time, Guaymíes could utilize the government facilities of the mining project (see Part 3 below). Related government programs of providing clean, reliable drinking water and of building latrines reached only a handful of Guaymí communities.

44. Some remaining strict adherents of the Mama Chi movement would not, on principle, participate in programs sponsored by non-Guaymíes; at least one of their communities was decimated by an epidemic of measles after its members had refused vaccinations.

45. A worker in the provincial health offices in David told me, in considerable detail, of decisions made not to provide the Guaymíes with adequate vaccinations. According to this source, scheduled trips sometimes were can-

celled because an assigned doctor simply did not want to be bothered when the day arrived. Further, local health officials decided that the Guaymíes did not need (or deserve?) the dosages of vaccines prescribed in the medical literature; so they did not bother to schedule boosters or did not worry about their timing. Responses to this informant's questions and complaints indicated that these officials had little concern for the possibility of epidemics in the Guaymí area. I had no way of independently verifying this information; I can only say that this report is consistent with the vaccination activities I observed and heard about in the Guaymí area itself.

46. I made no study of native Guaymí methods of health care. The Guaymíes have *sukias* (like shamans) who, among other things, are experts in folk medicine *(curanderos);* in addition, there are some people who are skilled in folk remedies, but are not considered *sukias*.

47. A 1934 law recognized as "indigenous reserves" the "unoccupied *(baldías)* lands" of the Cricamola, Cusapín, and Bluefield areas of Bocas del Toro; a 1952 law recognized the "Comarca of Bocas del Toro and that of the Tabasará [Chiriquí-Veraguas]," providing temporary delimitation of the Tabasará Comarca. A 1958 law, which replaced that of 1952, again provided that delimitation of the Tabasará Comarca would be temporary until "geodesic tasks actually under way are concluded." These temporary demarcations presumably followed the criteria of the 1952 and 1958 laws, namely, that the indigenous reserves would be constituted by "the regions presently occupied" by the indigenous people. These laws responded to pressures that arose in conjunction with the Cuna fight (in the 1930s) for their comarca, to Articles 94–96 of the Panamanian Constitution of 1946, and to the efforts at least since the early 1960s of various groups of Guaymíes, often led by Lorenzo Rodríguez, cacique of Chiriquí. See Sarsanedas (1978:79–83) for a summary of some Panamanian laws referring to indigenous lands and rights; see Lobo (1980a, 1980b) for more analysis.

48. In fact, even as the government referred to the "collective property" of indigenous lands, it was using a legal term that had no meaning either in the traditions of the Guaymíes or in the Panamanian legal system. Panamanian law recognized either private property or "national lands," lands that were untitled. Guaymí lands were national lands, under the direct control and ownership of the government itself.

All these legal provisions came in documents that clearly stated the government's overall goal of incorporating indigenous people into the national life. See Lobo (1980a, 1980b) for more detailed analysis of "incorporation" and its real meaning as assimilation.

49. In this meeting, not open to outsiders, presumably General Torrijos and Cacique Lorenzo discussed these questions in a somewhat more veiled and indirect way than I present them here.

50. He eventually hired a consultant to report to him on the work undertaken with respect to the comarca. But while she met with ranchers and campesino communities of Tolé, she would not meet with Guaymíes; and her report remained secret.

51. Guaymí elected representatives, usually quite ineffective at their jobs, stood out in a crowd; they generally weighed more than other Guaymí men, wore newer and better clothes, and sported fancy watches and radios. Their regular income of $300/month plus expenses seemed to turn the heads of many representatives, giving them a feeling of superiority to their poorer, more common relatives and neighbors.

Corregimientos in the Guaymí area tended to be arbitrary geographic areas not reflective of people's own grouping of themselves; electing someone to represent a corregimiento did not fit. A given corregimiento often included many members of one extended kin group, themselves closely aligned through family and economic ties with people of a neighboring corregimiento more than with neighbors within the same corregimiento. Factions, often already present, became more openly opposed through the process of electoral campaigns, which usually pitted one extended family against another— even within the same community.

Further, the government's own allocation of projects by corregimientos meant competition among corregimientos for scarce budgets. Rather than seek ways to work together, corregimientos pulled further apart.

52. The major exceptions to the above statement were the Cerro Colorado and Teribe-Changuinola projects (discussed below) and, to a lesser degree, the comarca.

53. By the time of my fieldwork, only a handful of Guaymí communities in Remedios and San Félix districts adhered to the Mama Chi cult. I knew of a few Mama Chi communities in Tolé District, but I covered very limited ground there; I suspect the movement was still fairly active in parts of San Lorenzo District, home of Samuel González, the Chiriquí Mama Chi leader who was granted General Torrijos' "personal" recognition as a cacique. In his 1975 fieldwork, Sarsanedas encountered enough Mama Chi adherents in Tolé to believe that the movement still carried considerable weight; and Cabarrús, doing fieldwork at the same time, conversed at length with the principal Mama Chi *predicador* (literally, "preacher") of Bocas del Toro, where perhaps

the movement continued fairly strong after it had greatly fallen off in much of Chiriquí.

The Mama Chi religion figured as "the traditional religion" in pronouncements of the Guaymí congresses. But the initiative generally arose not from Guaymíes who lived in the area, but among university students (some of whom I knew quite well). I don't think that these younger men had direct experience of the movement; and in their daily lives and conversations, they did nothing that might have marked them as adherents. I suspected that they put these phrases into pronouncements in an attempt to gain further legitimation for their hopes for Guaymí autonomy.

54. By 1980 a number of Guaymí groups maintained that the office of cacique was a "traditional" Guaymí leadership position. However, so far as I could determine, the office of cacique first emerged among the Guaymíes some time in the 1960s, and only began to command attention among the Guaymíes in 1969–70 when General Omar Torrijos granted government recognition to the caciques (see Young and Bort 1979:88–90, 93–94). Government recognition was not formalized on paper or by law.

Both Cabarrús (1979:44) and Young and Bort (1979:93) note strong similarities between the Guaymí office and the older Cuna model, although pro-cacique Guaymíes tend to deny that they have borrowed anything from the Cunas.

The Guaymíes had no mechanisms to name or replace caciques; while each of the three caciques claimed to be the victor in some election, the actual procedures seemed more some sort of power play, with the losers unable to find effective ways to protest being ousted (Young and Bort 1979:92; see Cabarrús 1979:35 for complaints of a former Bocas del Toro cacique). Guaymí caciques had no job descriptions, no listing of rights, duties, and powers; no structures or organizations through which they exercised their offices; no formal accountability to constituents or to the government. Within the local dynamics of the Guaymí area, caciques seemed to have only the power people gave them, power that not only varied from subgroup to subgroup, but even from time to time within the same subgroup. My impression is that the caciques enjoyed a fair degree of popular backing so long as they represented Guaymí interests concerning the comarca and carta orgánica; but when the caciques sought to exercise other kinds of authority, e.g., in the resolution of local land disputes, they could quickly find that their backing disappeared (see Young and Bort 1979:94).

While I speak in general terms, my research has more to do with the case of Cacique Lorenzo Rodríguez of Chiriquí than with the other two. I have good reasons to believe that the case of Cacique José Mónico Cruz of

Bocas del Toro was strikingly different from that of his Chiriquí counterpart, and I will later note some differences. And I think that the case of Cacique Camilo Ortega of Veraguas is somewhat more mixed, although he would to some degree be more like his Chiriquí colleague than like Mónico of Bocas del Toro.

55. Although I tried to get a better sense of his earlier activities, I was unable to find the informants I needed. In my meetings with him, Cacique Lorenzo showed little interest in indulging my strange requests for reminiscences about his past; Young and Bort seemed to experience similar problems (see 1979:89–90). Sarsanedas (1978:24) reported that Lorenzo was elected in 1969, imprisoned twice in 1970, and was a strong supporter of the Mama Chi movement.

56. The *corregidor* was a local official of the national government; his (or occasionally, her) main responsibility was to register births and deaths in the corregimiento. Corregidores sometimes helped solve minor disputes such as working out agreements for payment of damages to crops from cattle or pigs not kept under control by their owners (see Young and Bort 1979:90). The elected representative of the corregimiento appointed the corregidor.

57. As Young and Bort (1979:96) note, many jefes inmediatos were quite conservative in their views. Like the cacique himself, the jefes inmediatos had no job descriptions, structures, or organization. The cacique appointed them; in some fashion they were accountable to him. But the cacique had no mechanisms for monitoring their activities beyond their own reports; and he in turn seemed to be more concerned with their loyalty than with their actions.

In a couple of very diplomatic meetings with Cacique Lorenzo, several of us priests offered him some concrete information about things being done and said in his name, after he had assured us that such things in no way represented his approach. When the same actions by the same people continued unchanged in the following months, we surmised either that Lorenzo did not regard our concerns as all that important, or that he had little ability to influence his followers in these areas.

58. I ran across this very energetic ethnologist two or three times, but had no opportunity to talk with her at any length, and I saw no written work she may have done; I found it difficult to get a clear sense of what she was doing and why she was doing it. What I report, obviously, came from experiences and perceptions of people who disagreed with what she was doing. In that discussion, I have selected materials best supported by a variety of Guaymí informants, by people from CODEMIN, and by my own observa-

tions. She will appear again later in this book, in the discussion (in Part 3) of the impact of the mining project.

Apparently, this ethnologist worked under and was supported by the National Guard's military commander for Chiriquí Province; the personnel of the Department of Social Development of CODEMIN claimed to have no idea of what she was doing in the 1978 elections. Although her salary came out of the CODEMIN budget, she did not report to the Department, which had no control over her work. The Department thought the controversies surrounding her activities detrimental to its own efforts to gain Guaymí acceptance for the mining project, since people were aware of her association with CODEMIN. After failing in the attempt to sever her ties with CODEMIN, the Department of Social Development thought it had reined her in, keeping her from further involvement in the internal politics of the Guaymíes; however, she continued her seemingly free-lance work after the elections.

From things people said about her, I gathered that she operated from her own vision of what would be best for the Guaymíes, supporting the Chiriquí cacique and trying to influence him on some policy issues. Rumors (most of them uncomplimentary) circulated to explain her influence over Cacique Lorenzo, influence that quite probably came through her friendship with his principal wife and her access to higher levels of the National Guard.

59. Pointing to the number of signatures backing one's candidacy was a main feature in the low-key Guaymí campaigns. Guaymíes in the corregimientos of Hato Chamí, Hato Culantro, and Hato Julí made the same charges against her and the cacique.

60. Cuerima was also home to Cacique Lorenzo's candidate for the corregimiento of Hato Julí.

61. So far as I could tell, the jefe inmediato of Hato Pilón assumed his office by default; he was the only resident of the corregimiento who went to the cacique's meetings with jefes, generally held in Tolé District.

62. Throughout the election period, Torrijos and the National Guard remained neutral. When I asked this jefe what happened to this neutrality, he said I could know about it because I had a radio; he had none. Later that day I visited him in his home, where he was listening to a radio. When convenient, Guaymíes typically denied knowledge of things outside the range of their direct experience.

63. The government provided food supposedly for all Guaymí voters because many of them had to be away from home two or three days in order to vote.

Several other jefes inmediatos also kept the government-provided beef for their own voters, and the incumbent representatives used their own money to provide food for everyone else.

64. The note, delivered by the jefe's son, supposedly was signed by the cacique's candidate; however, the signature did not resemble his handwriting.

In the Guaymí area, school teachers organized the actual elections, which were technically under the neutral oversight of visiting corregidores; to guarantee neutrality, the government instructed corregidores not to work in their own corregimientos. Panama had no absentee ballots; corregidores and other election officials could vote in the corregimientos where they worked on election day.

65. The banner of the main opponent of his candidate flew on the jefe's home. One candidate's official poll watcher supported another candidate.

66. Virtually no one took seriously the third candidate, the incumbent representative. People liked him, but said he had done nothing during his six-year term; as expected, he placed a distant third in the balloting. In the final tally, the winner captured 46 percent of the 297 votes cast; the cacique's candidate received 41 percent, and the incumbent only 13 percent.

67. Kinship lines in the corregimiento were too complex to be reliable indicators of how people voted. For example, one young married man, living with his father who formed part of the jefe's group, was himself married to a close relative of the corregidor.

People expressed some satisfaction that with the new system of representatives, they could vote in their own corregimientos for people they knew; prior to the National Guard takeover in 1968, Guaymíes voted in latino towns where representatives of the principal political parties made empty promises and bought their votes with bottles of liquor. With elections in their own corregimientos, the Guaymíes enjoyed the diversion of a big gathering, perhaps reminiscent of their traditional *balserías*.

People did not close ranks around the victor. In Hato Pilón, the new representative made no attempt to reconcile his differences with the supporters of the cacique's candidate, and the jefe inmediato continued to sabotage attempts at local organization and development. When the representative called a meeting to put together the local committees that were to work with him on community projects, the jefe and his people stayed away and then complained that none of them were named to the committees. The jefe called his own meetings, then protested that the representative was at fault for the problems because he did not come. The new corregidor had no power over the jefe because the jefe refused to recognize him as a legitimate official.

The victors generally acted as though merely winning the election were the fulfillment of their goal, giving them prestige in a way perhaps analogous to being a renowned participant in the *balsería*. In Hato Pilón, the new representative purchased some sports equipment for the people, and bought rounds of *guarapo* (a sugar cane-based alcoholic beverage) whenever he visited the main caserío. But he did little else, and his own supporters did not pressure him to carry out projects. Guaymíes showed little commitment to elections as a way of choosing leaders they would follow.

68. For example, she was later a very visible presence when U.S. military transport helicopters and pilots, on loan to Civic Action of the Panamanian National Guard, hauled building materials from the town of San Félix to remote communities in the Guaymí area.

69. The jefe, undaunted by his critics, continued his efforts after the elections; he gathered signatures for a petition protesting the "illegality" of the new representative's opposition to the cacique, shown in his failure to make the jefe inmediato the new corregidor. This jefe and his counterpart from the corregimiento of Hato Culantro had returned from a pre-election meeting of jefes with Cacique Lorenzo proclaiming a new "law": the offices of jefe inmediato and corregidor were to be combined. The cacique later told me he had never given such an order, but had proposed this move and hoped that new representatives would take this step without awaiting the necessary changes in federal legislation.

70. I did no fieldwork in San Lorenzo District; my impression is that the comarca was an important issue there, but that people didn't particularly know Cacique Lorenzo.

71. Although Lorenzo of Chiriquí was the most conservative of the three caciques, there is little doubt that he was more liberal than these opponents gave him credit for (see Young and Bort 1979:96, 106 note 17).

72. Guaymíes of San Félix and Remedios faced few of the direct effects of the diminished Guaymí territorial base; latino ranchers had not made incursions as in Tolé. The Cerro Colorado project lay in the northern portion of Remedios District, and many Guaymíes of the area came to oppose the project; but they found little support from Cacique Lorenzo and his followers. The mining project lay at some distance to the east and north of the Guaymíes of San Félix, who had little concept of the effects they would experience.

73. As will become more apparent later on in this book, Cacique Lorenzo of Chiriquí, perhaps tired after long years of battle, exercised less and less leadership among the people as time went on. Sarsanedas (1978:92) quoted informants' views that the cacique's leadership had withered considerably as he adopted more ambiguous stances, to such an extent that he had very little support among younger Guaymíes.

74. However, the government tended to bypass the Guaymí representatives and deal directly with the caciques, to the frustration of a number of representatives (Young and Bort 1979:97).

75. I did relatively little fieldwork in Bocas del Toro. I worked with Cacique Mónico's delegation on the CEASPA-Guaymí report on the impact of the mining project (CEASPA y Comisión 1979). I went to Canquintú three or four times, where I was a guest of the Augustinian priests (for the Guaymí Congress of September 1979 and for later work with Catholic missionaries). I spent a little time in the towns of Bocas del Toro, Changuinola, and Almirante, as the guest of other Augustinians; and I accompanied the cacique for three to four days of walking from Canquintú up the mountains to the Continental Divide. My perceptions of his support in Bocas del Toro are based on these experiences, conversations with the priests who had known him for many years, and witnessing the extent to which he and his associates were able to mobilize Bocas del Toro Guaymíes to participate in major congresses. I suspect that further investigation would show more weaknesses in his leadership and organization than I here suggest; but I think the basic lines of my judgments would survive. See Young and Bort (1979:96), and Cabarrús (1979).

76. Earlier in his career, before Mónico saw what was happening, he was used by the Chiriquí Land Company as a labor recruiter and disciplinarian for their banana plantations. But with his advisers' and some others' help, he came to see the situation, made changes, and came away strengthened in his ability to recognize and resist manipulation. See Cabarrús (1979).

77. I suspect that the Bocas del Toro Chiriquí Land Company union allowed the Guaymíes to continue the practice of short-term work because in Bocas del Toro the company itself saw that it needed Guaymí laborers more than it did in Chiriquí, where it could draw more readily on the surrounding campesino and urban working people.

78. The prime mover of UIG was Ricardo Smith, an older Guaymí university student from Bocas del Toro who had earlier tried to found a pan-Indian movement in Panama, but ran into problems with the more adept,

better organized Cuna delegates. Some North Americans and Europeans active in international indigenous concerns knew Smith from international meetings. Like Smith, UIG's other principals were Guaymí university students residing in Panama City. In order to be among the small number of Guaymíes who continued their schooling to the university level, they had spent years living away from ordinary folks; no schools in the Guaymí area itself enabled students to get the background to enter the university.

Miguel Cruz, a close associate of Ricardo Smith, worked for several months as my field assistant while he gathered data for his own undergraduate thesis in agronomy. Cruz later represented the Guaymíes in a number of international meetings, including the 1980 Russell Tribunal in Rotterdam.

79. In fact UIG leaders, far from having a soft life in the capital, like most Guaymí university students lived very poorly in crowded sub-standard housing, with very little income, scratching for food, clothing, transportation, and other necessities. I knew them as dedicated champions of the Guaymí people even as they lived their way through major identity issues brought on by their years of isolation in latino worlds.

80. In 1979–80, the government reform of the National Assembly led to the creation of two or three elected legislators per province. The first province-wide elections, held in 1980, marked the first test of the strength and organization of the recently legalized political parties.

In the area of Bocas del Toro where I observed these elections, several corregimientos received the wrong lists of voters. Local voting officials adopted widely differing approaches to the problem; hundreds of people were unable to vote. While the National Guard was responsible for helicopter delivery of the election materials, it was unclear who had switched the lists and whether the mistakes were intentional; the prime suspects were local leaders of the Guard and of the Democratic Revolutionary Party (Torrijos' party). After these elections (as after any recent elections in Panama), many communities and party leaders throughout the country claimed fraud on the part of the government and its party.

Cruz and, even more, Smith, would disagree completely with my characterization of UIG; they maintained they had widespread support and large membership. I failed in my attempts to get more detailed information with respect to the active membership of UIG.

81. Several thousand Guaymíes took part in major congresses in Canquintú (September 1979) and Soloy (April 1980). Congresses followed procedures combining Guaymí and non-Guaymí approaches. People spent hours and hours listening to the reading of documents; a few people entered into ac-

tive, back-and-forth debate. Outside of formal sessions, many participants gathered in small groups and quietly conversed, Guaymí-style, about the matters under discussion. Occasionally some more traditional Guaymíes asked questions or made a point; but for the most part, they sat in silence, leaving the active part of the congresses to the younger, more latinoized participants.

Guaymíes traditionally avoided direct confrontations in meetings about a proposed course of action. After carefully listening to a proposal, one who disagreed offered an alternative, without making direct reference to the first proposal; the areas of disagreement could be deduced from the alternative proposal and the ways it took care of this or that issue. If people in a meeting did not perceive consensus around a line of action, the meeting ended without a decision; in the time before the next meeting, participants talked things over, subtly advancing their own proposals but still not attacking another's (see Young and Bort 1979:76–78, 94, 106 note 14). Congresses attracted many latinoized Guaymíes who engaged in open debate.

Although Guaymí supporters of congresses fairly bristled at the suggestion, it seems to me (and to other observers) that the congresses are borrowed from the Cunas, for whom congresses have considerably more historical or traditional weight (see Young and Bort 1979:93). Guaymíes bristled both because of what they viewed as the insult in the suggestion that they had to borrow a "traditional" form of meeting, and also, I suspect, because of the fact that they have a fair amount of distrust of the Cunas. In general, Cunas are much better organized than the Guaymíes; they have many more educated members (including a few doctors and lawyers), and much more control over their members. They are much better at getting what they want from the government, and they are much better known within and outside Panama.

82. This group, which will appear again in Part 3 of this book, was comprised of a handful of Guaymíes who manifested considerable arrogance with respect to "common" Guaymíes. They worked closely with CODEMIN to sabotage the Canquintú congress (Chapter 8); they lost their bid for control of the Soloy congress (Chapter 9); and they tried to make deals with the government to land good jobs for themselves.

83. See Part 3 below for discussion of the substantive issues of these congresses.

84. Young and Bort discuss the Intendente:

[E]xamining the shadows of the past, we must not forget that years ago a previous national government had appointed one Guaymí as *intendente* (manager or overseer—the equivalent of a provincial governor) of all the Guaymí. He still occasionally journeys from his permanent residence in Panama City to make his appearance on the local scene.

Officially, the *caciques* are responsible to the *intendente* under Panama's laws. . . . In the Guaymí case, the *intendente* is Guaymí but the principle is not accepted by the *caciques* or the populace and thus the *intendente* is virtually powerless. (Young and Bort 1979:91, 106 note 12).

The Intendente claimed to have a lively organization in Tolé of Chiriquí; but, so far as I could tell, his popular support was insignificant.

85. In addition to this ideological difference, Ricardo Smith of UIG and the leader of the Frente were personal rivals. At times, both of them seemed to want to give orders free from explanations and challenges, and could be very difficult to work with. In the small world of the Guaymíes of Panama City, UIG and the Frente had interesting connections. The Intendente's son was a principal of the Frente; Miguel Cruz, a principal of UIG, was married to the Intendente's daughter. Both Miguel and the Intendente's son lived in the Intendente's house on the outskirts of Panama City.

86. Part 3 of this book will explore this confrontation.

Chapter 4: Panama's Struggle for Control

1. Canadian Javelin, through its Panamanian subsidiary Pavonia, S.A., applied for a concession in February 1969 after geologist Paul Kents confirmed that Cerro Colorado was a substantial copper deposit. Kents said he went there on a hunch because he had explored a "Cerro Colorado" in Peru (E/MJ 1971:27); another version had it that Kents was led to explore Cerro Colorado by a report from a team of Canadians who surveyed the region for the United Nations (NYT 1973a). Canadian Javelin also said its founder and Chief Executive Officer, John Doyle, sparked the company's interest in Cerro Colorado, prompted by reports from his pilots that their compasses reacted strangely when they flew over Cerro Colorado (E/MJ 1972:61). Canadian Javelin competed with Placer Development, Ltd., for the concession, winning it by offering a premium of $51,000 to Placer's offer of $10,000 (E/MJ 1971:27).

2. Canadian Javelin sent the ore samples to Panama City for assay, corroborating the results in laboratories in Miami, Ottawa, and Toronto (NM n.d.:2).

The heavy tropical rains during the rainy season and frequent fog and high winds during the dry season made air travel risky. Canadian Javelin stopped using small planes after one crashed into the landing strip.

3. Doyle owned a hotel-casino in Panama; one might suspect he had a permanent welcome-mat out for Torrijos. Perhaps the premium of $51,000, obtaining the Cerro Colorado concession for Canadian Javelin over Placer Development, was a gloss for other transfers of money. Such activities would be consistent with the rumors about Torrijos' corruption, one of those things that "everyone knew" in Panama, but that was never clearly discussed in the media nor looked into officially.

4. The consortium was probably influenced by the sharp drop in copper prices, from an all-time high of $1.376 per pound on the London Metal Exchange in April 1974 to just $0.585 per pound by the end of December 1974. When negotiations broke off, prices were down to $0.575 per pound.

5. The Securities and Exchange Commission knew Doyle long before he began work on Cerro Colorado. In 1965, Doyle pleaded guilty to violating U.S. securities regulations by hyping his company's stock. He received a sentence of 36 months in prison, with 33 months suspended; but, rather than serve time, Doyle jumped bail (NYT 1973b). Consequently, the U.S.-born Canadian citizen had to avoid the United States. He flew circuitous routes back and forth between Canada and his residence in Panama.

In Panama, Panamanian shareholders of Doyle's hotel wondered why their dividends were so small although the hotel was normally booked to capacity (NYT 1973a). In Canada, too, Canadian Javelin was involved in various legal and business disputes.

6. As early as December 1972, *Engineering and Mining Journal* reported that Wright Engineering, Ltd., of Vancouver, B.C., was scheduled to submit a feasibility study by the end of 1972 (1972:61). The *Northern Miner* reported that the study was due early in 1973 (n.d.:1), but it was still pending in July (MH 1973a). In response to the Securities and Exchange Commission, a Canadian Javelin statement claimed that Wright Engineering had "completed a final technical and economic study dated September 25, 1973" (WSJ 1973c). I have found no earlier reference to the completion of this study, and no references to the contents or quality of the study.

7. By this time, Canadian Javelin had estimated the deposits at "two billion tons of drill-proven ore, one billion tons of probable ore, and a further one billion tons of possible ore, for a total of four billion tons in all categories, grading 0.65 percent copper equivalent" (WSJ 1975c).

8. In the Chamber of Commerce forum with CODEMIN, questioners implied that Panama had paid Canadian Javelin much more than the announced $23.6 million; CODEMIN gave no precise figure of the total

(including interest), saying only that it was considerably less than Canadian Javelin's demand of $125 million (Cámara de Comercio 1979:23–24).

Controversy concerning the access road provided some insight into the workings of Canadian Javelin. The SEC charged that Canadian Javelin could not account for $7.2 million allegedly spent on this road and on other properties in Honduras and El Salvador. According to the SEC, in 1972 Canadian Javelin contracted Grand Cayman-based Owl Investments, Ltd., to do studies, plans, and surveys for the road; but no one could determine what, if anything, Canadian Javelin received in exchange for payment of this contract. In 1973, Canadian Javelin paid an advance of $6.5 million to International Oceanic Construction Corp. and Almora, S.A., contractors for the construction of the road. These latter companies were both registered in the name of Roberto A. Torres, but the contracts were signed by Augustín de la Guardia. The SEC charged that these companies had no prior construction experience, no assets other than payments from Canadian Javelin, and were in fact controlled by John Doyle.

There was no way to determine how much money went to construction of the actual road, an unfinished one-and-a-half lane dirt and gravel access road of about 40 km. Canadian Javelin officials told the SEC that the work done on the road did not exceed $1.3 million; Panama's compensation package included payment of $5 million for the road (MH 1977). Canadian Javelin (1977:17) stated that $733,974 of the original advance of $6.5 million was returned in December 1975 and applied to the $870,000 purchase of properties in El Salvador and Honduras; these unnamed properties were initially offered to Canadian Javelin for $25,000.

From published material available, it is difficult to see how Canadian Javelin arrived at its claim of $125 million; presumably most of this claim was Doyle's calculation of what his company would have earned from the mining project. In mid-November 1973, Canadian Javelin reported drilling expenses of around $7 million (NYT 1973), although, by then, the major part of the drilling was finished. Other major expenses would have been the feasibility study from Wright Engineering, and the famous road. If one allowed $3 million for further drilling and other work on the site in 1974, and the company's highest claim of $5.8 million for the road, Panama's compensation still included $9 million for the mysterious feasibility study.

9. Ronald Müller coauthored (with Richard Barnet) *Global Reach: the Power of the Multinational Corporations* (1974), cogently and readably presenting the main issues of growing worldwide concern over the power of MNCs. In the wake of events in LDCs in the 1960s and early 1970s, and the investigations into MNC dominance of the Western world economy, LDC bargaining

power emerged as a major theme among government officials, business leaders, and academics of various persuasions. (For some examples, see the studies by these authors cited in the bibliography: Bosson and Varon, British-North American Committee, Carman, Davis, Mezger, Mikesell, Miller et al., Pardy et al., Radetski and Zorn, Robert, Roberts and McLean, Seidman, Sideri and Johns, Sklar, Tanzer, and Zorn.)

In the Ministry of External Relations, Xabier Gorostiaga, a Basque Jesuit priest and naturalized Panamanian, concentrated on political-economic analysis of the Panama Canal; later he turned his attention to the role of international financial centers (see Gorostiaga 1978). In 1977 Gorostiaga began CEASPA, with which I was associated during my time in Panama.

10. Zorn (1980:217ff) offers case materials that support the argument that majority ownership does not necessarily mean control of profits of a mining project.

11. If it took this counsel, Panama would be advised to study closely the ties of the MNC manager, to guard against hidden links with providers of equipment or outside services. These ties could be ownership links or the myriad ways of interlocking boards of directors.

12. Western Europe and Japan might have been interested in financing Cerro Colorado because they relied on imported copper and needed to guarantee future supplies. They also possessed the technology necessary for Cerro Colorado; export credits could have helped with the financing. In exchange, Panama could have guaranteed them Cerro Colorado's output, with prices to be determined by the market prices at the time of delivery.

In the mid-1970s, OPEC countries, particularly Iran prior to its Islamic revolution, might have been interested in Cerro Colorado both as an investment and as part of a strategy to restructure the international economic order. Brazil and Venezuela, needing copper for their own industrialization and interested in restructuring the economic order, might also have participated.

13. Müller and Gorostiaga also advised Panama to delay eight to twelve months before committing itself to contracts, in hopes that depressed copper prices would rise as the recession bottomed out; copper prices on the London Metal Exchange had declined from their historic high of $1.376 per pound in April 1974 to $0.568 per pound in May 1975. In fact, their projections of copper prices and the length of the recession were no better than those of most industry forecasters. In January 1976 London Metal Exchange prices averaged $0.541 per pound (although by May 1976 they had recovered to $0.686); the year-long average price only rose above $0.60 or so in 1979 and 1980.

The government would have had to mount a domestic campaign to reassure Panamanians that the delays in signing new contracts were temporary and deliberate, that intense MNC bidding continued, and that the result of going more slowly would be greater benefits for the people. Even with the delay, Cerro Colorado could still have begun production in 1980 or 1981.

Gorostiaga and Müller advised Panama to take advantage of the delay to complete final engineering studies, projecting an expenditure of $3 to $5 million. In retrospect, their estimate of the cost of engineering studies seemed extraordinarily low; a more realistic figure would have been in the range of $30–50 million. Mining MNCs usually contracted these complex studies to major engineering firms like Brown and Root, Seltrust Engineering, Fluor, or Bechtel.

14. In accord with Panamanian usage, henceforth I will refer to this state corporation only as CODEMIN (pronounced co-day-MEEN). CODEMIN, which officially came into being with the enactment of Law 41, 1 August 1975, reported directly to the executive branch of the government and not to any ministry; its initial capital came from a $5 million government-guaranteed loan from Citibank. CODEMIN had the

> principal aim of promoting the development of the mining-metallurgical Project Cerro Colorado. [It could] also undertake other activities in accord with special projects assigned to it by the Executive Branch. (CODEMIN 1977)

The government assigned it the additional responsibility of investigating Panama's geothermal resources for use in generating electricity.

15. LaFeber (1979:197–198) noted that González'

> source of power was compelling: frequently living in González's house, Torrijos entrusted his private financial affairs to his host. González's impressive clout was not often employed for reform programs. One close associate became Ambassador to Washington, and two nephews moved into the government as Foreign Minister and Finance Minister.

16. I could not confirm, independently of my sources for these speculations, that Rodrigo González took this trip in the way described. However, these sources were in a position to know, and other materials they provided me have withstood considerable scrutiny.

17. The *Latin America Economic Report* speculated that "pressure from U.S. interests with their eyes on a potential bonanza" may have been part of the rejection of Canadian Javelin. The same article noted that the government of Panama had reduced to four its list of possible partners; one of these was Texasgulf (LAER 1975:71).

If such U.S. pressure in fact took place, I do not know what person or what branch of the U.S. government would have been involved. Well after Texasgulf became Panama's partner, and over a decade before he would become president of the United States, George Bush joined its board of directors. He had stepped down as head of the CIA, a post to which President Gerald Ford named him in late November 1975. In 1980, Dr. Fogarty, chairman of Texasgulf, strongly backed Bush's bid for the Republican presidential nomination. I do not know what connection, if any, Bush had with Texasgulf before he became a director.

18. Torrijos died as reputedly one of the wealthiest people in Latin America; gossip about Rodrigo González, who managed Torrijos' money matters, almost inevitably included the contention that he was a "mafioso."

According to news reports, a number of U.S. multinational corporations, especially through the early and middle 1970s, considered demands of LDC leaders for payoffs and kickbacks a sufficiently normal part of doing business that they carried such information on their corporate books. Later, such information was used to prosecute a number of companies in U.S. courts. Texasgulf, for its part, was aggressively expanding and diversifying when it landed the Cerro Colorado contracts. However, nothing I uncovered in Texasgulf's history gives plausibility to this line of speculation.

In a famous lawsuit, the SEC charged Texasgulf executives with illegally using "insider information" to acquire stock options on the eve of the announcement of the Texasgulf bonanza at Kidd Creek in Ontario. Although the Supreme Court finally resolved this case against some Texasgulf executives (including Dr. Fogarty), business and legal analysts widely interpreted it not as a case of corporate corruption, but as an instance of the SEC's use of a lawsuit to change the accepted meaning of one of its own rules. See Patrick (1972).

19. González might have gone to Washington to get World Bank reactions to this strategy or to discuss the World Bank's willingness to assist in the development of the Cerro Colorado project; by 1975 the World Bank had begun to help finance nonfuel mineral projects as it moved toward a policy change announced in its 1978 Annual Report (World Bank 1979:20–21). There, he might have been apprised of a major problem in the Müller-Gorostiaga strategy: the financing. Only through a consortium of international banking firms could Panama have tapped the growing "petrodollar" market; OPEC nations proved to be very conservative investors, reluctant to tie up their capital in long-term, high-risk ventures unless persuaded by overriding political considerations. Banks in turn insisted on provisions for lender control over important aspects of the project's development and on agreements spec-

ifying the order of payment to all who had claims on revenues from the project; in such lists, the host government usually brought up the rear (see Radetzki and Zorn 1979).

Furthermore, banks and multinational mining firms were generally not inclined to participate in a project that separated financing, technology, management, and marketing. Financial interests commonly insisted that a major mining MNC be clearly in charge of LDC projects; LDCs had to allow the MNCs the latitude to make "sound business decisions" free from undue political considerations, or else forego the needed financing from multilateral and commercial lenders. Multinational mining firms rarely sold or rented their technologies and managerial expertise; even if they did, banks required the MNC managers to have more at stake in the project than just their management fees.

The above line of analysis starts from Mikesell's argument that "depackaging" or "unbundling" the needed resources, skills and other inputs for a major mining project is not acceptable either to potential MNC partners or to investors needed for financing (Mikesell 1979b:45–47). Perhaps Müller and Gorostiaga had in mind the Shah of Iran's success in signing Anaconda Co. to a management contract for the Sar Cheshmeh copper mine. But Iran needed no help from banks to finance the mine. And Anaconda, far from establishing a new MNC strategy, signed the agreement with Iran in the immediate aftermath of the nationalization of its properties in Chile; the company needed work for some experienced personnel (see Mikesell 1979b:43 note 9).

20. So stated Kenneth Kutz, Texasgulf vice president in charge of the international division, president of Texasgulf-Panama, and Texasgulf's chief negotiator for Cerro Colorado. In the Spring of 1978, before I went to Panama, I interviewed Mr. Kutz at Texasgulf's corporate headquarters in Stamford, Connecticut; Dr. Charles Fogarty, then chairman of the board and chief executive officer, kindly arranged this interview. Except where noted by reference to published materials, allusions to the views of Mr. Kutz are from this interview.

21. In the text, I will use "Consejo de Legislación, Assn." to cite the Association Agreement, "Consejo de Legislación, Adm." to cite the Administration Agreement, and "Consejo de Legislación, Arts." for the Articles of Incorporation. Roman numerals refer to clauses or articles; Arabic numbers and letters refer to subclauses or subarticles. I quote from the English version of the contracts, given me by Dr. Fogarty of Texasgulf; the official version was the Spanish, published according to Panamanian law as the entire issue of the *Gaceta Oficial* No. 18,022, dated February 6, 1976 (see Consejo de Legislación 1976).

The contracts between Texasgulf and the government of Panama provided the general framework for their relationship, spelling out in great detail the obligations and responsibilities of the partners. However, even with their precise legal language, the contracts could not delineate all aspects of the interaction of the parties; questions of interpretation remained, and some difficult issues were skirted through imprecise language and concepts in the hope that these issues would not become problematic in the relationship.

Both the government of Panama and Texasgulf offered these contracts as models of the new, more equitable relationship between multinational corporations and LDCs. Texasgulf executives talked frequently, publicly and privately, about their view of the contracts. CODEMIN, in its first Annual Report *(Memoria)* to the National Assembly of Panama, stated

> We believe that with these [contracts] the country has positively contributed to the inauguration of a new stage which augurs more modern and equitable relationships between a country on the road of development and a transnational corporation. With a realistic and pragmatic spirit, the country has made a valuable contribution to the underdeveloped world in its quest for viable channels toward development and independence. (CODEMIN 1976:5)

Different international groups (including the United Nations), meeting to discuss MNC–LDC relationships, tapped Jaime Roquebert of CODEMIN to present these contracts as the model new relationship between host countries and multinational corporations.

22. The sponsors proposed to finance the project according to a 70:30 debt-equity ratio; that is, 70 percent of project financing would be obtained through loans made directly to the operating company, and 30 percent would come from equity contributions of the sponsors.

23. Mr. Kutz of Texasgulf thought Panama found attractive the fact that the company had never been unionized and had never lost an hour of work to a strike; this attraction contained the implicit promise that Texasgulf, with Panamanian government help, would manage Cerro Colorado's labor force with similar success.

Sponsors regard as crucial their control of labor on a risky, large-scale mining project, especially during the highly vulnerable construction period and the first few years of operations. Sponsors finance mining projects through loans whose interest accumulates during the grace period of construction; inflation and cost overruns throw off the construction budget. Work stoppages almost inevitably result in even costlier financing. During the initial years of operations, sponsors hurry to work out technical problems and bring projects up to full capacity, so that they can generate the revenues needed to cover the heavy debt repayment schedules; again, work stoppages would be devastating.

24. Mr. Kutz said that only Texasgulf offered a plan to make sulfuric acid as a smelter by-product, instead of burning off sulfur wastes into the atmosphere; Texasgulf proposed to combine the sulfuric acid with phosphate to make the fertilizer. Consejo de Legislación, Assn. (I.2) stipulated that Texasgulf could own 49 percent of a separate corporation established to produce and market these by-products; Texasgulf would provide management and technology, and could retain its shares forever.

25. CODEMIN called this price "the most moderate of all the market projections available" (CODEMIN 1979d:34). In fact, the average London Metal Exchange copper price for 1984 was $0.625 per pound (E/MJ 1985:40).

Chapter 5: Limitations from the Transnational Dynamics

1. In the mid-1970s, Chile's state-owned Chuquicamata was the largest copper mine, with annual capacity of 400,000 metric tons. Peru's privately owned Cuajone mine was rated at 155,000 metric tons per year (Mikesell 1979a:8, 252); it was 88.5 percent owned by Southern Peru Copper Company, which, in turn, was majority (51.5 percent) owned by ASARCO, with Phelps Dodge and Newmont holding the main minority interests. The Bougainville mine in Papua New Guinea produced around 185,000 metric tons per year (ABMS statistics); this facility was 80 percent owned by Conzinc Riotinto of Australia (CRA), which in turn was 85 percent owned by RTZ.

2. The table provides Texasgulf's administrative fees during Cerro Colorado production:

Year of Operations	% of Gross Sales	% of Operating Profits
1st through 5th	1.5 %	2.5 %
6th	1.375 %	2.2 %
7th	1.25 %	1.9 %
8th	1.125 %	1.6 %
9th	1.0 %	1.3 %
10th	0.875%	1.0 %
11th through 15th and succeeding	0.75 %	0.75%

SOURCE: Consejo de Legislación, Adm. VII.3.

3. I based my calculations on Texasgulf's most likely case in its feasibility study, following Zorn (1977). Kenneth Kutz of Texasgulf maintained that

Zorn's analysis did not hold up. Jaime Roquebert of CODEMIN claimed that Zorn later retracted his analysis; Zorn chuckled as he recalled friendly arguments with Roquebert, but said he had no reason to go back on his analysis.

4. Texasgulf arrived at an opportune moment; in 1978, Robert McNamara and the World Bank announced the decision, already a growing World Bank practice, to increase funds available for LDC mining projects (World Bank 1979:20–21; see also Payer 1982:158–59). In Texasgulf's only other major base-metal mining project, the Kidd Creek zinc and copper mine near Timmins, Ontario (constructed 1963–66), Texasgulf had continued its long-standing practice of financing the development from its own earnings and ability to raise capital.

5. The Torrijos-Carter treaties did not provide Panama with the expected new revenues; see the discussion in Chapter 2. According to Mr. Kutz, by a "happy coincidence" Texasgulf was in a unique position for a U.S. corporation, because the President of the United States was personally involved in what was, for Texasgulf, a major "side issue": the canal negotiations. Panama, he surmised, "must have mentioned" Cerro Colorado in the canal negotiations, and the U.S. "must have some interest" in ensuring Panama's financial stability. Implicit in these statements was the conviction that Texasgulf could count on some support from the United States government.

Mr. Kutz even saw Panama's indebtedness as a potential asset; pragmatic lenders might well decide to help Panama finance a major mining project with high risk and high potential, rather than see Panama default on previous loans.

6. As the costs of constructing the Cerro Colorado project soared, Texasgulf proposed (for the time being) elimination of the smelter, and with it elimination of the phosphoric acid plant; Cerro Colorado would go to market with copper concentrates.

7. A high Texasgulf executive said these things to me in a 1977 telephone conversation that he initiated from his home. I cite them without precisely identifying their source because the call caught me by surprise, and I didn't think to ask him whether I could quote him. Circumstances kept me from later seeking his counsel on this point.

8. Texasgulf was involved in public debates with the government of the province of Saskatchewan over Texasgulf's potash operations, which the province wanted to take over. Frank Church's senate hearings on the involvement of the CIA and U.S. corporations in the overthrow of President Salvador Allen-

de of Chile (who had risked the wrath of the Kennecott and Anaconda copper companies) and his replacement by the repressive Pinochet regime seemed to support this Texasgulf official's statement to me about the political climate in late 1977.

9. Mr. Kutz, denying that Texasgulf had control over the board of directors through its veto power, was unable to provide me with a category of major decision-making that Texasgulf could not block. When all the conditions from different parts of the contracts were put together, the board of directors, by simple majority, retained unobstructed power of decision over the annual mining program, training and education programs, research and exploration programs, and transportation and distribution policies. In all cases, the board of directors would receive the recommendations of the administrator, giving Texasgulf control over the information on which decisions would be based (Consejo de Legislación, Adm. VI.2). Zorn (1977:245) makes the same point about Texasgulf's control of decisions. See CEASPA (1979a) for a chart depicting the levels of decision-making.

10. Specifically, Panama could not alter the taxes or exemptions granted by the contracts (Consejo de Legislación, Assn. XIX). Included here were exemptions from import duties on anything deemed necessary for the operation of the mining project (Consejo de Legislación, Assn. XV.1), despite provisions granting preference to goods of Panamanian origin whenever competitive "as to delivery, quality, quantity, availability and cost." The Panamanian preference clause was left to the interpretation of Texasgulf and its contractors (Consejo de Legislación, Adm. XIX).

11. As native North Americans have found out, this kind of preferential hiring mandate has no controls and is unenforceable (see Geisler 1982). The Colville Confederated Tribes of north-central Washington State, negotiating with AMAX, achieved agreement on strict hiring quotas with controls for the proposed Mt. Tolman molybdenum-copper mine on their reservation; but the project was cancelled before construction.

12. Texasgulf obtained further control over labor practices through the inclusion of "strikes and other labor conflicts" in the *force majeure* clause of the contracts. *Force majeure* allowed the parties to the agreement to fail to carry out contracted obligations without either side claiming a breach of contract or default; mainly included under *force majeure* were such events as wars, blockades, earthquakes, acts of God, "any cause . . . over which the affected party has no reasonable control" (Consejo de Legislación, Adm. XXV).

13. In the Fall of 1983, I interviewed Dr. Guy McBride, president of Colorado School of Mines and former director of Texasgulf. Dr. McBride kindly

allowed me to tape our conversation, and gave me permission to quote him, recognizing that he was speaking from memory and might be mistaken on some details.

14. Texasgulf's studies seemed to coincide with Canadian Javelin's overall estimates of the size and grade of the deposits.

15. Texasgulf maintained only the principal roads: from San Félix through Hato Chamí to Escopeta, and from Hato Chamí to Cerro Colorado; the others, rough access roads, were allowed to disintegrate from the effects of the weather.

16. The same clause specified the procedures to be followed in case neither Texasgulf nor CODEMIN wanted to go forward with the project, or in case only one partner wanted to proceed.

17. As Dr. McBride recalled, Texasgulf was

> assessing and reassessing and extending the feasibility study, contacting bankers all over the world, contacting people that knew about world copper markets and world metal markets . . . . At almost every board meeting . . . during that period, we heard some discussion of what was happening in the Cerro Colorado situation. What were we doing? We were doing this, we were doing that, we expect by such-and-such a date to have this pulled together, and we're going to meet with Panama on such-and-such a date, and after that we ought to have a better idea of whether Panama can get its money or not. That kind of discussion went on for a long time.

18. Dr. McBride observed,

> The simple question of what happens if Bell Telephone succeeds in replacing copper wire with glass—what does that do to the copper price? What if—that's one of the what-ifs. And if you're going to invest two or three billion dollars, you have to worry about things like that, because you're not going to get that money back in a hurry. Things can change, and you're left out on the end of a limb with an unamortized investment of several billion dollars.

19. Dr. McBride recalled that Texasgulf would have recommended against going forward with Cerro Colorado far sooner had it not been for the tenacity of Dr. Fogarty, whom he described as

> a man who was very much concerned about the future of the world as regards its supply of minerals. He felt that people were not paying enough attention to proper provision of minerals for the future . . . . He was simply reluctant to conclude, very reluctant to conclude, that this was not a do-able project, because it represented a very large deposit of copper. [The board of

directors worried that Texasgulf] was spending too much of management
time and effort on this project when it looked like it was not going to go.

20. Access to World Bank information can be a great help, since the Bank
(with its sister institution, the International Monetary Fund) has the leverage
to obtain considerable information that LDC governments are often unwilling to make public.

As an "international presence," the World Bank "consciously perform[s]
the role of guaranteeing the stability of the foreign corporation's investment"; its participation in a project places the institutional weight of the
Bank—and of its principal shareholders (the major countries of the west)—
behind negotiated agreements. Private lenders, bilateral aid agencies, and export credit institutions are invited to "co-finance" projects approved by the
Bank (Payer 1982:78, 5). World Bank and commercial loans

> are linked by (a) cross-default and other cross-reference clauses in the two
> agreements, which effectively provide a World Bank guarantee to the private
> lender; and (b) a written memorandum of agreement between the two
> lenders providing for exchange of information and consultation on matters
> affecting the implementation of the project or the borrower's ability to meet
> its repayment obligations. This provision assures greater than usual access
> by private lenders to the plethora of country and project information that
> the World Bank collects and analyzes in the normal course of its activities.
> (Payer 1982:184 note 1)

The cross-default provisions mean that a default on any part of the loans
(e.g., from the private lender) will be taken as a default on the whole package of loans (i.e., including the World Bank loan).

Raymond Mikesell, writing for the British-North American Committee,
agreed that World Bank participation would provide a major boost to foreign investors.

> [E]ven their modest participation in both loans and equity financing could
> be a powerful instrument for mobilizing private international loan financing
> and for giving greater confidence to potential private international lenders.

He adduced the same two reasons for this conclusion: reliance on "the project investigation and evaluation undertaken by the international agency," and
the "general belief that governments are less likely to default on loans in
which international agencies have participated." From the point of view of
an active defender of the role of multinational mining firms, Mikesell offered
a conclusion similar to that of Payer:

> International agency participation in project formulation and equity financ-
> ing should give private foreign equity investors considerable security against

expropriation or other contract violations which would affect the earnings of the enterprise. (All quotations taken from Mikesell 1979b:71)

Payer (1982:7) concluded:

> [T]he World Bank has deliberately and consciously used its financial power to promote the interests of private, international capital in its expansion to every corner of the "underdeveloped" world . . . . [T]he World Bank is perhaps the most important instrument of the developed capitalist countries for prying state control of its Third World member countries out of the hands of nationalists and socialists who would regulate international capital's inroads, and turning that power to the service of international capital.

Mikesell would adopt a different tone, but would clearly approve of the substance of this conclusion.

21. A note on some of the sources I use in the discussion of the World Bank's involvement in the Cerro Colorado project: 1) World Bank (1978) was a report on Panama's overall economic situation. This report, a preliminary draft of what might later become a public World Bank country report, was supposedly kept to limited distribution; but like so many World Bank limited-distribution studies, it was easy to obtain. 2) World Bank memoranda are cited from Posse (1980). Ana Victoria Posse, a Panamanian, somehow got access to many World Bank documents and memoranda relating to Cerro Colorado; she quoted liberally from them in a paper written for a graduate course at American University in Washington, D.C., and included some 24 photocopied pages as appendices. Ms. Posse was the niece of Dr. Aristides Royo, then-president of Panama. 3) In a December 1980 visit to the World Bank, I spoke with a couple of officials in key positions with respect to Cerro Colorado. These conversations were not for attribution; I refer to them here and there (as in the paragraph to which this note pertains) in this section. I asked one of these officials to let me study the documents used by Ms. Posse. He showed me one or two memoranda, but would not allow me to take notes or make copies; he insisted that the World Bank did not make such internal documents available to anyone.

22. The sponsors envisaged a town of around 40,000 (CODEMIN 1976:16). In private, an angry World Bank official argued that without good housing, numerous squatters would invade the area, creating problems for permanent employees; with inadequate living conditions, the project would suffer from high turnover of employees, especially foreign experts, and production would be adversely affected.

23. Texasgulf's tests revealed that the San Félix River had insufficient carrying capacity to handle 26.3 million metric tons of tailings each year; it pro-

posed to cover the added costs through its already-stretched 15 percent contingency budget. Mr. Kutz told me the company intended to adhere to U.S. environmental standards in Panama; but U.S. law prohibited dumping untreated tailings into rivers. Rio Tinto-Zinc employed this disposal method for its Bougainville project in Papua New Guinea, destroying the fish in the river, depriving people of agricultural land through the spread of tailings on shore, and threatening the marine life of the Empress Augusta Bay where the river emptied (Pardy et al. 1978:121–22).

24. The World Bank estimated that the more expensive electricity would increase the cost of power from Texasgulf's 19 percent of cash operating costs to 26 percent (World Bank 1978:74, 77); privately, a Bank official told me that the added energy costs could reach $200 million per year, equal to 85 percent of Texasgulf's proposed operating budget. If IRHE hurried into construction of Changuinola I, it would throw off its financial planning and overextend its technical capabilities, adding the risk of further price increases. The contractual provision binding Panama to ensure electricity to Cerro Colorado at the same tariffs as for all large industrial users (Consejo de Legislación, Assn IV.2.b) would amount to an unacknowledged subsidy of the mining project, denied by CODEMIN and IRHE officials (Cámara de Comercio 1979:55 ff., 70 ff.).

25. Texasgulf bore no legal responsibility for any problems created; in the contracts, CODEMIN had to "indemnify and hold harmless Tg. [Texasgulf], each of its subsidiaries and affiliates," its employees, officers, directors, agents, as well as anyone contracted for the project

> for and against any and all costs and expenses . . . incurred . . . in connection with any claim made for any reason relating to the Concession Area or the Project Area by [anyone] claiming to have a right or interest in . . . the Cerro Colorado Deposits or the Concession Area or Project Area. (Consejo de Legislación, Assn. XXVII)

In the Concession Area (750 square kilometers, which included the Project Area of 20 square kilometers), Texasgulf had a free hand to do whatever work it thought necessary (Consejo de Legislación, Assn. I.3). In and out of that area, Texasgulf acquired free right-of-way to all state-owned lands it needed; free use of earth, gravel, sand, timber, and stone from the Concession Area; free use of waters so long as no other users would be prejudiced; and free addition of necessary lands and rights of use to the Project Area (Consejo de Legislación, Assn. IV.1, 2). Texasgulf was well protected.

For its part, CODEMIN and the government had undertaken no studies, had no information on the extent of the problem, and kept affirming that "no Indians live there" (Pres. Royo in FT 1979:21). Texasgulf neither challenged these statements nor undertook its own studies; had it in fact adhered to U.S. norms, it might have looked into the specific provisions for assessment of the social impact of projects. See Part 3 for further discussion of questions relating to social impact assessment, relocation, and indemnification.

26. From 1974 through 1980, annual inflation averaged 10 percent as the increases in petroleum prices worked their way through the Western economy (U.S. Department of Commerce 1980:36; 1981:S-7). In the contracts, "the management agreement provides Texasgulf with no financial incentive to keep the project cost down since during the project execution [i.e., construction] its fees [of 1.25 percent of all construction costs] will increase with rising capital costs" (World Bank Memorandum of 24 August 1979, in Posse 1980:9). Without completion guarantees in the form of penalty clauses if Texasgulf brought the project to capacity production later than expected, the government of Panama would have no effective way to pressure Texasgulf. The World Bank thought that lenders would require substantial commitments from Texasgulf and from Panama for completion and cost-overrun guarantees; "substantial" meant "higher than the equity" of $480 million (World Bank 1978:78). These commitments could have been in the form of back-up financing to cover the unplanned additional costs that would arise from overruns or delays.

27. In Table 7, I recalculated the capital requirements for the Texasgulf project, incorporating estimates of omitted costs, higher inflation, and contingency lines. I used Texasgulf's own projections for the different aspects of the project (see Table 6), and the loan assumptions published by CODEMIN (CODEMIN 1979a:15, 21–22). I omitted working capital and income for year five, since they were almost equal. Even if my calculations were significantly off, they seemed to indicate more accurately than did the Texasgulf estimates the real costs of building Cerro Colorado.

28. Not even considered was what might happen if Panama also had to guarantee the loans made directly to the joint operating company, loans (with interest during construction) which could have totaled $2,730.6 million.

In a memorandum, the World Bank staff complained that both Texasgulf and CODEMIN were

> unwilling to consider any other needed infrastructure items [such as the ones mentioned on p. 107] for which financing will be required and insist[ed] that those items [were] not the project's but the Government's or that they should be financed by the private sector. (World Bank Memorandum of 5 December 1978, in Posse 1980:14)

The government, when asked to determine the sources and timing of additional funding needed for infrastructure, "according to World Bank sources was unable or unwilling to clarify this important matter" (Posse 1980:14).

29. Predictions of recoveries, future demand, and future prices are based on complex computer-run macroeconomic models of future economic patterns. Texasgulf projected that copper demand would grow by 4 percent per year from 1980 to 1990; the World Bank projected a 3.5 percent annual increase in demand from 1980 to 1985, dropping to 3.2 percent yearly from 1985 to 1990 (World Bank Memo of 19 April 1979, in Posse 1980:15). The table below, comparing the demand projections, uses two years of actual market-economy country copper consumption as starting places: 1976, the latest year available to Texasgulf for this part of its feasibility study; and 1980, for comparison.

Projections of Copper Demand, Market-Economy Countries
(Thousands of Metric Tons)

	1980	1981	1982	1983	1984	1985	1986	1987	1988	1989	1990
1976 Base:											
Tg	7,522	7,823	8,136	8,461	8,799	9,151	9,517	9,898	10,294	10,706	11,134
W B	7,378	7,636	7,904	8,180	8,467	8,763	9,043	9,333	9,631	9,940	10,258
Diff.	144	187	232	281	332	388	474	565	663	766	876
1980 Base:											
Tg		7,626	7,931	8,248	8,578	8,921	9,278	9,649	10,035	10,437	10,854
W B		7,589	7,855	8,130	8,414	8,709	8,988	9,275	9,572	9,878	10,195
Diff.		37	76	118	164	212	290	374	463	559	659

Actual Consumption of Refined Copper:
7,147   7,252   6,770   6,888

[Tg = Texasgulf; W B = World Bank; Diff. = difference]

SOURCES: Author's calculations, using 1976 base of 6,429.6 thousand m.t. consumption of refined copper and 1980 base of 7,322.7 thousand m.t. consumption; base figures from MA (1981). Actual consumption figures adapted from ABMS (1984).

More so than Texasgulf, the World Bank looked at the underutilized mining capacity brought on by production cutbacks with the world recession of the mid-1970s. With rising demand, closed or underutilized mines would be brought back to full production before new copper projects would be needed; "most mine production capacity utilization would only be restored to the historical level of 90 per cent after 1985" (World Bank Memo of 18 August 1978, in Posse 1980:15). While Chase Econometrics thought there was an underlying disequilibrium on the mining side because of the lack of investment in new projects in recent years (Elliott-Jones 1979), Metals and Minerals Research Service argued that an increase in the basic level of investment in new copper mines would be precipitous and destabilizing, and the exploitation in the medium range of major new deposits like Cerro Colorado was "exactly what the industry does not need" (quoted in CEASPA 1980:5).

The disagreements illustrate the difficulty concerning projections of growth of annual copper demand; expert projections for the mid-1970s to 1990 or 2000 ranged from 2.1 percent to 5.2 percent. Texasgulf's projection of 4 percent represented a choice that lay in the range of the average annual increase since World War II (4.3 percent per year from 1946 to 1980); the lower World Bank projection was still significantly higher than the average level of 2.8 percent per year from 1970 to 1980. Mikesell (1979a:186), discussing econometric models for copper, concluded that the models do not satisfactorily explain historical price movements or predict prices.

30. Copper prices, themselves dependent on copper demand, are the single most important determinant of the viability of a mining project. If Cerro Colorado produced its planned 182,954 metric tons of copper per year, one cent in the price per pound of copper would translate into $4.03 million in project revenues. Given the volatility of prices, the World Bank thought it prudent to use its own forecast as the upper limit (World Bank 1978:75). The table below compares the Texasgulf and World Bank price predictions.

Copper Price Projections
(U.S. Cents per Pound)

	1978	1979	1980	1981	1982	1983	1984
Constant 1977 $:							
Texasgulf	0.62	0.81	0.89	0.92	0.95	0.98	1.00
World Bank	0.58	0.60	0.62	0.83	0.92	0.94	0.96
Current Terms:							
Texasgulf	0.66	0.93	1.09	1.21	1.33	1.47	1.61
World Bank	0.62	0.68	0.75	1.00	1.25	1.35	1.47
Actual Prices:							
London Metal Exchange	0.618	0.901	0.993	0.795	0.672	0.722	0.625

SOURCES: World Bank 1978:75, ABMS, and E/MJ 1985.

31. Texasgulf's study identified potential markets in Japan, Western Europe, and North America for a total of 600,000 to 800,000 m.t. per year of Cerro Colorado copper concentrates; Texasgulf also had a list of potential customers for 195,000 to 290,000 m.t. per year of blister copper among refineries in Japan, West Germany, Great Britain, and North America (Texasgulf 1978:2-16 to 2-18). Of these, British Kynoch Metals, Ltd., part of the ill-fated consortium with Canadian Javelin, showed the most interest; negotiating on behalf of Société General des Minèrais of Belgium and Norddeutsche Affinerie of West Germany, the Kynoch group agreed to purchase all of Cerro Colorado's blister copper production for the first fifteen years and to provide contingency financing that would total $350 million over the first five years of production. However, the Kynoch group declined any equity participation (World Bank Memorandum of 19 April 1979, in Posse 1980:18).

Exact marketing terms and costs were never clarified, and the World Bank believed that beyond ordinary interest and commitment fees, the Kynoch group "would expect payment of 4–5 cents/lb over and above the normal refining charge for blister during the first 5 years of production. This would imply additional operating costs of U.S $18–20 million for that period" (World Bank Memorandum of 19 April 1979, in Posse 1980:18). "No tentative long-term sales contracts were negotiated, and it appears to be extremely difficult to obtain real take-off contracts at the present time"; La Caridad copper mine in Mexico, due to begin production within months, had still not obtained any sales contracts (World Bank 1978:75). Sales contracts were necessary because the loans from the Export Development Corporation would require that the sponsors assign "the proceeds of long-term sales contracts" as security for the lenders (letter cited in Miller et al. 1978:17). Privately, the World Bank maintained that Texasgulf simply had done no serious marketing studies.

32. I based the copper production figures on Texasgulf's anticipated 182,954 m.t. per year capacity; I calculated the diminished revenues using Texasgulf's projected $1.46 per pound.

The World Bank (1978:74) contended:

[t]he project is large and the processes involved are complex. Texasgulf, the operator, has no previous experience in mining low-grade copper ore in large-scale open pits, nor had it ever operated a copper smelter. No skilled manpower is available in Panama and the training requirements are great.

Texasgulf planned to use the new Outokumpu smelter technology from Finland. "Smaller plants using Outokumpu technology have been reported to experience technical difficulties" in Poland, Botswana, and Zaire (World Bank Memorandum of 18 August 1978, in Posse 1980:12). Texasgulf officials acknowledged that "they had not collected start-up data from similar operations" in the preparation of their study (World Bank Memorandum of 20 November 1978, in Posse 1980:13). The World Bank also found it strange that Texasgulf recommended "a single line plant, in order to minimize capital costs," despite the great size of the project; any problem would shut down the entire smelting process (World Bank 1978:74).

33. The World Bank separated "Pre-Tax" and "After-Tax" onto different lines; since in these cases both kinds of income came out the same, I put them together.

34. Jaime Roquebert even took this study to a U.N.-sponsored meeting in Africa, telling other third world delegates about Panama's success in its contract negotiations with Texasgulf and its "can't-fail" mining project.

35. 'Total financing," under the Texasgulf proposal then available, amounted to 70 percent of $1,600 million, or $1,120 million. The EDC planned a package combining 30 percent Canadian commercial loans and 70 percent EDC loans, offered to the joint operating company for partially fixed, partially floating interest rates projected to average around 10.5 percent. The Canadian government, through EDC, would underwrite the syndicated commercial loans, obtained at a floating interest rate 1.5 points above the London Inter-Bank Offering Rate (LIBOR). EDC would take advantage of its government-backed triple-A credit rating to obtain lower interest rates for its share, offered to the operating company at a fixed rate of about 9.5 percent. The loans were both to be for 21 years, including 6.5 years grace, with repayment over 15 years. The EDC would combine the interest rates of the components of its own loans, and add 0.5 percent to cover expenses and administrative costs. Loan information derives from LAWG (1980:24, 25–26) and World Bank Memorandum of June 1979, in Posse (1980:Annex I).

EDC interest rates, although lower than commercial bank rates, are generally higher than those of other major industrial-country export programs, by as much as 1.2 percent in 1978. On a $1,000 million loan, for example, 0.5 percent higher interest rates represent more than $60 million in added interest over the life of a twenty-year loan, assuming a five-year grace period, $25 million accrued interest during the grace period, and repayment over 15 years.

Developed-Country Export Financing: Interest Rates

	1977	1978
Canada	9.3%	9.2%
France	8.2%	8.2%
Federal Rep. of Germany	8.6%	8.6%
Italy	9.2%	10.3%
Japan	8.7%	8.0%
United Kingdom	8.9%	8.9%
United States	8.45%	8.8%

SOURCES: 1977 rates from Radetzki and Zorn (1979:89); 1978 from LAWG (1980:29, 30).

36. These analysts noted that Texasgulf went to Japanese sources for its design and technology for the copper-smelting process being installed in its Timmins, Ontario mine. Texasgulf had already announced that its testing had indicated that the Outokumpu flash furnace of Finnish manufacture was most adequate to Cerro Colorado's technical requirements, especially the need to recover the high amounts of sulfur present in the ore in order to avoid major environmental problems; the Canadian Noranda continuous smelter had been considered and rejected. Suitable 166-tonne capacity trucks were made in Canada; 16-cubic-meter shovels were not. Canadian mines usually used United States-made milling and concentrating equipment, "suggesting that competitive Canadian equipment is not available" (Miller et al. 1978:7).

37. The Trudeau Liberal government made the original EDC offer; the Clark Conservative government renewed it in 1979, and the Liberals reconfirmed it when Trudeau returned to power in early 1980. For further analysis of the Canadian political economy, see LAWG (1980:24–30) and Miller et al. (1978). For an excellent analysis of Canadian foreign aid policies and their effects, see Carty and Smith (1981).

38. CODEMIN (1979d:27), in an identical paragraph, dropped the phrase "in a strict sense," saying only that there was no requirement of government underwriting. The CODEMIN–Texasgulf contracts envisaged financing the mine on a project basis, i.e., using the joint operating company and its holdings as collateral for loans without implication of further guarantees from Texasgulf or the government of Panama (Consejo de Legislación, Assn. IX.2).

Although financing from other countries might have provided more favorable terms, several factors made the EDC offer attractive to Cerro Colorado's sponsors. EDC's may have been the only firm offer; no other was ever mentioned. Posse, citing "Panamanian authorities," said that EDC might provide "unlimited cost overrun financing" for items covered in the EDC part of the package; that is, EDC might have been willing to finance Canadian inflation as it affected Cerro Colorado (Posse 1980:17). Also, Panama probably hoped for better terms from EDC because of the close ties between the Canada Development Corporation (CDC), principal Texasgulf shareholder, and EDC. The boards of directors of both agencies were interlocked by representatives of two government ministries. (Rodrigo González, president of CODEMIN and of the joint operating company, told the Chamber of Commerce panel that EDC "has no relationship" with CDC; "they are two distinct entities" [Cámara de Comercio 1979:41].) However, this same relationship could have turned sour for Panama, since

> Texasgulf's relationship with the single most important financier of Cerro Colorado also provides the private company a significant measure of economic and political leverage should disputes arise in the future between Texasgulf and the Panamanian government. (LAWG 1980:30)

39. The RTZ Group's 1979 sales of $5.5 billion compared to Panama's 1979 gross domestic product of $2.8 billion; the RTZ Group's 1979 pre-tax profits of $992 million compared to Panama's 1979 central government spending of $934 million. Panamanian figures from *Panamá en cifras*.

40. Carty (1982:310) synthesized the "character" of Rio Tinto-Zinc:

> The creation of Rio Tinto-Zinc established its essential character from the outset; it has always been an international firm, reliant on the growth of European demand for metals, adept at wielding influence in the marketplace, and well-connected to sources of financial capital and political power. (Translation from unpublished English draft)

41. The Bougainville copper project is the world's closest parallel to Cerro Colorado: a large, open-pit operation mining low-grade copper ore, located in a tropical mountain range where there was no previous infrastructure.

42. Carty (1982:328–29) referred especially to the new canal treaties, providing for U.S. military presence in Panama until the year 2000 or beyond; Panama's economic dependence on foreign investment and its role as a transnational service platform; and the deepening of these same ties in proposals for an oil pipeline [already constructed] and a sea-level canal.

43. The last two paragraphs rely on and paraphrase Carty (1982 passim).

44. The Texasgulf–CODEMIN contracts had provided that the two spon-

sors pay for Texasgulf's feasibility study as it proceeded, splitting the costs in proportion to their equity. The RTZ–CODEMIN contracts made provision for the later "capitalization" of these RTZ expenses in the event either of a favorable decision to proceed with the project or of a future Panamanian decision to replace RTZ. ("Capitalization" meant that RTZ's expenses would be considered as part of its equity contribution.)

45. The hydraulic process presumably would have relied on the San Félix River to transport the overburden away from the project area, giving this process the same disadvantages of Texasgulf's proposal to use the river for tailings disposal. The process would save on equipment and fuel costs, as well as the costs of locating and building storage in the immediate area for the dry overburden.

46. High-grading lowers the operating costs per unit of production—if it costs about the same to extract and process 0.8 percent copper ore or 0.4 percent ore, high-grading begins with the 0.8 percent ore to generate better cash flow during the early years of mining. Texasgulf's mining plans took the grades of ore as they came, spreading the more profitable and less profitable production over the life of the mine.

A World Bank official used RTZ's proposal for high-grading as the basis of his statements to me that Texasgulf had not adequately tested the orebody, did not do sufficient drilling to know the full dimensions of it or the grade of ore in the subsections, and could not put together the best possible mining plan. He said RTZ was surprised that Texasgulf overlooked the high-grading, since the richest part of the ore (0.8 percent) lay near the surface and was amenable to this approach. He also faulted Texasgulf's studies of the overall processing requirements as inadequate to determine the kind of processing that would work best for Cerro Colorado ore and to map out the feeding of the ore to the processing plant. I asked Dr. McBride about these criticisms; he flatly denied that Texasgulf's geological and engineering work was in any way inadequate.

47. Despite various rumors, it proved difficult to confirm that RTZ and CODEMIN had decided to suspend the Cerro Colorado project. We finally got written confirmation of the rumors when the Fluor Corporation urged the Interfaith Center for Corporate Responsibility to withdraw its shareholder resolution regarding the Guaymíes; *American Metal Market* sought further confirmation in Panama City, from RTZ in London, and from the World Bank, and then broke the news (AMM 1982).

Before long, the operating company stripped everything salvageable from the camps and auctioned off the equipment—bulldozers, dump trucks, jeeps, beds and so on. CODEMIN, which had already reduced its Panama City staff enough to give up one of the two floors it occupied in the Banco Nacional office tower, cut back to one small office.

When the project went into mothballs, various sources speculated that with the presidential elections of 1984, Panama could once again consider its options. Even that speculation proved unrealistic.

Chapter 6: The World Copper Industry in Control

1. A sovereign nation could probably not be enjoined from passing new domestic legislation by contractual provisions; such provisions are "important to the investor from a symbolic point of view, as a deterrent to hasty unilateral action by the state to amend the agreement or override its provisions" (Zorn 1977:243). The Texasgulf-CODEMIN contracts were the first recent Latin American mining agreement to accept external arbitration of disputes; a Panamanian negotiator told Mikesell that if this provision were ever invoked, "the agreement is dead" (Mikesell 1979b:56, 58 note 4). No developed-country government would ever have accepted these provisions, which constituted denials of sovereignty (Miller 1978:34).

2. Mikesell synthesized this viewpoint:

> Foreign direct investment is more capable of providing politically independent management, whether the managers are nationals or foreigners. Top management and boards of directors of government enterprises not only tend to be political appointees, but are under constant pressure to put certain national economic and political objectives [the national dynamic] above that of running the mining enterprise with a view to maximizing gross profits. (1979b:42)

> International creditors usually look to future mineral exports of the mining project to service the debt. This means that the creditors will insist on the construction and management of the mine by an experienced international mining firm which has an equity stake in the venture. Unless the government enterprise has an exceptionally good reputation based on proven experience, public international development institutions such as the World Bank also require participation by an experienced international mining firm as a condition for financing the enterprise. (Mikesell 1979b:44)

3. The EDC financing of Cerro Colorado would have required assignment of proceeds of long-term sales contracts to repayment of the loans (Miller et al. 1978:17). As noted earlier, complex cross-default provisions would insure that LDCs gave highest priority to debt repayment above any national income needs.

4. The administrative fees, it was expected, would produce more income for Texasgulf than would the dividends on its 20 per cent equity share. The fees, essentially a method of computing the transfer of technology, seemed very high; "many aspects of the technology used in constructing and operating mining projects are widely known, and can be purchased by LDCs from numerous sources" (Zorn 1980:223, 222).

5. By the time the mining project was suspended, estimates of the cost of hydroelectric power had risen to $700 million (AMM 1982).

6. Zorn synthesized the problem of enclaves. Mining operations, located in distant areas of LDCs, tend not to be well integrated with the national economy; they are almost "separate political and economic units," with more direct links (for food and other supplies, for communications, for transportation) with other parts of the world than with the host country. Expatriate managers and host-country nationals, living together in isolated project communities, feel little sense of belonging to the nation; schools, hospitals, and other public facilities and infrastructure in the mining towns generally surpass in quality what is possible in the rest of the host country, further setting apart the mining population. In capital-intensive mining, multinational corporations are usually willing to pay wages "far higher than the generally prevailing levels in the host country." Higher wages attract laborers from other sectors of the economy, making it difficult for national industrialists to find and keep skilled workers; the wages serve as constant points of comparison for wage demands by workers in labor-intensive sectors of the economy, where productivity per worker is lower. Mineworkers form an elite within the labor force, a sort of upper class within the proletariat, isolated from and hostile to other sectors of the national labor movements. See Zorn 1977:213–14. Panama, host to United Fruit Company banana plantations and bisected by the Canal Zone, knew well the effects of enclaves.

7. Panama had no experienced personnel; its last significant mining project ended when the Santa Fe (Veraguas) gold deposits petered out late in the sixteenth century. Jaime Roquebert was, to my knowledge, Panama's only mining engineer; prior to his work on Cerro Colorado, he had done graduate studies at the Colorado School of Mines and had participated in the work of the United Nations Development Programme's mineral survey of Panama. Panama's only mining economist was still doing graduate studies at the Colorado School of Mines. Those charged with monitoring and ameliorating the social effects of the project had equally little experience.

8. In fact, one World Bank official, convinced that Texasgulf's work in Panama was so shoddy as to amount to thievery of its fees, privately asserted

that Texasgulf's refusal to increase its equity could only mean that the company would not stand behind its own studies. Texasgulf, on the other hand, concluded from the same studies that further efforts to develop Cerro Colorado would only waste more exploration capital and management time.

9. Part 3 includes some discussion of domestic criticism of Cerro Colorado.

10. Rio Tinto-Zinc's activities, especially in Aborigine-inhabited parts of Australia and in Namibia, have received considerable attention; see, for example: West (1972); Christian Concern for Southern Africa (1976); Roberts and McLean (1976); Roberts (1978); Counter-Information Services (n.d): Haywood (1979); PARTiZANS (1979); and Carty (1982). Several studies document different aspects of RTZ's mining project in Papua New Guinea, including: Pardy (1978); Bedford and Mamak (1975, 1976a, 1976b, 1977); Connell (1977); Gilles (1977); Mamak and Bedford (1974a, 1974b, 1977, 1978); Oliver (1973); and Treadgold (1978).

11. According to the contracts, CODEMIN

> shall have the right . . . to examine at all necessary times any and all of the records, reports, accounts and other documents related to the Project and all installations, activities and operations of [the joint operating company]. In like manner, [CODEMIN] shall be entitled to conduct technical inspections of the Project on behalf of the Nation to determine compliance with applicable laws and regulations of the Nation then in effect. (Consejo de Legislación, Assn. XXVIII; see also Consejo de Legislación, Adm. XXII)

The contracts made mention of no other Panamanian agency that had inspection rights.

12. Other LDCs have discovered that power once granted to a major semi-autonomous state corporation can be very difficult to modify later. In Zambia and Zaire, mining parastatals have such power that they operate basically independently of the government (see Seidman 1975, passim).

13. After the ratification of the Torrijos-Carter canal treaties in June 1979, General Torrijos resigned as chief of state, supposedly handing over his power to the civilian government led by President Aristides Royo; but Torrijos retained his position as head of the National Guard.

14. An official of the office of the Comptroller of the Republic said that only CODEMIN, of the many state agencies in Panama, refused to comply with the laws requiring submission of budgets and financial reports. I was part of a group of Jesuits who met privately with President Royo late in 1980; given that the mining project was far and away the most significant

development project of his government, we were surprised that the president seemed to know little more than what came from public relations announcements. He complained about the Catholic Church's activities raising questions about the project; he knew neither the basis of the Church's concern, nor any of the major problems connected with the mining project. He was also unaware of CODEMIN's harassment of church personnel. The expatriate financial consultants worked with the executive branch of the government on proposals to refinance some of Panama's foreign debt.

15. Kenneth Kutz said that one thing he found satisfying in the contract negotiations was the fact that both he as the chief Texasgulf negotiator and Rodrigo González as the chief Panamanian negotiator had the power to make a deal. To confirm immediately the acceptability of their agreement on some issue, each had only one telephone call to make: Kutz to Dr. Fogarty, González to General Torrijos.

The greatest damage from official corruption may not be the loss of some millions of dollars diverted from the public coffers, so much as the likelihood that major decisions are made to move forward some interest other than that of the nation itself. Leaders who seek personal gain through bribes and kickbacks must find it difficult to weigh the best interests of the majority of the people over against their personal gains.

16. As noted in Chapter 2, Torrijos' strategy of gaining and maintaining popular support included the placement of members of the Party of the People in government positions, giving them visibility but little or no real power. During the national debate on the Cerro Colorado project, local cadres of this party in eastern Chiriquí convinced their campesino supporters that the mining project would provide them an endless stream of high-paying jobs as well as an unlimited market for agricultural products.

17. Ninety per cent of copper use falls into four principal categories: the electrical industry, engineering, building or construction, and transportation industries; the remaining 10 percent includes domestic consumer products, ammunition, coins, artistic uses, and some use for agriculture (Bowen and Gunatilaka 1977:14, 305–06).

While copper ore smelting was utilized in Egypt by 3300 B.C. (Bowen and Gunatilaka 1977:1), major copper production only began as part of the industrial revolution, in the United Kingdom. For much of the fifteenth through seventeenth centuries, copper was in wide demand in Western Europe for coinage, for cannons (cast-bronze) and for numerous industrial, handicraft, and household uses. However, the development of iron-ore smelting brought about substitution of iron for copper in arms manufacture and in household uses, such as less expensive, easier to clean cooking pots that transmitted no taste to food. In the nineteenth century, developments in electricity and communications set the stage for today's main uses of copper.

18. Japan and the European countries import almost all their copper. In the period 1950–56, these countries averaged 5.3 percent of market-economy country (MEC) mine production; in 1980, their mine production had slipped to 3.8 percent (ABMS).

The United Kingdom was the world's principal copper producer through the eighteenth century and well into the nineteenth century. Midway through the nineteenth century, Chile began to challenge Great Britain, and has been a principal copper producer from the 1820s to the present. Major U.S. production began around 1845; since 1883, the United States has been the world's leading copper producer. As Western European and Japanese reserves were depleted, in the twentieth century major deposits have been opened in the copperbelt of central Africa, which straddles the border between Zambia and Zaire, and in Chile. In the centrally planned economies, the Soviet Union is the leading producer, now second only to the United States in world totals (Schmitz 1979:10–11). More recently in the present century, Canada, South Africa (including Namibia), Indonesia, the Philippines, and Oceania (principally Australia and Papua New Guinea) have also become major copper producers.

19. For example, by the 1860s Chilean exports of copper constituted around 40 percent of world production, providing about 65 percent of the needs of British industry and consumption. Chilean capital, or at least foreigners residing in Chile, controlled the mines. But the British government made strong complaints against Chilean legislation that favored, through export taxes, Chilean processing of their ores and utilization of Chilean shipping. The U.K. had smelters, but needed ore; British shipping carried finished products to Chile, and wanted return cargo. By 1864, under pressure to support "free trade," the Chilean government abolished customs ordinances that favored Chilean shipping, which in turn could no longer compete with the more advanced foreign competition. With no ability to sustain protectionist import barriers in international political negotiations, nascent Chilean industries were unable to compete with imports.

British industrialists proved able to control Chilean mining, limiting or extending it to suit their purposes, even without ownership of the mining properties, because they had a free hand to tax Chilean copper with transport charges, commissions, and smelting fees. In addition, they could manipulate prices in London; Chileans accused the British smelters of lowering copper prices upon notice of departure of shipments from Chile, then raising them once the copper had arrived and been purchased in the U.K. At that time, Chile had no other major market for copper. The world depression of the latter part of the 1870s further weakened the Chilean producers, who were unable to resist the transfer of ownership and control to foreign interests; by the early twentieth century, these foreign interests were principally U.S. corporations. (Example summarized from Frank 1969:61–70).

20. Research and development branches of multinational corporations (MNCs) are now creating new machinery for large-scale underground mining where the depth of the ore deposits or drainage problems make open-pit mining uneconomical or not feasible. These developments are also highly capital intensive.

The open-pit mines and mammoth processing facilities increased ecological disruption and the production of waste (solid, liquid, or gaseous). When developed-country governments came under domestic pressure to enact environmental controls governing such large-scale mining operations, the corporations claimed that the controls were too expensive, and found in them further motivation to look for supplies in LDCs where fewer effective environmental controls were in force.

21. The following table shows schematically some of the changed relationships between MNCs and copper-exporting LDCs.

Country	MNC	Year	Results
Chile	Kennecott/ Anaconda	1967	Acquisition of 25/51% interests in producing companies
Chile	Kennecott/ Anaconda	1971	Nationalization of remaining foreign interest
Zaire	Union Minière	1967	100% ownership interest acquired; management contract
Zambia	Anglo-American/ AMAX	1969	Acquisition of 51% equity interest
Zambia	Anglo-AMAX	1974	Increase in national control over management

SOURCE: Zorn (1980:219, Table 12.2).

Part of the background of these LDC movements was the growing concern over the concentration of economic (and thus political) power in the hands of a relatively small number of MNCs; see Barnet and Müller (1974) for a widely read expression of these concerns.

22. The acronym "CIPEC" derives from the organization's name in French and in Spanish: Conseil Intergouvernemental des Pays Exportateurs de Cuivre, and Consejo Intergubernamental de Países Exportadores de Cobre. Unless explicitly noted otherwise, I use "CIPEC" to refer to the four founding countries: Zambia, Zaire, Chile, and Peru.

23. Zorn described the principal problems relating to each objective. In summary: the first objective is in response to LDC needs both for foreign exchange (all the more after the oil price increases of the 1970s) and for government revenues, especially for countries heavily reliant on copper exports, as shown in the following table.

Export Dependence of Copper-Producing Countries
(Copper Exports as Percentage
of Total National Exports)

Country	1973–75	1975–77
Chile	66.4	55.6
Peru	20.0	18.5
Zaire	68.8	63.9
Zambia	91.9	91.6
Botswana	—	43.4
Namibia	67.4	65.0
Papua New Guinea	44.5	31.6

SOURCE: Zorn (1980:216).

The second objective aims at ownership for reasons of prestige, national pride, a sense of political and economic independence, and experience, as well as for revenues; control could be internal (majority of the board of directors) or external (statutes, regulations, government directives). The nation must have incorruptible government personnel with objectives consistent with those of the government. The third and fourth objectives need no summary. The fifth addresses LDC concerns to assert clearly their national sovereignty over natural resources, to avoid legal enclaves as under traditional concession agreements (in which MNCs received exemptions to the major laws of the land), and to achieve recognition of national courts for the resolution of disputes. See Zorn (1980:215–25). Mikesell (1979b:51) provides a similar list, in nine points, of LDC host-country demands in negotiations for mineral products.

24. Mikesell (1979b:56–58) offers a brief analysis of the Texasgulf-Panama contracts for Cerro Colorado as an example of successful compromise between demands of foreign investors and those of host governments. In my view, these contracts represented little compromise by the foreign investors; Texasgulf (and later RTZ) substantially obtained all of the items in Mikesell's investor list except for majority equity ownership.

25. Aluminum becomes a substitute for copper for many uses depending on relative costs of the two metals; presently, communications companies are using faster, more efficient fiber optics to replace copper transmission wires wherever possible. Several corporations have already explored for cheaper ways to extract copper from the ocean (see Tanzer 1980, Mezger 1980, Gluschke et al. 1979).

26. RTZ carried out the exploration, construction, and initial exploitation of the Bougainville mine when Papua New Guinea was still under Australian administration.

27. Mikesell (1979b:25–28) cited various surveys indicating the changes in exploration allocations. More than 80 percent of exploration expenditures of eighteen U.S. and Canadian MNCs "in recent years" have been in developed countries (DCs); between 1961 and 1975, fourteen European firms decreased the LDC share of exploration expenditures from 57 percent to 15 percent, down to 11 percent in 1976, recovering to 19 percent in 1977 because of renewed interest in Brazil. Bosson and Varon (1977:32) noted:

> This skewed distribution of expenditure is attributable to the stable political and economic climate of the industrialized nations in the eyes of the private investors rather than to any geological advantages. Countries such as Chile, Peru, Zambia, and Zaire would receive a much larger portion of the total exploration budget if allocations were made on strictly technical grounds.

28. From 1977 to 1980, the CIPEC share increased to 40.5 percent annually; Pinochet in Chile had turned back some of Frei's and Allende's reforms, and the Peruvian government had demonstrated that its nationalism had limits acceptable to MNCs.

29. Zaire was the weakest CIPEC link for refining; in the late 1970s, wars made it difficult to retain needed expatriates to oversee the technical details of processing. Before 1974, Peru refined less than 20 percent of its copper; now it refines around 60 percent. Landlocked Zambia, with its major transportation problems exacerbated because it was a front-line country during

Zimbabwe's war of liberation, exported only refined copper to the degree possible. (Percentages adapted from tables in ABMS, various years.)

CIPEC copper-processing statistics contrasted with those of LDCs producing other minerals. In 1970 the average amount of processing of nine LDC minerals in countries of origin was 29 percent; only 10 percent of LDC bauxite was transformed into aluminum within the LDCs (Bosson and Varon 1977:53).

30. In 1950, developed countries smelted 65 percent and refined 82 percent of market-economy country copper; in 1980 they smelted 57 percent and refined 70 percent (ABMS, various years).

31. With the low grade of contemporary copper mines, it would be uneconomical to transport the ore as it comes out of the ground; to my knowledge, all large copper mining projects include on-site concentration facilities.

By 1973, Japan, leading the way, imported at least 60 percent of its copper in the form of concentrates to be processed in its custom smelters and refineries (Mezger 1980:51). From 1960 to 1980, Japan increased its copper smelting by 6.8 percent per year and its refining by 7.3 percent per year. In 1980, Japan produced 15 percent of market-economy country smelted copper and 14 percent of MEC-refined copper. West Germany is the major European smelter; West Germany, Belgium, and Great Britain are all major refiners of copper.

On the international market, traders buy and sell only refined copper; producers and processors trade concentrates and blister through long-term sales contracts pegged to international prices for refined copper, less several cents a pound for processing charges, plus the traces of other minerals (e.g., gold or molybdenum) often present in copper deposits. These arrangements could favor MNCs, who could set any prices they wished for internal transfers from their production subsidiaries in LDCs to their processing subsidiaries in DCs; however, in contrast to the aluminum industry, the copper industry is not particularly vertically integrated; consequently the mining MNCs do not move the metal through their own facilities from mine to semimanufacture.

However, one must distinguish between U.S. producers and their European and Japanese counterparts. Anaconda, Kennecott, Phelps Dodge, and others in the U.S. have always been major smelters, refiners, and semimanufacturers as well as mining companies; Asarco, atypically, became involved in mining by integrating "backwards" from smelting and refining. In Europe and Japan, on the other hand, integration has tended to be "backwards," from trading companies to the latter stages of processing. As discussed in the example of increasing British control over Chilean mining (see note 19, above), those who control processing can, through this means, control the entire production process. Europe and Japan were major primary producers of copper in the last century; as their mining reserves were depleted, their facilities for processing ore were maintained and upgraded. The United States, with substantial reserves, continues to be a major producer at all stages.

32. The copper industry supports considerable research and experimentation because each ore deposit is unique and requires custom-designed processing. In addition, mining schools and research and development divisions of major MNCs constantly seek ways to design cost-effective techniques to extract more of the copper from the ore or to eliminate steps as through continuous casting.

33. Smelting too is subject to experimentation and technological changes. The Japanese have developed continuous smelting, which eliminates a step in this process, again cutting labor and energy costs. This kind of change, subsidized by the Japanese government, is part of the Japanese strategy to minimize the risks inherent in their high import dependency by doing as much smelting and refining in Japan as possible (Mezger 1975:72-73; Mezger 1980:66).

34. One indication of the problems of mining MNCs was the spate of takeovers by capital-rich petroleum MNCs in the 1970s and early 1980s: oil companies offered better possibilities for traditional financing of expansion or new investments. Not all mining people are convinced that modern projects must be implemented on such massive scales as proposed for Cerro Colorado; but, so far as I can tell, the little-voiced opinion that a project like Cerro Colorado could be viable by starting small and expanding gradually is generally considered heretical within the industry.

35. See Chapter 5 for discussion of the World Bank's role in financing mineral projects. As already noted, mining projects are also financed through developed-countries government agencies like Canada's Export Development Corporation or the U.S. Export-Import Bank, which offer government-guaranteed loans to promote the export of major capital goods. DC governments also provide political risk insurance to major MNCs and banks investing in LDCs, through programs like the U.S. government's Overseas Private Investment Corporation (OPIC).

Decisions about allocations from these DC agencies include their own political considerations, both domestic (as in problems faced by the EDC in Canada over its proposed financing of Cerro Colorado) and international (as through IMF pressures on Zambia in the late 1970s to conform to politically motivated proposals by the United States, which opposed Zambian support for Zimbabwean independence). All these measures serve to favor DCs and their MNCs, since no LDCs have corresponding agencies.

Part 3: Introduction

1. While commentators blasted away at many government programs and problems, usually they spoke only cautiously and vaguely about National Guard and government corruption; people shied away from investigating and reporting the widespread corruption within the Torrijos government.

2. From the 1978 announcement of Torrijos' "retirement" as head of government until his death in mid-1981, everyone in Panama assumed that the General would be the 1984 presidential candidate of his Democratic Revolutionary Party.

3. The Chamber of Commerce later published a complete transcript of the forum; of the forty-five or so questions (many of them composed of several sub-questions) included in an appendix, perhaps twenty-five received some attention during the forum (Cámara de Comercio 1979). I have no way of knowing whether many people other than the Chamber of Commerce organizers submitted questions for the forum; I saw beforehand some properly submitted questions that never found their way into the official pages of questions.

4. Representatives of CODEMIN argued that their majority on the board of directors of the joint operating company gave them control of the annual budget, "which is the essential element for the operations of each year," whereas Texasgulf had power over "technical questions and the daily management of the company." When the Chamber of Commerce businessmen remained unconvinced of CODEMIN's control of the project, CODEMIN moved the argument to a different point by asserting that the Texasgulf contracts contained the terms that enabled Panama to skip a stage that other mineral-producing LDCs had been unable to bypass, namely, that of granting open concessions under which multinational mining firms exercised absolute control for an unlimited time. Texasgulf would have to transfer the technology and know-how so that Panama could gradually assume complete control of the mining operation; after fifteen years of mining, the transfer would be complete and Texasgulf could leave as administrator (Cámara de Comercio 1979:33–35).

5. President Royo's economic consultants submitted their cautious recommendations in April, shortly after the Chamber of Commerce forum (Conse-

jo Consultivo de Economía 1979). In June, the national association of economists submitted a report (Gómez P. 1979), as did the association of construction contractors (Morales 1979). All these groups thought the project very risky for the government.

6. CODEMIN promised the Chamber of Commerce and the nation that it would gladly respond, in writing, to questions either not discussed during the forum or still left in the air; those responses turned out to be CODEMIN 1979c, a series of newspaper advertisements during June and July of 1979. See Chapter 4 for a sampling of these advertisements.

7. Despite CODEMIN's constant assurances that all their information was available to the public, none of us was able to get so much as a peek at the cover of this much-touted UN review. Some people within CODEMIN, after considerable conversation back and forth, finally acknowledged that they could not find anyone (except Herrera) who claimed to have seen the review.

8. I was one of the priests involved in these activities. See the methodological section of the Preface, and Chapters 7 through 11 (particularly Chapter 10), for treatment of the methods and activities of those who worked with the Guaymíes in these efforts.

Chapter 7: Impact of the Cerro Colorado Project on the Guaymíes

1. Chapter 3 provides essential background for an appreciation of the scope of these impacts; occasional reference will be made to some elements of this background. For this discussion of potential and actual impacts of the mining project, I used and expanded the materials of Gjording 1981a:23–32. In appendices of that monograph, I provided tables on which I based some of what I present here (see Gjording 1981a:46–48, originally prepared for CEASPA y Comisión Guaymí 1979). I adapted CODEMIN's published map of the project's facilities to fit with government maps and census information of Guaymí and campesino communities (see Figure 3); I pulled together other bits and pieces of published information on the location and land needs of the project. While I did not walk the entire area covered in these projections, I did walk and study a good part of it: most of the Corregimiento of Hato Chamí, much of the Corregimiento of Maraca, the Cricamola River system from Bisira (below Canquintú) to the Continental Divide, the road from San Félix to the mine area, and perhaps half the trial road from Hato Chamí to Nancito. I drove over the remainder of this road.

In all my calculations, the precise numbers are deceptive; all are approximations. But my discussion of these issues offers at least some feel for the scope of the problem, even should the details have needed later revision.

CODEMIN disputed my calculations, maintaining that a much smaller number of people and communities would have been affected. But CODEMIN did virtually no studies, published no information to support its contentions, and offered no insight into what it meant by "affected."

2. For convenience, I assumed the same route for the slurry pipeline for concentrates, electricity transmission lines, and the possible tailings pipeline.

3. The Colorado School of Mines Research Institute study noted that the road construction would involve "side-casting of superficial materials" into the Cuvíbora-Tabasará river system, but found this to be little problem: "It is not unreasonable to assume that the potential transport capacity of these rivers will be enough to wash the side-casted materials to the coast within two rainy seasons" (CSMRI 1977:XI–26).

The response of Texasgulf and of CODEMIN to Guaymí concerns about contaminated rivers missed the point; they stated that the only effect would be that year-round, the rivers would be muddy as they were anyway at the height of the rainy season, some two or three months of the year. But this response did not take into account that the rest of the ecosystem does not operate within the framework of a year-round rainy season. Local residents had to rely on the rivers during the months of the dry season each year.

4. The Changuinola I hydroelectric project suffered from virtually all the defects of the Cerro Colorado project with respect to planning and study of social impact.

5. But officials of CODEMIN were not convinced that money was the best way to compensate damages. In a January 1980 discussion with a Canadian delegation headed by Bishop Remi DeRoo, technical manager Jaime Roquebert said:

> In 1975, we gave $40,000 in compensation [for the damages done by Canadian Javelin, 1970–74]. Over half of this went to a bar [was spent in a bar] in San Félix, according to the owner. The bar is owned by a man who used to work [on the mining project].

Guaymíes who received lump-sum indemnification payments often regarded these as bonanzas and fell easy prey to unscrupulous merchants in the towns outside the Guaymí area. The bar owner mentioned by Roquebert located his business on the road leading from the Guaymí area to San Félix. He apparently had little trouble attracting Guaymíes flush with cash into long drinking bouts.

6. Some CODEMIN personnel argued that Guaymí acceptance of indem-

nification payments constituted ratification of the government methods used to arrive at the amounts. Apparently, any Guaymí who judged the compensation inadequate should have refused any compensation, even though no procedures existed (or were even accessible to the Guaymíes) to challenge the government's assessment.

7. My disorientation during my first days in Hato Chamí opened my eyes to the general impact of Cerro Colorado work on the population. I began fieldwork in Hato Chamí in December of 1978, after about three months in Hato Pilón of San Félix, a community some distance from Cerro Colorado. Although I found life difficult in Hato Pilón, because of the isolation, the feeling of not belonging, and the insecurity wondering if I was really doing fieldwork, I did become somewhat accustomed to life among the Guaymíes. Hato Pilón is near Cerro Mamita and Cerro Otoe, where Philip Young and John Bort did fieldwork. Young and Bort had given me names of friends and welcomed my trading on their own good names; the people of Hato Pilón knew Young and Bort. Also, although the Guaymíes had little experience of Catholic priests, they seemed to recognize early on that we were not from the government, we were not buying or selling, and we were not looking for women. They observed that we were friendly, we were happy to help them with some things, such as understanding the paperwork required to seek further education for their children, and we tended to live more or less as they did.

From my arrival in Hato Chamí, I felt disoriented. I could not get going in the morning; I worried about what to eat, and whom to see; I got discouraged every time I tried to interview someone and things did not go as I had hoped—perhaps the person wasn't home, or he or she was busy and didn't want to talk about what I wanted to talk about. It was as though these surroundings and these people had nothing in common with the people I had known and relied on in Hato Pilón. I was undone in less than a week, so I made a sudden return trip to Remedios.

There, through conversations with my surprised Jesuit companions, I saw that Guaymí life in Hato Chamí did not conform to my experience of Hato Pilón. The Guaymíes of Hato Chamí were not different; they didn't have different customs, language, or dress. Their day-to-day problems were similar, but the context was different. It seemed to me that Hato Chamí combined a Guaymí world with another world that in my view simply didn't fit there. More than I knew, it jarred me to drive to Hato Chamí instead of walking or riding my horse. It jarred me that a road, one with daily traffic, ran through the middle of the caserío. Day and night there was the background noise of the electrical generator for the camp; at night, I looked across the little valley to an area illuminated by electric lights. I was sometimes offered meals by the Hato Chamí cook, better meals than we ate in Remedios, and not at all typical of the food available in the Guaymí area. From Hato Chamí I could easily get a ride to San Félix or Remedios, even on a whim; I did not have to face the eight to ten hours of walking. I was constantly waving to mine workers as they went by in their vehicles, or running into them shopping at one of the small Guaymí stores or chatting with them after their dinner hour. All these things jarred me.

In my time in Hato Pilón, I think I had developed a sense of how people managed their lives in the Guaymí area. Hato Chamí did violence to that sense. From my arrival there, I felt the incongruity of the placement of this industrial project right in the heart of the Guaymí living space. This sense of incongruity never left me; I suspect it never left the Guaymíes either.

8. *Chácaras* are handmade knotted bags of all sizes, from tiny to huge, with a strap for shoulder or forehead, made of naturally dyed bark cloth or brightly colored store-bought thread. "Mr. Williams" was David Ruiz Williams, the Cuban-American vice-president of Texasgulf-Panama, the top in-country executive for Texasgulf.

Handbag-sized *chácaras* (about a foot deep) made of *pita* (a bark thread), with a bit of natural-dye geometric design, would ordinarily be sold for under $2.00. Elaborate ones of the same size, made of thread, with tight knots, would ordinarily be sold for around $20.00 to $30.00; the thread cost about $12.00. Large, simple *chácaras* of *pita,* perhaps 3–4 feet deep, ordinarily sold between $3.00 and $4.00. Some latino merchants in the towns along the Pan-American Highway bought *chácaras* at these prices, then re-sold them for 3 or 4 times as much. As *chácaras* moved toward Panama City, the prices rose even further; I saw $2.00 *chácaras* marked at $25.00 in tourist shops in Panama City. What I am calling the "depth" of a *chácara* is my translation of the Guaymí way of measuring their size: extended fingers in the middle of the bottom of the bag, measuring on one's arm where the top of the bag ended up.

9. The San Blas Cuna successfully formed cooperatives to market *molas* (designs made of appliquéd layers of brightly colored textiles) in Panama City; by organizing themselves, they kept a clear difference between prices to each other and prices to tourists. With the cooperatives, most of the final selling price went to the producer. In Hato Chamí, Mr. Williams' purchases did nothing to foster the organization of a handicraft cooperative among Guaymí women.

10. The Ministry of Public Works built two classrooms and a kitchen; the

work was high quality, and the construction appropriate to enable the school to withstand the velocity of the dry season winds. Acción Cívica of the National Guard, as a public relations project, built two more classrooms; the roof curled up and blew away with the first winds, and the walls developed large cracks even before the addition was used.

The head of security for the Cerro Colorado joint operating company, rather than the Guaymíes, brought about construction of a small health center in Hato Chamí, located a stone's throw from the better staffed and better equipped government-run health center of the Hato Chamí camp. He did not want Guaymíes coming to the camp to see the Ministry of Health infirmarian, who insisted on treating anyone who sought his services. The security chief had earlier brought the health center of the Escopeta camp completely under mining project control, with no government involvement; except for rare emergencies, the Guaymíes of the area were not allowed to use the Escopeta facilities.

11. Much work had been done before the National Guard used U.S. Army transport helicopters to haul the remaining supplies.

12. The school itself was the biggest and best equipped in the Guaymí area of San Félix or Remedios, with its kitchen and utensils to provide U.S. Agency for International Development food to the children.

13. A number of Guaymí communities established voluntary schools controlled by the local community; some of these schools later gained official recognition. The Bocas del Toro cacique helped his constituents organize many such schools, and demonstrated what he and they could do with little or no government help.

14. The Guaymí representative maintained he had no problems with the principal, but that she wanted to think there were problems—a fairly typical Guaymí statement that the other party was totally at fault.

15. Even the mining project's cooperation in hauling materials for the building of the school came to look quite self-serving when their publicity campaigns made prominent mention of their work to bring education to the Guaymí area. The school of Hato Chamí was used as a showpiece by CODEMIN and the joint operating company public relations people.

16. The problems associated with the school in Hato Chamí were replicated, indeed anticipated, in the caserío of Quebrada Guabo not far up the mine road from the San Félix River. This caserío also expanded along the edge of the mine road after the school was upgraded. The caserío of Boca del Monte, about an hour's walk south of Hato Chamí, also grew along the

mine road, with some added tensions and conflicts. However, Boca del Monte's self-appointed leader was unable to attract the resources for a permanent school, and the children walked each day to Hato Chamí.

17. The help included the transport of government-provided building materials in vehicles of the joint operating company, the voluntary free-time help of some personnel from the Escopeta camp in the work of construction, and the assigned help of CODEMIN-sponsored masonry trainees, using the construction of the school as a practicum. The head of CODEMIN's Department of Social Development maintained that the mixed signals of help on the school represented communication and cooperation breakdowns between CODEMIN in Panama City and the joint operating company personnel at the mine site. But she had no explanation for the help of the trainees, who were directly under her department of CODEMIN.

18. When I treat Guaymí responses below, I will return to the case of the people of Hato Rincón (see Chapter 8).

19. Some Guaymíes told me that the women had abandoned their husbands, who abused them, and had invited the attentions of the guardsmen. There were conflicting rumors as to whether the guardsmen paid directly for the favors of the women, or whether compensation was more in the form of lodging, meals, and companionship.

20. So far as I am aware, no particular penalty attaches to a Guaymí, male or female, who marries a non-Guaymí. The spouse can live in the Guaymí area without any major problem.

21. At this meeting, Guaymí concerns, given voice principally by men but echoed a few times by women, revolved almost exclusively around the fears of a large influx of outside men. Little was said about environmental problems and impacts; much was made of the social and cultural impacts. Some Guaymíes knew of the problems of prostitution and children born out of wedlock in the latino town of Tolé when it served as the base camp for workers who were building a stretch of the Pan-American Highway in the early 1960s.

22. Sponsors stressed the policies of no contact to the Cerro Colorado employees, and supervisors strictly enforced the policies; the two National Guard members were removed from the area. However, some employees commented privately that enforcement of the policies with only 100 workers was one thing, but quite another would be their enforcement once the construction work force increased to 3,500 or more. One worker thought the government would have to assign a security guard to each worker.

CODEMIN's president, Rodrigo González, one of those who told the Guaymíes there was nothing to worry about, privately acknowledged the major problems. CODEMIN officials formulated policies, but they had little idea how to enforce them.

Many Guaymíes privately criticized the behavior of one of the mine's watchmen at the San Félix River, a man whom they nicknamed *El Tigre* (The Tiger). They said that he was often drunk, and tried to trade rides to Hato Chamí (about eight hours' walk) for sexual favors from Guaymí women.

The Guaymíes and CODEMIN were unaware of a growing body of literature addressing the problems of boom towns, the rapid influx of a large, predominantly male work force into an area hardly prepared for their arrival, and the associated problems of social breakdown. This literature included documentation of the experiences of Bougainvilleans when RTZ built its Papua New Guinea copper mine, and showed that Guaymí fears were well founded; Bedford and Mamak (1976b:456), commenting on Bougainvillean natives' antagonism to outsiders and the repeated outbreaks of violence between groups in the migrant population, noted that

> increasing social disorder associated with the rapid growth of a predominantly male population housed in cramped, temporary camp accommodations, together with difficulties in obtaining employment, generated widespread dissatisfaction among Bougainvilleans with the kind of urban development taking place in their District.

One would have hoped that knowledge of problems elsewhere would have made CODEMIN officials cautious in their responses to Guaymí concerns and interested in looking further into the questions raised.

23. Virtually no Guaymí grasped the full implications of the Cerro Colorado project. The only person I met with some vision of that sort tried a number of times to hold community meetings in Hato Chamí to discuss these things; but he ran into many problems, especially factions among the Guaymíes of the area.

24. One of his defeated opponents claimed that the CODEMIN ethnologist cheated for the winner by preventing the opponent's official books for signatures of support (a kind of primary) from arriving until virtually the date for filing for the elections. See Chapter 3 for an earlier discussion of this ethnologist's affiliations and activities.

25. However, the godmother neglected to arrange for a priest; the oversight went unnoticed until everyone had gathered in Hato Chamí. The National Guard colonel ordered his helicopter to get a priest from Remedios; they

finally located the pastor, visiting in another part of the Guaymí area. He was furious about becoming involved in the manipulation of the representative, but saw no way out without creating political problems for the priests of Remedios.

26. Their experience of CODEMIN's care hardly instilled confidence in them; they enjoyed recounting the story of the ethnologist's fish-raising project. On their little plain was a small body of water. She arrived one day in a National Guard helicopter announcing that she was planting fish in the little lake, so that the people could raise them and increase their protein intake. She did not ask them about her plan, and they volunteered nothing. She dumped the fish from the helicopter. This little lake dried up each year. The people waited for the dry season, when they walked around the edges picking up the dying fish to take home for supper, ending what CODEMIN touted as a "pisciculture project."

27. I was always shocked to see Guaymí friends in San Félix; they seemed so different. People whom I had relied on for my basic survival in their own communities seemed transformed into people who hardly knew how to do anything. Members of the Cerro Otoe co-op, when gathered in their small building in San Félix, tended to act pretty much as they did at home; but in a mixed crowd of latinos and Guaymíes, these same Guaymíes seemed to shrivel up into passive beings with few competencies of their own.

28. It was not unusual for Guaymí families to seek extra food from each other; among themselves, the movement of food back and forth was an ordinary part of life, done without embarrassment and with dignity. Often children went alone to borrow.

29. The state determined who had what legal rights; the state determined that it owned mineral rights anywhere in the country, and that it was owner of all non-titled lands, including those of the Guaymíes (see Lobo 1980a, 1980b).

Chapter 8: Early Guaymí Opposition to Cerro Colorado

1. Although opposition to the hydroelectric project was, if anything, earlier and stronger than opposition to the mine itself, a few Guaymíes favored Teribe-Changuinola—whether because of government promises that the entire Guaymí area would receive electricity, or because they were far enough removed from the direct consequences of the project that they could be open to the government's urging that all Panamanians had to make appropriate sacrifices for progress and the common good.

2. CODEMIN periodically dispatched Marcelo Bruno, a Guaymí employee of the Department of Social Development in Panama City, to attend to the Bocas del Toro community of Suitche, about three hours' walk over the Continental Divide from Cerro Colorado. He supervised the work of community members in the construction of a small health subcenter made from rough wooden planks.

3. General Torrijos had retired from his position as head of government to concentrate on running the National Guard; it had been some months since he had made a public appearance. He was a friend of several of the mining people, and probably was on hand to visit with them as well as to enhance CODEMIN's credibility with the Guaymíes, for whom he was something of a folk hero.

4. Both of these publications, and reactions to Catholic Church activities promoted by them, will be discussed below.

5. Several other Guaymí communities of Chiriquí sent similar letters to Canquintú.

6. The resulting study is CEASPA y Comisión (1979), later published in Congresos Guaymíes (1980:52–87) and, somewhat abbreviated, in LAWG (1980:11–15, 19–23).

The grassroots pressure for including the mining project on the agenda of the congress came mostly from the residents of Valle de Riscó, an area which would have been flooded by the Teribe-Changuinola hydroelectric project. Ricardo Smith had a long association with several members of CEASPA; Miguel Cruz worked closely with Smith.

7. See the Introduction to the document that resulted (Congresos Guaymíes 1980:53):

> The conclusions arise from the analysis of the potential impact of the project in its economic, ecological, socio-cultural and politico-legal dimensions, all of these interrelated. . . . Nonetheless, as desired both by the Guaymí team [working on the document] and by CEASPA, it is explicitly noted that the Guaymí people themselves will define any political position with respect to the project.

8. This slide and tape presentation became part of the educational materials used in meetings with Guaymí communities (see below for some discussion of these meetings). Later, Canadian colleagues revised it with an appropriate beginning and ending, translated it into English, and published it for use in international solidarity efforts.

9. The official Acts of the Congress stated that 4,500 Guaymíes took part (Congresos Guaymíes 1980:90).

10. Manteca, from Cerro Iglesias of Remedios District, founded and headed a small Guaymí organization which never adopted a clear stance on major issues concerning the relations between the Guaymíes and the government of Panama; it was widely suspected of being a vehicle for the personal ambitions of Manteca, who seemed to many Guaymíes willing to sell out their interests in order to get a good government job. Frederico Santos, a Guaymí from San Lorenzo District who worked for the government rural development agency, was widely regarded as also an employee of "G-2," the intelligence division of the National Guard.

11. The CODEMIN document turned out to be CODEMIN 1979b, an inexpensive printing of a fancy booklet (CODEMIN 1979a) originally prepared for CODEMIN's major public relations campaign with the Panamanian press in early 1979. To the original presentation, which summarized the technical aspects of the project and the financial and economic considerations, CODEMIN had hastily inserted a loose page with a few paragraphs listing the social benefits. It did not address any issues of importance to the Guaymíes. Palacios had brought about thirty copies of the booklet; there were five hundred copies of the other document.

12. Both Manteca's direct arguments against the discussion of the projects and the use of the Guaymí document, and Smith's direct counter-arguments, went contrary to typical Guaymí procedures. In general, the congress delegates did not respond in kind by directly challenging his statements; rather, they followed Guaymí norms by presenting views without directly alluding to the disagreement.

13. The "Considerations" for the resolution on the hydroelectric project moved in the same direction with respect to IRHE, but made reference to specific measures and studies (Congresos Guaymíes 1980:92). The Guaymíes of Valle de Riscó sent a well-organized delegation to Canquintú; they had met a number of times, and knew what they wanted. They were especially angered that there was no discussion of the major projects.

14. It is very unlikely that the Roquebert would have allowed Palacios to interfere as he did in the congress. The technical manager always had great confidence in the project itself, and believed that all the problems could be resolved; he had little fear of people's concerns coming out into the open.

15. The Guaymí photographs in Núñez y Consejo 1979 had been taken in and around Hato Rincón, as had some of the slides used in the slide show;

the priest, one of my companions, also took along other unpublished slides of the people of Hato Rincón. The people, who had given their permission for the use of their photographs for non-commercial promotion of the Guaymí cause, enjoyed seeing themselves on the screen or on the printed page.

I took many of the photographs and slides referred to, and I worked with the group that put together the slide show. I also made the colored map. We sought to put together some audiovisual materials that would respond to the educational needs of the Guaymíes with whom we worked.

16. These links not only provided the Guaymíes with more choices about where to plant subsistence crops; they also provided a wider network of relatives with whom to carry on informal exchange, especially when there were difficulties at home.

17. A common latino misperception, shared by mining company workers and by members of the Department of Social Development of CODEMIN, saw the Guaymíes as a "nomadic" people who enjoyed packing up and moving. The people were aware of these latino misperceptions; their awareness contributed to distrust of CODEMIN statements that something was under study or being taken care of.

In fact, many Guaymíes spoke with enthusiasm about taking long trips within the Guaymí area, getting to know people and places with which they were unfamiliar. For those who could, a trip of a month or two was a popular way to spend the dry season, staying for an extended time with (distant) relatives. But these trips were very different from packing up and moving elsewhere.

The latino misperception may have been based on the fact that the Guaymíes, when more land was available, built nearby caseríos to allow sufficient fallow time for the lands they had used; but they would stay in the same area. They also used to solve land disputes through formation of new communities (see Young 1971:125). Such movements were not "nomadic," as though the Guaymíes were a wandering, rootless people.

18. The two Panamanian bosses staunchly defended the mine and the Torrijos government; in conversations with them, the Guaymíes were generally reticent about the extent of their problems and reservations concerning the mining activities. These two had organized a public letter from joint operating company workers in favor of the mine, criticizing the Catholic hierarchy for, in their view, opposing the project as part of the bishops' opposition to the Torrijos revolution. One of them tried, in vain, to get the Guaymí elected representative to take a similar letter around the area for Guaymí signatures.

The job as head of security turned out to include both meanings of the ambiguous term. The chief stressed that his job was to attend to "industrial security," i.e., the observance of work safety rules. But many mining company workers believed he was a member of the National Guard's G-2 section for military intelligence. He had some connection with the National Guard; once he told me how much he had enjoyed a stay in Israel as part of a Panamanian National Guard peacekeeping force.

19. The Guaymíes of Hato Rincón were aware, through comments they heard, that the principal personnel of the joint operating company had little or no respect for the Department of Social Development of CODEMIN.

20. She attributed the action of the people of Hato Rincón to the priests of Remedios; in fact, the people of Hato Rincón had anticipated that CODEMIN would not send anyone other than her, and they had decided upon this course of action.

21. The Guaymíes of Hato Rincón knew that the mining company offices at Escopeta had direct radio-telephone communications both with the CODEMIN offices in David, the provincial capital of Chiriquí, and with the CODEMIN and Texasgulf offices in Panama City. They figured that the mining people could respond more easily than they could.

22. Juan, one of the sons of the Rodríguez household (discussed in the Chapter 7 description of problems in Tebujo), was my principal informant about the responses of the Guaymíes of Tolé to the penetration road. With Miguel Cruz, I spent several weeks of April and May 1980 doing fieldwork in the area of Tebujo; we enjoyed the hospitality of the Rodríguez family.

23. The entire text of the Cerro Puerco resolution, in English, appears in Gjording 1981a:49.

24. Valid signatures in Panama are always accompanied by the national identity card *(cédula)* number.
    Except for a few sympathizers from campesino communities in Tolé District, no non-Guaymíes were present at these meetings. My information came from the published resolution itself and from conversations with Juan Rodríguez and other organizers, who showed me their notes summarizing some of the discussion as well as their drafts of the resolution.

25. Guaymíes often unselfconsciously referred to themselves as "naturals" *(naturales)*, using a seemingly derogatory latino characterization which contrasted "naturals" with "civilized."

26. Apparently, in the Mama Chi religion "God Jesus Christ" was a single name.

27. Even individual Guaymíes took some care to note that they did not oppose the government, i.e., that they were not engaging in the partisan political debates of the time.

The reference to "race" is, I think, both an expression of Mama Chi concern for the preservation of the Guaymíes and, implicitly, a rejection of the government goals of "integration" or "incorporation" of the Guaymíes into the national population.

28. In my translation of these materials, I have done some minor editing to correct grammar and spelling of the original documents. The orthography of these documents consistently reflects Guaymí Spanish—the addition of the letter *e* to some word endings (e.g., *generale* for *general*), the elimination of the letter *s* from the ending of others (e.g., *nosotro* for *nosotros*), the free substitution in writing of *f* and *p* (Guaymíes have difficulty with the pronunciation of *f*, usually substituting the sound of *p*), the elimination of syllables beginning words (e.g., *flotación* for *explotación*, *caba* for *acaba*).

People from Cangrejo took these notebooks to the priests of Tolé, asking them to help the people make known their protest against the government project; but no vehicle for their use was ever found.

29. I do not know exactly why they were opponents. Cacique Lorenzo, like most Guaymíes, had been a devotee of Mama Chi in the mid-1960s; the Mama Chi movement formed part of the "launching pad" that made him cacique of Chiriquí. The Mama Chis did not recognize the authority of this cacique, but had their own cacique, Samuel González, in San Lorenzo, himself made into something of a leader by General Torrijos' recognition of him. The Mama Chis opposed negotiations with the government, and opposed the comarca—all these things were seen as concessions to outsiders.

30. Sarsanedas (1978) presents a good discussion of these issues.

31. As with the Mama Chis, Cacique Lorenzo remained noncommittal. But Cacique Camilo Ortega of Veraguas Province made it clear that he and his constituents supported the land claims of the campesinos (who in Veraguas outnumbered the Guaymíes in the same area) and would seek to accommodate them in drawing up the carta orgánica, the code of laws that would regulate affairs within the comarca.

32. People in the Department of Social Development often grumbled that no one knew what Palacios was up to, and that they had lots of complaints about his work.

Chapter 9: Guaymí Opposition Coalesces and Gains Outside Support

1. CODEMIN personnel complained several times that the commissioners made no move to meet with them. However, despite their enthusiasm in Canquintú and their promises of help, neither CODEMIN nor IRHE offered invitations or resources.

2. The Guaymí Miguel Cruz, a University of Panama student from near Canquintú, worked at this time as my field assistant, under contract with CEASPA, while he gathered data for his senior thesis in agronomy; we did fieldwork together around Tebujo in Tolé. It will be recalled that Cruz worked closely with Ricardo Smith; Cruz was secretary to the Canquintú congress, Smith its president. Smith was a commissioner for negotiations with the government concerning the comarca; he was appointed by Cacique José Mónico Cruz of Bocas del Toro Province.

3. See Chapter 8, note 10, for some discussion of Manteca and Santos. Supposedly the organizers would be acting on behalf of Cacique Lorenzo Rodríguez of Chiriquí Province, nominal host for the congress. But this group had little use for Cacique Lorenzo (and vice versa), and rumors abounded in Chiriquí that the congress would try to unseat the cacique.

Lorenzo and his associates took no part in the organizing and did not attend the congress itself; they had not taken part in the Canquintú congress either. For some time, the Chiriquí cacique had played little active role in the affairs of the Guaymíes, and by early 1980 discontent with him was fairly widespread; but there were no mechanisms for naming—or "unnaming"— caciques. He always claimed illness; he did have some cataracts removed (with help from CODEMIN), but managed to move around when he really wanted to.

4. Transportation was a major problem. There was considerable confusion about times and places people should meet in order to be taken to Soloy; and fewer buses and trucks arrived than were needed. The Ministry of Public Works did little work on the road to Soloy, and the buses could get no farther than a spot still about two hours walk away. A dump truck took a number of people the rest of the way, but many walked in. People were still arriving late into the opening night; some only arrived the following day.

5. The Guaymíes had no established customs for congresses, which were not traditional meetings for them.

6. More than half the members of the commission knew in advance that they would be in agreement with the work Cruz did.

7. These samples, translated from my field notes, are either verbatim expressions of the people cited, or close paraphrases that attempt to capture both the point and the flavor of the speakers.

8. Four or five Guaymíes, principally those who had organized the congress, tried to sway the congress toward rejection of the study. Outside the meeting place, I openly listened in as one trio, led by Santos, insisted that the priests were interfering, criticized Smith's connection with a church-sponsored group in Panama City, and generally made it clear that they regarded most Guaymíes as too stupid to understand the real issues of the project. Two of them wanted to have the priests removed from the congress because they were outsiders; but the third noted that they themselves had arranged for a latino doctor to open the congress, had invited other latinos from the government, and could hardly begin requiring that all outsiders be forced to leave.

9. The phrase "light made by humans" referred to IRHE's promise to the Guaymíes of electricity. Coclé province, like all of Panama, was originally indigenous territory; perhaps the speaker chose that province because of the extensive archeological work documenting the rich indigenous cultures of that part of Panama (see Lothrop 1937, 1942).

10. See Wali 1983, 1984 on Bayano and its effects.

11. Moisés González, a priest from Tolé, sat near the circle of chairs of the resolution committee, along with a number of Guaymíes. Bruno objected to the presence of a foreigner and sought to force him to leave. However, the other members of the commission noted that, since the congress had allowed non-Guaymíes to be present throughout, including Bruno's employers from CODEMIN, they had no objection to Moisés listening in on their conversation.

On December 19, 1980, Moisés González drowned while trying to cross the swollen Tabasará River high in the mountains of Tolé. Guaymí participation in his funeral showed how this non-Guaymí had gained their respect.

12. See Gjording 1981a:49–50 for the complete text of the Cerro Colorado and Teribe-Changuinola resolutions.

13. Guaymí representatives delivered the resolutions of the Soloy congress to the daily newspapers, but no newspaper saw fit to publish them. It was widely believed in Panama that Rodrigo González, president of CODEMIN and of the joint operating company, was the principal shareholder of three of the four dailies; I was unable to verify this rumor.

14. It is difficult to guess the outcome of this debate had Manteca and friends succeeded in bringing the question to the floor of the congress. The delegate meeting was stacked against the government agencies; but in general, the Guaymíes tended to accommodate people who had traveled some distance to meet with them. When Smith informed the whole congress of the meeting, no one raised any objection to the decision. Nonetheless, Smith and associates probably did well to keep this decision away from the floor of the congress.

Manteca and his cohorts also fared poorly at Soloy. Several of us overheard them, at different times, commenting disdainfully about the "ignorance" and "stupidity" of the people who came to the congress, people who let themselves believe that anyone really cared what they thought about the mega-projects scheduled for the Guaymí area. The sale of beer on the last day of the congress, generally seen as a violation of unwritten norms of conduct for this kind of meeting, was widely attributed to them and further hurt their image as potential Guaymí leaders. The treasurer, who was mayor *(alcalde)* of San Félix District, could not account for quite a bit of the money collected for the congress; his financial report at the end omitted, as people reminded him, a number of contributions made by local communities. This led to months of controversy and weakened his possibilities as an emerging Guaymí leader.

15. The Panamanian Ministry of Government and Justice is somewhat similar to a combination of the U.S. Departments of Justice and Interior, or a parliamentary ministry for internal affairs.

16. Minister Rodríguez offered no guesses about whether anyone would respond to Guaymí requests for help, nor did he suggest how the handful of government gifts were to be distributed among more than 4,000 congress delegates.

17. A Guaymí commissioner for comarca negotiations told me during the congress that the minister had contracted a government lawyer to review for him all the documents pertaining to the negotiations. However, the minister would not provide the Guaymí commissioners access to her report.

Before the congress, Cacique Mónico of Bocas del Toro Province, after being rebuffed a number of times, finally managed to arrange one meeting with Minister Rodríguez. In that meeting, the minister made it clear that his ministry had far more important matters to deal with than the Guaymí comarca; in any case, he said, the Guaymí boundary proposals were nothing short of absurd.

18. Royo showed himself disturbed by the possibility of Guaymí violence. He had virtually no knowledge of the people or the area, had no advisors who were any help to him in these matters, and seemed to fear that the Guaymíes were capable of organizing something. Elsewhere in Central America during the late 1970s, the Sandinistas had overthrown Somoza (in 1979), and very active guerrilla movements were operating in El Salvador and Guatemala—the latter with majority indigenous participation. In fact, the Guaymíes could have done little or nothing.

19. The report read, discussed, and approved at Soloy included a recommendation that the Guaymíes ask help from the Panamanian Catholic Church or some international organization in the preparation, with Guaymí participation, of a study of all the effects on the Guaymíes of these projects (Congresos Guaymíes 1980:39).

20. These pastoral letters, and reactions to Catholic Church activities, will be discussed in the next chapter.

21. Gjording (1981a:50) provides an English translation of the text of this open letter.

22. RTZ officials in London seemed surprised to be asked detailed questions about their intentions with respect to the Guaymíes within days after breaking the news that RTZ was replacing Texasgulf. In the United States, the Fluor Corporation asked those who had filed the shareholder's resolution to withdraw it not only because it dealt with matters outside the control of Fluor (viz., the mining project's relationship with the Guaymíes), but also because the question was moot. Through telephone conversations with the Fluor spokesperson, we first received definite word that the sponsors had decided to suspend the Cerro Colorado project. In exchange for Fluor's written confirmation by telex both of the halt of the project and of Fluor's commitment to inform the shareholders should the sponsors anticipate renewed work on Cerro Colorado, those responsible withdrew the resolution. A trade newspaper, *American Metal Market,* after obtaining confirmation in Panama and in London that the sponsors were stopping the project, broke the story publicly (AMM 1982).

23. A number of local communities and regions used an inexpensive publication of Guaymí statements as a basis for their discussions (Congresos Guaymíes 1980). Judging from various commentaries, I think that the best organized Guaymíes were the 2,000 or more inhabitants of the Valle de Riscó, in the area of the proposed Changuinola hydroelectric project; I was unable to visit there, but I met many of their leaders at other meetings, and

spoke with a number of residents and with the priest who usually went there.

In eastern Bocas del Toro and in Chiriquí, church representatives attended most meetings that were larger than just one community or caserío. A priest from Canquintú and I heard some very flattering remarks (often given with wry humor because we were so obviously tenderfeet) from a number of Guaymí participants because we accompanied Cacique Mónico on the rainy 3–4 day trek to a regional meeting held just north of Cerro Colorado. CODEMIN sent its own people, who hiked in some 6–8 hours from the mine road. At the invitation of the delegates, CODEMIN's representative and we two priests briefly addressed the meeting. CODEMIN's delegate assured the people that Cerro Colorado and the government would take care of them. The other priest and I reminded them of Bishop Núñez' pastoral letter and of his talk at Soloy, and said we were there to accompany them, to listen, to learn, and to assure them with our presence that the church supported them in their struggles to take care of themselves.

Chapter 10: "Outside Agitators": The Catholic Church and Cerro Colorado

1. See the Preface for the composition of this group and its methodology.

2. In the Catholic Church, a pastoral letter is an official pronouncement by a bishop or a bishops' conference, and becomes part of the "magisterium" or teaching for the region over which the bishop or conference has jurisdiction.

3. When Núñez extended the invitation to include a priest from the Remedios parish, I happily accepted. I had just completed background fieldwork in San Félix District (presented in Chapters 3 and 7) and meetings in Panama City to organize our investigation of the Cerro Colorado project; I was ready to begin fieldwork in the project area, beginning with the Hato Chamí seminar. I had already reviewed some literature on the effects that generally accompanied major resource-development projects among indigenous peoples. I had also studied others' notes from fieldwork in the mine area around the time Canadian Javelin was leaving the project.

4. CODEMIN president Rodrigo González instructed the Department of Social Development to respond to Núñez' letter. Taking the letter as a personal attack, the Department drafted for publication a stinging repudiation of the questions he raised, but González insisted on a shrewder approach. Accordingly, CODEMIN publicly expressed gratitude that Bishop Núñez and the Catholic Church shared its concerns for the Guaymíes, and assured

him that all the problems raised were well under control. In addition, a representative of the Department travelled to David to invite Núñez to be part of an oversight committee that would be formed to ensure respect for the Guaymíes. Apparently, González intended to co-opt Bishop Núñez as part of a very visible but powerless committee, enabling CODEMIN to claim it was doing everything possible for the Guaymíes.

Núñez, who saw through the ploy, expressed interest in the committee. He even offered some suggestions about the powers it should have: access to CODEMIN's social-impact studies among the Guaymíes, the ability to contract qualified consultants, and the freedom to publish its work. CODEMIN never returned with a specific proposal.

5. At this time, Chiriquí Guaymí efforts to develop new social and political organization beyond kin networks concentrated almost exclusively on the comarca, with little or no mention of Cerro Colorado. But the Guaymíes of the Valle de Riscó were already organizing their opposition to the Teribe-Changuinola hydroelectric project.

6. It is important to emphasize that these discussions and evaluations were based on the project *as then conceived*. We discussed some ways of mitigating the negative impact of the project; but these ways would have required the sponsors to reconceive parts of the project itself, and throughout the entire process we saw no serious willingness on the part of project sponsors to re-think any part of the project in the light of Guaymí needs and interests.

7. Núñez' Presbyteral Council was a committee of priests elected by the priests' senate as consultants to the bishop; the council met regularly with the bishop, who used the meetings to maintain communications with his priests on developments in the diocese. Núñez y Consejo 1979 was published in English translation in *Survival International Review* of Summer 1979.

8. Although Núñez and his advisors feared that Cerro Colorado would prove disastrous to the Guaymíes, in the pastoral letter they tried to stay within the bounds of raising pointed questions. As discussed elsewhere, at the time the mining project was a political football in Panama, regarded both by the government of Torrijos and the political opposition as a make-or-break issue. Núñez wanted to avoid both confrontation with the government and manipulation by the reactionary opposition to the government.

9. The bishops also brought to the debate the international character of the Catholic Church, the possibility of gaining publicity and solidarity for their approach not only within Panama but elsewhere. The pastoral letters could only have created some space for discussion and action in Panama if they re-

ceived fairly widespread attention inside and outside Panama. As soon as the pastoral letters were published, groups in Panama mailed copies to groups in Latin America, Canada, the United States, and western Europe. Some of these groups, in turn, republished and further disseminated the letters; for example, Survival International in London published a rough but readable translation of Bishop Núñez' letter at their first opportunity, and LAWG made available a translation of the conference pastoral. Many people sent letters and telegrams of support to the bishops and to the Guaymíes; some also urged the government to slow down the project until the bishops' concerns had been met. This national and international attention to the themes of the pastoral letters further encouraged church workers in Panama to continue their own efforts with their constituencies, building up their confidence that these church documents provided them with protection should the government contemplate some form of reprisals. At the same time, the widespread attention put the government on notice that any actions it might take would have an impact beyond the boundaries either of the Guaymí area or of Panama itself.

Several factors influenced the dissemination of and support for these pastoral letters. The widespread publicity surrounding the mining project and its importance for Panama's future contributed to the attention paid to the pastoral letters within Panama. In addition, many individuals and groups took the international character of the church as a call to concern themselves with the plight of those they regarded as their brothers and sisters in many different parts of the world. Enduring expressions of this call are Catholic (and other Christian) efforts in the United States and Europe in solidarity with the poor and their struggles throughout Central America. Informal networks of communication and action frequently engage in activities along these lines. Such groups as Survival International, the International Work Group on Indigenous Affairs (IWGIA), the Anthropology Resource Center (ARC), and Cultural Survival dedicate themselves to monitoring the situations of indigenous peoples and their rights in various parts of the world; these groups sometimes rely on church-sponsored analyses of local problems. The Latin America Working Group (LAWG), in publishing translations of both pastorals, was carrying out part of the overall research and publication strategy discussed in the Preface of this book.

Others, besides being concerned for the poor of Panama should the copper mine be built, also supported these pastoral letters in the context of the intrachurch struggle over the meaning and use of the document written by the Latin American bishops at their January 1979 meeting in Puebla, Mexico (CELAM 1979). While theologians and others argued back and forth about the meaning of the different parts of the Puebla document, the main battle over its interpretation was decided by how the document actually came to be used in the life of the church in Latin America. Bishop Núñez, a participant at Puebla, became the first Latin American bishop officially to apply the Puebla document to a concrete local situation when he published his pastoral letter on the situation of the Guaymíes and Cerro Colorado; by making use of the liberation-oriented aspects of the Puebla document, Núñez implicitly endorsed that line of interpretation. The Conference pastoral letter, adopting the same implicit interpretation of Puebla, was probably the first post-Puebla official statement by a Latin American conference of bishops.

10. I did not gather information about divergent opinions of Panamanian church representatives with respect to the bishops' pastoral letters; but I have no reason to think that the Catholic Church in Panama attained a degree of unity and single-mindedness unheard of in other parts of the Catholic world. I suspect that the strong convictions of Archbishop McGrath reduced the maneuvering space of some bishops who were not so convinced as he with respect to the issues or their importance. I also suspect that a number of priests supported those parts of the bishops' messages that they could read as anti-government, while skating around such criteria as the preferential option for the poor. Some bishops, so far as I know, made no further public reference to the Conference's pastoral letter once they had signed it; and I assume that a number of priests and religious women neither read the letters nor made any use of them. Among Catholic laity, I imagine that Panamanians covered the expectable spectrum: from those who genuinely supported their bishops' activities, through those only vaguely aware of what all the discussion was about, to those who were convinced that the bishops had become involved in affairs about which they knew nothing.

11. Since few Guaymíes could read Spanish well, everyone involved with the pastoral letter had hoped it would be published in Ngawbere; but attempts at a published translation foundered.

12. People from the communities organized these meetings, set the dates, and asked for help from the priests. Experience showed that the priests, as outsiders, had no power of convocation among the Guaymíes, no matter the topic; only local people could arrange a meeting and have some assurance of participation.

13. Information for the map came from CODEMIN publications, the Chamber of Commerce forum, and fieldwork.

14. Some examples of CODEMIN publicity may be found in Chapter 4 above. The same publicity blitz represented CODEMIN's only fulfillment of

its promise to the Chamber of Commerce to provide written responses to any further questions regarding Cerro Colorado.

15. Texasgulf offered no responses to the questions raised by the Panamanian bishops, and Dr. McBride told me that Texasgulf's management never had occasion to discuss these matters with its board of directors, suggesting that the church's efforts created no difficulties for the corporation. I have noted elsewhere in this book that the contracts enabled Texasgulf to maintain that these problems were Panama's alone to resolve.

In the midst of all the controversy about the mining project came the major teachers' strike of 1979, which distracted public attention from Cerro Colorado while serving to focus much of the popular discontent with the economic measures of the latter years of the Torrijos revolution. In this strike, leaders of the teachers' union struck deals with the oligarchy opposed to the Torrijos government, transforming what began as a salary dispute into a referendum on educational reform and, more generally, on the government's inability to stimulate economic growth.

16. The text of Posse (1980), containing quotations from the World Bank's assessment of the mining project (referred to extensively in Part 2), did not come into the hands of CEASPA until some months after the publication of the pastoral letters.

17. CODEMIN (1980a:7 note 9) stated that the sponsors had "an inventory of 96 sites potentially utilizable as storage for the disposal of tailings, at least six of which have been studied in detail."

18. The overall organization of the mining project added to the Department of Social Development's powerlessness. At the project site itself, Cerro Colorado Copper Corporation—the joint operating company—made the decisions and carried them out; and the operating company was itself managed by Texasgulf, the real decision-maker. The on-site managers scarcely concealed their disdain for those they referred to as the *"niñas"* (little girls) of the Department of Social Development when they made one of their rare trips to the project site; the managers and workers knew who had power and who did not.

19. The investigative group also found comparative materials that would shed light on the prospects for the Guaymíes (e.g., Richard Bedford's and Alexander Mamak's writings; see the References in this book). By mid-1978, we had discovered that Rio Tinto-Zinc's copper project at Bougainville, Papua New Guinea, more than any other mining project in the world, closely paralleled the Cerro Colorado project. Both projects involved mammoth open-pit facilities to mine low-grade copper ore in tropical mountainous re-

gions that previously had no industrial infrastructure. Both affected a large number of indigenous people who were completely unprepared for the arrival of advanced industrial capitalism. When Texasgulf left Cerro Colorado, both projects even involved the same major mining corporation, Rio Tinto-Zinc. Although the arrangements differed, both involved governments which claimed to look out for the needs of the local populace; Australia, the administrator of Papua New Guinea when RTZ began work there, had no better record with indigenous minorities than did Panama. Unfortunately, in both projects the sponsors wanted to make decisions based only on technical considerations, ignoring until after the fact the social effects of these decisions. The major difference was that Bougainville was already producing copper, and RTZ had already begun trying to mitigate some of the disastrous effects; Cerro Colorado was still in the planning stages.

20. F. T. (Casey) Davis of the Colorado School of Mines Research Institute estimated that Cerro Colorado environmental- and social-impact studies would cost from one to ten million dollars (F. T. Davis, in conversation with Canadian delegation; see DeRoo et al. 1980).

Alongside the forty-eight volumes of economic, geological and engineering data and suggestions that comprised the Texasgulf-directed feasibility study sat a 332-page double-spaced volume, *A Reconnaissance Environmental Study of the Cerro Colorado Project in the Republic of Panama*. This study, supervised by F. T. Davis and prepared at a cost of $500,000, was "essentially a reconnaissance study of existing information on the environment in the potential impact area (CSMRI 1977:I-2); no field studies were undertaken. Chapter 6, the study's only discussion of the socio-economic situation of eastern Chiriquí, attempted no analysis of Cerro Colorado's potential impact on the Guaymíes, and included only one marginal reference to the published anthropological material on the Guaymíes (CSMRI 1977:VI-34). No one could explain to me why the Panamanian authors of Chapter 6 did not at least review the literature on the Guaymíes (e.g., Young 1971), in order to offer some enlightened guesses about the ways the mining project might affect them.

This study recommended that after the first year of construction, "specific studies should be made as to the possible degree of displacement of the Guaymí Indian population as a result of the project" (CSMRI 1977:III-3, No. 4). Within the same period, "an assessment should be made of potential bio-health hazards to humans in the Concession Area" and "impact assessments should be made following establishment of physical plant location and specifications" (CSMRI 1977:III-4, 12, 13).

Texasgulf, in arguing to delay these studies, disregarded its commitment to perform according to the highest standards of environmental responsibility in the development of Cerro Colorado, standards which Texasgulf maintained included, at minimum, compliance with United States codes. United States environmental law mandated social-impact studies as part of the environmental-impact assessment required before the sponsors could begin the project. The Panamanian sponsors, if they were even aware of this implication of Texasgulf's commitment, chose to ignore it also.

In October 1983, I was able to visit with Casey Davis in his home near Denver. Davis, by then retired from the Colorado School of Mines Research Institute, offered me invaluable insights into major mining projects while patiently answering my questions about the Cerro Colorado project.

21. The contracts stated that Texasgulf was "indemnified and held harmless" with respect to all expenses incurred in connection with "any claim made for any reason" relating to the concession and project areas and brought forth by anyone "claiming to have a right or interest" in the deposits or the area (Consejo de Legislación, Assn. XXVII); the entire burden of working out problems with Panamanians affected by Cerro Colorado rested on CODEMIN (cf. Consejo de Legislación, Assn. IV-2a). Texasgulf, in complying with national legislation, could also count on its ability to negotiate with the state in case the legislation appeared too restrictive (cf. Consejo de Legislación, Assn. XL, and Adm. XXXI—referred to in Chapter 5 above).

22. Texasgulf and CODEMIN engaged in practices and arguments typical of sponsors of large-scale projects in the third world or in indigenous areas in general. RTZ's Bougainville copper complex in Papua New Guinea brought in its wake serious environmental and social problems, unanticipated in studies prior to the construction of the project (Pardy et al. 1978:120–24). The struggles waged in Papua New Guinea concerning the development of the Purari River hydroelectric project resulted in part from negative experiences in Bougainville, just as some of the Guaymí resistance in Panama resulted from negative experiences of Cunas and Chocóes in the Bayano. In the following quotation on the Purari project, one could easily substitute "copper" and "Panama" for "power" and "PNG" (Papua New Guinea).

> While it may seem extraordinary that adequate attention is not paid to environmental and social planning, it may be understood in the light of the powerful outside interests in the scheme. Potential buyers of power, funding organizations, and experts in various fields are all only concerned with the economic and engineering feasibility of the scheme. They are only interested in the environmental and social consequences insofar as these affect the economic and engineering aspects, and certainly do not want to spend any more money than they are forced to. It is left to the host government to put up the money for these studies. In PNG, where the finance which has been invested in the feasibility study has been substantial for a small coun-

try's budget, there is clearly a reticence to sink more money into such investigations until it is certain that the scheme will be going ahead. But this
means that in practice a decision to go ahead will be made before a full
evaluation has been made. Even if the environmental damage and social
degradation are excessive, these will not be taken into account. (Pardy et al.
1978:126)

23. The only similar experience in modern-day Panama, the Bayano hydroelectric project (completed in 1976), showed that despite planning attempts,
poor management created problems that remained unresolved some years
later. These concerned social organization, economic production, lifestyle,
and standards of living among the Cuna and Chocó Indians affected by the
Bayano project (Alaka Wali, personal communication 1979–80; Wali 1983,
1984).

In the Bayano, IRHE refused to use the studies done under the auspices
of the Patrimonio Histórico de Panamá, the government agency concerned
with advancing knowledge of Panama's indigenous peoples. In place of the
quite thorough Patrimonio Histórico studies, IRHE contracted its own
quicker, more superficial, studies. The Patrimonio Histórico was never invited to look into Cerro Colorado. In 1980, CODEMIN hired from IRHE
the man who had directed work on the social impact of the Bayano project,
asking his help to organize its efforts among the Guaymíes.

24. On paper, the government had long had an office for indigenous affairs
under the Ministry of Government and Justice. However, only in the late
1970s was anyone appointed to head this office; after a relatively short tenure, the appointee resigned to pursue further studies in Mexico, amid
rumors that he could no longer tolerate the government's unwillingness to
come to terms with its problems with indigenous peoples.

25. See Bedford and Mamak (1976:452, 1977:27) for problems in Bougainville
resulting from the aborigines' perceptions that the government was an agent
of the mining company.

Experiences in other parts of the world indicated that indigenous people
could place little hope in social-impact studies undertaken by interested parties in a resource-development project. In August 1980, at Cornell University,
tribal representatives and outside experts discussed various aspects of social-
impact assessment for large-scale resource-development projects carried out
in tribal areas of the United States and Canada; in both countries, environmental and social legislation purports to protect the interests of people affected by such projects. Analysis of studies that complied with the legislation indicated to the participants that tribal peoples must exercise control
over such studies if their interests are to be safeguarded. But for such control

to influence the outcome of projects, tribal peoples also need negotiating power (see Geisler 1982). Some Guaymíes urged that the comarca be defined, with specific Guaymí rights regarding national development projects, and that then independent social-impact studies be undertaken for the Cerro Colorado project (Congresos Guaymíes 1980:39 and elsewhere).

Even if the people affected had control of the studies and had negotiating power, they might yet accept plans and impacts not in their interest. The Colville Confederated Tribes of Washington State, co-owners of the project, accepted a superficial social-impact assessment contracted by their partner AMAX for the (later suspended) Mount Tolman molybdenum-copper project, seemingly because of the interest of the Business Council (the tribal leadership) in having the project go forward as quickly as possible; their focus was on the narrowly economic benefits. (Information from my unpublished field research)

26. As the World Bank noted, omission of such studies as part of project planning meant that the costs of indemnification and of relocation would be excluded from the calculations of the project's costs, thereby altering the estimates (Posse 1980). It is difficult to know what it might have cost to do the needed social impact assessment. F. T. Davis of Colorado School of Mines Research Institute estimated the studies would cost ten million dollars; our investigative team put together a proposal for a study that would have cost about $100,000. Obviously, no estimates of the costs of the studies provided any guide to the costs of carrying out the studies' recommendations.

In 1982, the World Bank published a study that included recommendations "for meeting the human ecologic needs of tribal peoples" affected by development projects assisted by the World Bank (Goodland 1982:iii and Annex 1). A World Bank official assured me that these policies would be implemented should the Cerro Colorado project go forward. However, the other concerns of the World Bank in its involvement in a project like Cerro Colorado (see Chapter 5), as well as the difficulties encountered by the Anthropology Resource Center and others trying to influence the World Bank's anti-tribal support of the trans-Amazon Highway in Brazil in the late 1970s, made me skeptical about following his advice to leave all concerns about the Guaymíes in the hands of the World Bank.

27. According to Guaymí informants, CODEMIN field people made these claims very forcefully in meetings with Guaymí communities. In conversations with the priests, the CODEMIN personnel softened their wording a bit, arguing that "careful reading" of Núñez' pastoral letter revealed this underlying bias toward maintaining an impoverished status quo for the Guaymíes. When asked to demonstrate from the pastoral letter the basis for

this argument, they replied that they "inferred it from the document" *(se desprende del documento)*. Obviously, the priests disagreed.

28. CODEMIN made several different claims about this cassette: that it was a Remedios priest at a Guaymí meeting, that it was a Tolé priest at a Guaymí meeting, that it was a Tolé priest at a Sunday mass in town; but the priests had no idea what CODEMIN was talking about. CODEMIN personnel in Chiriquí and, later, in Panama City promised the priests a copy of this tape, which had the mysterious knack of disappearing every time they looked for it; no priest ever heard it.

On at least two occasions, Guaymíes working for the mining project taped open community meetings that included priests. Ironically, if CODEMIN people listened to these tapes, they heard the priests explaining that the radio programs warning of the dangers of sterility and death had no foundation other than conveying the desire of a small group of people to frighten listeners into general opposition to the government; the priests were able to counter opposition propaganda much more believably than CODEMIN. These stories of sterility and death never took hold among the Guaymíes; they appeared in no publications of or for the Guaymíes, and did not reach the floor (or, to my knowledge, the corridors) of the Guaymí congresses discussed above.

29. These events took place when the representative was running into his own disillusionment regarding his authority over the mining project (discussed in Chapter 7); in his anger at not getting his way, he kept the petition to himself. The representative told me about the petition and let me copy it.

The opposition of the mineworkers was difficult for the priests to counter. Virtually none of the workers had read the pastoral letters, even cursorily; their opinions regarding its contents and point of view were shaped by what they picked up from their bosses. They felt threatened; their jobs were at stake. The beginning of mine construction had already been delayed for several months, but CODEMIN never explained the problems; they were as much subject to the ups and down of conflicting rumors as were the Guaymíes. Few showed any great interest in hearing the church's side of the story; their minds were already made up. Even those with some openness, at best ended up confused, struggling with loyalties divided between their bosses, who they assumed knew things they didn't, and representatives of the church, who they thought might have been sincere but mistaken.

30. The watchman, obviously quite uncomfortable, acknowledged that nothing had happened to increase the dangers of landslides. In any case, the written permissions included the mining company's statement that the

unimproved road could be dangerous, along with its explicit denial of liability in case of any accidents.

A few days later, some priests tried again; this time the watchman showed them the slip of paper with the new orders. These orders detailed the categories of people who could no longer use the road: local merchants, cattlemen, and—on a typewritten line by itself, capitalized and spaced to cover much of the page—*R-E-L-I-G-I-O-S-O-S*.

31. I was one of these priests. At the Guaymí meeting, we had sat quietly listening to discussions (usually in Ngawbere, which we didn't understand) that principally revolved around details of Guaymí hopes for their comarca and carta orgánica. Of a number of regional meetings I attended, only at this one were we invited to speak; we said a few words about the church's support for the Guaymíes in their just struggles concerning their comarca and concerning the Cerro Colorado and Teribe-Changuinola projects. We mentioned no specifics about the projects, and we said nothing about the government.

Palacios also told this Cerro Colorado field boss about the poverty of the Guaymíes of Bocas del Toro, who did not even have beans to eat; the mine, which represented every kind of progress for the Guaymíes, would teach them to grow beans. We explained to him that the constant rains of Bocas del Toro, and not ignorance or poverty, kept the Guaymíes from cultivating beans; the beans rotted on the vines. He insisted that the mining project would nonetheless solve the problem.

32. Aristides Royo, president of Panama, personally overturned the decision to exclude the priests' vehicles from the access road after an unexpected discussion during his late 1980 visit to the Jesuit novitiate on the outskirts of Panama City. After turning off the television cameras, he spoke candidly of his dislike for the church's misguided opposition to Cerro Colorado, which would clearly bring great benefits to Panama; he referred to the recently published open letter written by Catholic bishops and missionaries working among the Guaymíes.

Knowing from several sources that CODEMIN told the president very little about the mining project, I politely challenged his statements about the Guaymíes, offering him information both from my fieldwork and from knowledge of effects of large-scale resource-development projects among indigenous peoples in other parts of the world. I also told him of our annoyance at the petty harassment we put up with at the hands of people who worked for his government. He seemed genuinely surprised to hear these things, and ordered his aides to set up a meeting with himself, Bishop Núñez, Rodrigo González of CODEMIN, and the priests of eastern Chiriquí. At this meeting (held after I left Panama), he overturned the decision to exclude our vehicles.

The head of security took a more subtle approach with the priests. Saying that he did not want me to wait for a ride in the company's vehicles when I went down to the town of San Félix or came back up to Hato Chamí, he asked me to write up for him my itinerary: all the Guaymí communities I would visit, the dates of those visits, and the names of the people I would be with. (A number of Guaymíes told me of his curiosity about where I went and what I did.) I pointed out to him that I walked or rode my horse to Guaymí communities, very few of which lay along the road. I also reassured him that I did not mind taking my chances on rides; the company was doing me a favor letting me hitch rides, and I did not wish to inconvenience them further. He implied that his job as head of security included keeping tabs on the activities of everyone in the entire Guaymí area around the project; I pointed out that the government imposed no restrictions on people's movements in the Guaymí area, and that I interpreted his work as industrial security or job safety.

33. Project representatives made statements whose nuances and tones are not suggested in this synthetic summary. Some regarded themselves as pro-Indian, felt great sympathy for the Guaymíes, and saw their efforts as necessary to bring them into the twentieth century for their own survival. Others saw themselves as realists, for "facts have to be faced: indigenous people are going to disappear, be absorbed into the national population" (from a conversation with a CODEMIN engineer). Some seemed clearly to look down on the Guaymíes, sharing the common Panamanian latino perception of them as lazy, stupid, drunken and undeserving, needlessly occupying vast tracts of land that could have been put to much better use by latino ranchers. And the few Guaymíes in the Department of Social Development's Panama City office, men who for years had enjoyed the amenities of life in the capital, tended to look down on their country cousins as embarrassing remnants of a last stronghold against "civilization." These differing nuances, all of which still had in common the conclusion that some form of integration or assimilation was inevitable and even desirable for the Guaymíes, fairly well reflected the range of viewpoints in Panama in general, where the nation's policies and attitudes toward indigenous people received little attention. Some Guaymíes countered with posters whose slogan read "We are not tired of being Indians"—*"No somos cansados de ser indígenas!"*

34. Only some while after the arrival of RTZ did CODEMIN find itself challenged from within regarding its perceptions of Guaymí problems and their cause. RTZ helped CODEMIN bring as a consultant Douglas Oliver,

an anthropologist who had worked in Bougainville (Oliver 1955, 1973). Oliver maintained that any indigenous group understood only too well its own interests and the potential threats to them. He argued that the Cerro Colorado project could not help but create severe problems for the Guaymíes; whatever other factors might be present, he had no doubt that CODEMIN had a serious Indian problem on its hands. CODEMIN, having little or no relevant literature of its own in English, gave him the translation of CEASPA y Comisión (1979) prepared for the Canquintú Congress; Oliver concluded that CEASPA understood very well the problems that Cerro Colorado would create for the Guaymíes, and offered the unwelcome suggestion that the Department of Social Development contract CEASPA's help.

At the end of 1980, CODEMIN and RTZ representatives attended the annual meeting of the American Anthropological Association in Washington, D.C., in hopes of addressing a symposium in which I gave a paper summarizing some of our work (Gjording 1983). They also contacted several anthropologists, including Anthropology Resource Center and Cultural Survival, putting out feelers about hiring someone to direct a social-impact assessment. CODEMIN and RTZ, probably unknowingly, found themselves talking with anthropologists who knew each other and talked over their concerns. They all gave the mining people the same responses: the need for Guaymí participation, freedom to publish the results of any contracted work, the importance of taking very seriously the studies already undertaken by Young, Bort, and me. Nothing came of these conversations.

35. On arrival, RTZ did legal research and concluded that the Guaymíes might well have some legal rights in Panama. With RTZ funding, the Department of Social Development contracted a Panamanian sociologist to begin field studies in Guaymí communities to be relocated (see CODEMIN 1980b:21). But CODEMIN kept these studies a closely guarded secret until after the project was suspended; I was never able to see them.

36. Richard Bedford and Alexander Mamak published a series of articles and short monographs on different aspects of the Bougainville project and its impact on the peoples of the area (see the References); these studies disputed at least the tone, and often the substance, of RTZ's claims. For example, RTZ established credit unions only after several years of intense pressure; it adopted preferential hiring practices because of problems in retaining its expatriate work force, and still had high turnover rates as it sought ways to adjust the practices of the Bougainvilleans to its work schedules.

37. Most of those who encouraged or took part in the harassment of church workers likely did so from some underlying feeling of being threatened. But

it seemed to us that León Palacios, the principal field representative of
CODEMIN's Department of Social Development, a former elected representative from one of the latino towns in eastern Chiriquí, engaged in his
efforts in hopes of furthering his political career both in the Party of the
People and in the government. If he could make himself visible as defending
progress, jobs, and the advancement of the poor of eastern Chiriquí, he
might build up something of a constituency for the future. Among the
Guaymíes, he worked most closely with Federico Santos, Martín Manteca,
and their little group.

38. Even before the pastoral letters were published, it became evident that
local bosses thought—wrongly—that I was going around the mine area to
hold meetings concerning Cerro Colorado, to persuade the people to oppose
the project. A friend in the mining camp assured me that the fact that I per-
formed no religious services made me all the more suspect, since the managers could see little reason for a priest to be among the Guaymíes other
than to try to persuade them to become active Catholics.

During the three months that I did fieldwork out of Hato Chamí, I met
a number of Cerro Colorado project workers and talked often with them. In
several conversations, in response to their questions, I tried to describe what
I was doing: visiting communities, getting to know people, and trying to get
a better sense of their lives and concerns. As noted in the Preface, in accor-
dance with the counsel I received from a number of people, including a few
in CODEMIN's Panama City offices and other branches of the Panamanian
government, I did not tell these project workers that I was an anthropologist, although my descriptions of my activities reflected what I was really
doing. Later, when project workers commented to me about what the
bishops had said in their pastoral letters, I could see that they had a very distorted view of these documents. In these conversations, I did what little I
could to offer what I considered a less distorted version, but I found little
openness to what I had to say.

I think the project workers and their managers had a set of expectations
about what priests should be doing, and my companions and I did not meet
these expectations. We were in no hurry to try to convert the Guaymíes;
rather, we were convinced that we should spend time to get to know them
and their lifeways, and to try to discover ways that Catholic Christianity
might make a contribution to their lives. When Hato Rincón community
leaders pressed me to do baptisms there, my companions and I finally decided I should acquiesce, motivated in part by the insistence of their requests, and in part by the opportunity it presented me to let the local project
managers hear that I had done something that they considered religious.

39. Working with the government and the National Guard, the sponsors had possibilities of passing new laws (for example, restricting non-Guaymí access to the Guaymí area) or even of changing tactics without any changes in the laws. Among the priests, as among the investigative team in general, were a number of foreigners whom the government could simply have deported, with or without going through legal processes.

Chapter 11: Assessments of the Guaymí-centered Opposition

1. Beginning in 1981, ignoring Guaymí objections, the government of Panama contracted with Northville Industries to have Morrison-Knudsen construct a petroleum pipeline from Puerto Armuelles in western Chiriquí Province to a new port in Chiriquí Grande of Bocas del Toro Province. A major stretch of this pipeline, and the Bocas del Toro port, lie in Guaymí territory. To build and maintain the pipeline, the contractors had to build an access road—the first road connecting Bocas del Toro Province with the remainder of Panama. The Guaymíes feared that the road would open the center of their Bocas del Toro territory to cattle ranches and latino peasants. Environmentalists complained that the pipeline did not have suitable controls, e.g., against oil spills in the unsullied Laguna de Chiriquí on the Caribbean side, site of breeding grounds for some rare turtles. The pipeline was to transport Alaskan oil across the isthmus, so that the oil could go to U.S. refineries on the Gulf and east coasts. See NYT (1981) and Solano F. (1981) for background information on the pipeline, and Congreso General Guaymí (1983) for Guaymí resolutions opposing the pipeline.

2. Young (1980c) later thought that the three-year "Plan Guaymí" informal education program of directed change might have provided the Guaymíes some further possibilities for organizing.

3. One reason for my saying "perhaps": the Guaymíes, except for some leaders, took part in Cerro Colorado activities without running into conflict with their kin groups and kin activities; while the organization of these activities transcended kin boundaries, people did not have to subordinate kin interests to wider ones.

4. In the 1982 Conference on Native Resource Control and the Multinational Corporate Challenge (see Swenson 1982), a number of indigenous participants echoed similar distrust of outsiders. At one point they insisted that non-indigenous peoples vacate the meeting area. We support people used this unscheduled time alone to begin a valuable discussion of some of our own difficulties in our positions as generally uninvited volunteers work-

ing with indigenous peoples. Part of this discussion, verified in our work
with the Guaymíes, was that we at times became the targets of the hostility
and frustration of indigenous peoples. Given that circumstances of power relationships and the need to keep open the channels of dialogue often prevented the native people from venting their frustrations with those who
caused them, they seemed at times to turn instead on those outsiders closest
at hand. Also, it seemed to us that their very history of unequal relationships
with outsiders prompted them constantly to test us, to our chagrin and pain.
While this discussion hardly healed the hurt and confusion of feeling
attacked by those with whom we sought to cooperate, it did help us to discover common threads in our experiences as outside support people, and to
provide ourselves with some explanations of what was otherwise very discon-
certing behavior.

5. However, as this book suggests, it is very unlikely that any other Guaymí
strategy would have caused the government to take them seriously.

6. These power struggles created problems for our group only in Panama
City, where we worked with Guaymíes who were favorable to Ricardo
Smith, Miguel Cruz, and the *Unión Indígena Guaymí;* any attempt to develop a close working relationship with the *Frente de Liberación Guaymí* threatened our association with these important partners. In the Guaymí area itself
these power struggles imposed few, if any, limitations.

However, at times we found ourselves faced with some ambivalent
choices, as for example with the invitation to send Guaymí delegates to the
Russell Tribunal in Rotterdam in 1980. Since the Guaymíes had no mechanisms for deciding whether to participate in the Tribunal or whom to send,
and since the invitation arrived very late, we had to find a quick way to work
with a small group of Guaymíes to see who, if anyone, would go. It was not
difficult to find someone who understood the issues and could articulate
them well in Spanish. But the invitation became an issue in one of these
power struggles as Guaymíes from one group insisted that they participate
without the other group or not at all. Later, Guaymíes who travelled to this
or other meetings returned to face criticisms from perhaps jealous, perhaps
skeptical, rank-and-file Guaymíes. Such meetings, so important in publicizing
the Guaymí case and in developing ties of solidarity, at the same time hurt
the leadership possibilities for the delegates.

7. The Panamanian bishops had earlier worked closely with the U.S. bishops
regarding the Torrijos-Carter canal treaties; in solidarity with the Panamanian bishops, the U.S. bishops' conference endorsed the treaties and publicly
urged their ratification in the Senate.

8. See Chapter 10, note 9, for a brief discussion of some of the uncertainties in the wake of the Puebla conference of the Latin American bishops.

9. In some of our early meetings, these strongly held conflicting opinions threatened to pull us apart. Later on, we had to overcome tensions and misunderstandings created by the volatile political climate surrounding the mining project. For example, a source of uneasiness for Panama City members of the group had to do with fears of what the Chiriquí contingent might be doing, and whether these activities in turn might provoke reprisals.

The fears were not invention; several times, rumors circulated in Panama City of possible government reprisals against people it saw as threatening the success of the mining project. Some of these rumors surfaced in a Panamanian newspaper, alarming us with the insinuated possibility of a Salvadoran- or Guatemalan-style "disappearance" of a Jesuit working in eastern Chiriquí, isolated from ready communication with Panama City where people might have exerted pressure for a "reappearance." These rumors—baseless, it turned out—seemed designed to see whether we really had the backing of Bishop Núñez, who in fact came forward immediately with strong public support.

Non-Panamanian permanent residents in our group had some reason to fear being deported, legally or not; for this reason (among others), I took part in Guaymí meetings only as an observer, never as one providing information.

10. Although we called CEASPA 1979b "a preliminary contribution" subject to revision in the light of further information, nothing came along to invalidate the principal lines of this initial analysis; we found that we could incorporate new details into the framework we had developed, as when we provided the bishops' conference with an update (CEASPA 1980) of our earlier background work for them.

11. Subsequently we learned that the obvious (to us) approach of keeping the entire project in its global context and, as a consequence, not confining our analysis to "social-impact assessment" or studies only of the Guaymí reality, represented something relatively unheard of in professional circles devoted to these analyses. In August 1980, when I took part in a Cornell University meeting on social-impact assessment, we found that most Canadian and U.S. investigations of resource-development projects adopted a perspective that tended not to avert to the global or national contexts in which the projects were to be carried out. Some groups had seen the necessity of studying the corporate sponsors of projects, but even here their perspective

tended to be confined to looking at a corporation's previous behavior in native people's areas. See Geisler 1982 for examples.

12. In 1975, at the invitation of an indigenous group founded by Guaymí Ricardo Smith, Douglas Sanders, a British Columbia law professor with expertise in international questions of indigenous rights, visited Panama to study the legal situation of the Guaymíes. His excellent report, written in English, remained little known.

GLOSSARY

Acronyms and Abbreviations Used in the Text

CDC	Canada Development Corporation (Canadian government holding company)
CEASPA	Centro de Estudios y Acción Social–Panama (Panamanian non-governmental agency)
CELAM	Consejo Episcopal Latinoamericano (Latin American Bishops' Conference)
CEP	Conferencia Episcopal Panameña (Panamanian Bishops' Conference)
CIPEC	Intergovernmental Council of Copper-Exporting Countries
CODEMIN	Corporación de Desarrollo Minero Cerro Colorado (Panamanian government mining corporation).
DC	Developed Country
EDC	Export Development Corporation (Canadian government agency)
IMF	International Monetary Fund
IRHE	Instituto de Recursos Hidraúlicos y Electrificación (Panamanian government electricity agency)
LAWG	Latin America Working Group (Toronto)
LDC	Less Developed Country
LIBOR	London Inter-Bank Offering Rate, a changing interest rate often used in the calculation of interest rates for international loans
MEC	Market-Economy Country
MNC	Multinational Corporation
m.t.	metric ton
NACLA	North American Congress on Latin America

RTZ	Rio Tinto-Zinc, Ltd.
SEC	Securities and Exchange Commission (U.S. government agency)
UIG	Unión Indígena Guaymí (Guaymí Indian Organization)
UNDP	United Nations Development Programme

REFERENCES

GENERAL REFERENCES

Abbott, Walter M. ed.
  1966 *The Documents of Vatican II*. New York: America Press.

Adams, Robert McC.
  1977 "World Picture, Anthropological Frame." *American Anthropologist* 79:265–79.

Alphonse, Ephraim S.
  1956 *Guaymí Grammar and Dictionary with Some Ethnological Notes.* Bureau of American Ethnology, Bulletin 162. Washington: Smithsonian Institution.
  1980 *Gramática Guaymí.* Panama City: Fe y Alegria.

Barnet, Richard J. and Ronald E. Müller
  1974 *Global Reach: The Power of the Multinational Corporations.* New York: Simon and Schuster.

Bedford, Richard and Alexander Mamak
  1975 "A Town Council Election in Bougainville." *South Pacific Bulletin* 25:45–50.
  1976a "Bougainvilleans in Urban Wage Employment: Some Aspects of Migrant Flows and Adaptive Strategies." *Oceania* 46:169–87.
  1976b "Kieta, Arawa and Panguna: The Towns of Bougainville." In *An Introductory Urban Geography of Papua New Guinea.* R. T. Jackson, ed., pp. 444–86. Port Moresby, P.N.G.: Univ. of Papua New Guinea.

1977   *Compensating for Development: The Bougainville Case.* Bougain-
         ville Special Publications No. 2. Christchurch, New
         Zealand: Univ. of Canterbury.

Bennett, Charles F.
   1968   *Human Influences on the Zoogeography of Panama.* Berkeley:
         Univ. of California Press.

Berger, Thomas R.
   1977   *Northern Frontier, Northern Homeland: Report of the Mackenzie
         Valley Pineline Inquiry.* Vol. 1. Ottawa: Minister of Supply and
         Services.

Berryman, Phillip
   1984   *The Religious Roots of Rebellion: Christians in Central American
         Revolutions.* Maryknoll, New York: Orbis Books.

Bidwell, Charles T.
   1865   *The Isthmus of Panama.* London.

Bort, John R.
   1976   "Guaymí Innovators: A Case Study of Entrepreneurs in a
         Small Scale Society." Ph.D. dissertation, Anthropology De-
         partment, University of Oregon.
   1977   "Coping with Productive Fluctuation: A Ceremonial-Based
         System among the Guaymí Indians of Panama." Paper pre-
         sented at Northwest Anthropological Association meeting,
         April 1977, Victoria, B.C.

Bort, John R. and Mary W. Helms, eds.
   1983   *Panama in Transition: Local Reactions to Development Policies.*
         Monographs in Anthropology No. 6. Columbia, Missouri:
         Univ. of Missouri Museum of Anthropology.

Bosson, Rex and Bension Varon
   1977   *The Mining Industry and the Developing Countries.* A World
         Bank Research Publication. New York: Oxford Univ. Press.

Bowen, Robert and Ananda Gunatilaka
   1977   *Copper: Its Geology and Economics.* New York: John Wiley and
         Sons.

Bray, Wayne D.
   1977   *The Common Law Zone in Panama.* San Juan: Inter-American
         Univ. of Puerto Rico.

British-North American Committee
1976   *Mineral Development in the Eighties: Prospects and Problems.* A report prepared by a group of Committee members on the basis of a document provided by Ian MacGregor with a statistical annex by Sperry Lea. Washington: British-North American Committee.

Canadian Javelin, Ltd.
1977   *Annual Report 1976.* Montreal.

Carman, John S.
1979   *Obstacles to Mineral Development: A Pragmatic View.* Bension Varon, ed. Elmsford, New York: Pergamon.

Carneiro, Robert L.
1960   "Slash-and-Burn Agriculture. A Closer Look at its Implications for Settlement Patterns." In *Men and Cultures.* A. F. C. Wallace, ed. Philadelphia: Univ. of Pennsylvania Press.

Carty, Robert, Virginia Smith and LAWG
1981   *Perpetuating Poverty: the Political Economy of Canadian Foreign Aid.* Toronto: Between the Lines.

Castillero Calvo, Alfredo
1967   *Estructuras sociales y económicas de Veragua desde sus orígenes históricos, siglos XVI y XVII.* Panama City: Editora Panamá.
1969   "Política de poblamiento en Castilla del Oro y Veragua durante los orígenes de la colonización (1502–1522)." *Lotería* 160:67–89.
1971   "La independencia de Panamá de España—factores coyunturales y estructurales en la Capital y el Interior." *Lotería* 192:4–18.
1973   "Transitismo y dependencia: el caso del Istmo de Panamá." *Lotería* 210:17–40; 211:25–56.

Castillero Reyes, Ernesto J.
1968   *Chiriquí: Ensayo de monografía de la Provincia de Chiriquí.* [First published 1949.] Panama.

CELAM (Consejo Episcopal Latinoamericano)
1970   *The Church in the Present-Day Transformation of Latin America in the Light of the Council.* Vol. 2: *Conclusions.* Texts of the Second General Conference of Latin American Bishops, Medellín, Colombia, August 26–September 6, 1968.

Official English Edition. Bogotá: General Secretariat of CELAM.

1979   *Evangelization in Latin America's Present and Future.* Final Document of the Third General Conference of the Latin American Epicopate, Puebla de los Angeles, Mexico, January 27–February 13, 1979. John Drury, transl. In *Puebla and Beyond: Documentation and Commentary.* John Eagleson and Philip Scharper, eds., pp. 111–285. Maryknoll, New York: Orbis Books.

Connell, John ed.
1977   *Local Government Councils in Bougainville.* Bougainville Special Publications No. 3. Christchurch, New Zealand: Univ. of Canterbury.

Davis, Shelton H.
1977   *Victims of the Miracle: Development and the Indians of Brazil.* Cambridge: Cambridge Univ. Press.

Farnsworth, David N. and James W. McKenney
1983   *U.S.–Panama Relations, 1903–1978: A Study in Linkage Politics.* Boulder, Colorado: Westview Press.

Figueroa Navarro, Alfredo
1980   *Dominio y sociedad en el Panamá colombiano (1821–1903): Escrutinio sociológico.* 2a edición. Bogotá: Ediciones Tercer Mundo.

Fogarty, Charles F.
1976   "The Story of Texasgulf." Address to National Meeting of The Newcomen Society in North America, November 12, 1975. New York: Newcomen Society.

Frank, Andre Gunder
1969   *Capitalism and Underdevelopment in Latin America: Historical Studies of Chile and Brazil.* New York: Monthly Review Press.

Gandásegui h., Marco Antonio
1974   "La concentración del poder económico en Panamá." In *Panamá, dependencia y liberación.* Ricaurte Soler, ed., pp. 99–183. San Jose, Costa Rica: Editorial Universitaria Centroamericana (EDUCA).

Gandásegui h., Marco Antonio, A. Saavedra, A. Achong, I. Quintero
1980   *Las luchas obreras en Panamá (1850–1978).* Panama City: Centro de Estudios Latinoamericanos (CELA).

Geisler, Charles C., Rayna Green, Daniel Usner, Patrick West, eds.

1982   *Indian SIA: The Social Impact Assessment of Rapid Resource Development on Native Peoples.* Natural Resources Sociology Research Lab Monograph No. 3. Ann Arbor: Univ. of Michigan.

Gilles, P.J.

1977   "Environmental Planning at Bougainville Copper." In *The Melanesian Environment.* John H. Winslow, ed. pp. 358–64. Canberra: Australian National Univ.

Gjording, Chris N.

1981a   *The Cerro Colorado Copper Project and the Guaymí Indians of Panama.* Cultural Survival Occasional Paper No. 3. Cambridge, Mass.: Cultural Survival.

1981b   "Panama: The Guaymí Indians make their stand against mining, oil and construction companies." *Multinational Monitor* 2(5):27–30.

1982a   "The Social Impact of a Multinational Corporation on the Guaymí of Panama." In *Indian SIA: The Social Impact Assessment of Rapid Resource Development on Native Peoples.* Charles C. Geisler, et al., eds. pp. 371–411. Natural Resources Sociology Research Lab Monograph No. 3. Ann Arbor: Univ. of Michigan.

1983   "The Guaymí People and Cerro Colorado." In *Panama in Transition: Local Reactions to Development Policies.* John R. Bort and Mary W. Helms, eds. pp. 19–52. Monographs in Anthropology No. 6. Columbia, Missouri: Univ. of Missouri Museum of Anthropology.

Gjording, Chris N. and Alaka Wali

1982   "Panama." In *Background Documents.* Prepared for the Conference on Native Resource Control and the Multinational Corporate Challenge: Aboriginal Rights in International Perspective, Washington, D.C., October 12–15, 1982. Sally Swenson, ed., pp. 23–25. Boston: Anthropology Resource Center.

Gluschke, Wolfgang, Joseph Shaw, and Bension Varon

1979   *Copper: The Next Fifteen Years.* Natural Resources Forum Library. Published for the United Nations. Dordrecht, Holland: D. Reidel Publishing Co.

Goodland, Robert
1982   *Tribal Peoples and Economic Development: Human Ecologic Considerations.* Washington: World Bank.

Gorostiaga, Xabier
1978   *Los centros financieros internacionales en los paises subdesarrollados.* Mexico City: Instituto Latinoamericano de Estudios Transnacionales.

Gudeman, Stephen
1976   *Relationships, Residence and the Individual: A Rural Panamanian Community.* Minneapolis: Univ. of Minnesota Press.
1978   *The Demise of a Rural Economy: From Subsistence to Capitalism in a Latin American Village.* London: Routledge & Kegan Paul.

Gutiérrez, Gustavo
1973   *A Theology of Liberation: History, Politics and Salvation.* Maryknoll, New York: Orbis Books.

Guzmán, Louis E.
1956   *Farming and Farmlands in Panama.* Department of Geography Research Paper No. 44. Chicago: Univ. of Chicago Press.

Helms, Mary W.
1975   *Middle America: A Culture History of Heartland and Frontiers.* Englewood Cliffs, N.J.: Prentice-Hall.
1979   *Ancient Panama: Chiefs in Search of Power.* Austin, Texas: Univ. of Texas Press.

Jackson, R.T., ed.
1976   *An Introductory Urban Geography of Papua New Guinea.* Port Moresby, P.N.G.: Univ. of Papua New Guinea.

Jaén Suárez, Omar
1971   *El hombre y la tierra en Natá de 1700 a 1850.* Panama City: Editorial Universitaria.
1973   *Presencias imperialistas y dependencia ístmica en la segunda mitad del siglo XIX.* Estudios históricos del Centro de Investigaciones Sociales y Económicas. Panama City: Universidad de Panamá.
1979   *La población del istmo de Panamá del siglo XVI al siglo XX.* 2a edición. Panama City.
1981   *Hombres y ecología en Panamá.* Panama City: Editorial Universitaria y Smithsonian Tropical Research Institute.

LaFeber, Walter
 1979   *The Panama Canal: The Crisis in Historical Perspective.* Expanded edition. New York: Oxford Univ. Press.

LAWG (Latin America Working Group)
 1980   "Panama's Copper and Canadian Capital: The Social and Economic Impact of the Cerro Colorado Project." *LAWG Letter* 6(4-5):1–30.

Lewis, Oscar
 1964   *The Children of Sánchez.* Harmondsworth, Middlesex: Penguin.

Linares, Olga F.
 1968   *Cultural Chronology of the Gulf of Chiriquí, Panama.* Smithsonian Contributions to Anthropology No. 8. Washington, D.C.: Smithsonian Institution Press.

Linares, Olga F. and Anthony J. Ranere, eds.
 1980   *Adaptive Radiations in Prehistoric Panama.* Peabody Museum of Archaeology and Ethnology. Cambridge, Mass.: Harvard University.

Lothrop, Samuel K.
 1937   *Coclé: An Archaeological Study of Central Panama.* Part I. Memoirs of the Peabody Museum of Archaeology and Ethnology Vol. 7. Cambridge, Mass.: Harvard.
 1942   *Coclé: An Archaeological Study of Central Panama.* Part II. Memoirs of the Peabody Museum of Archaeology and Ethnology Vol. 8. Cambridge, Mass.: Harvard.

McCullough, David
 1977   *The Path Between the Seas: The Creation of the Panama Canal, 1870–1914.* New York: Simon and Schuster.

McCullum, Hugh and Karmel McCullum
 1975   *This Land is Not For Sale. Canada's Original People and Their Land, a Saga of Neglect, Exploitation, and Conflict.* Toronto: Anglican Book Centre.

Mack, Gerstle
 1944   *The Land Divided: A History of the Panama Canal and Other Isthmian Canal Projects.* New York: Alfred Knopf.

MacLeod, Murdo J.
 1973   *Spanish Central America: A Socioeconomic History, 1520–1720.* Berkeley: Univ. of California Press.

Mamak, Alexander and Richard Bedford
    1974a   "Bougainville's Students." *New Guinea and Australia, the Pacific and South-East Asia*, March/April:4-15.

    1974b   *Bougainvillean Nationalism: Aspects of Unity and Discord*. With the assistance of Leo Hannett and Moses Havini. Bougainville Special Publication No. 1. Christchurch, New Zealand: Univ. of Canterbury.

    1977   "Inequality in the Bougainville Copper Mining Industry: Some Implications." In *Racism: The Australian Experience*. Vol. 3. 2nd ed. F. S. Stevens and Edward P. Wolfers, eds. pp. 427–55. Sydney: Australia and New Zealand Book Co.

    1978   "Race, Class and Ethnicity: Industrial Relations in the South Pacific, with Special Reference to Fiji and Bougainville." In *Rank and Status in Polynesia and Melanesia: Essays in Honor of Professor Douglas Oliver*. Publications de la Société Océanistes No. 39, pp. 45–60. Paris: Musée de l'Homme.

Manduley, Julio
    1980   "Panama: Dependent Capitalism and Beyond." *Latin American Perspectives* 7:57–74.

Merrill, William C. et al.
    1975   *Panama's Economic Development: The Role of Agriculture*. Ames, Iowa: Iowa State Univ. Press.

Mezger, Dorothea
    1975   "The European Copper Industry and its Implications for the Copper-Exporting Underdeveloped Countries with Special Reference to CIPEC Countries." In *Natural Resources and National Welfare: The Case of Copper*. Ann Seidman, ed. pp. 60–91. New York: Praeger.

    1980   *Copper in the World Economy*. Pete Burgess, transl. New York: Monthly Review Press.

Mikesell, Raymond F.
    1975   *Foreign Investment in Copper Mining: Case Studies of Mines in Peru and Papua New Guinea*. Published for Resources for the Future, Inc. Baltimore: Johns Hopkins Univ. Press.

    1979a   *The World Copper Industry: Structure and Economic Analysis*. Published for Resources for the Future. Baltimore: Johns Hopkins Univ. Press.

    1979b   *New Patterns of World Mineral Development*. Washington: British-North American Committee.

1980a   "Mining Agreements and Conflict Resolution." In *Mining for Development in the Third World: Multinational Corporations, State Enterprises and the International Economy.* S. Sideri and S. Johns, eds. pp. 198–209. New York: Pergamon.

1980b   "The Role of Foreign Private Investment in Future LDC Mining Projects." In *Mining for Development in the Third World: Multinational Corporations, State Enterprises and the International Economy.* S. Sideri and S. Johns, eds. pp. 297–307. New York: Pergamon.

Miller, C. George

1978   "Investment Attractiveness: One Aspect of Competitiveness." In *International Competition and the Canadian Mineral Industries.* Centre for Resource Studies Proceedings No 2. pp. 25–38. Kingston, Ontario: Queen's University.

Miller, C. George, Nancy D. Olewiler and Peter R. Richardson

1978   "Cerro Colorado: A Case Study of the Role of Canadian Crown Corporations in Foreign Mineral Development." Centre for Resource Studies Working Paper No. 13. Kingston, Ontario: Queen's University.

NACLA (North American Congress on Latin America)

1979   "Panama—For Whom the Canal Tolls?" *NACLA Report on the Americas* 13(5):2–37.

Oliver, Douglas

1955   *A Solomon Island Society: Kinship and Leadership among the Siuai of Bougainville.* Boston: Beacon Press.

1973   *Bougainville: A Personal History.* Melbourne: Melbourne Univ. Press.

Pardy, Rob, Mike Parsons, Don Siemon and Ann Wigglesworth

1978   *Purari: Overpowering Papua New Guinea?* International Development Action for Purari Action Group. Fitzroy, Victoria, Australia: International Development Action.

Patrick, Kenneth G.

1972   *Perpetual Jeopardy. The Texas Gulf Sulphur Affair: A Chronicle of Achievement and Misadventure.* New York: Macmillan.

Payer, Cheryl

1974   *The Debt Trap: The IMF and the Third World.* New York: Monthly Review Press.

1982   *The World Bank: A Critical Analysis.* New York: Monthly Review Press.

Radetzki, Marian and Stephen Zorn
1979   *Financing Mining Projects in Developing Countries: A United Nations Study.* Published in cooperation with the United Nations. London: Mining Journal Books Ltd.

Radin, Paul
1933   *The Method and Theory of Ethnology: An Essay in Criticism.* New York/London: McGraw Hill 1933; republished, with Introduction by Arthur Vidich, 1965.

Rippy, J. Fred
1931   *The Capitalists and Colombia.* New York: Vanguard Press.

Roberts, Janine
1978   *From Massacres to Mining: The Colonization of Aboriginal Australia.* London: CIMRA and War on Want.

Roberts, J. and D. McLean
1976   *The Cape York Aluminium Companies and the Native Peoples.* Book III of *The Mapoon Story.* Fitzroy, Victoria, Australia: International Development Action.

Russell Tribunal
1980   *Report of the Fourth Russell Tribunal on the Rights of the Indians of the Americas.* Rotterdam, November 1980.

Sauer, Carl O.
1969   *The Early Spanish Main.* Berkeley: Univ. of California Press.

Schott, Joseph L.
1967   *Rails Across Panama: The Story of the Building of the Panama Railroad, 1849–1855.* New York: Bobbs-Merrill.

Schmitz, Christopher J.
1979   *World Non-Ferrous Metal Production and Prices, 1700–1976.* Totowa, N.J.: Biblio Distribution Centre.

Seidman, Ann, ed.
1975   *Natural Resources and National Welfare: The Case of Copper.* New York: Praeger.

Sideri, S. and S. Johns (eds.)
1980   *Mining for Development in the Third World: Multinational Cor-*

porations, State Enterprises and the International Economy. New York: Pergamon.

Sklar, Holly, ed.
1980 *Trilateralism: The Trilateral Commission and Elite Planning for World Management.* Boston: South End Press.

Soler, Ricaurte, ed.
1974 *Panamá, dependencia y liberación.* San Jose, Costa Rica: Editorial Universitaria Centroamericana (EDUCA).
1976 *Panamá: nación y oligarquía, 1925–1975.* Panama City: Ediciones de la revista Tareas.

Stevens, F. S. and Edward P. Wolfers, eds.
1977 *Racism: The Australian Experience.* Vol. 3 (2nd ed.), *Colonialism and After.* Sydney: Australia & New Zealand Book Co.

Steward, Julian H.
1945 *The Circum-Caribbean Tribes.* Vol. 4 of *The Handbook of South American Indians.* Smithsonian Institution, Bureau of American Ethnology, Bulletin 143. Washington: Smithsonian Institution. [Republished in facsimile edition by Cooper Square Publishers, New York, 1963.]

Swenson, Sally, ed.
1982 *Background Documents.* Prepared for the Conference on Native Resource Control and the Multinational Corporate Challenge: Aboriginal Rights in International Perspective, Washington, D.C., October 12–15, 1982. Boston: Anthropology Resource Center.

Tanzer, Michael
1980 *The Race for Resources: Continuing Struggles over Minerals and Fuels.* New York: Monthly Review Press.

Tilton, John E.
1977 *The Future of Nonfuel Minerals.* Washington: The Brookings Institution.

Torres de Araúz, Reina
1980 *Panamá indígena.* Panamá: Instituto Nacional de Cultura, Patrimonio Histórico.

Torrijos, Omar.
1973 *La Batalla de Panamá.* Buenos Aires: Editorial Universitaria.

Treadgold, M. L.
    1978   *The Regional Economy of Bougainville: Growth and Structural Change*. Development Studies Centre Occasional Paper No. 10. Canberra: Australian National Univ.

U.S. Department of Commerce
    1980   "Commodity Prices—Producer Prices." *Business Statistics 1979*. Washington: U.S. Government Printing Office.
    1981   *Survey of Current Business*. Vol. 61, No. 12.

Wali, Alaka
    1983   "The Bayano Corporation and Social Change: The Regional Consequences of Macrodevelopment." In *Panama in Transition: Local Reactions to Development Policies*. Monographs in Anthropology No. 6. John R. Bort and Mary W. Helms, eds. pp. 103–27. Columbia, Missouri: Univ. of Missouri Museum of Anthropology.
    1984   "Kilowatts and Crisis among the Kuna, Chocó, and Colonos: National and Regional Consequences of the Bayano Hydroelectric Complex in Eastern Panama." Ph.D. dissertation. Anthropology Department. Columbia University.

Wallerstein, Immanuel
    1974   *The Modern World-System: Capitalist Agriculture and the Origins of the European World-Economy in the Sixteenth Century*. New York: Academic Press.

West, Richard
    1972   *River of Tears: The Rise of the Rio Tinto-Zinc Mining Corporation*. London: Earth Island Ltd.

West, Robert C. and John P. Augelli
    1976   *Middle America: Its Lands and Peoples*. 2nd ed. Englewood Cliffs, N.J.: Prentice-Hall.

Wolf, Eric R.
    1974   *Anthropology*. New York: W. W. Norton & Co. [First published by Princeton Univ. Press, 1964.]
    1982   *Europe and the People without History*. Berkeley: Univ. of California Press.

World Bank
    1978   *Panama's Development in the 1980's: A Special Economic Report*. Washington: World Bank.
    1979   *Annual Report 1978*. Washington: World Bank.

Young, Philip D.

1968   "The Ngawbe: An Analysis of the Economy and Social Struc-
        ture of the Western Guaymí of Panama." Ph.D. dissertation.
        Anthropology Department. Univ. of Illinois.

1970   "Notes on the Ethnohistorical Evidence for Structural Con-
        tinuity in Guaymí Society." *Ethnohistory* 17:11–29.

1971   *Ngawbe: Tradition and Change among the Western Guaymí of
        Panama*. Illinois Studies in Anthropology No. 7. Urbana, Ill.:
        Univ. of Illinois Press.

1976a   "Guaymí Nativism: Its Rise and Demise." *Actas del XLI Con-
        greso Internacional de Americanistas*. Vol. III. México, 2 al 7 de
        septiembre de 1974:93–101.

1976b   "The Expression of Harmony and Discord in a Guaymí Ritu-
        al: The Symbolic Meaning of Some Aspects of the *Balsería*."
        In *Frontier Adaptations in Lower Central America*. Mary W.
        Helms and Franklin O. Loveland, eds. pp. 37–53. Philadelphia:
        Institute for the Study of Human Issues.

1978   "El movimiento de Mama Chi entre los Guaymíes y sus conse-
        cuencias sociales." *La Antigua* 7(11):45–75.

1980a   "Notes on Guaymí Traditional Culture." In *Adaptive Radia-
        tions in Prehistoric Panama*. Olga F. Linares and Anthony J.
        Ranere, eds. pp. 224–32. Cambridge, Mass.: Peabody Museum
        of Archaeology and Ethnology.

1980b   "Guaymí Socionatural Adaptations." Paper presented at Natu-
        ral History: Studies in Panama and Central America. A Sym-
        posium sponsored by Missouri Botanical Garden. Panama
        City, April.

1980c   "Plan Guaymí and the Emergence of a Symbol of Solidarity."
        Paper presented at The 79th Annual Meeting of the American
        Anthropological Association, Washington.

Young, Philip D. and John R. Bort

1976a   "Edabáli: The Ritual Sibling Relationship among the Western
        Guaymí." In *Ritual and Symbol in Native Central America*.
        University of Oregon Anthropological Papers No. 9. Philip D.
        Young and James Howe, eds. pp. 77–90. Eugene, Ore.: Univ.
        of Oregon Press.

1976b   "The Traditional Guaymí Decision-Making Process." Un-
        published paper.

1979   "The Politicization of the Guaymí." *Journal of the Steward An-
        thropological Society* 11(1):73–110.

Young, Philip D. and James Howe, eds.
> 1976 *Ritual and Symbol in Native Central America.* University of Oregon Anthropological Papers No. 9. Eugene: Univ. of Oregon.

Zorn, Stephen
> 1975 "Mining Policy in Papua New Guinea." In *Natural Resources and National Welfare: The Case of Copper.* Ann Seidman, ed., New York: Praeger. pp. 410–38.
> 1977 "New Developments in Third World Mining Agreements." *Natural Resources Forum* I:239–50.
> 1980 "Recent Trends in LDC Mining Agreements." In *Mining for Development in the Third World: Multinational Corporations, State Enterprises, and the International Economy.* S. Sideri and S. Johns, eds. New York: Pergamon. pp. 210–28.

NEWSPAPERS AND MINING PUBLICATIONS

ABMS (American Bureau of Metal Statistics)
> 1957 *Year Book of the American Bureau of Metal Statistics for 1956.* New York: ABMS.
> 1961 *Year Book of the American Bureau of Metal Statistics for 1960.* New York: ABMS.
> 1965 *Year Book of the American Bureau of Metal Statistics for 1964.* New York: ABMS.
> 1969 *Year Book of the American Bureau of Metal Statistics for 1968.* New York: ABMS.
> 1973 *Year Book of the American Bureau of Metal Statistics for 1972.* New York: ABMS.
> 1977 *Non-Ferrous Metal Data 1976.* New York: ABMS.
> 1981 *Non-Ferrous Metal Data 1980.* New York: ABMS.
> 1984 *Non-Ferrous Metal Data 1983.* New York: ABMS.

AMM (American Metal Market)
> 1979a "Panama Eyes 20% Sale of Cerro Colorado." October 5.
> 1979b "Texasgulf Rules Out Increasing its Cerro Colorado Stake." By Lynn Poretz. October 17.
> 1981 "Cerro Colorado's Decision Pending." April 16.
> 1982 "Panama's Cerro Colorado Project Placed on Hold." By Roberta Yafie. January 8.

E/MJ (Engineering and Mining Journal)
 1969a "This Month in Mining." Vol. 170(7):142.
 1969b "This Month in Mining." Vol. 170(10):112.
 1970 "This Month in Mining." Vol. 171(1):102.
 1971 "Hunch Leads to Huge Copper-Moly Find in Panama." Vol. 172(3):27.
 1972 "Canadian Javelin Eyes Production at Major Copper Find in Panama." By George P. Lutjen. Vol. 173(12):60–63.
 1976 "Texasgulf and Panama Sign Agreements for Cerro Colorado Copper Project." Vol. 177(4):23ff.
 1977 "Panama: A Major Mine Takes Shape at Cerro Colorado. Vol." 178(11):192–96.
 1985 "Copper: A Year of Paradox." By Simon D. Strauss. Vol. 186(3):40–43.

FP (Financial Post [Canada])
 1975 "Javelin Blunted." March 20.

FT (Financial Times)
 1979 "Men at the Top—Profile: President Aristides Royo, Financial Times Survey–Panama." By Hugh O'Shaughnessy. April 3.

LACR (Latin America Commodities Report-London)
 1981 "RTZ Seeks New Labour Laws." August 14:5.

LAER (Latin America Economic Report, London)
 1975 "Progress Report: Panama's Cerro Colorado Mine." May 9:71.

MA (Metallgesellschaft Aktiengesellschaft)
 1954 *Statistical Tables on Aluminium, Lead, Copper, Zinc, Tin, Cadmium, Magnesium, Nickel, Mercury and Silver.* 42nd Annual Issue—1938, 1946-1953. Frankfurt am Main.
 1961 *Statistical Tables on Aluminium, Lead, Copper, Zinc, Tin, Cadmium, Magnesium, Nickel, Mercury and Silver.* 48th Annual Issue—1951–1960. Frankfurt am Main.
 1971 *Metal Statistics 1960–1970.* 58th Edition. Frankfurt am Main.
 1981 *Metal Statistics 1970-1980.* 68th Edition. Frankfurt am Main.

MH (Miami Herald)
 1973a "Gold, Copper Finds Stir Panama Economic Hopes." July 17.
 1973b "Panama to Negotiate with Canadian Firm." July 18.
 1975 "Investors Welcome, Panama Boss Insists." By Don Bohning. March 23.
 1977 "SEC Questions Company's Latin Projects." February 16.

MJ (Mining Journal)
    1973   "Developments at Cerro Colorado." June 29:531.

MM (Mining Magazine)
    1974   "Feasibility Studies Outline Cerro Colorado Development."
                By David Hargreaves. August: 86ff.

MS (Montreal Star)
    1975   "Copper . . . as Vital as Oil." By Alan Riding. March 15.

NM (Northern Miner)
    n.d.   "Canadian Javelin's Copper Deposit Could Be Panama's Big-
                gest Industry." [Late 1972.]
    1975   "Javelin Settles with Panama Government." Sept. 4.
    1978   "Texasgulf Confident about Metals' Future." May 4.

NYT (New York Times)
    1973a   "Javelin's Mine Strike Rich in Ore and Controversy." Nov. 19.
    1973b   "Canadian Javelin is Sued for Fraud." By Robert J. Cole. Nov.
                30.
    1973c   "Trading Reinstated in Javelin Shares." December 7.
    1975   "Panama is Planning Payment to Javelin." March 22.
    1981   "Panama Oil Pipeline Job is Assigned." By Eric Pace. March
                19.

TC (The Citizen [Ottawa])
    1975   "Texasgulf Awarded Rights to Copper Before Final Bids." By
                Paul Gessell. July 19.

TGM (Toronto Globe and Mail)
    1974   "Canadian Javelin Plans Consortium to Develop Panama Cop-
                per Property." December 17.
    1975a   "Panama to Pay Total of $23.6 Million to Javelin for Cerro
                Colorado Deposit." August 29.
    1975b   "Texasgulf-Panamanian" Deal. Oct. 9.
    1975c   [No title available.] Dec. 5.
    1978   [No title available.] July 25.

TS (Toronto Star)
    1975a   "Panama Takes Over Javelin Copper Find." March 21.
    1975b   "Texasgulf Plans $200 Million Deal with Panama." October 9.
    1977   "More Charges Brought Against Javelin." February 5.

WSJ (Wall Street Journal)
    1973a   "Canadian Javelin Plans Panama Copper Output in about Two
                Years." July 18.

1973b   "Canadian Javelin Special Receiver is Asked by SEC." November 30.

1973c   "Canadian Javelin Ltd. Disputes Allegations in SEC's Civil Suit." December 6.

1975a   "Panama Says Talks with Canadian Javelin Collapsed." March 7.

1975b   "Canadian Javelin Ltd. Confirms its Group Halted Panama Talks." March 10.

1975c   "Panama to Take Over Big Copper Project Being Developed by Canadian Javelin." March 21.

PANAMANIAN MATERIALS: REPORTS AND PUBLICATIONS FROM DEPENDENCIES OF THE PANAMANIAN GOVERNMENT

CODEMIN (Corporación de Desarrollo Minero Cerro Colorado)

1975   *Proyecto Cerro Colorado.* [Summary.] By Irneldo Pérez M. Panama City: CODEMIN.

1976   *Memoria que presenta [CODEMIN] a la honorable Asamblea Nacional de Representantes de Corregimientos.* Panama City: CODEMIN.

1977   *Memoria que presenta [CODEMIN] a la honorable Asamblea Nacional de Representantes de Corregimientos.* Panama City: CODEMIN.

1979a   *Resumen del proyecto Cerro Colorado* [1]. Panama City: CODEMIN [Spring, 1979].

1979b   *Resumen del proyecto Cerro Colorado* [2]. Panama City: CODEMIN [Summer, 1979].

1979c   Newspaper advertisements; a series of thirty full-page advertisements placed in Panama's major daily newspapers during June, July, and August.

1979d   *Memoria que presenta [CODEMIN] a la honorable Asamblea Nacional de Representantes de Corregimientos.* Panama City: CODEMIN.

1980a   *Cerro Colorado y el medio ambiente.* By Rubén Dario Herrera P. and Irneldo Pérez M. Panama City: CODEMIN.

1980b   *Memoria que presenta [CODEMIN] a la honorable Asamblea Nacional de Representantes de Corregimientos.* Panama City: CODEMIN.

1981   *Memoria que presenta [CODEMIN] a la honorable Asamblea Nacional de Representantes de Corregimientos.* Panama City: CODEMIN.

Consejo Consultivo de Economía
1979   "Informe y recomendaciones del Consejo Consultivo de Economía a propósito del proyecto minero de Cerro Colorado." [Report to the Government, April 23.] Panama City.

Consejo de Gabinete
1980   "Acuérdase la celebración de un contrato, un acuerdo especial y se dictan otras medidas [entre CODEMIN y Rio Tinto-Zinc Corporation Limited]." *Gaceta Oficial* No. 19,085 (June 6). Panama City.

Consejo de Legislación
1976   "Autorízase a la Corporación de Desarrollo Minero Cerro Colorado [CODEMIN] para celebrar unos contratos de asociación y administración [con Texasgulf]." *Gaceta Oficial* No. 18,022 (February 6). Panama City. [In the text, "Consejo de Legislación, Adm." is the "Administration Agreement"; "Consejo de Legislación, Assn." is the "Association Agreement"; and "Consejo de Legislación, Art." is the "Articles of Incorporation."]

Estadistica y Censo, Dirrección de
n.d.   *Panamá en cifras* (published in various years).
1960   *Censos nacionales de 1960.* [Published in various years]
1970   *Censos nacionales de 1970.* [Published in various years]
1980   *Censos nacionales de 1980, cifras preliminares.* [Published in various years]

IRHE (Instituto de Recursos Hidraúlicos y Electrificación)
1979a   "Complejo hidroeléctrico Teribe-Changuinola, fase de prefactibilidad." Resumen. MS Panama: IRHE.
1979b   "Consideraciones en torno al suministro de energía eléctrica a las minas de Cerro Colorado." Documento preliminar, 8 de marzo. MS Panama.

Ministerio de Comercio e Industria
1975   *Código de Recursos Naturales.* Panamá.

ADDITIONAL BOOKS, UNPUBLISHED REPORTS, AND OTHER MATERIALS HOUSED IN THE CEASPA ARCHIVES, PANAMA CITY

Alvarado, Luis
1979   "Reporte de la posible contaminación de ríos y aguas subter-

ráneas adyacentes a la explotación minera de Cerro Colorado."
Study commissioned by CEASPA. Panama.

Cabarrús, Carlos R.
1979 *Indígena y proletario*. Serie el indio panameño no. 2. Panama
      City: Ediciones Centro de Capacitación Social.

Cámara de Comercio, Industrias y Agricultura de Panamá
1979 *Foro sobre proyecto minero de Cerro Colorado*. Biblioteca em-
      presarial no. 5. Panama City: Cámara de Comercio.

Carty, Robert
1982 "Rio Tinto-Zinc viene a Panamá." In *El pueblo guaymí y su fu-
      turo*. CEASPA y Comité Patrocinador del "Foro sobre el
      Pueblo Guaymí y su Futuro," ed. pp. 301–31. Panama City:
      CEASPA

CEASPA (Centro de Estudios y Acción Social—Panamá)
1979a "Análisis de los contratos de la mina Cerro Colorado." *Diálogo
      Social* 110:24–28.
1979b *Cerro Colorado: su impacto social y económico—un aporte pre-
      liminar*. Avances de investigación no. 3. Panama: CEASPA.
1980 "Informe sobre el estado actual del proyecto minero de Cerro
      Colorado." Draft study. Panama City: CEASPA.

CEASPA y Comisión Guaymí
1979 "The Guaymí People and Cerro Colorado." [Transl. by
      LAWG].

CEASPA y Comité Patrocinador del "Foro sobre el Pueblo Guaymí y su
      Futuro," ed.
1982 *El pueblo guaymí y su futuro*. Panama: CEASPA.

CEP (Conferencia Episcopal Panameña)
1979 "Los obispos hablan de Cerro Colorado." Carta pastoral. Pan-
      ama: Conferencia Episcopal Panameña, 11 de mayo. [English
      transl. by LAWG]

Christian Concern for Southern Africa
1976 *Rio Tinto-Zinc in Namibia*. London.

CSMRI (Colorado School of Mines Research Institute)
1977 *A Reconnaissance Environmental Study of Cerro Colorado Project*.
      Study contracted by Texasgulf. Golden, Colorado: CMSRI.

Comisión Interagencial para el Estudio de la Población Guaymí
1978 *Estudio socio-económico de la población indígena guaymí de Pan-
      amá*. Panama City.

Comité Pro Defensa Integral de Chiriquí
  1979   "Congreso analítico sobre el proyecto minero de Cerro Colorado." [Document distributed by anti-Cerro Colorado group.] David (Chiriquí), Panama.

Congreso General Guaymí. Directiva ed.
  1983   *Pasos en la lucha: documentos de la lucha guaymí desde el congreso de Soloy (1980) hasta Alto de Jesús (1983)*. [Documents of Guaymí meetings.] Panama City.

Congresos Guaymíes de Canquintú y Soloy. Mesa Directiva ed.
  1980   *Documentos de congresos guaymíes sobre los proyectos Cerro Colorado y Teribe-Changuinola*. [Guaymí-sponsored documents concerning Cerro Colorado and Teribe-Changuinola projects.] Panama City.

Counter-Information Services
  n.d.   *The Rio Tinto-Zinc Corporation Limited Anti-Report*. London.

DeRoo, Bishop Remi, Robert Carty and Tony Clarke
  1980   *Canada and Cerro Colorado: Report of an On-Site Investigation into the Social and Economic Impact of Panama's Cerro Colorado Project*. Toronto.

Dirigentes Guaymíes
  1980   "Carta abierta al Presidente de Panamá." *Diálogo Social* 128:2.

Elliott-Jones, Michael F.
  1979   "Why Copper Prices are going to Triple over the Next Decade." [Text of a Speech by Michael Elliott-Jones, Vice President, Research and Development, Chase Econometric Associates, Inc., Acapulco, Mexico, October 15.]

Gjording, Chris N.
  1982b   "Cerro Colorado: conflictos y contradicciones entre Panamá, corporaciones transnacionales y el indígena guaymí." In *El pueblo guaymí y su futuro*. CEASPA y Comité, ed. pp. 225–300. Panama: CEASPA.

Gómez Pérez, José A.
  1979   "Evaluación económica del proyecto minero de Cerro Colorado." Conferencia dictada bajo auspicios del Colegio de Economistas de Panamá. MS Panamá (13 de junio).

Haywood, Steve
  1979   "Rio Tinto Stinks." *Time Out* (London). June.

IMF (International Monetary Fund)
   1979   "Informe de la misión de revisión y consulta del Fondo
             Monetario Internacional" [Private report of IMF mission to
             government of Panama].

Lobo, Enrique
   1980a   "La nueva política indigenista (o bien: acabemos con el in-
             dio)." *Diálogo Social* 123:15–18.
   1980b   "El pueblo guaymí y el gobierno panameño (o bien: acabemos
             con el guaymí)." *Diálogo Social* 125:22–25.

Morales B., Francisco J.
   1979   "Cerro Colorado en cifras: informe sobre el proyecto de Cerro
             Colorado." Presentado a la Cámara Panameña de la Construc-
             ción. June 14. Panama City.

Núñez, Daniel E.
   1978   [Letter to the Editor]. *La Estrella de Panamá*. Septiembre.

Núñez, Daniel E. y Consejo Presbiteral
   1979   "El indígena guaymí y Cerro Colorado." Pastoral Letter of
             April 19. David (Chiriquí), Panama. [English translation pub-
             lished in *Survival International Review* (Summer 1979).]

PARTiZANS (People against Rio Tinto-Zinc and Subsidiaries)
   1979   "The Unacceptable Face of RTZ." MS London.

Posse, Ana Victoria
   1980   "Cerro Colorado Mining Project." Unpublished paper.

RTZ (Rio Tinto-Zinc)
   1973   *Rio Tinto 1873—Rio Tinto-Zinc 1973*. London: RTZ.
   1981   "Summary. Feasibility Study" [for Cerro Colorado].

Sanders, Douglas
   1975   "Report to the National Indian Association of Panama."

Sarsanedas, Jorge
   1978   *Tierra para el Guaymí*. Serie el indio panameño no. 3. Panama
             City: Ediciones Centro de Capacitación Social.

Solano Frias, Sergina
   1981   "El oleoducto transístmico." *Diálogo Social* 135:20–21.

Texasgulf, Inc.
   1978   *Feasibility Study* [for Cerro Colorado]. Summary Volume.
   1980   *Annual Report 1979*. Stamford, Conn.

INDEX